ובכן, תן כבוד, ה׳, לעמך, תהלה ליראיך...שמחה לארצך – במהרה בימינו.

And so too, O Lord, grant honor to Your people, praise to those who revere You… [and] joy to Your land – speedily in our days.

– High Holy Day prayers

אונזערע תכלית איז צו טאן, ניט דוקא אויפצוטאן.

Our purpose in life is to do, not necessarily to accomplish.

– Rabbi Chaim of Volozhin

… We could not believe what we saw, what a delightful scene, where God's spirit hovers over it, where entire households go out to their work until evening. We witnessed people, some of whom were beginning to sprout white hairs in their beards, their payot and their ẓiẓit swaying back and forth, marching with their sickles over their shoulders and working with incredible speed and strength; their women assisting them in gathering stalks and bundling sheaves… . And what are the children doing? Some of them gleefully heave the bundles over their shoulders and pile them up in designated places, leaving them to dry in the fields until it is time to gather them into their homes. The rest of the children fly like shadows throughout the valley, tending to their flocks. As the evening approaches, they all return home.

From "Ekron," published in 1886 in *Knesset Yisrael,* a Warsaw journal edited by Shaul Pinchas Rabinowitz

Rebels in the Holy Land

Mazkeret Batya -
An Early Battleground for the Soul of Israel

Sam Finkel

Library of Congress Cataloging-in-Publication Data
Finkel, Sam.
Rebels in the Holy Land : Mazkeret Batya, an early battleground for the soul of Israel / Sam Finkel.
p. cm.
Includes bibliographical references.
ISBN 978-1-59826-861-4
1. Mazkeret-Batyah (Israel) 2. Jews--Israel–Mazkeret-Batyah–History. 3. Land settlement--Palestine–History. 4. Palestine–Emigration and immigration. I. Title.

DS110.M36.F56 2012
956.94'7–dc23
2012000181

ISBN 978-1-59826-861-4

Distributed by:
Feldheim Publishers
www.feldheim.com

Graphic Design: Ben Gasner Studio
Graphic Artists: Bat-Chen Grossman, Nili Boim, Mindel Kassorla

Printed in Israel

בס"ד

Rabbi Zev Leff

Rabbi of Moshav Matityahu
Rosh HaYeshiva–Yeshiva Gedola Matityahu

הרב זב לף

מרא דאתרא מושב מתתיהו
ראש הישיבה-ישיבה גדולה מתתיהו

D.N. Modiin 71917 | Tel: 08-976-1138 'טל | Fax: 08-976-5326 'פקס | ד.נ. מודיעין 71917

Dear Friends,

I have read the manuscript about Mazkeret Batya by Shmuel Finkel. Mr. Finkel details the founding and settling of Mazkeret Batya in the context of the First Aliyah to modern Israel. He makes it clear that the original settlers were for the most part strictly observant Jews who wanted to settle and develop the land, fulfill its unique mitzvos and earn a respectable living from agriculture.

He also documents the roots of the Shemittah controversy and the valiant efforts of the farmers of Ekron–Mazkeret Batya to fulfill this mitzvah properly against those in opposition from many quarters.

This book is an eye opener that destroys many secular myths and stereotypes. It is a true Kiddush Hashem in properly portraying the image of the true founders of modern Israel, people who were loyal to Torah, Am Yisrael and Eretz Yisrael.

I commend Mr. Finkel for his efforts. May he reap the rich reward that is destined for those who sanctify G-d's name publicly.

Sincerely,
With Torah Blessings

Zev Leff

Rabbi Zev Leff

Map Index

* *Andrees Allgemeiner Handatlas* (Bielefeld: Velhagen & Klasing, 1896), p. 91a. *Courtesy of The National Library of Israel, Eran Laor Cartographic Collection, Jerusalem.*

** C. R. Conder, *Map of Western Palestine in 26 Sheets from the Surveys Conducted for the Committee of the Palestine Exploration Fund [cartographic material] by Lieutenants C.R. Conder and H.H. Kitchener R.E. during the years 1872-1877* (London: Photozincographed and printed for the Committee of the Palestine Exploration Fund at the Ordnance Survey Office in Southampton, 1880). Sheet 16 (Esdud – Ashdod). *Courtesy of the Palestine Exploration Fund, London.*

****Central Zionist Archives, Jerusalem.*

Whence they came. *First Map:* A familiar region filled with Slavic names. The pioneers hailed from a farming colony adjoining the town of Rushany (Rozhinoy). Their first stop was the train station in the town of Wolkowysk, to the northwest. The red lines signify railroad tracks. What followed was a harrowing, twenty-day journey.

Where they were going. *Second Map:* An alien world filled with Arabic names. This is one section of a much larger map of the Holy Land, drawn by a British team of surveyors and cartographers just a few years before the farmers arrived. The pioneers came ready for hard work, with hopes of success and spiritual fulfillment.

Wasilischki
Ostrino
Dembrowo
Schtschutschin
Skidel
Kamenka
Mikelewitschi
105
Dubno
Ditwa
Lebeda
Ischtscholno
Bjelizy
Sheludok
Roshanka
Orle
Wseljub
Ljubt
Stat. Njemen
Nowogru
323
Korel
Ochonowa
Djatlowo
Nowojelnja
Wensowez
282
Dworez
Jawor
Potschenow
Mosty
Schara
Peski
Rogosniza
Kremjaniza
Deretschin
Moltschad
Gorodi
230
Stol
Derewnoje
Wolkowysk
Golynka
Isabelin
Selwa
228
Oserniza
212
Polonka
Sherebilowka
Slonim
Mal. Loperiza
Iwaschkewitschi
Schilowitschi
Podorosk
Shirowizy
Meshewitschi
Roshany
Bitten
Ostrowo
Lyskowo
Domonowo
203
Kossowa
Schara
186
Chorowo
Selez
Prushany
Bobrowitschi
161
Telechany
Kartus-Keja
Beresa
Peski
Os. Tschernoje
Maletsch
Sporow
Signewitschi
Ssositowo
168
Chomsk
Motol
Kanal
Ogiński

Nalibok
Rubeshewitschi
Koidanow
Samochwalowitschi
Derewnaja
Stankow
Poljany
Sinjawka
Negorjeloje
Oscro
Sasulje
Duditschi
Jeremitschi
Turez
Stolbzy
Usda
Loscha
Schazk
Mir
Nowyj Swershen
Pyryschewskaja
Ischkold
Mogilno
Njemen
Gorodeja
Pjasetschna
Neswish
Wynija
Kutschinka
Snow
Pogorjelzy
Kopyl
Gresk
Swojatitschi
Grosow
Klezk
Timkowitschi
Sluzk
Romanowo
Semjeshowo
Medwjedischki
Morotsch
Wisna
Tschishewitschi
Loktyschi
Starobino
Lan
Gonzewitschi
Deniskowitschi
Chotenitschi
Malkowitschi
Chorostow
Miljewitschi
Woluta
Bobrik
Bastyn
Lenino
Djatelowitschi
Pogost
Slutsch
145
236
201
230
237
147
180
149

E
F
G
Sand Dunes
es Suarki
Ărab er Rŭmeilât
el Melâlhah
el Khŭrbeh
Tell el Khŭrbeh
Khurbet Lezka
Tell el Murreh
Nahr Sukereir
Khurbet Sukereir
Wâdy el Khubb
Burkah
Minet el Kŭlâh
Esdŭd
el Batâni el Gharbîyeh
el Batâni esh Sherkîyeh
Kh. Berdeghah
Khurbet Yâsîn
Khurbet Ghŭwâdeh
Khurbet Dîar el Kabeh
Beit Darâs
Tell Abu Heraizeh
es Sûâfîr esh Shemâlîyeh
Khurbet Marbeh
Khurbet Beizeh
Khurbet Hatâs
Khurbet Khaseeh
es Sûâfîr el Gharbîyeh
es Sûâfîr esh Sherkîyeh
Hamâmeh

H
I
J
Wâdy Deirân
el Kubeibeh
Zernûkah
Khurbet Selmeh
Nââneh
Tell el Batîkh
Barriyeh
Tell Jezar
Abu Shusheh
Electric Telegraph
Âkir
Wâdy Rahles
Khurbet Metât
Mughâir Summeil
Khurbet Summeil
el Mughâr
el Mansûrah
Kh. Umm Kelkhah
Wâdy Katrah
Katrah
Shahmeh
Khurbet Nîna
Wâdy el Murubbâh
Khuldeh
Kh. Kefr Âna
Kh. Beit Fâr
Wâdy es Sûrâr
Ârâb es Sûtâneh
Tell Butâshi
el Mughârah
Wâdy el Mukheizin
Kh. el Mukheizin
Wâdy el Mekenna
Kh. el Mekenna
Kezâzeh
Sitta
Deir el Ashek
Khurbet Fered
el Kheimeh
el Mesmiyeh
et Tineh
Khurbet Ammûrieh
el Bureij
el Kustineh
Mughallis
Tell et Turmus
Khurbet Jelâs
Khurbet es Sâfi
Tell es Sâfi
Khurbet Atraba
Kh. Deir el Bâtin

Table of Contents

צבי
פייגע רחל
שרה
אפרים

DEDICATIONS

THIS BOOK IS DEDICATED TO
THE MEMORY OF OUR FATHER

SIDNEY FINKEL

לעילוי נשמת אבינו

ר׳ שבח בן ר׳ שמואל ויענטע פינקל ז״ל

A SURVIVOR

ארמי אבד אבי

A MAN WITHOUT A COUNTRY,
WITHOUT A FAMILY, WITHOUT A PENNY

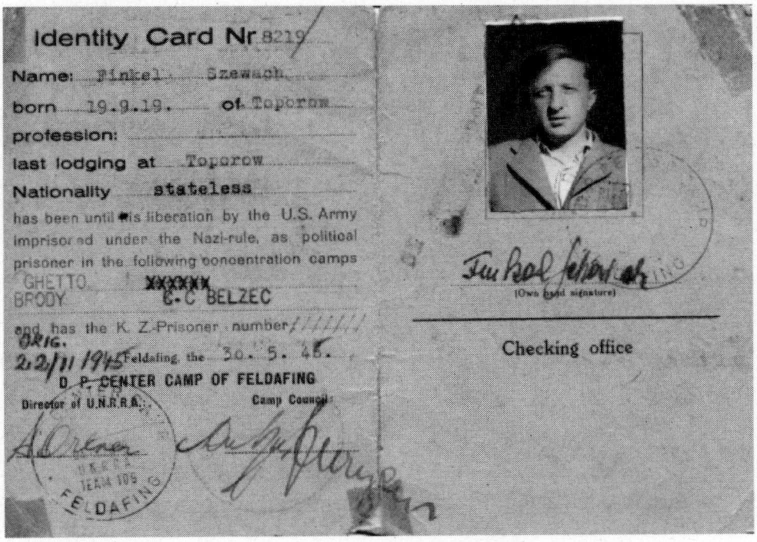

Identity Card Nr 8219

Name: Finkel Szewach

born 19.9.19. of Toporow

profession:

last lodging at Toporow

Nationality stateless

has been until his liberation by the U.S. Army imprisoned under the Nazi-rule, as political prisoner in the following concentration camps

GHETTO XXXXXX

BRODY C-C BELZEC

and has the K. Z.-Prisoner number

ORIG. 22/11 1945 Feldafing, the 30. 5. 45.

D. P. CENTER CAMP OF FELDAFING

Director of U.N.R.R.A.: Camp Council:

U.N.R.R.A. TEAM 109 FELDAFING

(Own hand signature)

Checking office

Our father knew what it felt like to have everything. His father was a learned Jew and a respected leader in their small shtetl in Galicia. They had status, wealth and security. There were siblings and cousins.

When Father was a teenager, the Soviets nationalized the family business. Under Communism, he and his family were social outcasts. He was conscripted into the Red Army and shipped far away from home. A year later, he was transferred to a slave-labor battalion that was attached to Soviet army units. He survived aerial bombings, bullets, physical and mental exhaustion, hunger, and the malnutrition that caused him to lose his teeth and even (temporarily) his eyesight.

The Germans murdered his parents and four of his brothers and their families. His youngest brother survived the entire war while hiding in an underground bunker, only to be murdered by Ukrainian nationalists two weeks after the war was over.

He returned to his hometown right after the war and found everything was gone. Everything but his memory. There weren't even graves to cry over.

He had one overarching dream – to keep that memory alive.

He refused to sink into self-pity, bitterness or depression. He immigrated to America, reuniting with his sister, the only other member of his family who was still alive. She had managed to leave on the last boat out of Europe to America before the onset of the war.

Father started a family of his own, naming his children after his slain parents. He refused to be intimidated by his poverty, lack of formal education and broken English, and eventually went into business for himself, investing every penny he had saved up from working as a manual laborer in a lumberyard. With sweat and tears, he built a thriving lumber business for himself, keeping alive the memory of his father's successful lumber firm in Poland. He resisted the temptation to which many fellow Jews succumbed, especially refugees – to assimilate into the American melting pot – choosing instead to send his children to Jewish day schools, even when he was still struggling financially.

Another memory he kept alive was that of shouldering

responsibility for the community at large. Like his father before him, who had served as the lay head of his local *kehillah* and had donated large amounts of money to charity and to build the local beit midrash, our father was a member of the board of directors of the Talmudical Academy of Baltimore (Yeshivas Chofetz Chaim) and contributed money to yeshivot, the Associated Jewish Charities of Baltimore, local synagogues, the Religious Zionists of America, Israel Bonds, and many individuals who were in need.

Shortly before he made *aliyah* from Baltimore, he was outraged upon learning how a Jewish educator had passed away suddenly, leaving his widow and children destitute and bereft. In collaboration with Rabbi Herman Neuberger of Ner Israel Rabbinical College, and the Associated Jewish Charities of Baltimore, he set up a fund that provides every single family in Baltimore whose breadwinners are *mechanchim* with a $250,000 life insurance policy. Since his moving to Israel in 1999, four bereaved families have benefited from that fund.

The idea of preserving memory, the force behind Father's intense desire to survive, was one of the inspirations behind the writing of this book – for the book's purpose is to keep alive the memory of the early religious pioneers, who were forgotten by history. Father would have felt quite at home if he could have gone back in time and spent a day in Mazkeret Batya. He would have enjoyed the sing-

וַיְבִאֵנוּ אֶל הַמָּקוֹם הַזֶּה וַיִּתֶּן לָנוּ אֶת הָאָרֶץ הַזֹּאת
אֶרֶץ זָבַת חָלָב וּדְבָשׁ:

song learning of Mishnayot, and would have been absorbed in a Talmud *shiur.* As a man who relished hard work and never shirked manual labor or getting one's hands dirty, Father would have admired the pioneers who spent all day sweating in the fields under the hot sun. He would have been proud of the farmers whose concern for their Jewish brethren persecuted in Russia was what brought them to the Holy Land in the first place.

Father eventually settled down in Israel, and his only regret was that he didn't do so earlier. He loved attending *shiurim* at the Great Synagogue in Jerusalem, and listening to the melodious *musar shmuess* of Rabbi Shalom Schwadron at the Gra Synagogue in the city's Shaarei Chesed neighborhood, or playing chess with one of the boys learning in a local yeshivah. He was especially gratified to be visited by his grandchildren, all of whom live in Israel.

His life story embodied it all: destruction and renewal, death and rebirth. Like little Mazkeret Batya, Father was a microcosm of Jewish history. May his memory be a blessing to us, and may his penchant for preserving memory be an inspiration to all who knew him.

Sam Finkel and Sharon (Finkel) Green

ת.נ.צ.ב.ה.

THIS BOOK IS DEDICATED TO
THE MEMORY OF OUR MOTHER

GENIA FINKEL

לעילוי נשמת אמנו
גולדה בת ר' יצחק אלחנן
ושרה עטיל אייזנברג ז"ל

Just four days shy of eleven months since the passing of our father (and just before concluding the eleven-month period of saying Kaddish), our dear mother passed away.

True to her Yiddish name, Golda, Mother had a heart of gold. Until a tragic fall brought her to the hospital in great pain three weeks before her death, she had the most beautiful smile and was constantly singing. She had a mischievous twinkle in her eyes and a good sense of humor. She was the quintessential warm and giving Yiddishe mama. Her joy belied her tragic past.

Genia Eisenberg was born to a well-to-do family in Szydłowiec, a town in central Poland near the city of Radom. Her parents, followers of Rabbi Yiẓchak Finkler, the rebbe of Radoszyce, owned and operated a leather factory. Her mother, Sarah Ettel, was very dedicated, dignified, and refined. Her father, Yiẓchak Elchanan, was warm, loving, and charitable. And her saintly grandmother Miriam, always reading Psalms, instilled in her Yiddishkeit.

Goldaleh remembered a charmed childhood. She was a beautiful girl who loved elementary school and excelled in her studies. She skated on the frozen pond outside the town's castle and got together with her numerous cousins.

Mother's recollections of the terrible years that followed were murky, often incoherent. Her father built a bunker underneath the leather factory. The family hid there for six weeks, only to be betrayed by a Polish neighbor and arrested by the Gestapo. The Germans forced them at gunpoint to trample on the Torah scrolls kept in her father's office. About fifteen years old at the time, Mother was separated from her parents and never saw them again.

Mother, her sister Chaya Dina (Helen), and her brother-in-law Mottel (Max) bribed their way into the Nazi slave labor camp in Skarzysko-Kamienna. There, at least, they would have something to eat (though everyone was malnourished, and Mother later developed osteoporosis). Mother worked twelve-hour shifts, performing quality-control checks on explosives later used in German bombs. Any worker who didn't meet his daily quota was hanged the next morning. Risking her life, Mother allowed some defective material to pass through quality control. That was her form of resistance. Despite the long hours, she helped take care of Helen and Max's baby, Shraga Feivel. Tragically, the toddler died shortly before the war ended.

When the Red Army liberated the camp in 1945, Mother fled through the forests and reached the American sector. For the next few years, she lived in a displaced-persons camp in Garmish, Germany.

On her first Friday of freedom, Mother couldn't bring herself to light Sabbath candles. She was filled with bitterness and rage over the injustices she'd witnessed. "How could God have allowed all this to happen?" she wondered. Then she asked herself: "If my mother could speak to me right now, what would she tell me?" And she knew the answer. She lit the candles, and she did so every Friday thereafter.

Mother married in 1953, and God blessed her and Father with two healthy children. She took wonderful care of us. She gave and gave, spoiling everyone (including the dog). As the Sabbath approached, the house smelled fresh and clean. The linens had been changed, and heavenly aromas wafted from the kitchen.

Mother rose around five-thirty every morning and devoted all her time to the family. A perfectionist, she kept the house spotless. She rarely went straight to bed, but fell asleep in a chair, exhausted from the day's work of cleaning, shopping, laundry, and cooking gourmet meals. Her homemade chocolate cookies were so delicious that neighborhood children and adults alike would drop in and take a few from the cookie jar.

Mom was the sweetest, warmest person we knew. Her affection was so effusive. She would ask how many servings you wanted, and before you answered, one serving was already on the plate. If you said, "One," then she added another. If you said, "No thanks," she somehow didn't hear. She wanted nothing more than to see her family happy.

She had exquisite taste in clothes and home furnishings. Had Baron Edmond de Rothschild hired her to select his wardrobe and decorate his palatial residence, he would not have been disappointed. And she was

עֹז וְהָדָר לְבוּשָׁהּ וַתִּשְׂחַק לְיוֹם אַחֲרוֹן

very smart, insightful, and idealistic.

Mom taught us the importance of etiquette and of expressing appreciation. She was extremely compassionate, unable to see anyone in pain. She nursed sick birds back to health.

But the Holocaust was always on her mind. Stories we would have preferred not to hear were sometimes served along with dinner. Like many of her contemporaries, she was plagued with survivor's guilt and suffered from anxiety.

Her true nature of happiness and good cheer were felt most during her last years. Young at heart, she couldn't understand why she was being sent to the senior center to be with "old people."

Mom was constantly humming such classic Yiddish songs as "Shayne Vee Dee Levuneh" (Beautiful as the Moon). She enjoyed visits from her five grandchildren, but nothing gave her more nachas than looking adoringly at a picture of her great-grandson, Sinai, named after her late husband.

The Talmud (Menachot 29b) records that when Moses saw prophetically that Rabbi Akiva would meet such a terrible end, he protested. God replied, "Silence! Such was My original intent." The Gaon of Vilna explains that God originally intended to create a world based on strict justice, but He foresaw that such a creation could not endure, so He tempered it with mercy. However, says the Gaon, special people can live with strict justice, and they and the world are all the better for it. We would like to think our mother was such a person.

Sam Finkel and Sharon (Finkel) Green

ת.נ.צ.ב.ה.

Acknowledgments

The lion's share of appreciation goes to **Achiezer Arkin**. It was his film about the struggle of the Mazkeret Batya farmers to observe *Shemittah* and his book *Nachshonei ha-Shemittah* that inspired me to bring this story to the English-speaking public. Achiezer gave me *carte blanche* to use his book and provided me with much of the source material. His warm encouragement fueled my enthusiasm, alleviated some of the loneliness, and was like an oasis in the desert.

My account of the journey of the farmers from Pavlovka to Palestine was taken from *Yesud Ha-Ma'alah* by **Yechiel Brill**. I have culled heavily from *Mazkeret Batya* by **David Neiman** for information regarding the details of daily life on the *moshavah* as well as for biographical information on the settlers.

In addition, I have relied on the work of a number of historians, such as **Ran Aaronsohn**, **Simon Schama**, **Ehud Luz**, **Mordechai Eliav**, **Avraham Sternberg**, **Arnold Blumberg**, and **Mordechai Naor**.

In spite of all the research placed in my lap, this book was not easy going for me. I am not the type who can sit and write for hours, focusing easily on the task ahead. Neither am I used to long, drawn-out projects. This has been a draining and lonely experience with many more valleys than peaks. There have been quite a few times when I felt ready to throw in the towel. The bottom line is that I could not have finished this book were it not for the assistance of many people.

The initial jolt I needed to begin the project came from **Dr. Don Brand**.

When negative emotions started to flood me, I was helped on countless occasions by my wise friend **Claire Gutstein**. She guided me out of the many rough spots with enough wisdom and patience (thank God!) to ignore me when I said that I couldn't complete the project.

There were many others who helped me along the way, quite often at crucial junctures. I am very grateful to **Daphna Shimshoni**, the director of the Eran Shamir Village Museum, Mazkeret Batya, for her time and assistance in obtaining important documents. She made the museum a friendly place for me and her invaluable historical insights are incorporated in this book.

Dr. Yerakh Tzur spent much time with me, poring over old military maps and atlases of eastern Europe, trying to piece together the first leg of Yechiel Brill's journey with the Pavlovka farmers. Tzur also devoted hours to review and comment on parts of the manuscript. I am indebted to him for his time, expertise and great analytical skills. I would also like to thank **Dr. Shaul Stampfer** of Hebrew University for answering questions regarding European Jewish History.

I am grateful to **Ayelet Rubin**, head of the Eran Laor Cartographic Collection of The National Library of Israel, for providing me with old maps of Europe and Palestine.

My friend **Yechiel Greenbaum**, one of the most amazing sources of information about Jewish books and authors, made himself available to find pertinent articles or obscure sources for content and photographs.

Rabbi Dr. David Katz of Baltimore, a Torah scholar and professor of history at Johns Hopkins University, enlightened me regarding Baron Edmond de Rothschild's thinking and the philosophy of the rabbis of the Chovevei Ẓion movement. He introduced me to the writings of Dr. Ehud Luz and reviewed part of the manuscript.

My thanks go to **Rabbi Gedaliah A. Rabinowitz** (we both did our research in the Hebrew University's National Library of Israel reading room) for sharing with me some of his knowledge and insights.

And thank you to **Rabbi Meir Schlezinger**, founder and *rosh yeshivah* of Yeshivat Shaalvim, **Dr. Yossi Avneri** of Moshav Gimzu, **Dr. Menachem Friedman** (who lives in Mazkeret Batya), and **Dr. Arie Morgenstern** for historical information.

My gratitude goes to **Mrs. Rita Lubinsky** and **Rabbi Yaakov Yehuda Salant** (a descendant of Rabbi Zundel Salant) for their help in translating the German-language material and to **Rabbi Lipa Rabinowitz** for translating the Yiddish material. My appreciation to **Rabbi Berel Wein** for making the time to discuss some of the technical aspects of producing a book, for recommending to me the editor Charlotte Friedland, and for his insights into the historical period of the late nineteenth century.

A number of people graciously permitted me to incorporate their material. They include **Rabbi Amihud Yiẓchak Meir Levin** of Netanya, and **Rabbi Raphael Reichman**, dean of Yeshivas Me'ah She'arim, who kindly consented to share with me his original letter from Rabbi Mordechai Gimpel Yaffe. I offer my thanks to the writer **Tsur Shezaf** of Tel Aviv. I extend my appreciation to **Shaul and Ruth Dagan** for permission to use excerpts from their book, *On the First Road to Zion: Stories of the First Aliyah Colonies.*

Thank you to **Rabbi Simchah Hakohen Kook**, chief rabbi of Rehovot, for answering my questions about his uncle, Rabbi Avraham Yitzchak Hakohen Kook; and **Rabbi Ben Zion Kugler** of Keren Ha-Shvi'it regarding the statistics of the Shemittah of 5768/2007-2008; **Rabbi Aharon Goldberg**, grandson of Rabbi Shlomo Zalman Auerbach, who explained to me his grandfather's position regarding Shemittah and the *Heter Mechirah*; **Dr. Uri Rottenberg** for his help in obtaining rare photos of rabbis and obscure historical information about the Chassidic founders of Zikhron Yaakov; the librarians at Yad Izhak Ben-Zvi and **Adi Ofer** of its publishing house; the librarians of the National Library of Israel and to **Rachel Misrati** from the JNUL archives department. I want to express my appreciation to the librarians of Michlelet Herzog and **Reuven Kopler** of the Central Zionist Archives. Special thanks to **Adi Rubin**, curator of the Museum of Rishon Le-Ẓion, and to **Yehoshua Shofet** of Keren Ha-Shvi'it. Thank you to **Rabbi Avishai David** of Beit Shemesh for lending me his (hard to obtain) copy of *Heter Tarmat.*

Others who have helped me along the way were **Dr. Moshe Koppel**, **Rabbi Danny Gutenmacher**, **David and Phyllis Strauss** (whose enthusiasm and insights were a big boost for me), and **Tzvi Willner** (who accompanied me to Mazkeret Batya and took some photographs for this book).

My thanks to **Vered Shatil** – Vered made the beautiful maps for the book. I wish to acknowledge the superb work of **Charlotte and Yiẓchak Friedland**, who edited the book.

The beautiful graphics of this book is a testament to the conscientious professionalism and supervision of **Ben Gasner**, who is also a wonderful and caring friend. The bulk of the graphics was done by **Bat-Chen Grossman** who put her heart and soul into the book! What she accomplished exceeded my wildest expectations. I would also like to thank the other members of the staff, who contributed greatly to this book, **Nili Boim** and **Mindel Kassorla.** Special mention to **Rabbi David Kahn** of Feldheim Publishers for taking a personal interest in this book and making sure that it would come to fruition.

I am grateful to my parents for instilling in me a love of the Land of Israel by making my Bar Miẓvah there right after the Six Day War. Thanks to the farmers of Beit Chilkiah and Yesodot who introduced me to their special blend of old-fashioned Yiddishkeit and Israeli agriculture. And thank you to **Ahron Horovitz**, founder of the Derech Ereẓ tour guide school, whose program introduced me to Mazkeret Batya.

And most importantly, I would like to thank the Almighty for choreographing the whole project from start to finish.

Sam Finkel
Jerusalem
February, 2012/ Shevat 5772

finkels2@zahav.net.il

Foreword

This book is not just about Mazkeret Batya. It's about appreciating what it means to live in Israel.

The "Israel experience" has become a rite of passage for young Diaspora Jews. They leave home for an extended period, such as a year, and live in a foreign country. Many study here. It's all very exciting – the Old City of Jerusalem, Masada, kayaking in the Galilee. But something is missing. Wherever they go, whatever majestic scenery their bus may be passing, they're too busy chatting on their cell phones to be awestruck by what they're witnessing.

They've "skipped the first chapters," so they don't get the story.

Whenever I turn on the faucet here in Israel, I'm amazed, because not long ago the country had no indoor plumbing.

When I walk down the streets of Rechavia, the Jerusalem neighborhood where I live, I appreciate everything I see, because back in the 1920s, the area was nothing but rocky desolation. Every tree, every building, every road today is a miracle.

People take it for granted that there are fine restaurants all over Israel. But not long ago there were soup kitchens instead, and people were starving.

Everything we have today in Israel might very well not be here if not for a few hardy (some say crazy) Jews who loved Ereẓ Yisrael so much that they put their lives on the line to settle it – for themselves and for us.

This book is meant to be experiential. I want you to immerse yourself in the story and experience the colonizing of the Holy Land firsthand. Don't just read about the protagonists – join them. Put yourself in their shoes. Try to feel what they felt when they saw the coastline of Ereẓ Yisrael for the first time. Experience the dread of getting past hostile immigration officials, the concern of a mother hoping her child won't die of malaria, and the thrill of seeing stalks of wheat swaying in the wind and Jews returning to the soil of the Holy Land.

Imagine the sanctity the settlers felt when they ushered in the Sabbath, and their joy and fear as the yearlong agricultural Sabbath loomed.

Then your Israel experience will be much deeper.

Mazkeret Batya also encapsulates the history of Israel. Should the country be religious or secular? Nationalist or universalist? What role should Diaspora Jewry play in building Israel? How should we relate to the Arabs? How to apply Jewish law to changing circumstances, and how to unify the Orthodox community? All the major issues facing the State of Israel began in this tiny village. To understand the twenty-first century, we have to step back into the nineteenth.

If this book helps provide that understanding, by placing Israel in its moving historical context, then the five years of work I've put into it will all have been worthwhile.

Rebels in the Holy Land

Prologue

Discovering Mazkeret Batya

Mazkeret Batya is located along Israel's coastal plain, five kilometers (3.1 miles) southwest of the city of Rehovot. As in other Israeli small towns, the landscape fills the eye with red-tile roofed homes and gardens bursting with flowers, bounded by creeping vines. The children of Mazkeret Batya play in broad, open areas and run through freshly cut grass. While most of the structures are of recent vintage, the community has managed to retain the charm of an historic old town. There is a rural feel to the place, and a walk through the village easily banishes the tensions of city life.

Rothschild Street, the town's main thoroughfare, is named after Baron Edmond de Rothschild, whose largesse formed

Founders Street, Mazkeret Batya. The town has 11,000 residents but not a single traffic light.

the central economic pillar of the settlement. Along this road, just a block away from Founders Street, are four old buildings. One of them has been converted into a café. The buildings are referred to as *kazarmes* (perhaps from the Latin word for "house of weapons" – or the Russian word for "barracks"), as they physically resemble military barracks. They were the first structures built back in 1884 to house the colony's first families. Tucked between two of the kazarmes is the town's museum.

It was in the museum building that my love affair with Mazkeret Batya began. The year was 2005, and I was participating in a program that trained people to become licensed tour guides in Israel. Our lectures focused on the period known as the First Aliyah (1882-1903), and we visited Mazkeret Batya, as its establishment was during that era.

Framed photographs of the founders of this community lined the walls of the museum. As I gazed at their faces, I was shocked: Here were men with beards and *payot,* men who prayed three times a day and studied Torah morning and evening. Who knew that the earliest pioneer settlers had been fervently Orthodox Jews?[1] I was even more amazed to learn that they had been skilled farmers back in Russia. There were Jewish farmers in Europe?

Like so many others, I had always believed that the early pioneers came to Palestine to build a new society based on socialism and the secular Jewish "Enlightenment" (*Haskalah*), rejecting

Faces of Mazkeret Batya

traditional Jewish practices. I had also thought that the primary motive of the early pioneers was to escape anti-Semitism and to abandon the "*galuti*" (Diaspora-like, in a derogatory sense) Jewish means of livelihood. I thought that non-religious pioneers in Palestine were the first Jews in modern times to engage in manual labor and farming. I was so wrong!

Family portraits of early residents revealed the faces of hopeful young religious couples, pious parents and children, not secular ideologues. They had come to Palestine imbued with the mission of planting Torah – more than any other crop – in its stubborn soil. (See Afterword: "Idealists or Opportunists?," p. 312.)

Even the broad outline of their story was extraordinary. In 1882, ten men in the tiny hamlet of Pavlovka, in White Russia (today Belarus), were presented with a proposal: Baron Rothschild in faraway Paris was willing to support their establishing a farming colony in Palestine. The anti-Semitism that was so endemic in Russia had not overtly affected this relatively secluded Jewish village. The people were successful farmers, economically and politically stable. Why would they be willing to separate from their families for a long time and give up their livelihoods to make the arduous trek to a distant land, to a neglected corner of the Ottoman Empire?

Chaim and Guta Glick with son Noach

Yet these indomitable ten farmers – and a *melamed* (teacher) – established the sixth[2] Jewish agricultural colony in the Land of Israel. The colony was initially named Ekron, because it was located adjacent to the Arab village of Aqir. The Arabs were known to have retained the ancient names of places in which they settled, and it was assumed that Aqir was a derivative of Ekron, the ancient Philistine city. A few years later, when Baron Rothschild visited Ekron, he renamed it Mazkeret Batya, in memory of his mother, Batya Rothschild.

Yisrael Arkin and daughters

And there was more, much more that left me incredulous. Our guide led us to an old building, a farmhouse that had been converted into a screening room. We watched a short docudrama about the fierce struggle of these farmers with their patron in 1889. The issue was working the land during the *Shemittah*

(Sabbatical) year. According to Jewish law, there is an agricultural cycle of seven years in the Land of Israel. Every seventh year it is not farmed, similar to the day of rest on the seventh day of every week, a year-long Sabbath. The Baron wanted the farmers to abide by the *Heter Mechirah* – a legal leniency that would circumvent the Shemittah prohibition by temporarily selling the land to Arab farmers. Some (albeit a minority) of the leading authorities on Jewish law in Europe accepted this procedure as legitimate, but the Ashkenazic rabbis in Jerusalem did not.

The farmers faced a dilemma. For five years, they had worked hard and succeeded in creating a beautiful farming community, by then numbering over 100 souls; they were on the threshold of economic independence. Should they follow their own religious principles and accept the counsel of their spiritual leaders in Jerusalem? Or should they accept the ruling of the European rabbis, guaranteeing that Baron Rothschild would continue to favor them with his financial support? Their answer – to refrain from farming during Shemittah – demonstrated a brand of spiritual heroism overlooked by later generations.

Why Are They a Secret?

The reason of why this group of pioneers has been ignored in our history books is disquieting. After all, they certainly merit attention.

Most of Israel's history textbooks gloss over the First Aliyah period and concentrate on the Second Aliyah (1904-1914), which formed the basis of Israel's secular, socialist character. One of Israel's distinguished experts on its modern history, Mordechai Eliav, writes the following in the introduction to his two-volume work *Sefer ha-Aliyah ha-Rishonah* (The Book of the First Aliyah):

> ... despite its significance with regard to the history of the Yishuv [the pre-state Jewish community in Palestine], the First Aliyah did not gain the fame it deserved in the historiography of the Yishuv and the Jewish national movement. There are no significant differences between the numbers of immigrants in the First and Second Aliyot. Even more people returned [to the Diaspora] from the Second Aliyah than from the First. But the Second Aliyah attains

> this shining halo of pure pioneering to the point that one gets the misleading impression that [its participants] were the ones who began the period of new Jewish settlement in the land. The aura of the First Aliyah was relegated to the corner. Some even relate to the achievements of the First Aliyah with a bit of scorn and disparagement.[3]
>
> ... It is fitting to re-emphasize that the majority of settlers [of the First Aliyah] observed the commandments and nearly all of the first settlements had a definite religious character at the onset of their establishment.[4]

Perhaps we know so little about Ekron because these pioneers did not fit the mold of the subsequent chaluẓim who became the role models for the future State of Israel. Successive waves of immigration to Palestine brought thousands of non-

Comrades in arms. Fervently Orthodox pioneers came in all sizes and genders.

observant Jews, as well as Jews who were anti-religious. The goal of the Zionist movement that developed in the early twentieth century was to create a secular, nationalist society – a religious, social, and historical break from the European Jewish world. The role models these Zionists wanted to bequeath to their children were the self-assured, revolutionary, and bronzed chaluẓim whose ideals were derived from the modern socialist and nationalist movements.

There were also non-religious pioneers who settled in

"Chaluẓim building road." Postcard, British Mandate period. What about the Orthodox pioneers who preceded them by three decades?

Palestine during the First Aliyah period; they came from the ranks of the BILU movement.[5] However, the "Biluim" – as the movement's members were called – were the major exception; the majority of the first groups of settlers were religious Jews. Eliav writes:

> In all respects, the Biluim were different from the rest of the people of the First Aliyah. In practice, only a handful of them made *aliyah,* and their sole achievement was just one settlement. Over time people have unjustifiably identified the whole First Aliyah movement with the Biluim, while in reality they were only a small segment of that Aliyah.[5A]

Unsung hero. Yosef Weidenfeld, a founder of Rosh Pina

In the glossy history encyclopedia published by Ma'ariv/Revivim, *The Great Periods in the History of the Land of Israel* (similar in style to the Time/Life *American History* series), two full pages are devoted to the Biluim, along with two long sidebars in the volume titled *A Province in the Teetering Empire.* One sentence, tucked away in the body of the text about the First Aliyah, informs us that most of the First Aliyah settlers were religious. Ekron/Mazkeret Batya is never mentioned, and there is no discussion in those pages of the major role played by the meticulously observant Jews in this period of agricultural colonization. In truth, the early settlements of Ekron, Petach Tikva, Rosh Pina, Yesud Ha-Ma'alah, and Bnei Yehuda[6] were all established by such Jews.

The lack of awareness of Mazkeret Batya's history is not limited to the non-religious population. Many religiously observant Jews are unaware of its history. There is an ideological issue here as well:

For many non-Zionist Orthodox Jews Mazkeret Batya is too closely associated with Chovevei Ẓion (Lovers of Zion), the pre-Zionist movement whose goal was to settle Jews in Palestine. Chovevei Ẓion's leadership was composed of both religious and non-religious Jews.[7] Mazkeret Batya is also associated with Rabbi Shmuel Mohilever, who believed that the resettling of the Jewish masses in the Land of Israel would solve many of the problems that beset the Jewish people at that time. Rabbi Mohilever was indisputably one of the great Torah sages of that era and he was one of the founders of the Chovevei Ẓion movement.

Conversely, to many religious Zionists, the founders of Ekron/Mazkeret Batya were too intimately linked with the "old-fashioned" Old Yishuv – the Jewish community established in Palestine prior to 1882 – and with their anti-Chovevei Ẓion rabbis.

העלייה הראשונה

1903-1882

ב"1882 הגיעו לארץ אלפי יהודים ממזרח אירופה, בעיקר מרוסיה ומרומניה. רובם היו חברי תנועת "חיבת"ציון", שהתארגנו לעלייה בעקבות **"סופות בנגב"**, הפרעות בדרום רוסיה, והחליטו לעלות לארץ וליישב אותה. בארץ"ישראל, השוממה ברובה, שלטו בזמן ההוא התורכים (**האימפריה העות'מנית**). רוב התושבים בה היו ערבים, והיהודים המעטים שחיו כאן היו דתיים, שהתפרנסו מ"כספי החלוקה" (העולים כינו אותם "היישוב הישן").

בעקבות הפרעות ברוסיה עולים ארצה כמה אלפי יהודים ב"1882.

ע"לי **העלייה הראשונה** לא רצו להצטרף ל"יישוב הישן". הם ביקשו להקים בארץ"ישראל חברה יהודית חדשה, חברה לאומית ועובדת. הם רצו להיות איכרים ולהתיישב התיישבות חקלאית באזורים בלתי מיושבים על"ידי יהודים.

אנשי העלייה הראשונה שואפים להקים בארץ חברה יהודית לאומית ומקימים מושבות חקלאיות.

בעזרת תרומות של יהודים מרוסיה ומרומניה קנו העולים אדמות, ועליהן הקימו **מושבות חקלאיות**. במשך שנה אחת הכשירו המתיישבים את הקרקעות במשותף, ואחר"כך חילקו אותן ביניהם, וכל משפחה הקימה משק לעצמה.

Misleading. From a history digest on the First Aliyah for Israeli high school students. It contrasts the Old Yishuv, described as religious and financially dependent on contributions from abroad with the New Yishuv of the First Aliyah, which "wanted to establish . . . a new Jewish society – nationalistic and working." No mention is made that the vast majority of the early pioneers of the New Yishuv were religious. The truth is that all but one of the first twelve settlements were >

established by observant Jews, and two were even established by Jews from the Old Yishuv.

In short, the pioneering farmers of Ekron/Mazkeret Batya do not fit the mold of today's ideological constructs. On the one hand, they differed from the Old Yishuv in that they refused support from the Diaspora-funded Chalukah pipeline, actively attempting to sustain themselves through agriculture.[8] On the other hand, they broke ranks with the pioneers of the other settlements by making the strict observance of Shemittah a greater priority than the settlement of Palestine: they threatened to return to Russia if they could not observe the Sabbatical year!

What most characterized the founders of Mazkeret Batya was their avowed dedication to those special commandments known as the *mizvot ha-teluyot ba-arez* – commandments linked to the Land of Israel. They viewed living in the Holy Land as a privilege and farming its soil as an opportunity to fulfill the land-linked mizvot. Observance of the Torah's commandments took precedence over Jewish nationalism and was their primary motivation for coming to Palestine.

They were keenly aware that their establishment of a model colony could pave the way for other European and Russian Jews to make their new homes in Palestine rather than in America. It was their love of Klal Yisrael (the Jewish people), and their love of Erez Yisrael (the Land of Israel), that drove them.

And they suffered terribly in many ways for these allegiances. It was this aspect of their story – brave, dramatic, and heartrending – that inspired me to write this book. My goal is to transcend ideological and partisan biases and acknowledge the true story of the pioneering days of Israel, for the founders of Mazkeret Batya occupy a unique niche in the history of our people.

Chapter 1

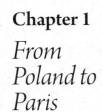

From Poland to Paris

It was the summer of 1881. Like a tsunami, anti-Jewish pogroms spread throughout southwest Russia, bringing devastation in their wake. Fueled by the rumor that one of the conspirators involved in the assassination of Czar Alexander II was a Jewish woman, the czarist government provided a "green light" for anti-Semites to set out on a rampage of burning and looting. Jews in over 166 communities throughout the Ukraine watched helplessly as their homes and businesses went up in flames. No one in these modern times anticipated such unbridled hatred and violence.

For many Jews, the mayhem signified that there was no future for them in Russia. Between 1881 and 1914 more than

On the run. Two panic-stricken refugees, carrying *tallit*-wrapped Torah scrolls, escape a pogrom in Heimlase, Russia. *Painting by the Jewish artist Stanislaus Bender*

two million Jews emigrated to the *"goldeneh medinah"* (the golden land), the United States of America. For tens of thousands of Russian Jews, the first leg of their long journey to the New World began by fleeing south to cities such as Brody and Lvov. They were located in Galicia, a province of the neighboring Austro-Hungarian Empire, where the government had a much more tolerant attitude toward the Jews.

There, huddled together without a roof over their heads, they were met by a number of Jewish dignitaries who represented individual wealthy Jews, ready to assist their brethren.

America replacing Israel as the Promised Land. Uncle Sam as Moses leading the Jews out of Egypt (Russia). Caricature from *Der Groisser Kundes*, New York, 1913.

Additionally, representatives of Jewish communal organizations from western Europe came to Galicia to survey the situation. Among those who came to provide relief were Baron Samuel Montague, a leader of British Jewry, Sir Lawrence Oliphant, and representatives of the French worldwide social welfare assistance organization, Alliance Israélite Universelle. Only two Polish Jewish leaders paid a call to Brody: Shmuel Mohilever,[9] the chief rabbi of Radom, and the writer, Shaul Pinchas Rabinowitz[10] of Warsaw.

Rabbi Mohilever was a person whose wide-ranging interests went far beyond the confines of Radom and who cared deeply about all his fellow Jews. Representing no one, he traveled there at his own initiative and expense.[11] As early as 1871, he began writing some of his thoughts on the question of Jewish return to the Land of Israel:

> Since we see that we have not merited to hasten the redemption through our deeds … if the earlier [generations] with all their great righteousness did not merit to hasten a miraculous redemption for themselves, we certainly would not be capable of meriting this – this is something that no one who thinks logically can deny. …[12]

The human wreckage and misery that he witnessed in Brody made him believe that now, more than ever, God was signaling to His people that it was time to leave the European and Russian Diaspora and return home.

> Don't you see the hand of God in all that has occurred to us? It has been close to a decade since God has made us drink from the bitter cup in most of Europe. People of ill repute have risen against us to persecute us and falsely accuse us. And a voice calls out and

proclaims, "Children, return to your homeland! Throw out your gods of silver and gold! Come and take shelter in My shade, in the land of your forefathers."[13]

Visionary. Rabbi Shmuel Mohilever was described by a contemporary writer as a man "... of great stature and thin of flesh. His face is pale and thin. His forehead is wide and wrinkled, and his eyes are blue, penetrating and expressive of grief and worry. ... He is bent when he walks and seems to be counting his footsteps. His few words spring from the depths of his heart as 'the waters of the Shiloach, which run gently.'" Regarding the future redemption of the Jewish people (which he believed would be in the near future) he wrote, "The redemption that we are awaiting ... will come about through natural means and will be on a very low level."

The two men furnished emotional support to the refugees; they knew their language and spoke to their hearts. But they failed in achieving their primary objective – to convince the representatives of Western Jewry to redirect the flow of emigration from the United States to Palestine. The representatives had a simple question for which the rabbis had no answer: How could a barren country like Palestine, lacking the necessary infrastructure, be capable of absorbing such a large number of refugees so quickly?[14]

Rabbi Mohilever would not allow himself to be quickly deterred or discouraged. Something needed to be done.

In 1882, Rabbi Mohilever organized a Jewish colonization society in Warsaw – the first of scores of local chapters later known as the Chovevei Ẓion movement. While in Warsaw, he persuaded Rabbi Yosef Ber Soloveitchik[15] of Brisk and Rabbi Eliyahu Chaim Meisel[16] of Lodz to sign a public proclamation with him, calling on rabbis to issue a warning to their communities "... about the serious nature and danger to Judaism that would result from mass emigration to America. A dry piece of bread [in Russia] even without tranquility, God forbid, where fulfillment of the Torah is possible, is preferable to all the wealth and charm of America."[17]

The proclamation called for Jewish communities to take some concrete steps to establish a presence in Palestine:

Signatories.
Top: Rabbi Eliyahu Chaim Meisel
Bottom: Rabbi Yosef Ber Soloveitchik

> They should establish groups in every city, and every group should consist of at least ten men in which each one of them [pledges] to contribute 1,000 silver rubles each. And with their total sum of 10,000 silver rubles they should purchase land and build homes ... they should prepare [in advance] for all their needs ... they should seed [their fields] at least one year before they arrive [in Palestine]. Toward this end, they should select one or two men to travel there. ...[18]

When it became known that secular Jews (later known as Biluim), were heeding the call, Rabbis Soloveitchik and Meisel withdrew their names from the proclamation and no longer wanted to promote immigration to Palestine.[19]

Two Visionaries Meet at a German Spa

In late summer of 1882, Rabbi Mohilever traveled to western Europe to garner support for the Chovevei Ẓion movement. He visited Vienna, then Germany, but he failed in winning any rabbis and philanthropists over to his cause. His next destination was Paris, where he wanted to meet with the representatives of the Alliance Israélite Universelle and convince them to renew their colonization activities in Palestine. Physically ill and emotionally drained, he took some time off to relax at the mineral springs spa of Zaiden, near Mainz, Germany.

Yechiel Brill, the restless editor of the Hebrew-language newspaper *Ha-Levanon,* was also taking time off in Zaiden. Brill, who had taught himself Hebrew, was a highly opinionated and vocal journalist. He wrote strongly worded editorials, many of which criticized the Jewish leadership of his day. Loathing deceit and duplicity, he pulled no punches.

But there was another side to Brill: he was an idealist ready to make huge personal sacrifices for the sake of bringing Jews back to the Holy Land. At first, he opposed mass *aliyah*:

> [Palestine's] best fields are taken by the *fellahin* (Arab peasant farmers) and the Bedouin, who devastate them. Only for a lot of money would they be willing to sell their inheritance. [Therefore] the only fields for sale in this country are those that have poor soil or bereave their inhabitants [i.e., due to malaria]. If we indeed settle Jews in such fields, without a doubt they will leave before

the first year is out. And because there is no real commerce to speak of or sufficient employment opportunities, by bringing Jewish people here, all we will accomplish is an increase in the number of poor people who are already living lives of pain and shame here that stem from their having to live on handouts sent to them out of the generosity of the people who send them the money, whether willingly or under coercion. ...[20]

Yechiel Brill. Brill is an acronym for **B**en **R**abbi **Y**ehuda **L**oewe, otherwise known as the Maharal. Born in Tulchin, Ukraine, he spent time in Bucharest, where he was a student of Rabbi Meir Leib ben Yechiel Michel (the Malbim). In 1855, he immigrated to Palestine, where he was employed as corresponding secretary of Kollel ha-Perushim in Jerusalem. He established *Ha-Levanon* in Jerusalem in 1863, making it the first Hebrew newspaper to appear on a regular basis in Palestine. He re-established the paper, first in Paris (1865), then in Mainz (1871) as the Hebrew-language supplement to Dr. Meir Lehmann's *Der Israelit*. Brill may have been the first to propose that Jews undergo agricultural training prior to *aliyah*.

Brill changed his mind after the pogroms of 1881. The devastation he witnessed visited upon the Russian Jews turned him into a supporter of Chovevei Ẓion.[21] He began writing about the novel idea of sending professional Jewish farmers[22] to

Bread of affliction. Old Yishuv soup kitchen in Jerusalem

colonize Palestine. That occurred more than a year before Rabbi Mohilever's efforts met with any success:

> ... in our opinion, if we want to establish Jewish settlements in the Holy Land, we will succeed if we first send up to Zion our brothers who have been farmers in the colonies that they have in southern Russia ... [selecting] those who have already mastered the skills needed to work the land prior to their arrival in the Holy Land. [It is they who] will work the land which we will acquire for them. ... [23]

Fate would have it that these two men who deeply believed in the return of the Jews to the Land of Israel would meet in a spa in Germany and forge an important working relationship. Brill urged Rabbi Mohilever to send fifty experienced Jewish farmers from the Ukrainian Jewish farming communities to build farms and infrastructure, after which they would send for their families.[24]

The Baron's Inner Circle

Spiritual advisor. Rabbi Ẓaddok Kahn was the chief rabbi of Paris from 1869 until 1890.

Financial advisor. Michael Erlanger, a Chovevei Ẓion activist, administered the Baron's philanthropic activities starting in 1877.

Rabbi Mohilever went on to Paris, where he met with the Russian Jewish magnate Horace Günsburg and with representatives of the Alliance, but neither showed any interest in his proposals. He fared no better with other wealthy Jews to whom he was referred.

Just two days after Yom Kippur in 1882, Brill happened to be in Paris on business and met with a very disheartened Rabbi Mohilever. Brill looked at the rabbi's remaining prospects and realized they would be fruitless. That very day, Brill went to see the chief rabbi of Paris, Ẓaddok Kahn.[25] Next on Brill's list was Michael Erlanger, a leader of the Alliance.[26]

The spiritual advisor of Baron Edmond de Rothschild, Rabbi Kahn had developed a close and highly influential relationship with him. According to one biographer:

> ... the truth is that back then, the first and only person to influence Rothschild in regard to Palestine was none other than the Grand Rabbi of France, Rabbi Ẓaddok Kahn. ... Needless to say Rothschild did not receive people who wanted to interest him in their projects unless he had been informed definitely on the subject beforehand by someone whose opinion he valued and respected. This important function was performed by Rabbi Ẓaddok Kahn.[27]

Brill spoke passionately about Rabbi Mohilever to both men, pointing out the rabbi's selflessness.[28] His speculation that Rabbi Kahn would respond favorably was on target. The energetic and influential modern rabbi was deeply moved by the ardor of the rabbi from the Old World. He promised to ask the Baron to grant Rabbi Mohilever an audience.

Two days that seemed like an eternity passed without any word from the Baron. But on September 27, the eve of the holiday of Sukkot, Rabbi Mohilever received a message that the Baron had agreed to meet with him at 2:00 in the afternoon on the first day of the holiday.[29] The timing seemed odd: travel was prohibited on Jewish holidays, and the rabbi would have to walk for over three hours from his lodgings in the Jewish neighborhood in the center of Paris to the Baron's residence on the city's outskirts. Was this simply the only time the Baron had available, or was it perhaps an expression of the Baron's sentiments that he was not enthusiastic about meeting with yet another eastern European *schnorrer*? Was it a serious offer to meet with him?

Chapter 2
The Rabbi and the Baron

Rabbi Mohilever gazed up at the massive entrance of Rothschild's magnificent residence. Physically ill, exhausted from hours of walking and emotionally drained, he now faced the moment of truth. Escorted by Rabbi Ẓaddok Kahn and Michael Erlanger, he was ushered into Edmond de Rothschild's study.

In his own words, Rabbi Mohilever described that fateful meeting with the Baron:

Imposing. The Baron's palatial residence at 41 rues du Faubourg-Saint-Honoré. The building could accommodate up to 1,800 people in its reception rooms and ballrooms. Two critics of architecture and interior design who visited in 1889 claimed that it was the most princely residence they had seen in all of Paris.

> At the appointed hour when we entered his office, the Baron extended his hand to me and with a cold gesture motioned to me to sit in the chair next to his desk. A few minutes went by, and then he asked me, in a cold tone that was only out of courtesy, "Rabbi, about what are you inquiring?"[30]

Although the extended Rothschild family was actively involved in helping the Jewish poor – and it made sure that Edmond would be no exception[31] – Jewish communal work was not one of Baron Edmond de Rothschild's priorities. Moreover, he opposed the idea of colonizing Palestine.[32] Rabbi Mohilever realized that if he did not break the ice quickly, he would lose the Baron forever. His account continues:

> His [cold] attitude did not encourage me much, and I certainly was not the first rabbi to turn to the Baron [for assistance]. Many rabbis from many countries, in rabbinical attire like mine, had come to him for help. Most of them came for themselves, and a few came for some group or society. So how could I influence him to take me seriously? For a brief moment, I was flabbergasted, but then I suddenly reminded myself of the great purpose for which I had come, and I did not pay attention to my weaknesses or fragile state of health. I encouraged myself and told him:
>
> "Forgive me, Your Honor, the Baron, if I communicate to you as I would address my own congregation. I am a rabbi from the

old school, and I am accustomed to speaking through simile and parable."

A smile [suddenly] passed over his lips, and with a friendly face and a warm and heartfelt tone of voice he said to me, "I will gladly listen to you."

I said: "For years I was troubled by this vexing question: Why was Moses, of all people, chosen to be the leader of the Jewish people, to take them out of Egypt, when he suffered from such a debilitating speech impediment? As a political leader and representative, he had to speak to the king and to government officials. The most basic requirement of a spokesperson is to be a good communicator. Exactly what Moses was not!

"... I was perplexed by this question, but only [now] during my trip to see you do I – as an emissary to perform a *mizvah*... suddenly realize the answer.

"Moses was chosen to be not only the political leader of the Jewish people, but the giver of the Torah. God chose him not only for the exodus from Egypt but to bring them to Mount Sinai to receive the Torah. If Moses was charismatic and eloquent, knowing how to influence people and be persuasive, the cynics would have claimed that the Torah was not from God but rather from Moses, who knew how to seize the moment and mesmerize people into believing. But if the Jews accepted the Torah from a stutterer and one heavy of speech, it is a proof that God was speaking through Moses, that Moses was the *messenger* and not the sender.

The main man. Baron Edmond de Rothschild (1845-1934) was only 37 years old when he met Rabbi Mohilever, who was 58. An avid art collector, he had obtained etchings and drawings from the time he was 14 years old. That collection, now in the Louvre, is considered one of the museum's finest. He loved archeology and was fascinated by biochemistry as well. (He financed the National Institute of Biochemistry in the 1890s.)[33] He had also been an advisor to one of the Rothschild family's banks and possessed a solid knowledge of finance, but he semi-retired from the world of banking at age 28 to devote himself more fully to his other pursuits. It is strange that Jewish (and especially Israeli) history books usually portray him as a genial and generous old grandfatherly type, whereas most of his life's work in Palestine was accomplished when he was a young man. He was physically robust, and at the age of 40 he was determined to scale the Matterhorn – and he did. Edmond de Rothschild was a Renaissance man, with the time and resources to pursue his many dreams.

"My lord Baron, before this very table that you are sitting at come representatives of many countries – some of them quite powerful, who have power of attorney on behalf of great financial institutions. They come with different proposals: about building railroads or canals, or the colonization of desolate lands. They all come to you armed with a wide array of facts and a wealth of information regarding the topic they want to discuss with you. With their power of eloquence, they can explain and try to impress you with their plans and proposals – why they would be so profitable to you and beneficial for mankind.

"I also come to you with a proposal from my people, a proposal that is so important that the spirit of our people depends on it – the settling of the Land of Israel. But I am a man of heavy tongue and have great difficulty communicating to you the great reward [this proposal has] for you and for our people.

"If you accept my proposal and heed the request of your people to revive this desolate land, it is only because the lot of this ailing and oppressed people has touched your heart. And if you do not pay attention to my words, and you send me away empty-handed I will not regret my difficult journey with all its aches and pains – because I fulfilled the obligation that was placed upon me, and I have carried out my mission."

It seems that my words made a strong impression on the Baron, and when I laid out to him the specifics of the proposal, he listened with great interest and intense seriousness.[33]

The moving rabbinic parable had broken the ice. The rabbi went on, describing the difficulties that the Jews of Russia were experiencing, and he articulated the noble yearnings and hopes they had regarding the settlement of Palestine. Rothschild told Rabbi Mohilever, "If you came to me for financial assistance for this enterprise, you name the figure, and I will give it. If you are trying to convince me of its merits, then hold off – I need to give it a lot of thought and even test out the thesis to see if it is feasible."[34]

The Baron's words reflect the conflicted feelings he had about Jewish settlement in Palestine. Undaunted, Rabbi Mohilever replied, "We make no claim to guarantee the success of this venture, since it has been 2,000 years since we were exiled from our land and haven't worked it. But we hope that God will bless our project and fulfill our wishes."[35]

Though the Baron appeared hesitant about assisting the enterprise, his conversation with Rabbi Mohilever represented a major shift in his thinking about the Jewish nation's potential for resettling the Land of Israel. He said that if a few farmers would be willing to come to the Holy Land on their own initiative and funding, and prove over the course of a few months that they were capable of supporting their families in Palestine, he would help them establish a colony there.

Where history was made. To Rabbi Mohilever's credit, he was not intimidated by the Baron's opulence and power. However, he was taken aback by Rothschild's initial coldness. The rabbi mustered all his strength and pressed for the cause he so deeply believed in.

Rabbi Mohilever's reality came straight from the biblical prophets and transcended the glamorous trappings of nineteenth-century Paris. His words of fire were drawn from the spirit of the Bible and the Talmud he knew so well. Rothschild was also a man of vision, but he moved more slowly in his contemporary, business-oriented world. He was an uncompromising realist, taking his cues from the concrete world of finance.

But he was ready to try, to make a tentative start. And while he would eventually furnish extensive financial support and exert control over many of the new settlements in Palestine, he always insisted on anonymity. Never officially mentioned by name, he would become known throughout the settlements and the Jewish world simply as Ha-Nadiv Ha-Yadua – the Well-Known Benefactor – acknowledged yet secret. He did not want to attract the attention of the Turks, the French government or the press.

The meeting lasted only thirty minutes, half of which was consumed by Rabbi Kahn's translation from French to Yiddish and back. Nonetheless, it changed the course of Jewish history.

Not to lose momentum, Yechiel Brill wrote up a step-by-step plan detailing how a farming colony would be set up just a few days later, at the conclusion of the Sabbath. He asked Rabbi Mohilever to pass it on to Rabbi Kahn.

Rabbi Mohilever met with the Baron a second time and reached an agreement on the terms of the project. It was up to the rabbi to find and select suitable candidates – ten or twelve experienced farmers. They would travel to Palestine at their own expense, temporarily leaving their families behind. The Baron agreed to support these families until they were reunited with their husbands and fathers.

When the farmers arrived in Palestine, they were to proceed to the Mikveh Israel school,[35A] where expenses for their room and board would be covered by the Baron. Their stay at Mikveh Israel would be a trial period. They were to be supervised there by an agronomist hired by the Baron, who would train them in Palestinian farming methods and conditions for two to three months and then determine their suitability for this venture. Their expenditures for land, farm equipment, and upkeep during the first year would be granted as a loan.[36]

The potential historic impact of the venture was obvious to all. This project, if successful, would serve as a flagship settlement that would be the standard-bearer for future colonies in Palestine for the oppressed Jews of Russia.

Much like many newlyweds, neither Baron Rothschild nor Rabbi Mohilever fully foresaw the nature of the relationship they were getting into. The rabbi's first impressions of the Baron were of a man of great aristocratic bearing and benevolence. But he may not have fully perceived the Baron's stubborn belief "…that he, not they [the settlers] knew what is best for them. His brand of paternalism was of the most pronounced variety, and he would not tolerate any infraction of his absolute authority."[37] This is not to say that the Baron was arrogant, but he definitely was autocratic. He was ready to give his heart and fortune for them, but he demanded total obedience in return. The Baron, in turn, had no idea that the farmers who were soon to volunteer for this experiment would come with their own stubborn set of values and ideals.

Rabbi Mohilever's meetings with Baron Rothschild spelled a successful end to a long and exhausting trip. He had obtained a pledge of support from one of the richest Jews in the world.

Now he would have to find the farmers.

Rothschild's Daunting Considerations

While Rabbi Mohilever spoke, the Baron's mind was racing with many practical questions about the formidable obstacles that would have to be overcome.

The Ottomans: A farm could not be started without land, and an official Turkish deed (*kushan*) was necessary for entitling a farmer to ownership. Wary of European intrusions into their empire, the Ottomans viewed any organized European effort to build in their domain with justified suspicion. At the time, they were attempting to quell the Greek and Balkan nationalists who were trying to secede from the empire. The last thing the Ottomans wanted was to import a new nationalistic movement into their territory.

National and International Relations: How would France's national interests be affected if Rothschild's philanthropy incited the Turks against them? And how would such a venture affect France's relationship with its Jews, who had obtained full civil rights in 1791? Would it lead to accusations of dual loyalty?

Personal Relations: How would it affect Rothschild's relations with his associates, even with members of his own family? Would they view him as some sort of eccentric, pouring the family fortune into a barren, neglected province of the Ottoman Empire?

Technological and Economic Challenges: Rothschild was quite interested in agriculture and technology. The French had experience in colonizing North Africa, and Algeria was under their control. What ideas could be borrowed from there?

What could be grown in Palestine that would make enough money to guarantee that the farmers could become self-sufficient?

What kinds of drills and pumps would be needed to draw water from the depths and get it out to the arid fields? What kinds of plows and farming equipment would work in Palestine?

What building materials would be needed to create the infrastructure?

What experts needed to be sent, and how was the administrative structure to be set up?

How would the money be channeled – through the Alliance or perhaps some other vehicle?

Spiritual Needs: What about synagogues, schools, and slaughterhouses, and the personnel needed to man them? For what kind of spiritual environment should they aim?

Chapter 3
In Search of a Few Good Men

"May God Watch Over Us."

The fate of Russian Jewish refugees who yearned to settle in Palestine was at stake. Before Rabbi Mohilever left Paris, a letter arrived from Rabbi Kahn:

> Beloved master and rabbi, in the name of all my friends who are here, I would like to add the following: This project must set forth *with great care and deliberation,* so that – may God watch over us – no mishaps may come out of this. The candidates must be chosen with *great discernment* so that there is hope that this project will end well.[38]

The question as to whether Jews were capable of farming the Land of Israel was quite serious. By the time Baron Rothschild met Rabbi Mohilever in 1882, Petach Tikva, the first modern attempt by Jews to set up a farming colony in Palestine,[39] had been all but abandoned. Gei Oni (later renamed Rosh Pina), also founded in 1878, fared even worse: it lasted for only one year. Rishon Le-Ẓion, Jewry's third attempt, established two months before the historic meeting in Paris, was floundering, its financial resources totally depleted. It was simply uncharted territory, and Rabbi Kahn was right to urge caution.

Although Arab farmers had successfully cultivated the soil, the weighty question of whether European Jews were capable of adapting to the climate and environmental conditions of the Middle East hung over them. Had two millennia of Diaspora in the northern climes destroyed their chances?

Poster kids. Postcard reads: A farmer's children in Petach Tikva

For Rabbi Mohilever there was another challenge – finding experienced Jewish farmers who were committed to scrupulously observing the religious laws connected to farming the Land of Israel. His dream was to find candidates

who could prove that even after long hours with the plow and hoe, one could still make time for prayer, Torah study, and charitable deeds.

Rabbi Mohilever and Yechiel Brill left the French metropolis with Rabbi Kahn's letter, which contained a summary of the meeting with the Baron. They arrived triumphantly in Vilna (Vilinius)[40] and shared the news of the Baron's promised financial assistance with the Chovevei Ẓion supporters who flocked to see them. Although Brill had written about Jewish farming colonies in the Ukraine, they still had no clue as to where to start the search for religious farmers in the vast steppes of southern Russia. Unfortunately, neither did any of his visitors and well-wishers.

One man, a lawyer from Warsaw and a friend of Rabbi Mohilever, Dr. Yisrael Yasinovsky,[41] casually mentioned that he had heard there were religious Jewish farmers living not far away, near the town of Rozhinoy, in White Russia. Brill was encouraged by the fact that the rabbi of Rozhinoy was an enthusiastic supporter of settling the Land of Israel. Rabbi Mohilever entrusted Brill with the mission of traveling to Rozhinoy to recruit the farmers. Before Brill left, he asked the rabbi to pledge that in the worst-case scenario – if the farmers had to leave Palestine and return to Russia – he would pay their way home. To this end, Rabbi

What they left behind. A typical thatched home in Pavlovka (photo taken many years after the farmers left for Palestine)

Mohilever agreed to deposit 1,000 "shekels" (see caption, p. 27) with a third party, to be used for travel expenses.[42]

With a letter of introduction from Rabbi Mohilever, Brill reached Rozhinoy on October 19 and met with the town's rabbi, Mordechai Gimpel Yaffe.[43] Rozhinoy was an old, established Jewish community and its rabbi was a respected Torah sage who had authored a number of scholarly works.[44] The venerable Rabbi Yaffe had given his blessings to numerous projects that encouraged Jews to settle in the Land of Israel ever since the proclamation of Rabbi Ẓvi Hirsch Kalischer (1795-1874) back in 1862.[44A]

Rozhinoy's rabbi. Rabbi Mordechai Gimpel Yaffe who studied at the Yeshiva of Volozhin

When Rabbi Yaffe heard of Brill's mission, he was elated. He told Brill about a small farming colony just outside Rozhinoy called Pavlovka. Rabbi Yaffe invited Yerucham Fishel Pines,[45] an important member of the Rozhinoy community who was well acquainted with the Pavlovka farmers, to join him and Brill in the selection process. They made their way to the village with due haste.

The three men interviewed any farmer who expressed interest in the project. After careful scrutiny, they selected the following individuals (these photographs depict the men at later stages in their lives):[46]

Yaakov Arkin, age unknown
Somber, his forehead heavily creased, Arkin was an introverted man who kept his feelings and thoughts to himself. He feared God and devoted set times for Torah learning and he was involved in communal affairs.

Moshe Maller, 32
This pious Litvak knew the entire book of Psalms by heart and an interpretation for every word of it. Woe to any child who encountered him and couldn't explain a verse or word of Psalms to his satisfaction.[47]

Ẓvi Arkin, 34
Younger brother of Yaakov. Studied in a *cheder* and after marriage worked in a textile factory.[46A] He later changed direction and dedicated his life to working the soil. He truly considered himself a "man of the field." One of his descendants, Achiezer Arkin, wrote a book and produced a documentary about the Shemittah controversy that would engulf his great-grandfather and his colleagues.

Yaakov Laskovsky, 34
Tradition has it that Laskovsky was the most religious of all the founders. He excelled in strength and courage; feared no one, including Arab marauders. He later proved to be too much for Rothschild's administrators, who had him expelled from the colony. Lived many years in America, but in his old age returned to his true love – the Land of Israel.

Ephraim Skolnick, 49
Born in Rozhinoy. After completing *cheder*, he became a farmer in Pavlovka. He was also active in communal affairs.

Chaim Moshe Press, 31
A sociable individual, he was well known for his hospitality and generosity. He would later serve as the butcher to his fellow pioneers, offering them meat for the Sabbath on credit.

Dov Rudovsky, 33
Born in Rozhinoy. Received a traditional Jewish education. In 1885, he would be elected by his fellow pioneers to chair the *bikkur cholim* (medical) and *chevrah kaddisha* (burial) societies of the colony they founded. Gentle in spirit but capable of enduring the rigors of a new life in the Holy Land.

Yechezkel Levin, 20
Worked as a farmer until the last day of his life. He has many descendants who are farmers in Israel. A dignified and pious Jew, he started preparing himself to greet the Sabbath early in the afternoon and would prohibit his family from doing any form of farm chores that might result in the desecration of the Sabbath.[48]

No picture available

Baruch Ẓvi Bernstein, 42
Born in Rozhinoy. After Bernstein finished *cheder* his father taught him his first trade – carpentry. (Baruch later had all his daughters marry carpenters!) He later switched to farming. He saw building the Land of Israel as a holy vocation. A tough advocate, he became a fierce fighter on behalf of his settler colleagues.

No picture available

Yehoshua Rubinstein, age unknown
Born in Rozhinoy. He later moved to Pavłovka where he was engaged in farming. His farming skills qualified him to be picked by Brill as one of the candidates to be sent to Palestine. According to the book *Mazkeret Batya* he was the first member of this pioneer group to pass away.

These ten formed the nucleus of the first colony established by Baron Rothschild in the Land of Israel. They were heads of families totaling 101 people: fifty-four males and forty-seven females. Everyone was extremely happy with the qualities of the men they had chosen, and praise was not in short supply.

Brill wrote that "[The farmers are] all physically strong, peace-loving and brotherly … all of them have worked the land since their youth. …Besides agriculture, some knew how to build homes of wood, one knew woodwork, two were lumberjacks, and two were weavers of wool."[49]

Rabbi Mohilever stated that they had been "working the soil since their youth [and were] extremely decent and God-fearing men."[50]

Rabbi Yaffe wrote that they were "…honest, guileless people who work their own land by the sweat of their brows and with great toil; not even a scintilla of iniquity was ever heard regarding them."[51]

Although Brill described many of their qualifications, he did not state *why* the farmers wanted to give up their prosperous farms in Russia – farms that had been painstakingly established by their parents a generation earlier[52] – to embark on the treacherous venture in Palestine. None of them were members of any chapter of the Chovevei Ẓion society. What made them so eager?

Camouflaged currency. Enlargement of Russian silver ruble, 1878. That's what Brill probably meant by "shekel."

Achiezer Arkin has made it his life's work to publicize his family's history. He says that his ancestor and the others who constituted one of the first groups of modern-day settlers in the Land of Israel were devout and pious Jews who prayed three times a day. To him, the obvious answer is that they took the prayer *"Let our eyes behold Your return to Zion in mercy"* to heart. Their love of the Land of Israel and their desire to fulfill the agricultural miẓvot motivated them to take up the challenge. They were ready to leave their secure surroundings for a life they could barely imagine. (See Afterword, p. 312)

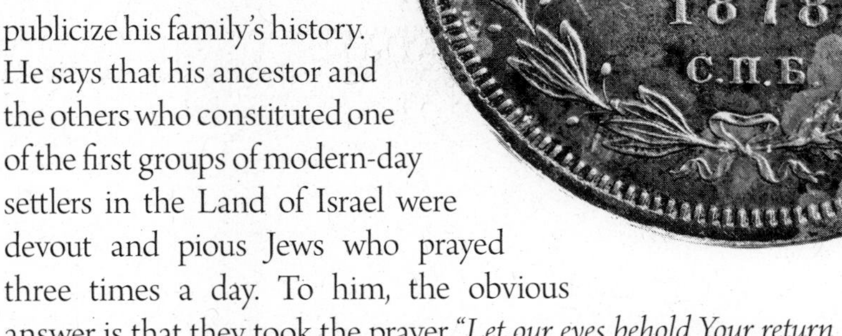

It's on the map! Segment of a detailed military map commissioned by the Austro-Hungarian monarchy, showing Rozhinoy (Różany) with Colony Constantinova (Kol. Konstanynowa) to the southwest of Rozhinoy and Colony Pavlovka (Kol. Pawlowa) to the southeast. The map was produced sometime in the last two decades of the nineteenth century and was probably used by the military during World War I.

Chapter 4 *The Contract*

To delineate the responsibilities and obligations of all the parties, Yechiel Brill drew up a contract with the following eleven clauses:[53]

1. Each one of us is making *aliyah* to the Holy Land at his own expense and of his own volition. [We are in agreement that] there is no coercion or entrapment.
2. When we arrive in the Holy Land, we will spend approximately two to three months at the Mikveh Israel school near Jaffa and work the land there and learn the essentials of planting saplings and vegetable gardening from the agronomist who was sent there [by the Alliance] … and if the agronomist finds us suited for agricultural work, we will stay in the Holy Land and settle on the land there, as will be explained below. But if the agronomist does not see any or all of us as suitable for the task, then we have no claims against the Alliance, ________,[54] Rabbi Shmuel Mohilever or Yechiel Brill.
3. If we are found suitable, the Alliance will grant us land in Mikveh Israel that will be large enough to grow sufficient amounts of wheat to make bread for our families and fodder for our animals.
4. The Alliance will supply us with the seeds we need to sow the fields and vegetable gardens for the first year.
5. The Alliance agrees to build homes for each family as well as barns for the livestock. The Alliance will dig a well in the area of land that is designated for us, and purchase the mechanical pump required to bring the water to irrigate the fields.
6. [The Alliance] will also assist us in acquiring animals and plowing apparatus.
7. During the trial period and subsequently during the first year, the Alliance will house us in the quarters that already exist at Mikveh Israel and pay for living expenses until the first harvest.
8. After our homes are built and the fields are awaiting harvest, we will send for our wives, our relatives, and all the members of our households according to the number of people we will delineate below … We understand that the travel expenses for our family members are not the responsibility of the Alliance.[55]
9. Re: all expenditures that the Alliance has spent on our behalf from the day of our arrival in the Holy Land until the first

harvest – we accept as a full obligation to return the monies to the Alliance according to the due date that the Alliance will determine.

10. Rabbi Mohilever agrees to guarantee 700 shekels in government promissory notes for the farmers if the Alliance fails to abide by its agreements.
11. When we settle on the homestead that will be given to us, the Alliance officials in Mikveh Israel may intervene in our personal affairs only when it comes to matters between man and his fellow man. But in matters between man and God, they have no right to intervene and dictate: "This you may do and this you may not do." We will abide only by the directives of those who are halakhic authorities – and through that we will be successful.

This final clause is highly significant. Brill included it because he was concerned about the cultural and religious differences between the pious eastern European shtetl Jews and their semi-assimilated brethren in France. It clearly identified the farmers as devout Jews who would not compromise their religious beliefs or practices. Five years from the signing of this document, this clause would play a major role in the history of their settlement.

The agreement was finalized and signed by the ten farmers on either October 19 or 20. Symbolically, the weekly Torah

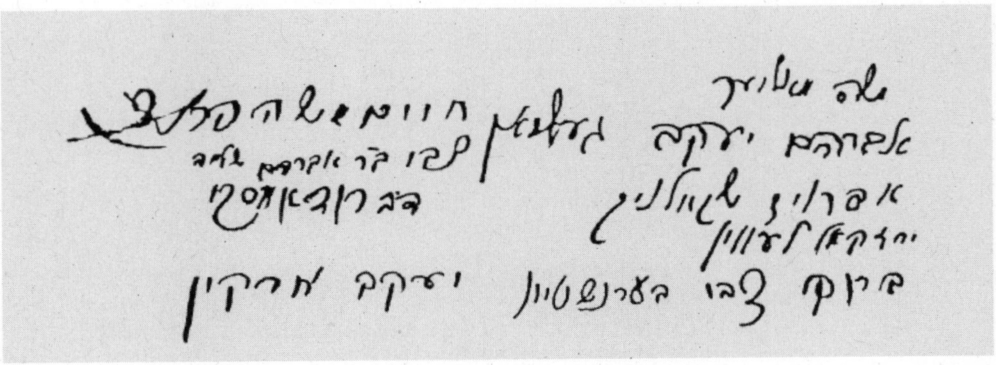

What's wrong with this picture?[56] Signatures of the Pavlovka farmers who signed the contract, as displayed in the Eran Shamir Village Museum, Mazkeret Batya

reading reflected the historic proportions of this enterprise. That week, they read in the Torah portion of *Lech Lecha*: "And God said to Abraham: Go you from your country and your birthplace and your father's household to the land that I will show you" (Genesis 12:1).

Brill told the farmers to put their affairs in order and be ready for the journey to Palestine in just two weeks.[57] Just before Brill left Pavlovka, Rabbi Mordechai Gimpel Yaffe implored him to accompany the farmers to the Holy Land himself to ensure the project's success. Brill replied that it was highly unlikely he would go, for he would have to stop publishing his newspaper, *Ha-Levanon*, which was his family's sole means of support.

Rabbi Yaffe and Yerucham Fishel Pines of Rozhinoy, Rabbi Yosef Ber Soloveitchik of Brisk and Rabbi Chaim Eliezer Wachs of Kalish (formerly the rabbi of Tarnogród) contributed money to cover some of the farmers' travel expenses.[57A]

Within a few days, Brill returned to Vilna and sent a report to Rabbi Shmuel Mohilever with the good news that he had found the men singularly fit for the job. This detailed report, which included the agreement the Pavlovka farmers had signed, was to be forwarded by Rabbi Mohilever to Rabbi Ẓaddok Kahn in Paris.

Despite the Baron's promise of support and the signed agreement in hand, Brill was apprehensive. He had heard about Shmuel Hirsch, the director of the Mikveh Israel school, on whom the farmers would have to depend. While he does not record precisely what he was told, the reports clearly made him uneasy.

Brill asked Rabbi Mohilever to send a letter to Rabbi Kahn, requesting that Hirsch be sent orders to receive the Pavlovka group warmly. But anxiety continued to plague him. What if Hirsch – even with the letter from Kahn – wouldn't let them into Mikveh Israel? The entire venture could be over before it began!

Brill made a difficult decision. He carefully penned a letter to Rabbi Mohilever:

> Being aware of the reputation of the director of Mikveh Israel, I am afraid that if we send the farmers unescorted we will not achieve our stated aims. **I am therefore volunteering to escort them as far as Jaffa and personally hand them over to the director.** But I will do this only on the condition that you, Rabbi Mohilever, accept responsibility for my household, which is financially depen-

dent on me, and see to it that they will not suffer from want during the time I am away… [58]

Within a week, Brill received this reply from the rabbi:

I copied your report word for word and sent it by post to Rabbi Ẓaddok Kahn in Paris. However, I left out your name and did not inform him as to the identity of the author. I just wrote that I'd sent a special, reliable and intelligent man [to find the candidates] and that there was no need to doubt the report's veracity. The reason I did not let on as to who my agent was is that I feared you might be a little suspect in his eyes. But when you bring the men yourself to the desired destination, you can inform him of this yourself. [58A]

Brill's nemesis. Shmuel Hirsch, the Alliance's administrator of the Mikveh Israel school.

It was plain that Rabbi Mohilever trusted Brill, but he wasn't so sure if others did. Brill recorded this embarrassing letter in his book *Yesud Ha-Ma'alah,*[59] which he wrote after he returned to Europe from his journey to Palestine.

Ten days passed with no word from Paris. The designated day of departure for the Holy Land came and went. And there was more bad news: the only available port of embarkation was Trieste, a city in northeastern Italy. That route would cost the pioneering farmers much more than what they had collected for their travel expenses. Brill wondered, how could he get the money to make up the difference?

It's Now or Never

A telegram from Rabbi Mohilever arrived on November 7, telling Brill to come at once to Radom. He set out the very next day and arrived at Rabbi Mohilever's home shortly before midnight. The rabbi seemed deeply agitated. With dark foreboding in his eyes, he showed Brill a letter that he'd received from Dr. Yisrael Michel Rabinowitz, a Chovevei Ẓion activist in Paris. Dr. Rabinowitz wrote that he had spoken to Rabbi Kahn, who told him that the reason he had not responded to Rabbi Mohilever was that the Baron had left Paris quite suddenly on personal business for an unspecified period of time. Rabbi Kahn advised Rabbi Mohilever to postpone the project for a year!

If we wait a year, we might as well abandon the project, Brill thought gloomily. His response to Rabbi Mohilever was decisive and unwavering:

> The farmers have already sold their household items to cover travel expenses. Who will compensate them? And who knows if they will still be willing to go in a full year from now? We cannot wait even a month for the Baron's return.
>
> Now is the season for plowing in the Holy Land. If we arrive after that time has passed, others – the *fellahin* – will plow all the fields in Mikveh Israel, and our farmers will not have any fields to plow. And if there is no plowing, there is no harvesting, and they will not be able to bring over their families the following summer. And what will they live off for two years? For they have abandoned their fields [in Pavlovka], and the fields they are supposed to receive in Mikveh Israel will be given over to others! My advice is not to delay.[60]

That fateful suggestion would make the entire venture even more precarious, but it outweighed the greater risk of losing the farmers. Rabbi Mohilever mulled over Brill's words. Responding to Brill's bravado, he was cautious and defensive:

> If I were willing to accept upon myself this responsibility… [the consequence would be] that if the fathers and the sons [of the farmers] should later scream about the terrible misfortune that befell [their loved ones] who made *aliyah* to the Holy Land – all their cries, outrage and indignation would be directed *toward me* [not to Rabbi Kahn]. Only if you [Brill] would be willing to accept that kind of responsibility would I not then object to your taking them to Palestine, even before Rabbi Kahn's approval.[61]

Brill was shocked at this response and later wrote:

> …Not only did he refuse to take moral responsibility, but he even withdrew his promise to guarantee the 700 shekels as collateral for each one, should things not work out.…When I heard Rabbi Shmuel Mohilever utter those words, I was devastated, and I had an inkling of what lay ahead of me.

Now Brill had to make another difficult decision: should he

take the whole gambit upon his shoulders? After a suspenseful few moments, he answered, "I am ready to recover [from this surprise], and I will 'try to be a man where there are no men.'"[62] He was relieved when Rabbi Mohilever gave him his word that regarding Brill's household in Mainz, the rabbi would take care that it not suffer from want, "and that I [Brill] need not fear hearing news of its distress reaching me in the Holy Land."

Less than a week later, Brill returned to Rozhinoy to inform Rabbi Yaffe that the promised 700-shekel collateral would not be forthcoming. The rabbi was crestfallen at first, but after a short while, he perked up and even gave Brill some encouragement. "Your accompanying them is a greater guarantee than the 700 shekels they were supposed to receive." Rabbi Yaffe then spoke to the farmers and convinced them to go even without the monetary guarantee. They all agreed.

Brill and the farmers then decided on the date they would leave for Palestine. It would be on Saturday evening, following the Sabbath of the Torah portion *Va-Yeẓei*: "And Jacob left Beersheba, and he went to Haran" (Genesis 28:10). It would be a good week to embark on the longest journey of their lives.

The Jewish Return to Zion

Persecution and messianic stirrings (which often go hand in hand) galvanized the determination of Jews to return to their homeland. The expulsion of Jews from Spain in 1492 forced many to find refuge in the Ottoman Empire, and some of them found their way to Palestine, with Safed as their center. Safed also drew many Kabbalists, with Rabbi Yiẓchak Luria perhaps the greatest among them.

Poor and proud. Ashkenazim from the Old Yishuv. Often the subjects of vintage photographs, which required long exposures and extensive set-up, were models dressed to play the role. Perhaps that was the case of these seven "Ashkenazi Jews" photographed at the Mediterranean Hotel in the Old City in 1867 by a member of Lt. Charles Warren's expedition team. *Source: Lenny Ben David,* Jerusalem Post, *August 10, 2012, Weekend Magazine*

He taught that practical actions could bring the Redemption nearer.

When the Chassidic movement was founded by Rabbi Yisrael Baal Shem Tov in the middle of the eighteenth century, it was greatly influenced by Rabbi Luria's teachings. "They saw that leaving the Diaspora [and connecting to] the holiness of the land, and its settlement were means of bringing about the Redemption."[63]

It was not long before the movement desired to establish Chassidism in the Holy Land and for that center to have an

Four hundred years. Regiment of Ottoman soldiers standing in formation. The Ottoman Turks conquered Palestine in 1517 and had ruled it ever since.

influence on the rest of world Jewry. In Iyar 5537 (May 1777) Rabbi Menachem Mendel of Vitebsk led a contingent of 300 people through Poland, the Ukraine, Podolia, and Romania, and across the Black Sea to Turkey, reaching Akko on 5 Elul 5537 (Sunday, September 7, 1777).

Rabbi Eliyahu of Vilna, known as the Vilna Gaon, also impressed upon his students the importance of settling the Land of Israel as a precursor to the coming of the Messiah.[64] His vision incorporated three main elements: the ingathering of the Jews, the establishment of Jerusalem as the Torah center of the world, and the expansion of the Yishuv.[65] One of his students, Menachem Mendel of Shklov, led a group of seventy people (later known as the Perushim) from Lithuania in the winter of 1808 and arrived in Safed in Elul 5569 (August 1809).

These beachheads of the Chassidim and the Perushim laid the groundwork for the Ashkenazic community that would later be called the Old Yishuv.

The Old Yishuv was urban and dependent on what was known as the Chalukah, monies collected from Diaspora Jews, for its survival. There were approximately 26,000 Jews living in the four holy cities of Jerusalem, Hebron, Safed, and Tiberias (with a few in Jaffa and Haifa)[66] prior to the First Aliyah in 1882. Non-Jews, mostly Arabs, numbered between 300,000 and 500,000.[67]

There was almost no Jewish farming.

Another twist on the road to Zion was based on the modern concept of nationalism. When the Greeks and the inhabitants of the Balkans rose up in revolt against their Ottoman rulers in the early nineteenth century, Rabbis Yehuda Alkalai[68] (1798-1878) and Ẓvi Hirsch Kalischer[69] saw these nationalistic stirrings as a heavenly sign that the time had come to revive the long-dormant national aspirations of the Jewish people and return to its homeland. Their ideas were implemented much later, in the wake of the pogroms of 1881-1882, when Rabbi Mohilever established the Chovevei Ẓion settlement movement.

At a time when most eastern European Jews were living in overcrowded towns and cities within the Russian Pale of Settlement, agriculture appealed to the romantic notions of the nineteenth century. It was assumed that the surest way to strike roots in the ancient Jewish homeland would be to cultivate its soil. Moreover, farming was thought to be therapeutic and a means of weaning Jews from businesses considered to be unsavory – occupations that had been forced upon them during their long sojourn in exile, professions that some leaders saw as corrupting their souls. Manual labor, intertwined with nature's seasons and rhythms, was viewed as a path toward purity and wholesomeness.

But was it feasible? In the late nineteenth century, creating an agricultural settlement for Jews in the Land of Israel was like creating *ex nihilo* – something out of nothing.

Ironically, a boost for the idea of Jewish agricultural settlement came from a very unlikely source. In the two decades prior to the settlement movement of Chovevei Ẓion, a German Protestant group known as the Templers[70] established settlements in and around Haifa,[71] in Jaffa, and in Emek Refaim (Valley of the Giants)[72] near Jerusalem.[73] Jewish leaders and thinkers were aware of this movement's activities and accomplishments. If German gentiles could till the soil of Palestine, why couldn't Jews, to whom the land was promised by the Almighty Himself?

The failure of the first two Jewish attempts to set up agricultural settlements – Petach Tikva and Gei Oni – signaled apprehension in the minds of all those promoting a Jewish return to the land. Determined not to repeat the mistakes of the past, Rabbi Mohilever, Brill, and the Baron agreed that they needed to locate professional farmers for their venture to succeed.

In their Sunday best. German Templer community in Palestine

The Litvish Hitchhiker's Guide to Palestine

Chapter 5
Faltering First Steps

The farmers had a long and arduous journey ahead of them – 2,446 kilometers (1,520 miles) – "as the crow flies" from Pavlovka, White Russia, to Jaffa, Palestine. In reality, the distance was much greater.[74]

What routes were available? Were they dangerous? Where could travelers find lodgings? How would they get food and money? Did they need passports or other travel documents? (See appendix VIII.) Our intrepid pioneers left no written records of their adventures, but Yechiel Brill wrote a firsthand account of their journey.

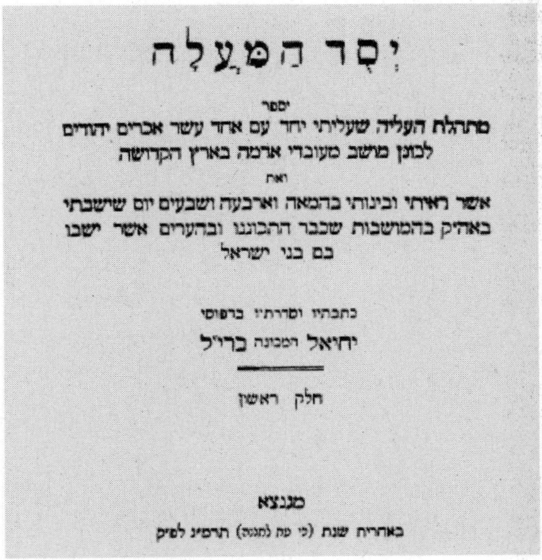
יְסֻד הַמַּעֲלָה

יספר

מהלך העליה שעליתי יחד עם אחד עשר אכרים יהודים

לכונן מושב מעובדי אדמה בארץ הקדושה

ואת

אשר ראיתי ובינותי בהמאה וארבעה ושבעים יום שישבתי

באה״ק במושבות שכבר התכוננו ובהערים אשר ישבו

בם בני ישראל

כתבתיו וסדרתיו בדפוס

יחיאל המכונה בריל

חלק ראשון

מגנצא

באחרית שנת (כי עת לחננה) תרמ״ג לפ״ק

Read all about it! Yechiel Brill's amazing travelogue, *Yesud Ha-Ma'alah,* chronicles the journey he took with the ten farmers and a *melamed* to the Holy Land in 1882.

Normally, before embarking on a trip to a foreign land, a traveler applies for a passport and an entry visa. Brill did not obtain these documents for the farmers. Later, they were denied entry into Palestine precisely because they were missing these essential documents. The reason Brill didn't obtain entry visas for them was simple – Jewish immigration to Palestine from Russia was against Turkish law.

The Turkish consul in Russia had been monitoring events and informed his government that a mass exodus of Jews from Russia to the United States was under way. He feared, however, that they might change direction and head for Palestine. The Ottomans did not want any of these "potential troublemakers" to make their home in Palestine.

"Uncle Abdul doesn't want you." A somber-looking Sultan Abdul Hamid II, ruler of the Ottoman Empire, was opposed to the emigration of Jews, because he feared they were being used by the European powers as a "Trojan horse" to infiltrate his empire.

On April 28, 1882, the Turkish general consul in Odessa issued an announcement barring Russian Jews from settling in Palestine. The statement was publicized in the Russian Jewish newspaper *Ha-Meliz*:[75]

Misinformation. "The Ottoman government will not harm Jews who wish to settle in the land [of Israel] and will even assist them. …" Eliezer Ben-Yehuda rebuffed reports that the Turkish sultan was against Jewish immigration to Palestine. The pioneers discovered the hard way that his "clarification" was erroneous. *From a letter to the editor of* Ha-Meliẓ, *April 26, 1882*

מאסקווא, 26 אפריל.

להמו"ל מ"ע „המליץ".

נגד השמועה שנתפרסמה במה"ע כי שר החיצון בקונסטאנטינופול הודיע להגענעראל-קאָנסול בארעסא כי לא יאבה השולטן לתת ליהודים לבוא להאחז בפלשתינא, מצאתי לנכון לפרסם דברי ה' בן-יהודא מירושלים שהגיעני היום לאמר:

„מלכות השולטן לא תרע ליהודים החפצים להאחז בארצה ועוד תטה להם חסדה, וכן הגיד השולטן למלאך אוסטריא היושב בסטאמבול, והדבר נדפס במה"ע „Levant Herold" היוצא שמה. וכן אמר לי בשמו גם האדון נסים בכר מורה בית הספר אשר כוננה פה חברת כל ישראל חברים".

שנ"ה יאָנאם.

The Turkish general consul in Odessa issued a request via telegraph to the foreign minister in Constantinople for clarification regarding the position of the Turkish government concerning Jewish immigration from Russia to Palestine. The reply of the foreign minister has now arrived. It completely negates the rumor that the sultan is in favor of Jews' settling in Palestine. The foreign minister forbids the general consul to issue passports to anyone who wishes to settle in Palestine.[76]

Brill was probably aware of the prohibition concerning Russian immigration to Palestine and reasoned that, under the circumstances, there was no purpose in drawing attention to themselves by applying for passports and visas that wouldn't be granted.

Brill apparently did not consult with anyone on this matter. He couldn't contact Michael Erlanger or other leaders of the Alliance Israélite Universelle who had influence with the Turkish authorities, because he hadn't asked permission from the Baron or the Alliance to make arrangements for the trip.

Who Knows Eleven?

At 4:00 on the frigid winter morning of November 21, 1882, Brill left his lodging in Volkovysk[77] and made his way to the railroad station to meet the farmers and begin their journey. He expected to find the ten men who had been selected, but he found eleven men waiting for him.

> … They added another person, whom I neither had seen before nor would have desired to take along. (I'd heard that he had left farming to become a *melamed*. He also did not possess that quality of innocence like the rest of the farmers.) They decided to add him

without my knowledge or consent, saying that they needed him to correspond with their families, because they themselves did not know how to write.[78]

Minyan man. The *melamed* Avraham Yaakov Gellman

An oral tradition posits another reason altogether for the appearance of Avraham Yaakov Gellman, the *melamed*. The farmers were devout Jews who insisted that they pray with a proper prayer quorum of ten men, a *minyan*. Should one of them fall ill, or not be present for any reason, they would need a back-up "minyan man."[79]

Shepherd without a Flock

The steam locomotive chugged out of the station at 6:00 a.m. The men traveled for nine long hours to Sosnowiec, their last stop in the Russian Empire. To avoid arousing suspicion, Brill remained while his charges went on to Szczakowa on the Austro-Hungarian side of the border. The next evening, when he got a letter that they arrived safely, he crossed the border into Prussia to solicit donations. Then he crossed the border again, this time entering Galicia. By the time he arrived in Szczakowa the next day, the farmers were gone. The shepherd nearly lost track of his sheep, but a chance meeting with a drunk saved the day. Brill writes:

> I ... traveled to that city [Szczakowa] and arrived there about midnight. ... Only one place still had a light on inside. I entered and found people sitting there, staying up late drinking wine. ... One man dozing against the wall ... told me while still half asleep that toward evening he'd seen men slowly walking by, carrying full sacks on their shoulders and inquiring about a snow-covered road that led to a certain village. If they'd made it there, I would find them in the house of a Jewish milkman.
>
> I journeyed to this village and arrived at two o'clock in the morning, and my eyes lit up when I saw my men, [though they were] lying there, trembling. When they looked up and saw me, they suddenly rejoiced![80]

Their odyssey had just begun. In the weeks and months ahead, the little band would encounter challenges that would test their mettle beyond all expectations.

Chapter 6
Vagabonds in Vienna

The next leg of their journey was Vienna, Austria. In 1882, the city was a cultural metropolis of 726,000 residents and the capital of the Austro-Hungarian Empire. Vienna could boast of its great culture and architecture – it even hosted the world's oldest zoo. Just a year earlier, a student by the name of Sigmund Freud had received his medical degree from the University of Vienna.

Center of culture. The elegant Schönbrunn Palace Garden Gloriette, built in 1755

Two hours before sunrise on November 24, eleven pious Jews with sacks over their shoulders, accompanied by their watchful escort, entered this cosmopolitan city. Imagine the awe of the farmers (who lived in thatched-roof cottages) as they gazed upon the city's magnificent marble edifices. They were nearly out of money, so they did what Jewish travelers had done for centuries (and still do to this day). Brill writes:

> Since I did not know where in this great, big city there was a small hotel that would welcome visitors of our ilk, I took the advice of a fellow Jew from Cracow who was traveling with us and we followed him to a *beit midrash* on Schiff Street that belonged to Galician Chassidim.

The *beit midrash* was closed, and they had no choice but to sleep on the street like vagrants.

> In the city of Vienna, the custom is that ten o'clock in the evening is gate-closing time for the various [apartment building] courtyards. From that time onward until the morning light, anyone who wants to enter must pay the gatekeeper ten kreuzer [pronounced *kroit-sər.* Ten kreuzer then was equivalent to U.S. $1.00 today.] And I couldn't afford at that time to pay 120 kreuzer [$12] to open the gate.[81]

There we sat or stood until daybreak on the city street at the gate of the courtyard. The laborers who arise early in the morning to get to work walked past us and saw a group of strange-looking men – each one of us standing with a sack slung over his shoulder – wondering to themselves whether we were a bunch of convicts en route to a remote land. Well, we certainly did not see ourselves that way!

At seven o'clock the gatekeeper opened the gates, and, following the advice of the Jew from Cracow, we sneaked in, one by one, so that the gatekeeper would not catch on and block us from going to the *beit midrash*. At the conclusion of the *davening*, the mercy of the *shammes* was aroused. For a small fee, he found us places to stay in Jewish homes close by. I took leave of the group and made my way to a Jewish hotel that would suffice, that is, for a locale where no one recognized me. I tried to check in at a more respectable hotel belonging to a noted scholar, but I was told that there were no vacancies. The reason for this is that his wife scrutinizes the people checking in and is able to discern which of the guests are men of Torah scholarship. So when such a guest arrives and asks if there is a place to stay, she will say "No!" She is afraid that such a guest will discuss Torah with her husband, who is under her thumb, and he won't carry out her work assignments.[82]

One kreuzer, 1881, Austria. In those days it could purchase a mug of beer. Worth approximately ten cents in today's U.S. currency.

The men who saved the day.
Left: Emanuel (Menachem) Mendel Baumgarten
Right: Baron Albert Salomon Rothschild

After Brill got some sorely needed rest, he recounted the money and realized that they had spent a large amount just to reach Vienna. The port of Jaffa was still far away. He then remembered that he had a relative through marriage living in Vienna, the writer Emanuel (Menachem) Mendel Baumgarten.[83] One of the leaders of the Viennese Jewish community, he agreed to meet with Brill.

Their meeting was cordial, and Baumgarten offered to contact Baron Albert Salomon Rothschild[84] on Brill's behalf. Two days later, Baumgarten had a letter from Rothschild

Magyar money. One Hungarian florin in 1882 was worth approximately $10 in today's U.S. currency. In those days, one florin could feed a family for a week. With two florins, one could purchase a small cow.

for Brill to present to Baron Morforno, owner of a steamship company in Trieste. In the letter, Rothschild asked Morforno to discount the tickets as much as possible for the farmers.

Baumgarten also purchased six train tickets from Vienna to Trieste worth 99 florins. (Presumably, Brill had just enough money for the other six.) If he should still be short of money in Trieste, Brill was to wire Baumgarten, who would then contact the Baron again for additional funding. As Brill was about to take leave, Baumgarten added that at about noontime Brill should expect a delivery of twelve woolen cloaks to keep the men warm from the cold winter winds as they crossed the ocean.

The "Hidden Ẓaddik"

But not everyone was as supportive as Emanuel Baumgarten. Another Jewish notable so disappointed Brill that his record of their encounter is venomous.

> Then I went to the house of … the rabbi of the "Congregation of Orthodox Jews of Hungary, Bohemia, and Moravia in Vienna," who is called a *ẓaddik*.… I said to him: "I have heard that you are the head of the Ahavat Ẓion [Lovers of Zion] Society which was organized to promote the settlement of the Land of Israel, and I am presently ascending to the Holy Land with eleven Jewish farmers to settle them upon God's land – to till it and to bring forth bread from the earth. It is my hope that these men will be a noteworthy example in the Jewish world, that they will correct an erroneous belief among our leadership – that the Jewish people can never again be a people that works its land, and that the land of its forefathers will remain desolate forevermore.…
>
> "This attitude has struck roots – poisonous roots in the minds of our leaders – either because of all the despair or because of all the affluence. But all this will change when people find out that a settlement of Jewish farmers has been established in the Holy Land, and the Land of Israel will yield its produce to those who till it, producing food in abundance."

Brill concluded his spiel with a flourish:

> "And now, my lord, Rabbi, head of the Ahavat Ẓion Society: It is not money or clothing that I have come to request from you for my men.... I am asking that you invite these men to your home and give them some words of encouragement and solace ... in order to strengthen their resolve, so they will be able to weather the tribulations of the Land of Israel that they might encounter in their first days there.
>
> "I would also like to suggest that in order not to let them leave you empty-handed, purchase for them, for just five florins, cured meat that can be utilized for celebrating the joys of the Sabbath as they cross the ocean."
>
> ... The rabbi responded to my last comment as follows: "Here in the sinful city of Vienna it is impossible to obtain kosher Viennese cured meats in accordance with Torah law." So I then asked him: "Is it possible that the cured meat that I have eaten in my hotel, which is located across from your house – and that you, my dear rabbi, also eat – is that also not kosher according to Torah law?" And the "ẓaddik" was as silent and unresponsive as a deaf man.[85]

Tearful in Trieste

The farmers and Brill departed from Vienna on the morning of November 27, accompanied to the train station by Baumgarten and a Jewish student Brill had befriended in the hotel. For the next twenty-four hours, they rode on the train until they arrived at the port city of Trieste.

Trieste, located on the coast of the Adriatic Sea, was the exclusive maritime portal of the Austro-Hungarian Empire. The steamship company Austrian Lloyd[86] provided regular passenger service from Trieste to Alexandria, Jaffa, and Beirut and also brought mail from Europe to the Middle East. The Pavlovka pioneers planned to travel to Palestine on one of these ships.

A beautiful seaport dating back to Roman times, Trieste had striking white, chalky rock formations juxtaposed with the beautiful turquoise waters of the Adriatic. When the farmers set their eyes upon the vast waters, they joyfully recited the blessing traditionally said upon seeing an ocean or other natural wonder: *Blessed art Thou ... Who performs the act of Creation.*

But their main concern was that they still had a long journey ahead, and not enough money to complete it. After making the necessary lodging arrangements, Brill made his way to Baron Morforno armed with the letter from Baron Albert Rothschild. Morforno looked at the letter and told Brill that he could give him only a 50% discount on the fare from Trieste to Alexandria.

"A journey of a thousand miles..." Likely route from Pavlovka to Palestine

Brill returned to his hotel room and counted his funds again: he was about 600 francs short of what was needed to complete the journey to Jaffa. (A franc was worth about $4 in today's U.S. currency,[87] so he was short the equivalent of $2,400.) It was time to take Baumgarten up on his offer. Brill wired him – and twenty-four hours later, 600 francs arrived, courtesy of Albert Rothschild!

Although Brill had enough money for the steamship tickets, he needed yet more for food. Whether it was a mark of his character or a sign of sheer desperation, Brill mustered the chutzpah to approach a former adversary!

> ... I paid Rabbi M. a visit. When I told him my name, he looked at me as if he didn't know me (but he did!), for I was the man who had waged a fierce battle against the dealers who sold *etrogim* from Corfu[88] – and I did not spare him either for certifying those etrogim as kosher.
>
> I briefed him about my trip and beseeched him to make an appeal to his congregation to contribute to the community chest on behalf of my men, so they could be supplied with food for the next few days in Trieste as well as provisions for the journey. The rabbi replied that although he had no influence on his congregants (he was telling the truth!), he would do what he could to help.
>
> Then I went to the home of Mr. Chertkowitz, a wealthy man who was the head of the Alliance Israélite Universelle in Trieste. I made the same miniscule request of him. He promised me that he would bring up my request before the heads of the community.
>
> ... The rabbi later told me ... that his congregational officers were not interested in his appeal on behalf of my men, but one woman was interested in contributing ... ten florins. ...
>
> The next day I went to Mr. Chertkowitz, and he, too, told me that the heads of the community were unresponsive to his appeal. ... Then he put his hand in his pocket and took out five florins and said ... "Please take this contribution from me."[89]

Did the Jews of Trieste think that the idea of Jewish colonization of Palestine was a pipe dream, or that Brill and his strange group of men were charlatans? They were likely mistaken for yet another group of scholars, en route to a life of Torah study.

They would go hungry from the time they reached Jaffa until their arrival at Mikveh Israel, Brill calculated. Determined not to let that happen, he wrote two letters – one to Rabbi Mohilever and the other to Baron Edmond de Rothschild – describing the situation and the need for additional funds. Then he wrote two more letters:

> From Trieste, I also corresponded with Rabbi Ẓaddok Kahn and Michael Erlanger. In my letters, I informed them that I had finally selected the men whom they had promised to give an *achuzat nachalah* – a homestead in the Holy Land – and I was personally escorting them until they got settled.
>
> Because I had heard that in Jaffa the authorities did not allow "these kinds of people" [i.e., Russian Jews] … to disembark, I beseeched [both men] to be so kind as to telegraph[90] the director of Mikveh Israel, [asking him] to await [the farmers'] arrival at the seaside on the 10th of December – the day the Austrian ship would arrive in Jaffa – so he would represent them and advocate on their behalf with the immigration official….
>
> Now, I had an ulterior motive besides the purpose stated in my letter to Paris. I was afraid Rabbi Kahn might have changed his mind about sending the chosen men to the Holy Land. But when he learned that they were already at the seaport in Trieste, he would say "It's done," and he would order the director in Jaffa to accept the men I was bringing to Mikveh Israel.[91]

Bon voyage! Jews in Trieste embarking for the Holy Land (circa 1920s). The Pavlovka farmers and the other pioneers of the First Aliyah paved the way for the thousands who followed.

In fact, Brill's concern about a change of heart in Paris was unfounded, for Rabbi Mohilever had received official approval in writing from there. He sent a letter to Brill informing him of this development, but it didn't arrive in Trieste until well after Brill had departed with his men for Palestine.[92]

On the High Seas

The fateful day finally arrived. They were leaving the European continent. Brill recorded his sentiments with the flair of a seasoned writer:

> After I prepared provisions for our trip as best I could, we left our hotel at ten o'clock in the morning on the 20th of Kislev [December 1] to go down to the boat that would take us to Jaffa. We did not go to the boat by wagon [but by foot], and the strong wind that blew on that day carried us on its wings, and it was as if the breeze appreciated the heavy loads we carried on our shoulders – just like the Jews who left Egypt.
>
> About noontime, the sailors began raising the anchor of the boat from the water. As I gazed around me, I saw groups of men, women, and children – travelers and their escorts – some exchanging kisses, others crying because it was so hard for them to leave their loved ones behind. And there we were, standing all alone and shivering in the wind and the snow.
>
> Whom did we have here to bid us farewell? My wife and children were in Mainz. Knowing that today I would be departing from Europe, they would be crying bitterly that the great sea would be separating us. My heart was pounding – who knew if I was leaving them for good? Who knew if I was going to my death?
>
> … While I was standing there, depressed and aching inside, I suddenly saw Mr. Chertkowitz in front of me! The wind and the snow did not stop this elderly man from coming to the boat and seeing us off! This distinguished gentleman parted from us with an abundance of tears. And I could see that the Judaism that Mr. Chertkowitz had absorbed during his childhood in Moran, his birthplace, had not completely dissipated during the forty years he'd lived here in Trieste! As he left us, I looked at the coast to see if Rabbi M. would be there to see us off, as he had promised – but he was not there. And the ten florins that he'd promised me also stayed peacefully put.[93]

Brill faithfully recorded details of the voyage in *Yesud Ha-Ma'alah*:

> At one o'clock in the afternoon, the boat began making its way across the Adriatic Sea, and the winds were howling and swaying

the ship back and forth the way a nanny would rock a cradle with a sleeping infant. Many of the passengers, including my men, had fallen on their faces because they were seized by terrible seasickness. But I, who had traveled the seas many times, was among the few who were able to stand on their feet, teetering like a drunk on the boat's deck. I braced my men so that they should not be frightened by the raging sea, and [I told them] that the waters would soon be restored to their former calm.

By sunset, the sea quieted down from its turbulence, and my men's spirits were uplifted, and they got up to pray and to welcome the Sabbath. I thought that there were no other Jews on board and that the storm had been on our account![94]

And then I realized ... that there were people among us who found it easy to desecrate the Sabbath in public, to eat forbidden foods even when they were [precariously] on a ship in the heart of the sea. If they ever had to say *Kaddish,* they ... would be better off if the dead prayed for them! As we prayed, another two passengers joined us – but from their appearance, you might never guess that they were Jewish. They stood with us until the prayer leader recited *Kaddish,* and they recited along with him word for word.[95]

CORFU – On the 22nd of Kislev [December 3], we anchored off Corfu. The Greek inhabitants of the island brought fruits (for which their island is famous) to our ship in their sailboats and sold them to the passengers at cheap prices. They also did not jack up the prices of large etrogim that were completely ripened and could be eaten raw. I bought one of those for ten kreuzer. I was thinking to myself, "If that Greek man knew I was a Hebrew, instead of asking for ten kreuzer [i.e., about $1], he would demand ten florins [$100] for the etrog – the price they get in Trieste before the Sukkot holiday."

The ship was anchored off Corfu for four hours, and some people boarded the ship to continue on to Alexandria. I recognized among the new passengers one person who was Jewish, and the next day he introduced himself to us. When he saw that we were standing in prayer and that some of my men were crying, he approached them and told them that he too was Jewish, and he gave out one franc to each one of them.

He did not join us while we were praying. (Maybe he was embarrassed in front of the passengers who were sitting with him at the same table on the top tier.) Only on the eve of the 25th of Kislev, when he observed that all my men were standing at the door of my cabin to hear the blessings over the Chanukah candles, he also came in to watch this sight – which seemed so foreign to him![96]

ALEXANDRIA – On the 25th of Kislev [December 6], at four o'clock in the afternoon, our ship anchored off the coast of Alexandria. Since the boat would be docking here for two days, I disembarked onto dry land, hoping to try to obtain documents for my men in Alexandria from the police that would verify that they were born in countries under the rule of the [Turkish] sultan.[97] My concern that the authorities would not let them disembark at Jaffa did not allow me to sleep. But my wish was granted through the assistance of my friend Chaim Mizrachi and with the help of the "item that answers all things"[98] [i.e., money].

On the 27th of Kislev, I returned in happiness to my men on account of the certificates that I was able to get on their behalf, and I sat with them in order to teach [them] how to reply in Arabic when they would be asked their names and their city [of origin]. And they kept practicing what they had learned until we got to Jaffa. We left Alexandria at eleven o'clock in the morning, and the next morning we arrived at Port Said, where the ship remained anchored until noon.[99]

Etrog City. Corfu was the main supplier of etrogim to European Jewry until etrogim from Palestine took their place. *From a postcard printed in Munich circa 1902*

Chapter 7 *Barred from Palestine*

The farmers and Brill observed another Sabbath aboard the ship and lit their fifth Chanukah candle at the day's conclusion. The air of excitement mixed with apprehension was palpable. All strained their eyes to catch their first glimpse of the Holy Land.

Then suddenly, land! Brill recorded that breathtaking moment:

> ... At the break of dawn on the 29th of Kislev [December 10], we saw from the distance – about an hour away – the houses of Jaffa perched on the hilltop. Hurrah! It has been about nineteen years since I have seen her – from the time I had to leave her with just the shirt on my back to travel to Constantinople to plead my case against the pasha (governor) of Jerusalem, who closed down my printing press. I called out with all my heart: "If only I had wings, so that I could fly to the dry land, kiss her stones and roll in her dust!"
>
> I thought to myself – will I find in Jaffa my dearest friend, Rabbi Yoel Moshe Salomon? (Because I was so preoccupied, I forgot to send a telegram from Alexandria to inform my relatives of my impending arrival in Jaffa. So I hoped [at least to] find there my friend, who lives most of the year in that city.) If only I could find you, and we could thank God together, "*for He has kept us alive and sustained us and brought us to this auspicious time.*"
>
> I was absorbed with these pleasant thoughts and musings while standing on the ship's stern and staring at the city – and I did not sense that the boat had anchored! My men had already tied up their sacks and bundles and were standing at the exit ramp. When they saw that many of the passengers had descended to the rowboats that would take them to shore, and I was just standing there like a man under the influence of wine, they called out to me: "Why are

Dawn of a new era. First glimpse of the Holy Land from the sea you just standing there? Hire a rowboat and let's get to the city!"[100]

I responded to their call like a man just aroused from his sleep. I gazed at the boatmen creating mayhem as they coaxed the travelers to come ashore with them. I approached them and inquired about their fare for bringing me and my men ashore. They asked me: "Do these men have valid passports? We are under orders not to allow to descend [to our boats] any Jews 'like these'[101] whom the government has barred from entering Palestine and Syria." I replied that these men had certificates from Alexandria stating that they were natives of lands under the rule of the sultan. So the boatmen took the documents and looked at them. Then they looked at my men, and the boatmen's facial expressions said, "These guys are from Russia."

Dear friend. Yoel Moshe Salomon (1838-1912) was a prominent member of the Old Yishuv in Jerusalem and one of the founders of Petach Tikva. He was one of three business partners (including Yechiel Brill) who set up the first Hebrew newspaper in Palestine, *Ha-Levanon.*

While I was still conversing with the boatmen, a Jewish advocate from Jaffa ... arrived and got involved in our discussion. He hinted to the boatmen that here was a genuine opportunity to make some money. To me, he said, "These men cannot go ashore with the passports they are holding. However, if you give. ..." I got angry with

Mayhem! In this 1880 engraving showing pilgrims disembarking from a steamship in Jaffa, Orthodox Jews figure predominantly in the lower right corner.

Jaffa boatmen. Steamships anchored about a kilometer (two-thirds of a mile) from the shore

Welcome mat. Passengers on the Jaffa landing pier

that fellow and turned to one of the boatmen to take us ashore on his boat. He took the passports ... and sent them off with one of his friends in another boat to have them inspected by the [immigration] official.

When the interceder saw that his plan had been foiled, he took another boat and hurried to get to shore ahead of us. He called out to me from the distance, "Now you will see what I am going to do to you!"

This low character was true to his word! When we came ashore, we were received by the immigration official and a policeman. After [the official] returned the passports to my men, he ordered the rowboat man to return them to the steamship from which they had come.[102]

Brill looked for Shmuel Hirsch from the Mikveh Israel school in Jaffa, but he was nowhere to be found. He wondered whether Hirsch had ever received instructions to meet them here.[103]

I asked everyone I encountered, including my friend Rabbi Yoel Moshe Salomon, if they'd happened to see the director of Mikveh

Gateway to Palestine. The ancient port of Jaffa, as it looked when the farmers docked there. *Image by nineteenth-century photographer, Felix Bonfils*

Israel in the city. And they told me, "Yes! He's at Sir Yosef Moyal's[104] store." I went there and told [Hirsch] all that had happened to me and asked him if he'd ever gotten a telegram from Paris about us. He told me that he did receive the telegram a week ago and requested permission from the pasha of Jerusalem, through the French consul there, to grant the men from Russia [entry into the country, so they could] enroll at Mikveh Israel on a certain date. Unfortunately, his request was denied.

And so I pleaded with Sir Yosef Moyal to go to the chief immigration official and beseech him with a "gift" to allow my men to come ashore. My friend, Rabbi Yoel Moshe Salomon, whispered in my ear that this official was his loyal friend.

> Moyal and the director were moved by my pleas and went together to the immigration official. The officer responded that he could not fulfill their request, because the pasha in Jerusalem already knew about the matter – so how could he allow men to whom the pasha would not grant entry to come ashore?[105]

We can only imagine the deep sadness and dread felt by the disappointed farmers who had come such a long way and reached the very gates of Palestine, only to be denied entry. The distraught group was herded back to the ship.

Searching for a Crack in the Ottoman Wall

Brill was not ready to concede defeat and turn back. If need be, they would enter Palestine through the "back door." Salomon suggested that Brill allow an advocate to take his place in accompanying the men to Haifa, their ship's next port of call, and try their luck there. Then they could take the land route (a three-day journey) to Mikveh Israel, bypassing the immigration officer in Jaffa. With any luck, Ottoman incompetence would allow them to slip through.

Brill liked the idea. He boarded the ferry along with two advocates and some friends. But on the way to the steamship, he suddenly had a change of heart. He had taken responsibility for these men, left his home and family behind, and journeyed all the way to Palestine with them. How could he hand them over to strangers at the last minute?

The steamship had begun to depart, and the small boat could not catch up with it. Brill shouted to the captain, and the eleven frightened farmers on deck cried out to the sailors in desperation. The ship finally came to a standstill, but its entrance ramp remained drawn. Undaunted, Brill scaled the wall of the ship. No one was sure if he would lose his grip and fall into the depths, but he miraculously reached the top and climbed on board. With his remaining breath, he blessed God, Who *"performed a miracle for me in this place."*[106]

When he saw his men, he burst into tears of anguish. All of this might not have happened were it not for the jilted advocate. Brill – the ultimate idealist – couldn't fathom how one Jew could betray his fellow Jews to the non-Jewish government.

Why hadn't he simply played the game and allowed the advocate to operate in the usual fashion?

Regrets were pointless now. Perhaps they would fare better in Haifa. They arrived that evening at Haifa Bay. Here too, the ferry boatmen asked for passports, but unlike in Jaffa, they didn't ask too many questions. An advocate by the name of Yosef Morgenstern appeared, offering his services. Brill had learned his lesson: he decided to cooperate with the bizarre "system." The immigration officer at the port approved their entry, and they all made their way to the advocate's home to spend the night.

Close to midnight, Brill was suddenly handed a telegram in Arabic from Shmuel Hirsch. Hirsch wrote that after the ship departed from Jaffa, he had been successful in obtaining permission from the pasha in Jerusalem for the entry of ten men. Therefore, the group should board the steamship on Wednesday, when it would depart from Haifa for Jaffa, so they could enter legally.[107]

The telegram was very problematic. Brill knew that Hirsch wasn't fluent in Arabic. Moreover, Hirsch must have been aware that the Turks intercepted mail and telegrams. He smelled a setup. A note written in Arabic would make it very easy for a postal clerk to report them. In addition, Brill had informed Hirsch in Jaffa that he had eleven men with him. Why would Hirsch seek permission for only ten?

The telegram must be a forgery, Brill decided. He suspected it was the work of the jilted advocate, scheming to lure the farmers back to Jaffa. Then he would blackmail them into paying for his services or risk being shipped back to Port Said.

It wasn't until later that Brill learned that Hirsch was indeed the author of the telegram! Why had he written in Arabic? Under Turkish law, all telegrams sent after sundown had to be in the language of that province. Brill discovered that Hirsch had received the pasha's permission around noon but hadn't bothered sending the telegram until evening.

The next morning, Brill hired a wagon to take his men to Jaffa. Suddenly the Haifa advocate appeared and told him that the local ruler (*kaikam* in Turkish) would not permit his men to leave the city on their own recognizance. The *kaikam* had deduced from the telegram that the passports the farmers brought were forged. The police arrived, arrested the men, and took them to jail. On their way to the lockup, the farmers blamed the Jaffa advocate.

Brill was again in anguish. He went out to the street and desperately turned to anyone who would listen and offer him some guidance. The locals told him that the Haifa advocate (their host!) – a man whose lust for money knew no bounds – was conniving behind their backs.

The Bobbsey twins. Turkish naval police

Subsequently, the advocate came to Brill around noon with a contrived look of exhaustion on his face, as if he had been working hard on their case. He told Brill he'd found a solution. If Brill could come up with forty[108] francs ($160 in today's U.S. currency) for each man, the police chief would "close his eyes" and not notice the men leaving the jail and making off to Jaffa.

Unfortunately, there was no money left for bribes. Brill contacted the Alliance representatives in Haifa, who tried to convince the police that the telegram was a forgery – but to no avail. The men were going to be sent to court in Jaffa.

On Wednesday, the last day of Chanukah, the steamship was anchored in the bay and the farmers were escorted by the police onto the small ferryboats. Brill telegraphed Hirsch, informing him of their impending arrival in Jaffa. It seemed that the whole project was doomed.

The next day, when the steamship arrived in Jaffa, the boatmen had some good news: The pasha of Jerusalem had sent word that the men could now legally enter the country.

But their troubles were not yet over.

When they came ashore, Hirsch was again absent.[109] The immigration officer asked Brill how many men were with him, and he replied, "Eleven." The bureaucrat was curt. "The entry permit is for ten men, not eleven. If one of them goes back to the ship, the remaining ten may remain ashore. Otherwise, not even one of them may remain here!"

This time, Brill knew what to do:

> I left my men sitting on the rowboat and went back into town to see Sir Yosef Moyal. He accompanied me to the coast and begged the immigration officer to take one of the men into custody until it would become clear what to do about him, while allowing the rest to come ashore. The official acquiesced and took the eleventh man into custody – the *melamed* whom the other farmers had added without my knowledge – because none of *them* wanted to go to jail. I directed the remaining ten to the hotel owned by the interceder Chaim Bakker. He promised me that he would find a way to get the prisoner released … and he succeeded! May his name be remembered for good![110]

The farmers had finally arrived. With gratitude to God in their hearts for answering their prayers, they bent down and kissed the soil of the Holy Land.

Chapter 8
No Hope in Mikveh Israel

It was in mid-December 1882 when the farmers moved to their temporary home at the Mikveh Israel school.[110A] Much like a principal giving his students the once-over on the first day of school, Shmuel Hirsch asked each farmer his name, how many were in his household, and about his farming experience. Then he wrote down all the information in a small notebook.

After the farmers were dismissed and sent to their temporary lodgings, Brill asked Hirsch: "I would like to know what they wrote to you from Paris about my men, and what is to be done with them." The reply to this simple question was disconcerting: "The word from Paris was that I should find lodging for them here, but if there isn't enough room, I could either rent them a house in Jaffa or bring them to Rishon Le-Ẓion. Right now I am leaning toward the second option."

Brill was agitated. What was Hirsch talking about? The clear understanding had been that they were supposed to be staying in Mikveh Israel.[111] Hirsch seemed uneasy with the prospect of having to live alongside Jewish farmers from Russia.[112]

Whipping out Rabbi Ẓaddok Kahn's letter to Rabbi Mohilever, Brill pointed out that it was quite explicit: the farmers were to be housed in Mikveh Israel. Period.

As the "guardian" of his charges, Brill felt it was his duty to protect them from exploitation – even by Jewish communal workers. Moreover, he felt that his farmers would not fit into the Rishon Le-Ẓion lifestyle. Although the residents of Rishon were Orthodox, they were known to be influenced by the *Haskalah* and were not as strict in observing Jewish law as the group from Pavlovka. Perhaps Hirsch, as a semi-assimilated west European Jew, could not tell the difference.

Brill, who was "old-style" Orthodox himself, tried to help Hirsch understand. "These men never lived in the cosmopolitan city of Paris as we have. They are simple farmers who walk in the path of God, and I cannot allow them to be in a place like Rishon."

As Brill continued to give an informal lecture on cultural sensitivity, Hirsch suggested that if the farmers were going to stay at Mikveh Israel, they should go to the market, shop, and cook for themselves.

"That suggestion does not follow the spirit of Rabbi Kahn's letter," Brill retorted. "Besides, if they have to travel an hour every day to the *shuk* and cook for themselves, that will take time away from their work. That might become a pretext for you to say that they are a bunch of loafers."

Hirsch suspended the conversation to give Brill a brief tour of the school, showing him a recently constructed building that was to be the synagogue. They continued their negotiations in the school library. The Baron's people had told Brill that the farmers would be given land to cultivate in Mikveh Israel. Where would his men be working?

"In Paris, they don't know what is going on over here," Hirsch replied with annoyance. "I have designated that the wheat fields go to the *fellahin* from the village of Yazur, where they work as sharecroppers for a three-year period. Now, since last year was a Shemittah year, we desisted from plowing and harvesting, as required by Jewish law, even though the *chacham bashi* (Sephardic chief rabbi of Palestine) offered to find a *heter* (legal alternative) to enable us to plow and harvest in the Sabbatical year. So I have a moral obligation to allow the *fellahin* to work the fields this year, because I did not allow them to work during the Shemittah year."[113]

Brill was not impressed. "This 'moral obligation' should not be an impediment for us. I will take it upon myself to appease the *fellahin* by offering them compensation of 100 or 200 francs so they will forgo their sharecropping rights for this upcoming season."

Hirsch resorted to elitism: "We Europeans have come to this land to sow the seeds of civilization. It is our moral obligation to show the natives that 'yes' means yes and 'no' means no."

The verbal duel continued until Hirsch revealed his fear that once the farmers started working the fields of Mikveh Israel, they might settle there permanently! He couched his objection in terms that implied he was interested only in their welfare. "Besides what I have already mentioned, there is another reason it is not a good idea for your farmers to settle in Mikveh Israel. The Turkish sultan designated these fields for the use of the Alliance Israélite Universelle for a period of only 100 years.

By the end of two Jubilees [fifty-year periods in Jewish law], the fields will return to the Ottoman government. Your men want a place they can call their own for posterity."

Brill countered: "The political situation will probably change, not in the next 100 years but within the next fifty.[114] This is not the time to talk about permanent settlement anyway. Let's cross that bridge when we come to it."

Director Hirsch's intent was only too clear. Brill later wrote of that first meeting:

> God knows how much *tzures* (difficulties) and anger is in store for me here. I was hoping to return to my family and my work in Mainz by the beginning of 1883. But if not, so be it. I can see where the director's head is. There is no way he is going to let my men settle here. I made it my job to be with them until they get their land and settle down. Now, I wonder, where will that homestead be?[115]

Approaching his protégés, Brill concealed his apprehensions while playing the role of a supportive coach.

> My brothers! I want you to know that this man who is in charge of Mikveh Israel is a very "enlightened" and educated fellow. Be careful not to step out of line with what he asks of you and not to infringe on his honor. Do whatever he tells you; even if he works you too hard at times, don't lose your temper. He's testing your mettle to see whether you have it in you to do agricultural work. Remember! If he says you don't pass muster, you could be sent back to Russia empty-handed! Please be careful. And may God help us![116]

Their First Sabbath in the Holy Land

Returning to his room in Jaffa that night, Brill was drained. He wanted to pour out his heart to his friend Yoel Moshe Salomon, but the latter was bedridden with malaria.

Friday evening came, and Brill ushered in the Sabbath. The following afternoon, after praying and having his Sabbath meal, he walked to Mikveh Israel to look in on his charges.[117]

Instead of finding the farmers in the large room the director had shown him two days earlier, Brill saw them squeezed into two tiny rooms without any flooring – "neither stone or wooden boards." Hirsch had placed them in the school's tool sheds. There were no beds, no pillows, and no blankets. The men slept on eleven sacks of straw placed on two wide benches that rose a few inches from the ground. They weren't even provided with sheets to cover the burlap sacks.

Brill refrained from commenting on this sorry sight and focused instead on inquiring as to how the farmers were managing. They recounted that immediately after his departure they had been sent out to do hoeing in the fields, even though they were tired from their exhausting journey to the school.

Jaffa sunshine. Brill wrote that there were "gardens, orchards, and houses all along the way" from Jaffa to Mikveh Israel. This is incidental testimony that the Arabs had developed the area and its citrus industry. They were exporting "Jaffa" oranges to Europe.

They also told him that on Friday, before Sabbath eve, they were allowed to go to the public bathhouse in Jaffa to wash up (their first thorough personal hygiene in weeks), and as soon as they returned to the school, they were put back to work. Hardy souls that they were, the men seemed ready to endure physical hardship; but what upset them was that the minimum necessities of Sabbath observance – a cup of wine for *Kiddush* and two loaves of bread – had not been provided.

Brill returned on Sunday. Before going out to assess how they were faring in the fields, he went to the director's office to bring him along. They went to the *pardes,* the orchard, where his farmers were laboring, and what they saw made Brill ecstatic:

> The director was dumbfounded to see how

> eleven Jews had worked on a piece of land equal to about one hectare [2.47 acres], using a type of hoe they had never used in Russia, from early morning until a little after noon. *Fellahin,* who were accustomed to this type of work, would have never been able to accomplish so much even in two days, even if we were talking about twenty-two of them! Then I asked Azulai, their Jewish overseer: "Are they suitable candidates for farming?" And he answered me that he realized from the start that these men had been tilling the earth since their youth.[118]

On the way back to his office, Hirsch told Brill that he was so busy with his work at Mikveh Israel that he did not have the time to scout out potential properties to purchase for the farmers, again noting that land was available in Rishon Le-Ẓion. If that was not acceptable, Brill would have to search and purchase the land himself. Brill told him that he was not sent here to be their real estate agent, but if he had to be the person to buy the land, so be it.

When Brill visited the farmers on Tuesday, they were furious. They told him that on the previous day, the director had summoned them and asked if they'd left Russia because of the pogroms. And why, he wanted to know, did they want to settle in Palestine?

Extensive. View of Jaffa from the orange groves

They replied that they had not experienced the suffering of most Russian Jews: the organized violence had not spread to their tiny, isolated village of Pavlovka. The reason they had come to Palestine was that they had been promised a homestead in the Mikveh Israel colony, where they could build homes and settle down. They wanted to set an example for their fellow

Jews, they staunchly asserted, by demonstrating that "in our own times the Holy Land will yield its fruits as a blessing to her sons who have returned to cultivate her."

Hirsch may have been moved by their stirring words, but his reply was devoid of sentiment. He told them that they shouldn't

Fieldwork. Students at Mikveh Israel

even think they could own land in Mikveh Israel, but that they had the option of living in Rishon Le-Ẓion.

The farmers responded that if they were not given land in Mikveh Israel, they would go straight back home. That night, they could not sleep. They suspected that *Brill* had deceived them just to bring them to Palestine. There was no place for them in Mikveh Israel, and the money they were promised in case they needed to return to Russia was never given to them. They were trapped!

When Brill showed up, they berated him, declaring, "We are lost! Totally lost!"

Brill was equally furious. Why did Hirsch have to frighten them like that? What kind of game was he playing with these honest men? He shouldn't have broached the topic with them at all, Brill thought bitterly, at least not until their three-month trial period was almost over.

Composing himself, Brill tried to mollify the distraught men. Perhaps they misunderstood what Hirsch was telling them, because he didn't speak Yiddish, but rather pure German. Now, if they sometimes misunderstood Brill, who knew their language, and had been in their company for quite some time, how could they be certain that they understood Hirsch? He told them that he would go immediately to the director and ascertain exactly what he had told them the day before.

Brill went to find Hirsch and notes sarcastically that he "saw him strolling in the garden."[119] Brill told him that tomorrow he was going to investigate a real estate lead for his men. He then asked Hirsch whether this business about not letting them stay in Mikveh Israel was based on orders from Paris or his own sentiments. In any case, he demanded, why did he have to upset the farmers?

Hirsch justified himself by saying that he was only trying to give them good advice, and he was sincerely interested in promoting their welfare, because he saw that they were simple, wholesome farmers since their youth and that they weren't "lazy like their brothers in Russia."

Brill returned to Mikveh Israel on the Tenth of Tevet (a fast day on the Jewish calendar) with a man from Jaffa named Yaakov Maimon, who was quite knowledgeable about local real estate and knew of land for sale in Wadi Chanin (the area that is now the town of Nes Ẓiona). Hirsch's manner was not friendly. Without knowing anything about Maimon, Hirsch suddenly blurted out: "I just want to warn you that lawyers can't run over me the way they do other people. I want nothing but the truth from you, and if you should ever express a single falsehood to me, I'm going to get you good!"[120] Brill was aghast, and Maimon was in shock.

Maimon was quick to respond: "Have you ever heard anyone say I operate like a crafty lawyer? Go ask anyone from Jaffa – Jews, Christians, or Muslims. They will tell you I'm not at all like one of those shysters!"

Maimon turned to Brill and told him that he did not come to Mikveh Israel to be insulted; he would return to Jaffa immediately. Brill pleaded with him to stay, telling him that Hirsch was just toying with him. Maimon relented and set out for

Wadi Chanin with Brill and J. Dugourd, Mikveh Israel's non-Jewish French gardener, along with two of the farmers from Pavlovka.

When they reached the farmland three hours later, Dugourd turned over the soil in several places to determine its quality. They examined the wells, measuring their depth. One well was nine meters (29.5 feet) deep, and the other, seven (23 feet). Dugourd then drew some water from the wells and took a sip from each of them. He thought the water quality was good, and he filled up a bottle to bring back to Hirsch, who wanted a chemist to analyze the sample.

They then headed for the citrus grove, where the oranges were just beginning to ripen. Brill observed the faces of the Arab peasant workers and was put off by their complexion. They looked sick, and he was concerned that the local swamps were breeding grounds for malaria and other diseases. He asked them, in Arabic, about the health conditions in the area, and their replies only aroused more concern. Nevertheless, he turned to the two farmers from Russia and was ready to tell them they'd just come upon a real "*metziah*" – a great find. He asked them what they thought. In a soft but firm reply, they told him they were not interested.

Brill was perplexed. "In Russia, do you have citrus groves or vegetable gardens like you find here?" Their reply would be repeated – with justification – on many more occasions.

> [We are wheat farmers!] What use do we have for citrus groves and orchards? Do we need fruit for a Sabbath meal compote? We need bread to eat and clothing to wear; and this type of land will not support us. Now, if you cannot get us land in Mikveh Israel as you promised us, we want to go back to Russia. And you are the one we will ask for money for the return trip![121]

With another hope dashed and a possible insurrection brewing, Brill placated them and played for time. He told the farmers they were fortunate for not settling in Mikveh Israel, where they would not be under their own authority but under the militaristic regime that was in charge there. But they were not convinced

Brill wrote:

> [They] saw me as a deceiver. I realized that they actually wanted to live in Mikveh Israel because it was so close to Jaffa. Mikveh Israel was the only place they were acquainted with in Palestine, and it was what they favored.... They were in a mournful spirit.[122]

A short while after the farmers began working at Mikveh Israel, one of them, Chaim Moshe Press, fell seriously ill. A doctor was called in to examine him. Shaking his head, the physician declared that if the man wanted to live, he had better pack his bags and return to Russia, for the climate was affecting him adversely. Although it appeared that his life was at stake, Press was undaunted: "We are like a barrel that is made up of wooden slats. If even one is removed, the entire barrel will fall apart. If I return to Russia, what will become of our group? But if I remain here with my friends, [that alone] will solidify us – and [at the very least] I will merit to be buried in the Holy Land."[123] Press recovered and, ironically, outlived all the other founding farmers, and possibly even the doctor who had predicted his demise.

That Darn(el) Bread

A February 1883 entry in Brill's travelogue records that he received an unexpected visit from two of the farmers. They had gone to see land in the Arab village of Dir'an. Their facial expressions were grim. He asked them, "How was your visit? Did you strike water there?"

They replied, "When we dug to a depth of about fifteen meters (forty-nine feet), we hit solid bedrock, and our pickaxes broke. With no tools left, we returned to Mikveh Israel." Then one of the farmers pulled a piece of bread out of his pocket. It was so dark that, in Brill's words, "it was impossible to describe it."

"This is the second time they fed us such bread in Mikveh Israel," the farmers complained. "We can't take it anymore!"

Brill examined the bread. It contained grain from the darnel plant, known as *zunin* in Hebrew. A member of the grass family, darnel resembles wheat, but it is a weed with poisonous fungus. It grows in grain fields throughout the Middle East. Since darnel and wheat grains are so similar, the two can be combined to produce a ground meal that can ruin a person's health.[124]

Regarding this bread, Brill quoted the Mishnah in *Kilayim*, the tractate that delineates which seeds are prohibited by the Torah to be sown together in a field: "Wheat and darnel do not constitute a forbidden admixture" (*Kilayim* 1:1). Brill wryly noted that although it may be permissible to *sow* the admixture, regarding human consumption, "… if you add even a little bit of darnel flour into wheat bread, it becomes inedible for humans. And if you add a lot, it becomes unfit even for a dog." When he saw the revolting bread, he was thoroughly disgusted with Hirsch. After holding back for nine weeks, Brill was now ready for an all-out war.

On February 16, he sent the following "tell-all" letter to Rabbi Ẓaddok Kahn:

Imposter. Darnel grass, a noxious weed

> Distinguished Sir,
>
> … I know that Mr. Hirsch has blackened my name, and I have found it necessary to clear it. I have no problem going to Mikveh Israel and personally reading to Hirsch this letter that I am writing to you now.
>
> From the moment the farmers and I arrived here, it became apparent to me that Hirsch does not want them to settle here…. I restrained myself from pointedly asking Hirsch why he did not arrange to have the agronomist teach them how to work the land here, how to plant trees and grow vegetables, which is why they came to Mikveh Israel in the first place. Instead, he sent them off to hew stones! I also held myself back from telling Hirsch how the farmers were complaining about the tasteless meals and the fact that they are served meat only on the Sabbath. Instead, I urged my men to bear with the situation.
>
> Three weeks ago, after returning from prospecting the southern part of the country, the farmers complained that for a period of ten days they were being fed black bread mixed with darnel grain. Only after Hirsch was told that the farmers sent someone to Jaffa to buy bread for them did he give an order that they receive better bread. (He gave them the bread they feed the animals – which the animals themselves were not so fond of!) I thought that this was just due to oversight, but when they complained to me again this past Sunday, I could not restrain myself any longer, and I went to Mikveh Israel and found Hirsch's assistant, Mr. Benschimol, and

> told him: "Look here at this bread that they are feeding the farmers. They don't get meat at all during the weekdays, and even the rice dish they aren't getting anymore. If they don't receive bread that is fit for human consumption, they will die of starvation!"
>
> Then just yesterday I went to tell Hirsch that I'd found a good prospect for the farmers to purchase. He was in the city and I found my men furious. They recounted that Hirsch had held a meeting with them last Tuesday and told them that there just wasn't any good land for sale in Palestine, and that if they didn't want to die young, they were better off packing their bags and returning to Russia.
>
> These innocent farmers were dumbfounded. They told Hirsch that if he meant what he said, then he should give each one of them 600 francs to cover travel expenses, and compensate their families for the loss of income incurred while they were away from their homes. Hirsch told them he would write to Paris about that.[125]

Brill was correct in his suspicion that Hirsch had complained about him to Rabbi Kahn in Paris. After receiving the complaints, Rabbi Kahn wrote to Rabbi Mohilever that Brill was becoming a nuisance and hindering the project. Kahn told Rabbi Mohilever that Brill should be sent home.

Six weeks later, Brill received two letters whose words cut him deeply.[126]

> The Austrian steamship brought me two letters. One was from Rabbi Mohilever, while the other was from my wife. I opened the second letter first. My wife recounted her most recent troubles, which helped me forget the previous ones. How was she going to get the money to buy matzah for Passover? Whatever she could sell or pawn, she did. The creditors had obtained a court order to confiscate my printing press. She was a half-year in arrears in paying rent on our house, and they had taken the housewares as collateral. The children had been expelled from school because they couldn't pay tuition. My only daughter and my wife were in need of medical care, and a kind Christian who was one of the leading citizens of the city had summoned a doctor to pay them a visit.... I put this letter with the other pains I have in my chest.[127]

As I opened Rabbi Mohilever's letter, I thought to myself that at least this one would provide me with some solace. He did, after all, promise to look after the finances of my family while I was away. (The same promises were made by Rabbi Kahn and Michael Erlanger of the Alliance Israélite Universelle. But during the entire time that I was away, my family in Mainz received only the paltry sum of 400 marks.)

… Dear reader – if my story till now has not yet satiated you with bitterness, Rabbi Mohilever's letter will fill the cup. Rabbi Mohilever wrote:

"… I received a letter from Rabbi Ẓaddok Kahn the other day.… He informed me that it looked like they were close to purchasing a good piece of real estate for the farmers. Rabbi Kahn assures me that the Benefactor is committed to building homes for our men in the Holy Land.…"

Rabbi Mohilever further wrote that my mission in the Holy Land is completed and that there is no longer reason for me to tarry there. "If it is indeed true that good-quality fields were purchased, then it's time for my friend to return home, especially in view of the hints of Rabbi Kahn that your intervention there does not please the Benefactor. I am unfortunately unable to elaborate."[128]

The very next day, Brill confronted Hirsch acrimoniously:

Why did you lie to Rabbi Kahn about me? When did I ever meddle in your affairs at Mikveh Israel? Such slander and outright falsehood! Is this what I get in return for doing your work for you? I went around to the Arab villages [scouting for land to purchase] for nearly forty days.[129] During the day, I would travel by horseback – sometimes for twelve hours straight – and in the evenings, I would lie down between camels and donkeys on the ground. I was doing your work with all this traveling, but you are the one who gets the good salary for all my labors! And what have you done to repay me for all this? Just slander and gossip![130]

When Brill finished his speech, he burst out sobbing, and Hirsch turned pale. In an unusually soft tone, he asked, "Didn't you complain to Kahn about the bread? And what is this that I read in the newspaper that you came here to take the place of the deceased Carl Netter?" (Carl [Charles] Netter was the founder and former director of Mikveh Israel.)

As to the bread, Brill replied, he had a moral obligation to look after the welfare of his men. And as to the second charge, he had witnesses who could vouch for him that he was constantly aching to finally complete his mission and return to his family. He had absolutely no desire to replace Hirsch in Mikveh Israel. One look at Brill's agonized face, and Hirsch knew he was telling the truth.

Chapter 9

This Year (1883) in Jerusalem

A few days before Passover (April 16/9 Nissan), Brill took a break from scouting for farmland to make a pilgrimage to Jerusalem for the holiday. He traveled by stagecoach on the relatively new Jaffa-Ramle-Jerusalem highway that had been constructed by the Ottoman government in the late 1860s.

Superhighway. The road to Jerusalem started off on the coastal plain at Jaffa. That road, the first built in the country since the Crusaders, was not completed until 1869. "When the first wagon arrived in Jerusalem, throngs of people streamed to Jaffa Gate to view this marvel."[131]

Road construction for horse-drawn carriages was relatively new in Palestine at that point. Transportation had been by horse, donkey, or camel, for which a narrow path would suffice.[132]

On the first day of *Chol ha-Moed* (the "intermediate days" of the holiday), three of the farmers walked the entire length of the road from Mikveh Israel to Jerusalem. They met with Brill and told him that Hirsch had not granted them permission to leave the school for the holiday, but they had ignored him. Hirsch had allowed them to supervise the baking of the matzah but was enraged when they'd refused to eat rice like

Left: Entrance to Bab El Wad (today Shaar Ha-Gai), where the ascent through the Jerusalem hills begins. (1894) *Right:* Carriage on the Jaffa-Jerusalem road near Abu Ghosh. (1900)

How the Western Wall appeared to the Pavlovkans. There was a narrow alleyway between the Wall and the homes of very poor Arabs. There were certain designated times when men and women could pray separately. The Turks would not permit the erection of a partition, even a temporary one. It wasn't until after 1840 that regular prayer services with a quorum became commonplace.[133]

the rest of the resident students in the school. (Unlike many Sephardic Jews, Ashkenazic Jews are forbidden to eat rice on Passover.) Before the holiday, they'd pleaded with him to give them money (8.67 francs each) for a visit to a *mikveh* (ritual pool), as is customary before Sabbaths and holidays. Hirsch had acquiesced.[133A]

The foursome made their way to the Kotel (Western Wall), where they kissed its ancient stones and poured out their hearts to God. It was their most spiritually uplifting moment since the day they'd arrived in Palestine.

Jerusalem – Nineteenth Century

Their appearance in Jerusalem startled Brill, who feared that the farmers would tell the religious residents of Jerusalem about their hardships. Jerusalem's Old Yishuv population was split on the question of Jewish settlement in the countryside. Many people opposed Jewish agricultural colonization, and Brill was afraid that the farmers' complaints would strengthen their arguments.

Unfortunately, his worst fears materialized. The news spread quickly that the farmers from Pavlovka were being "worked to

The Jewish Quarter.
Left: Lemonade vendor
Center: Jewish business closed for the Sabbath
Right: Jerusalem Jew

Left: The *shuk*
Right: Street scene – Jewish Quarter

death" at Mikveh Israel. It didn't take long before the farmers got the addresses of several advocates – lawyers who also served as real estate agents – who promised that after Passover they would show them fields for sale. As they had no money for lodgings, the farmers slept in the street. Brill was terrified that with the last day of the holiday approaching, they would line up at the entrance of the synagogues and ask people to invite them for a meal.

Jewish Quarter with the domed Churvah Synagogue on the right

So as not to appear as a delinquent guardian, Brill arranged for them to eat three meals at the hotel at which he was a guest. He managed to locate everyone but the *melamed*, who was snagged by a gracious host before Brill could track him down.

The only game in town. Brill doesn't tell us in which hotel he stayed, but it's a good bet that he was a guest at the only Jewish (and kosher) hotel in Jerusalem, owned by the Kaminetz family. Known as the Jerusalem Hotel, it was established in the 1880s and located on Jaffa Street. The hotel was the first in Jerusalem to offer European-style bread (instead of pita). Jewish tourism to the Holy Land lagged three decades behind Christian tourism. (Mark Twain visited Palestine with the first U.S. tour group in 1867.)

After Passover, Brill wanted to resume his search for farmland, but he understood from Rabbi Mohilever's letter that his days in Palestine were numbered. He made one more attempt to salvage his mission, touring the Galilee region (starting May 8) to search once again. Instead of taking the sea route from Jaffa's port to Haifa, he traveled by land – quite a dangerous option at the time. He hired a horse from an Arab who insisted that his lad (an employee) accompany Brill for his protection. "That is, for the protection of his horse," Brill dryly notes in his memoir.

Trekking. Jewish hikers in the early twentieth century

His description of the Galilee is most fascinating. As the sun was about to set, he arrived at the tomb of a Muslim considered by the Arabs to be a holy man. To perpetuate his memory and encourage travelers to stop and pray there, the Turkish government had constructed lodging for overnight travelers. The proceeds from the local produce purchased by the pilgrims were channeled back into paying for upkeep of the tomb.[134] At the Muslim site, the strictly Orthodox Brill was informed that he could obtain whatever food he desired, and he was assigned a room, a mattress, and a blanket.[135]

Caesarea. Fragment of large, conical stone in the Hippodrome, where the Romans held chariot races

Leaving at five o'clock in the morning, he made his way to Caesarea, where he stood in stunned silence for an hour and a half. Steeped in rabbinic lore and Jewish history, Brill knew well that Caesarea had once been the Roman seat of government

in Palestine. The decrees that had emanated from there caused great agony to the Jewish inhabitants. And now it was in ruins – a fitting symbol of the vanished Roman Empire!

This Roman metropolis, with its once magnificent edifices, was now pastureland for sheep brought by Arab shepherds to drink from the city's ancient cisterns. The city was desolate, even its ruins were in jeopardy, because stonecutters were chiseling away at the ancient structures. The stone would be sent to Jaffa, where it was used for construction.

"*Ekron tay'ah'ker* – 'Ekron will be uprooted' (עקרון תיעקר) – this is Roman Caesarea, which was the metropolis of the Roman kings," Brill noted, quoting from the Talmud (*Megillah* 6a). With joy, he recited the traditional blessing for this occasion: *Blessed art Thou, Lord, our God, King of the Universe, Who uprooted the enemies of Israel from this place.*[136]

The Romans were long gone, but Brill believed that this desolate land would one day – hopefully in the near future – be home to perhaps thousands of Jews. Little did he realize that Ekron was to be the name of the settlement that his farmers would soon establish.

In his travels, Brill visited a settlement that had been founded recently by Romanian Jews of the Chovevei Ẓion movement near the Arab village of Samarin. It later developed into the town of Zikhron Yaakov. Brill also visited Tantura, Haifa, and Akko.

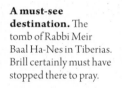

A must-see destination. The tomb of Rabbi Meir Baal Ha-Nes in Tiberias. Brill certainly must have stopped there to pray.

Then it was on to Safed. This leg of the trip was very dangerous, as there were many Arab marauders in the area. During this miserable journey, Brill fell off his horse due to heat exhaustion and "the numerous mosquitoes that swarmed around me without letup."

From Safed, he made his way to another newly founded Jewish settlement, Rosh Pina. Originally named Gei Oni, after the adjacent Arab village Ja'una, Rosh Pina was an agricultural settlement founded by ultra-Orthodox Jews of the Old Yishuv of Safed. Inexperienced as farmers, they had planted potatoes and despaired when they saw nothing growing out of the ground, until someone pointed out to them that potatoes are root vegetables that grow beneath the soil.[137] By the time of Brill's visit, Gei Oni had already been abandoned by its founders and was reestablished by Chassidic Jews from Romania.

Unsung hero. David Kosviner, a founder of Rosh Pina

From there, he traveled to Tiberias, where he slept in a tent that was bound on one side by the *chamei Teveria*, the famous hot mineral springs, and on the other side by the tomb of Rabbi Meir Baal Ha-Nes. He stayed on for a few days in Tiberias, remaining for the Sabbath.[138]

On May 28, he left Tiberias before the break of dawn and arrived in Shefar'am[139] around noon. There, he writes, "I went to see [the ruins] of the synagogue that according to legend was the seat of the Sanhedrin (the legislative body of ancient Israel) when it was in exile." From there, he made his way to Haifa, then sailed back to Jaffa. He'd had an uplifting trip but had not found suitable land for his farmers. He returned to them crestfallen and empty-handed.

Chapter 10
Farewell to Yechiel Brill

By the end of May, 1883, Brill concluded that there was no reason for him to remain in Palestine. His friends concurred, for his family had been deprived of a husband and father for many months. Brill was certain he had done his best, but he was not satisfied with the result.

> Just as I received no recompense for coming here, I will not be penalized for leaving. I did all that was humanly possible. Let God do what is good in His eyes. May the Owner of the vineyard come and remove the thorns and small foxes [i.e., the administrators] that are ruining the vineyard of the Lord of Hosts![139A] But where will I flee, where will I go? Where will I take my humiliation? What will become of my toil and effort on behalf of settling the Land of Israel these past nine months?[140]

The farmers had been encouraged to leave their homes to build a new life in Ereẓ Yisrael, and now Brill was shamefacedly leaving them there with nothing but broken promises. They, too, were on the brink of leaving.

> That night seven of the farmers came to me and told me that they had suddenly come to the realization that the director was not really interested in their welfare after all. A fight broke out between them and the director, and they refused to go out to work in the fields until he promised to keep his word and purchase land for them. He, in turn, frightened them by threatening to throw them out of Mikveh Israel if they continued to behave brazenly. They responded that they would make their way to Paris to cry foul over what had been done to them … because they could no longer eat the bread that Mikveh Israel was providing them … because they wanted to be given one franc per day to buy and cook their own food … because he was making them work seven times harder now than in the winter … because … because … because.…[141]

Although Brill was heartbroken and bitter, not once did he record questioning why God had not helped him succeed in what he considered a holy mission. At three o'clock in the afternoon of June 4, Brill prepared to embark on a steamship bound for France. Accompanied by his sister Yocheved and his comrades Michel Katz,[142] Yoel Moshe Salomon, and Yechiel Michel

Pines, he descended the stairs that led to the beach where a rowboat awaited to take him to the steamship.[143]

Suddenly, while aboard the rowboat, they heard someone call out, "Passport! Passport! Who is traveling?" Brill answered that he was the only one traveling and handed the Turkish policeman his passport. The immigration official recognized Brill and did not even bother to check the passport. He merely jotted down the date of exit and shook Brill's hand, inquiring, "What is your final destination?"

"Paris."

"Do you plan to return to us?"

"Yes."

Brill lied. He was too embarrassed to tell the truth. He loved the Land of Israel and his companions very much, but he doubted that he had the stomach or the financial resources to return ever again. Holding back his tears, he begged his friends to hurry back to shore. When he saw them approaching the shoreline, he envied them because they were privileged to live in the Holy Land, while he had just spent 174 days there.

One week later, he reached the European mainland, anxious to return home.

> As morning broke on June 11, the first day of Shavuot, I disembarked in Marseille. ... I walked to the synagogue, and after

From ship to shore. Rowboats in Jaffa Harbor with steamship in the background

> prayers were concluded, I searched for and found Sir David Malka. I implored him to invite me to dine at his table, because this city, with 3,000 Jewish inhabitants and numerous Jewish visitors, does not have a single kosher food establishment![144]

After the Shavuot holiday, Brill reported to Rabbi Ẓaddok Kahn in Paris. He muddled through that painful task and then set out for Mainz. There, he was finally reunited with his family. He straightened out his neglected financial affairs and began writing the chronicle of his journey to Palestine, *Yesud Ha-Ma'alah.*

Brill recorded not only the events that had transpired, but also his deeply felt opinions concerning everything that had occurred and the people he'd encountered. He had no hesitation in writing severe criticisms of the people with whom he disagreed. The cultural and religious clash between him and Mikveh Israel's director, Shmuel Hirsch, was inevitable, and, as we have seen in previous chapters, Brill spared no words in his severe criticism.

In *Yesud Ha-Ma'alah,* Brill clearly expresses his belief that Hirsch never wanted to help the religious Russian farmers settle in Palestine, doing everything he could to frustrate them in the hope that they would return to Russia. *Yesud Ha-Ma'alah* is replete with Brill's sarcastic and critical references to "the director."

Historian Ran Aaronsohn offers a different interpretation of events.[145] He points out that the Baron would have trusted Hirsch, for he was "a disciplined, hard-working, and highly capable man. Hirsch's major efforts on the Baron's behalf were in the areas of manpower and financial management, in which he had no peer." Moreover, Hirsch was steeped in French culture and easily mingled with Rothschild and the French Jewish elite. Brill was regarded as an eastern European outsider whose exposure to Western culture was skin-deep. While Brill may have seen himself as a bridge between the "simple" religious Russian farmers and the secular French Jews, the French Jews did not. When Brill and Hirsch sent conflicting reports to Paris, Hirsch was clearly the more believable source. And then there was Brill's abrasive personality.

Who was telling the truth? Brill's charges, published in his book and in his newspaper articles, were rarely refuted (aside for the one time Rabbi Kahn attacked him for portraying Hirsch as someone bent on undermining Jewish resettlement in Palestine). Did Rothschild's associates strategize that the best defense was to ignore him?

The tired typesetter. Newspapers must reach the public quickly, but the typesetter's work is painstakingly slow and laborious. Israeli stamp from 1963 commemorating the centennial of the founding of the Hebrew newspaper *Ha-Levanon.*

When Brill openly attacked the Alliance, he lost all credibility. In the November 29, 1883, issue of the Hebrew-language newspaper *Ha-Maggid,* he accused one of the Alliance's people of being a "Sanbalat" – a reference to the leader of the Samaritans who tried to prevent the rebuilding of the Second Temple when the Jews returned to the Land of Israel from Babylonia. The French Jews thought Brill was referring to Shmuel Hirsch. Rabbi Kahn angrily denounced Brill's assertions in a letter to *Ha-Maggid.* Brill clarified that he was referring to someone else and made veiled allusions to Michael Erlanger, one of Rothschild's chief advisors. After these public attacks in the press, Brill's standing with the secular French Jewish establishment reached an all-time low.

Four months after Brill returned to Europe in exasperation, Shmuel Hirsch, the man he had accused of eternal stonewalling, purchased 3,600 Turkish dunams (828 acres) of land for the farmers from Pavlovka. Located near the Arab city of Ramle, the land was registered in the name of Michael Erlanger of Paris.

In 1884, Brill moved to London. Two years later, he began republishing *Ha-Levanon* under extremely difficult conditions – doing his own typesetting in a dimly lit and cramped room. Only twelve editions came out. In July 1886, Yechiel Brill died suddenly of a stroke. He was 50 years old.

"A Man of Pure Heart and Mind"

Regardless of the establishment's opinion of him, Yechiel Brill was the catalyst who brought the farmers to Palestine. He was the right man in the right place at the right time.[146]

It was his idea to recruit pioneers from the ranks of experienced Russian Jewish farmers – the single factor that distinguished this initiative from its predecessors, making a positive outcome viable. The clear, focused, and achievable objective that Rabbi Mohilever presented to Baron Rothschild was Brill's concept. Rabbi Mohilever might not have even thought of meeting with Rothschild were it not for Brill.[147] In his introduction to the Ben-Zvi Press edition of *Yesud Ha-Ma'alah,* Getzel Kressel sums up Brill's contribution: "The bringing of the eleven farmers to the Land of Israel was due to the personal initiative of Yechiel Brill. He endangered his life in a one-of-a-kind endeavor that is almost unparalleled in the annals of our new settlement in the Land of Israel."[148]

Ironically, for all of Brill's efforts, until as late as 2007 there wasn't a single street in the whole town of Mazkeret Batya that bore his name. In many ways, Brill was a tragic figure. His contemporaries shied away from him. Even historians seem to avoid him.

Yet his passing stunned Jewish communities from London to Jerusalem. Eliezer Ben-Yehuda wrote an eloquent obituary

Mr. Hebrew. Eliezer Ben-Yehuda, editor of the Palestinian Hebrew newspaper *Ha-Ẓvi.*

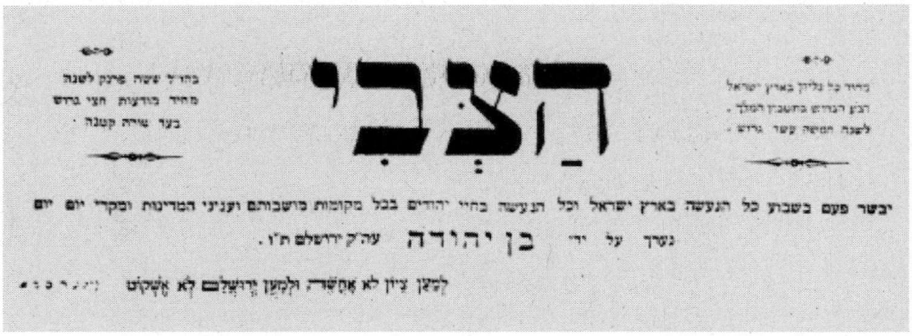

when Brill passed away, even though the two were poles apart ideologically. Despite their differences – Brill championed traditional Orthodoxy, while Ben-Yehuda was an outspoken secularist – Ben-Yehuda spoke from the heart. The obituary is a testament to Brill's heroic and bitter life. It appeared in the December 31, 1886 (4 Tevet 5647) edition of *Ha-Ẓvi.*

"The Cedar of Lebanon Has Been Cut Down"

"What comes from the heart touches the heart." What follows are excerpts from Eliezer Ben-Yehuda's articulate and moving obituary for Yechiel Brill, "The Cedar of Lebanon Has Been Cut Down":

> Terrible news has confounded us – that Rabbi Yechiel Brill, publisher of *Ha-Levanon,* was suddenly "cut down from the land of the living" in London, his residence for the last few years, on the

15th of Cheshvan (November 13, 1886).

Rabbi Yechiel Brill was born in the city of Krislova, Volhynia.[149] His father had him marry at a young age, but he later divorced. He then moved to Jerusalem and married the daughter of Rabbi Yaakov Sapir (of blessed memory), who was famous for his travels to Arabia, Yemen, and India. He took to studying the holy tongue in earnest in the home of his father-in-law, and eventually he became an outstanding writer. Together with his friends Rabbi Yoel Moshe Salomon and Reb Michel Cohen, he established an independent printing press in Jerusalem. They began printing a periodical called *Ha-Levanon,* which circulated for a year or so, until it was shut down.

Ben-Yehuda recounts Brill's efforts to ensure success for the farmers he brought from Russia, then continues:

…We are all aware that Brill was involved in many fights and had many adversaries; even the most sincere men saw his character flaws, for he was the pugnacious, combative type. However, all of these men did not know Brill to the full extent; they did not know of the true goodness of his heart, of all the hardships he encountered in his difficult life, which left their mark on his personality. Thus, they have a distorted opinion of him. But we knew him, and we knew well of his dear, pure soul; therefore, it is our duty to correct all those who disliked him – for he was trustworthy, a man of pure heart and mind.

He exhibited a level of compassion that many men cannot achieve; he was a man of faith and sincere love. He was a man of excessive strength and motivation, valor and courage. However, he had been stricken by so many hardships and troubles since his childhood. He suffered from poverty and misery his entire life; he led a forceful and difficult war against life's tragedies, during which time he witnessed much corruption. He saw that too many men preferred falsehood over truth. He encountered the recklessness and charlatanism which was in vogue, while genuine knowledge and talent were shunted to the side. He saw that bragging and flattery were used to work one's way to the top and were an easier path to take than the humble path of truth, and that the path of truth was entangled and inseparable from poverty and sadness. He therefore became a miserable man, facing the world with a scowl.

His bitterness at times added venom to his words; everything he wrote and said was filled with acrimony and poison. He bit like a snake and stung like a scorpion. His humor was sharp and offensive. This character of his only served to increase the number of his adversaries,

Muckraker. Yechiel Brill (1836-1886)

which made life's troubles even more difficult for him; the harder the battle became, the bitterer he became. He did not see any good in any of his work; it seemed that every project he took upon himself had turned into a detriment. The settlement of Ekron, which he carefully nurtured and toiled for, investing all of his energy and courage into the colony for which he sacrificed his reputation and status, turned its back on him and said: "I do not know you."

He felt compelled to leave for London in order to build a new home for himself; he established *Ha-Shulamit*, but his bitterness did not allow him to manage his periodical with peace of mind. Instead, he led a dedicated war against the heads, officers, and knights of the city, which brought him to the verge of bankruptcy. We do not justify this war of his by any means, for he went so far as to humiliate philanthropists and men of good faith; we will say, however, that his intentions were pure and that in his bitterness he did believe he was fighting for truth and justice.

His fate was similar to the fate of many Jewish writers; he died poor and is survived by a wife and children who live in poverty. The few who did love the man will undoubtedly help his family and not leave them to starve. However, we do hope that all those he provoked and upset during his lifetime will not hold a grudge against the man – but will rather see his good deeds and honest intentions.

Chapter 11 *The Chosen Land*

For nearly half a year, Yechiel Brill had searched for suitable farmland for the farmers, but none of his efforts met with success. Sometimes Hirsch simply rejected his proposals; at other times, Hirsch insisted on contacting Paris at every stage of the negotiations – a process that delayed the decision by months, souring any chances for a deal to be finalized.

By June 1883, Brill was gone. It was now up to Hirsch to find the farmers a place of their own – or continue to put up with them. Hirsch swung into action, eventually recommending several possible purchases. Between Hirsch and Brill, nineteen properties were investigated, each of them rejected for one reason or another. Many were vetoed by the farmers themselves. Back in Paris, the Baron and his associates were getting impatient. By summer's end, Hirsch received this sharp letter:

> August 24, 1883
> Paris
> Dear Mr. Hirsch,
>
> I have just come out of a meeting with Baron de Rothschild, and he is very distressed that this time again there has been no closure regarding a purchase of property. He has ordered me to telegraph you immediately to purchase at once the vacant land of Safed (which belongs to Abu Hai), if this will suffice the Radomers[150] [i.e., the farmers from Pavlovka], or purchase the land adjacent to Rishon Le-Ẓion – or any land, for that matter.
>
> If only this matter would come to an end and these men would settle down! The chief rabbi [Kahn], who just recently received a desperate letter from the Radomers, has requested of me to communicate to you (via telegraph) that you should comfort these men and give them words of encouragement.
>
> Michael Erlanger[151]

With the Baron breathing down his neck, Hirsch put pressure on the farmers to pick a plot of land. The farmers were facing a test. As beneficiaries of the Baron's largesse, it was unseemly for them to be choosy. But despite their gratitude to the Baron, they were determined not to settle on land they could not farm.

Field of dreams. Wheat field in the northern Negev

They were wheat farmers and they knew that wheat requires heavy, rich soil. So they stubbornly waited until they found land that was suitable for them.

The fact that the wheat harvest in Rishon Le-Ẓion was dismal did not deter the Baron's men from urging the farmers to settle there. But the farmers would not be lured into compromising their real needs for a short-term solution. Sandy soil, the kind found in Rishon Le-Ẓion or Zikhron Yaakov, would not do. The Parisians wanted facts on the ground; the Russians wanted a solid foundation on which to grow their crops. Patience on both sides was wearing thin and coming close to the breaking point. The farmers were threatening to return to Russia – and they meant it.[152]

An astute communal leader, Baron Rothschild felt it was imperative to prevent the farmers from leaving Palestine. He directed Erlanger to telegraph Hirsch at once:

> August 31, 1883
> Paris
>
> … The Radomers are giving you and us lots of trouble. Mr. de Rothschild does not want them to return to Russia under *any* circumstances. He wants them to settle down whatever way possible … He believes that if they, who are experienced farmers, return to Russia – then no Jew from Russia will even think of ever going to the Land of Israel. And since he is concerned with new

outbreaks of violence [in eastern Europe] ... he says we have to think of the future. He wants me to impress upon you the importance he attaches to establishing Jewish settlements in Ereẓ Yisrael. He is not far off. So many things can occur [even here] in civilized Europe. Brute force prevails over justice ...

The bottom line – keep searching. Get others to assist in the search. Do your best to acquire for them property they can call their own ... I repeat – Mr. de Rothschild will not agree to the return of the Radomers to Russia under any circumstances!

Michael Erlanger[153]

Ramle. Built circa 705-715 CE, Ramle was the only city the Arabs constructed in all of western Palestine that wasn't built upon a pre-existing settlement. The tower on the right, known as the "White Tower," was the remaining minaret of the giant White Mosque built in the eighth century. Though located nearby, the Jewish farmers preferred to do their shopping and business in Jaffa, which was four hours away. Ramle was a major stop on the Jaffa-Jerusalem road. *Lithograph by David Roberts, 1839.*

With determined resistance coming from the farmers, Hirsch decided to let them take the initiative into their own hands. One of the farmers, Ephraim Skolnick, recalled:

The Baron's reply in the telegram [to Hirsch] was "Hasten to purchase land for them." Then Hirsch "spoke to our hearts" and gave us permission to scout out a good piece of land ourselves, until we eventually found the land.... It was chosen by Reb Yaakov Arkin and me after we had surveyed it, and it looked just right.[154]

The fields they favored were situated near the Arab village of Aqir (Arabic pronunciation: *Ah-ger*), about one hour (nine kilometers/5.6 miles) southwest of the Arab city of al-Ramla (Ramle) and about five hours southeast of Jaffa. The soil in this

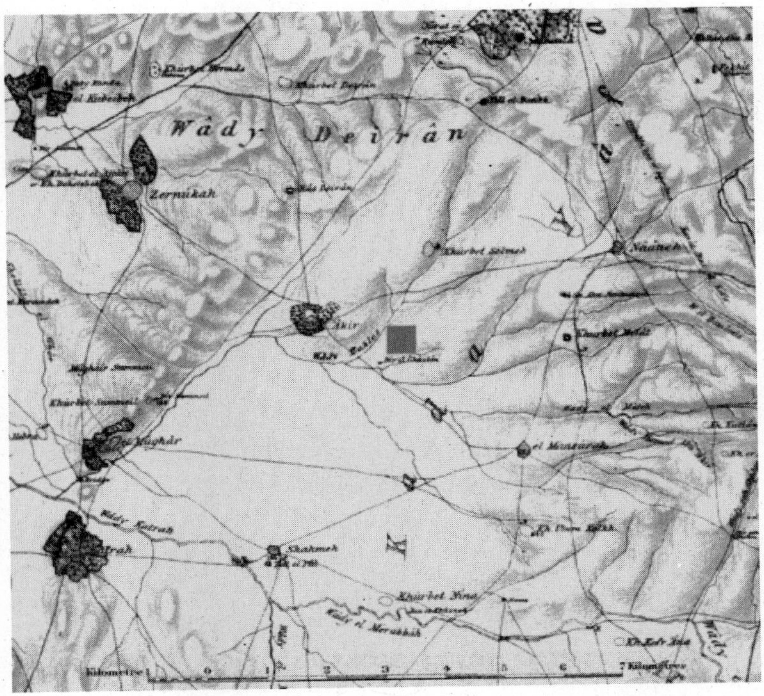

A little geography. One section of a much larger map of the Holy Land drawn by the Palestine Exploration Fund (PEF), a British team of surveyors and cartographers, just four years before the farmers arrived. In the center is the town of Aqir (spelled Akir). The area the farmers chose is designated by the square to the right of Aqir, about two kilometers (1.3 miles) east. The dotted, shaded areas around Aqir and other towns designate orchards. The large dotted area at the top of the map is the orchard district of the city of Ramle. There were no roads except from Jaffa to Jerusalem via Ramle. Part of this road can be seen as the dark line going southwest from Ramle. The thin lines are either paths or dried streambeds. *The Survey of Western Palestine (1872-1877), sheet 16, Esdud – Ashdod.*

locale was very rich and heavy – perfect for growing wheat. Moreover, the land they found was "…a fertile plain that didn't contain a single hill."[155]

The farmers were true pioneers: They selected a piece of land that was perfect for farming but otherwise barren. There were no homes, no buildings, no water, no infrastructure, and no schools. They had to build everything from scratch.

In several villages surrounding the proposed site lived 5,000 Arabs, not including a relatively large population of Arabs residing in Ramle. According to a British survey at the time, their closest neighbors were:

> Nâàneh – "a small mud village on low ground."
> El Mansûrah – "a mud village of moderate size."
> Shahmeh – "Resembles the last (Nâàneh). It has a well to its south."[155A]
> Ramleh – "a town containing about 3,000 inhabitants of which number more than two-thirds are Moslems. The majority of the homes are of mud … The town is surrounded by fine orchards and olive-groves, enclosed in hedges of prickly pear."[155B]

Now, after a search that took ten long months, it was up to their patron, the Baron, to purchase the land for them.

Ottoman Xenophobia

Jewish reacquisition of ancestral lands was an exceedingly drawn-out and tedious affair – and prohibitively expensive. The Turkish ban on European Jewish immigration and land purchase made it exceedingly hard to obtain a *kushan* (deed) and a *rukasiyye* (building permit).

This heavy hand on European Jews was an outgrowth of a wider ban on land purchases by non-Ottoman citizens.

When Napoleon Bonaparte invaded Palestine in March of 1799, he nearly succeeded in wresting the land from the Ottomans who had ruled it for nearly 400 years. Although he was finally defeated during the siege of Akko, Palestine would never remain the same.

As a result of the French invasion, the Holy Land became the focal point of European political, religious, and historical interest. More importantly, the French Middle Eastern campaign revealed that the once mighty and feared Ottoman Empire was hardly more than a paper tiger. The Ottomans, keenly aware of this, were alarmed at the prospect of European subversion and infiltrations into their empire, especially on the western frontier.[156]

Constantinople perceived the Russian Jewish "refugees" as potential spies and saboteurs. In addition, these so-called farmers could have a deleterious effect on the work ethic of the native population. When Elie Scheid, the Baron's superintendent of the colonies in Palestine, paid his first courtesy call to the pasha (governor) in Jerusalem, his reception was less than cordial:

> Mutessarif Mehmed Sharif Rauf Pasha told me: "Do you really believe the Jews will give themselves over to working the land? Never! They will only spoil the Arab peasants by their lifestyle. I will work with all my strength to see that the colonies do not reach fruition."[157]

Rothschild and his associates used all the resources and back channels at their disposal to overcome the first hurdle – obtaining the legal rights to acquire land.

One more concern that was on the Baron's and his associates' minds: The purchase of land was a delicate and volatile matter, one that had the potential to aggravate Arab-Jewish relations. A case in point was Petach Tikva: On March 29, 1886, sixty *fellahin* from the village of al-Yahudiyya attacked that settlement, causing the death of a woman and significant damage. The dispute was over land. The fields of al-Yahudiyya had been confiscated from their owners by Arab creditors after they had failed to make the interest payments on their loans. The fields were subsequently sold to the Jewish colony of Petach Tikva. In the eyes of the *fellahin*, this was robbery: their ancestral land had been forcibly taken from them. This type of scenario was often repeated with different variations.[158] Fortunately, this would not be the case regarding Aqir, but negotiations had to be conducted deftly and with caution.

A Frantic Purchase

Hirsch learned from his real estate agent that he would be acquiring 3,600 dunams (one Turkish dunam = 919.3 square meters, or 0.23 acres) for 70,000 francs ($280,000 in today's U.S. currency) from a wealthy Christian Arab landowner from Jaffa named Alfred Ruk.[159] But when the Baron's men carefully surveyed the area, the useable land amounted to only 2,800 dunams, raising the cost to twenty-five francs per dunam, a very high price for land at that time.

Hirsch delegated all the legal work to Avraham Moyal, one of the Jewish communal leaders in Jaffa.[160]

All land purchases had to be registered with the Turkish authorities. In whose name should the deed be recorded? Rothschild's first impulse

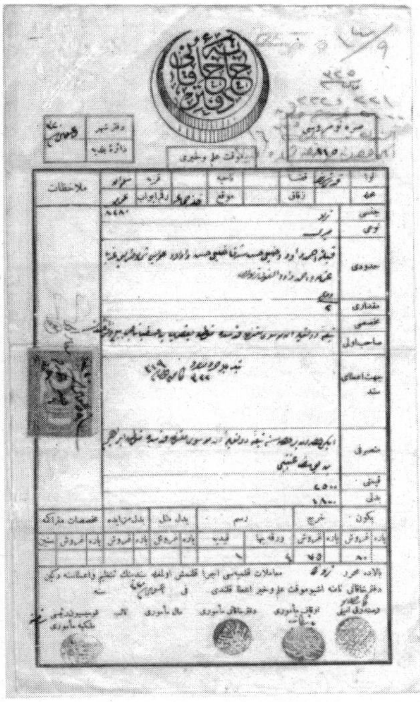

"This land is your land..." *Kushan*, a Turkish land deed. It took every bit of expertise and diplomatic pull that the Baron's men had to purchase a small plot of land for the Jews from Russia.

was to deed it to the farmers, since he had promised them that the land would be theirs. But at the last minute, he changed his mind. His reason was partly technical: To purchase land you had to be a Turkish subject, and the Turks were not issuing citizenship to Jewish refugees from Russia.

A more subtle reason was "educational." As the Baron wrote in a letter to Hirsch, the land should be registered in such a way as "not to immediately grant them full ownership, but that they should acquire it by the sweat of their brows." This decision was to have major repercussions.[160A]

Ironically, while nearly all the previous, failed attempts at purchasing property were clearly documented, the one that finally succeeded is somewhat vague. Even the date of the acquisition is in question.[161] Yet the land was clearly sold, and the deed was titled to Michael Erlanger, head of a "Paris-based charity," a designation approved by the Ottoman authorities. Later, when it became feasible, Erlanger transferred ownership directly to Rothschild. The purchase of the land was a major feat, accomplished only through the political savvy and expertise of the Baron's professionals.

From Aqir to Ekron

What should they name their new settlement? In nineteenth-century Palestine, the early pioneers and their financial backers sought to link their new communities to the Bible: it was a declaration that the Jewish people had finally returned to its homeland. For others (especially the *maskilim*), such names were part of the romantic Jewish notion of "renewal" harking back to pre-exilic Jewish history, when Jews were vanquishing their enemies rather than being humiliated by them.

When the Arabs conquered Palestine from the Byzantines in the seventh century, their custom was to retain the original names of the towns and villages, albeit with an Arabic twist. (This practice later proved to be a major boon for archeologists and historians.) For example, the city of Betar was renamed Bettir. It didn't take much imagination to see the resemblance between Aqir and the Philistine city of Ekron. Some say that it was Michael Erlanger who came up with the idea. In a November 1883 letter he sent to Hirsch, he identified Aqir with the ancient Philistine city of Ekron (Tel Miqneh).[162]

But was Aqir named after this Philistine city-state? The actual site of ancient Ekron is 8.5 kilometers (5.28 miles) to the south. Because of this distance, Yehuda Ziv, author of *Rega shel Makom,*[163] concludes that the naming of the village had no connection with Ekron, but alluded to a local holy man (regarded as a prophet) named Aqir, who was buried there.

In contrast, Dr. Yoel Elizur, an expert in biblical geography and Semitic languages, asserts that "the connection between [Philistine] Ekron and *'āqer* is indisputable, since neither ancient nor Arabic toponyms [place names] of the root *'qr* are known in other regions of the country."[164]

In any case, the farmers were also involved in naming their fledgling settlement. For them, the name Ekron signified something beyond a Philistine metropolis. It had another biblical allusion, found in the book of Zechariah (9:7):

וְהָיָה כְּאַלֻּף בִּיהוּדָה וְעֶקְרוֹן כִּיבוּסִי׃

"… and it shall become like a prince (*aluf*) in Judah; and Ekron – like the Jebusite."

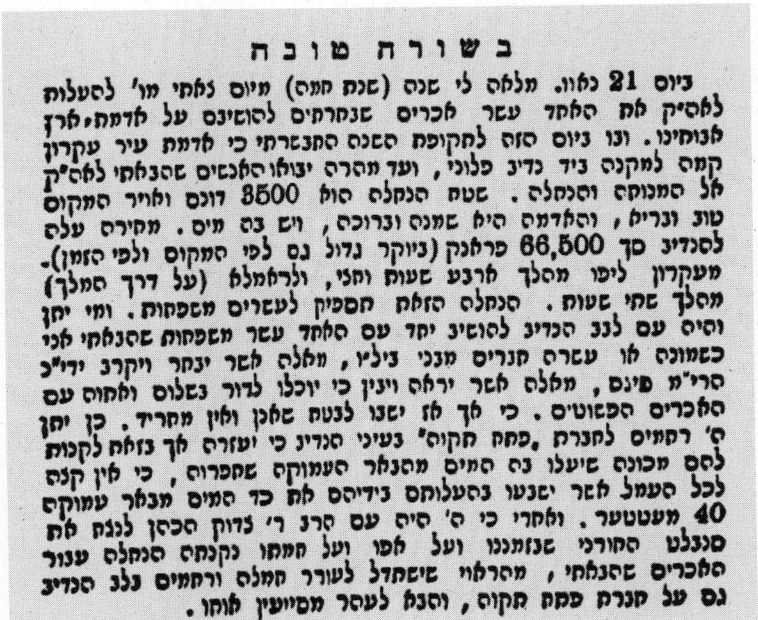

בשורת טובה

ביום 21 באב. מלאה לי שנה (שנת חמה) מיום צאתי מו' להעלות להסיע את האחד עשר אכרים שנבחרים להושיבם על אדמת ארץ אבותינו. וגו ביום הזה לתקופת השנה התבשרתי כי אדמת עיר עקרון קמה למקנה ביד הנדיב פלוני, ועד מהרה יבואו האנשים שהבאתי לארץ אל המנוחה והנחלה. שטח הנחלה הוא 8500 דונם ואויר המקום טוב ובריא, והאדמה היא שמנה וברוכה, ויש בה מים. מחירה עלה להנדיב סך 66,500 פראנק (ביוקר גדול גם לפי המקום ולפי הזמן). מעקרון ליפו מהלך ארבע שעות וחצי, ולרמלה (על דרך המלך) מהלך שתי שעות. הנחלה הזאת תספיק לעשרים משפחות. ומי יתן והיה עם לבב הנדיב להושיב יחד עם האחד עשר משפחות שהבאתי אני כשמונה או עשרה חברים מבני ביל"ו, אלה אשר יבחר ויקרב ידי"ד הרי"מ פינס, אלה אשר יראה ויבין כי יוכלו לדור בשלום ואחוה עם האכרים הפשוטים. כי אך אז ישבו לבטח שאנן ואין מחריד. כן יתן ה' רחמים לחברת "פתח תקוה" בעיני הנדיב כי יעזרה אך בזאת לקנות להם מכונה שיעלו בה המים מהבאר העמוקה שחפרוה, כי אין קנה לכל העמל אשר יגעו בהעלותם בידיהם את כד המים מבאר עמוקה 40 מעטער. ואחרי כי ה' היה עם הרב ר' צדוק הכהן לנגח את הנגלט החורבי שבזמננו ועל אפו ועל חמתו נקנתה הנחלה עבור האכרים שהבאתי, מהראוי שישתדל לעורר חמלה ורחמים בלב הנדיב גם על חברת פתח תקוה, והבא לטהר מסייעין אותו.

יחיאל בריל.

Good news! Announcement of the land purchase for the new colony of Ekron, published in *Ha-Maggid*[164A] by Yechiel Brill, who could only write about it from afar. He was informed of the purchase exactly one year from the date he set out with the eleven farmers for the Holy Land.

This enigmatic verse has been interpreted in various ways. The *Targum* of Yonatan ben Uziel (the Aramaic translation of the books of the Prophets) homiletically expounds on the last words – "and Ekron – like the Jebusite" – as follows: "Ekron will be filled with Jews like Jerusalem." (Jebus was the name of a city conquered by King David, who renamed it Jerusalem and established it as the national Jewish capital.)

The Talmud (*Megillah* 6a) interprets the words "*ke-aluf bi-Yehuda,* like a prince in Judah" as a prediction that "the circuses and theaters of Edom" (i.e., Rome) will be transformed from centers of bawdy entertainment into study halls where the "princes of Judah" (i.e., the Torah scholars) will teach spirituality. (The Hebrew word *aluf* can refer to a chief/prince, or to instruction/teaching.)

The farmers from Russia, who had sacrificed so much to get to this point, could now dream that their little settlement would one day transform a land desolate of Jews and Judaism into a center for Jewish refugees and a holy place of Torah learning. Although the pioneers loved farming, to them, the greatest accolade still belonged to the *talmid chacham* – the Torah scholar.

They had decided upon a name for their grand experiment. But where exactly would the farmers live until they could construct housing appropriate for their families? A resident of Aqir, Ibrahim Afuna, sold Hirsch a few windowless mud dwellings that surrounded a courtyard. These would serve as homes for the pioneers for the next few weeks. The farmers were now going to live in a totally alien world, surrounded by Palestinian Arabs, and at their mercy.

Chapter 12

The Eleven Àbâyehs

The eleven pioneers finally had their land. With hope in their hearts, undoubtedly mingled with natural trepidation, they moved into their mud huts in Aqir.

In his book *The Arab Village,* Moshe Stavi draws a portrait of a typical Arab village on Israel's lowland plain (*shefelah*):

> A number of mud huts, low and hunched over, are densely built together as a group, like a flock of sheep huddled together during a storm. A home is built side by side with a pen, a henhouse built under the belly of a barn, an oven rests on the lap of a cowshed, and a dovecote holds up a shed. They all cling to each other, climbing and rising and settling with each other, resting and dozing during the tiresome, hot summer days ... and merge into a lump of sun-eaten mud, which shares its hue with the color of the earth surrounding the village, and provides a home for all the living creatures that dwell there.
>
> When nearing the village, a passerby can smell the scent of water – well water, a pond and trough, and the swamp waters that surround the trough and are inhabited by an opulence of flies and mosquitoes; the tumult and noise of the sheep, cattle and camels, and humans who come to pump water and fill their basins ...
>
> The well is the most basic necessity of the village; the village could not exist without it.
>
> In the hind part of the village, near the ruins of a wall or cactus fence ... lies the village garbage dump, which is a recep-

Home, sweet home. Arab homes made out of mud bricks – home of the Pavlovka farmers for five weeks.

> tacle for the village's refuse: oven ash and residue, trash and garbage, carcasses.... All the buildings' ... bricks were made of mud and straw.... [165]

We don't know how the farmers managed to communicate with their Arab neighbors, but somehow they did. They actually developed friendly relationships with the Arabs, who were kind and helpful to their Jewish neighbors. There were so few Jewish farm settlements at the time that the presence of the Russian Jews did not rouse the ire of local Arabs.

Palestinian Yiddish

The lingua franca of east European Ashkenazic Jews in the nineteenth century was Yiddish, a language peppered with words from the wider societies in which the Jews resided.

The same process occurred when European Jews started coming to Palestine. They began to borrow words from Arabic and Turkish, creating a Palestinian Yiddish with its own peculiar flavor. Below is a sampler (taken with permission from Mordecai Kosover, Ph.D., *Palestinian Yiddish,* Jerusalem:Rubin Mass, 1966). Arabic appears in bold italics, and Yiddish in italics.

Ya-ret, *khvolt gevèn Baron Rotš'ld!* =
I wish I were Baron Rothschild!

Charām! *Farvos hoste dos ge-ton!* =
It's a sin! Why did you do it?

Vu geyt men du? ***Yam du-gri*** =
Which is the way to go? **Straight ahead**

Records indicate that "Together they ate bread with salt and drank the water of their well. This resulted in a covenant of peace between the residents of Aqir and the people of Ekron that lasted until the days of the rioting [the Arab revolt of the 1930s], when the Arab residents of the village were under enormous pressure from outside agitators."[166]

Shmuel Hirsch knew the farmers' Russian Jewish garb would

grab the attention of their new Arab neighbors, so he made sure to supply each farmer with two necessary accessories to his wardrobe: an *àbâyeh* and a *kăfiyyeh*.

When the men ventured out of Aqir and into the fields to survey their permanent homestead, they found one *churvah* (ruin) and the remains of an animal pen. The pen was to be

Dress for Success

The àbâyeh was a shoulder mantle, similar to a *tallit*, but without fringes. The usual àbâyeh was made of woven camel hair, goat hair, or coarse wool.[167] It was somewhat similar to a blanket that was draped over the shoulders like a cape. It was also used to veil the face, protecting the wearer from cold winds. These garments were multipurpose, also serving as blankets at night and as a sack for carrying things to the market.[168] It would have been an amusing sight to observe the Russian farmers muttering to each other in Yiddish from under their àbâyehs.

The kâfiyyeh is a large square head cloth, folded diagonally to form a triangle.[169] Traditional Arabs, like their traditional Jewish counterparts, wear a skullcap, with a kâfiyyeh on top, secured on the head by a double-ringed cord, usually black. It would not be surprising if the religious Jewish farmers wore the same.

As a result of their adaptation to their new cultural surroundings, the Jewish farmers earned the nickname, "The Eleven Àbâyehs."[170]

Tallis-man. Elchanan Bolkin arrived in Palestine from Bialystok in 1882 and opened the first textile factory in the country. It manufactured *tallitot* and àbâyehs. When Baron Rothschild toured the factory in 1887, he ordered 300 àbâyehs to be distributed to the colonists.

Photo op. Shimon Peres (later the prime minister and ninth president of Israel) sporting an àbâyeh and kâfiyyeh while riding a camel in the 1950s. Peres was appointed by Prime Minister David Ben-Gurion to organize a research expedition from Revivim to Uhm Rash Rash (Eilat).

used for the oxen recently purchased for them. Eventually, they moved into the *churvah*.

"The Radomers Are Plowing!"

The Baron acted quickly and appropriated 28,000 francs ($112,000 in today's U.S. currency) to cover general expenses for the settlement. With that money, his administrators purchased fifteen pairs of oxen, three horses, four mules, three female donkeys, two camels, and two wagons.[171]

With the advent of the first rainfall (sometime in the first half of November 1883) the pioneers hitched their oxen to the plows and began plowing furrows in the rich earth.[172] Their joy was indescribable – this was the fulfillment of their dreams! It was almost a year from the day they had departed from the Volkovysk train station.

המליץ

№18.

Front-page news. Though it took four months to hit the press, the Ekronians' first days at work made the front page of the March 14, 1884, edition of *Ha-Meliz*. Their brethren in Russia were keenly interested in what was going on in the Holy Land. The correspondent was Yechiel Michel Pines.

Wasting no time, Shmuel Hirsch cabled Michael Erlanger in Paris with the news. Erlanger was elated:

> Paris, 16 November 1883
> Dear Mr. Hirsch,
>
> Your telegram from the 12th of this month has brought me great pleasure. THE RADOMERS HAVE COMMENCED PLOWING. They have indeed begun working! I immediately passed the telegram on to Mr. de Rothschild, who was also very pleased. There is no doubt that you are no less pleased now that you know they are in a place of their own....[173]

No doubt, Rabbi Shmuel Mohilever (who by now was the new chief rabbi of Bialystok) could also breathe a sigh of relief.

In that first winter of 1883-1884, they planted wheat,[174] barley, and lentils. Ran Aaronsohn estimates that the fields cov-

Groundbreakers. Yosef Graf plowing in his vineyard along with Yosef Goldstein in Zikhron Yaakov.

ered an area of 2,000 dunams (460 acres).[175] To demarcate their property, the farmers dug a trench one meter deep, one meter (3.28 feet) wide, and about 1.4 kilometers (.869 miles) long at the perimeter of the settlement and planted cacti plants.[176]

Not everyone was involved with plowing and sowing. Two farmers worked full-time bringing in fertilizer with one of the wagons, while two farmers used the other wagon to bring stones for construction.[177]

They moved out of the mud houses of Aqir and into tents near the solitary ruin resting on their land. On their first Sabbath there (December 21, 1883), the Torah reading, appropriately, was *Va-Yeshev*[178] which begins with the verse: "And Jacob settled in the land of the sojournings of his father, in the land of Canaan" (Genesis 37:1). The following Sunday night, they lit their first Chanukah candle in the Holy Land. The wandering Jews of Pavlovka felt they had come home at last – even if "home" was just a tent.

Chapter 13
A New Home

The electrifying news reached Pavlovka: the farmers had land to call their own! The year-long wait and worry were over. Their families now knew they were going to leave their familiar surroundings and remake their lives in a faraway, strange new world – a world they had only dreamed of.

But it would take another year for the farmers to send for them. The eleven pioneers wanted to be more firmly established in Ekron and have at least a few buildings in which to house their loved ones. In the meantime, their wives and children and some of their elderly parents prepared for the journey to the Holy Land.

Moreover, news of the fledgling colony encouraged others to join them, resulting in several lightning-bolt weddings among idealistic youth. When departure time came, it was exciting news all over the Jewish world, as described in the following article in *Ha-Maggid.*[179]

RUSSLAND [Russia]
Rozhinoy: Rosh Chodesh Elul, 5644 [August 22, 1884]

We have some good news, this time concerning the eleven farmers who were escorted two years ago by Mr. Brill to the Holy Land from the colony [Pavlovka] near our city – news that is as refreshing as a splash of cold water on a weary soul, especially for those for whom the goal of settling the Land of Israel is very dear.

Last week four extended families departed for Palestine, totaling over forty people, with the support of the Benefactor [Rothschild]. Soon, the remaining seven families will follow. For ten days prior to their trip, they had nothing but celebrations over the "tying of knots" of *tenaim* [engagements] which they quickly performed prior to their departure. Many young ladies who had difficulty finding a husband due to their poverty and for other sundry reasons have now entered into marriages with young men who have trades and are highly energetic. One of them is a *chazzan/shochet* [cantor and animal slaughterer]. These men married the women even without a dowry, so they could travel to the Holy Land with them and work its soil.

Mazal tov! A typical young couple from Ekron

The farmers were determined to build homes for their families before they arrived, yet they faced another major obstacle: the Ottoman Turks flatly refused to issue permits to foreigners for the construction of residential structures. (This policy would remain in effect until 1887.) It didn't matter that the land had been purchased and deeded, or that farmers were already residing there (in tents) and had begun to plow and sow the land. The Ottomans were adamant: no permits for residences.

Although licenses for human housing were hard to come by, arranging for animal accommodations was relatively easy. So the Baron's representatives were clever and applied for permits to build *barns*. The permits were issued.

Then the pioneers got to work quickly. Stones for the foundations and walls were hewn from the soft sandstone quarry of al-Mŭghâr ("the caves"), a village 12 kilometers southwest of Ramle, and hauled to Ekron. In record time, four structures were built, each two stories high and thirty-nine meters (128 feet) long. Each story was separated by thick, wooden beams, which served as the ceiling for the first floor and the floor of the second.[180] The structures, nicknamed *kazarmes,*

Not quite a bungalow colony. One of the four remaining *kazarmes* left in today's Mazkeret Batya. Four large families crowded into this building.

were completed in 1884 and became the nucleus of the new settlement. These four buildings exist to this day.

Local folklore has it that sometime later the pasha toured the area and saw these elongated buildings. He couldn't recall issuing any permits for human habitation. He was told that these were the barns he himself had authorized. When he went inside and saw stairs leading to the second story, he was outraged. How, he demanded, did the farmers expect a cow to climb up those stairs?

But the farmers had a ready response: The first floor was indeed for the animals. The steps were there to enable people to carry the hay and fodder to be stored on the second floor. The pasha's anger subsided. He liked the answer – these Jews were quite clever! The founders poured their distinguished guest a brimming cup of Turkish coffee, and by the end of the drinking ritual, everyone was in good spirits.[181]

Ekron was the first Jewish settlement to receive construction permits. In contrast, the residents of nearby Gedera (funded by Chovevei Ẓion) had to live for a long time in caves.

Noah's Ark?

There still is some controversy about whether the families and cows actually resided together in those early days.

According to historian Ran Aaronsohn, the settlers indeed shared space in the *kazarmes* as the upstairs neighbors of their livestock. David Neiman, in his book *Mazkeret Batya,* concurs.[182] He writes that living in close proximity to the flies commonly found near animals made eye diseases more prevalent in Ekron than in other colonies.

Achiezer Arkin vehemently disagrees, asserting, "... utter nonsense. The settlers never shared their homes with the livestock!"[183] While Arkin would admit that odors emanating from the barn wafted into the family living room, and there were plenty of flies, the settlers never had to turn their home into a "Noah's Ark," with the animals and their manure directly beneath them.

The farm animals were (*eventually* – according to some) put into the barn in the backyard, some 50-100 meters (55-109 yards) from each house. The reason for the proximity was that the building permits eventually issued for the construction of real housing were very limited. The community was allowed to build structures within an area of only two dunams (approximately half an acre) of land.

In the fall of 1884 and throughout 1885, the families that were left behind began making their way to Ekron in small groups. The relatives included Avraham Shlomo Arkin, the father of Ẓvi and Yaakov; Tamara, the mother of Avraham Yaakov Gellman (the *melamed*); and Yechezkel Levin's parents. Levin's father passed away shortly after his arrival, but his family considered it no small privilege for him to be buried in the Holy Land.

Worth the wait. Ephraim Skolnick and family. It took up to two years before the founders of Ekron reunited with their loved ones.

Like their husbands and fathers before them, they too departed from Trieste on a steamship and endured the rough waters and the accompanying motion sickness and nausea. On one such stormy voyage, one of the women, Hinda Liba Arkin, daughter-in-law of founder Ẓvi Arkin,[184] was pregnant and began experiencing contractions. Crouched on a makeshift birthing stool, she gave birth to her first child, Pesha Leah. Like the biblical Yocheved, the mother of Moses, who was born "between the walls" of the Egyptian border, the baby became a symbol of the transition between two worlds.

Over 100 were heading for Ekron – a far cry from the "ten to twelve farmers" the Baron had in mind when he first discussed the proposal with Rabbi Mohilever in Paris.

Initially, fourteen families were crowded into the four original buildings. Four years later, ten single-family units were built.[185] Surrounded by spacious fields, the original group of families lived a cramped existence akin to the residents of an inner city tenement.

Each family had four small rooms; two on the first floor, and two on the second. Remember that the typical, traditional Orthodox nuclear family was large – and the in-laws also frequently lived with these families. At least it was better than living in tents. In fact, some families did have to endure living in tents until permanent structures could be built.

The family units were not equipped with kitchens or bathrooms: those were separate units, situated in the backyard. There was no indoor plumbing. Buckets of water were carried by animals from a well located at the edge of the settlement.[186]

Difficult as these conditions were, the farmers and their families knew they had overcome enormous obstacles. With the financial and political support of Baron Rothschild, they had achieved their goal: at last, they had established a viable farming settlement in the Land of Israel! What could be better?

Chapter 14
The Strength to Endure

It had been two grueling years since the ten farmers, the *melamed,* and Yechiel Brill had left the Volkovysk train station in the wee hours of a wintry night. But they had made a start: wheat was growing in the fields, some houses were constructed, and a well was dug.

Until now, we have focused on the eleven pioneers as a unit, viewing their communal accomplishments. Let's meet a few individually to see how their strong and colorful personalities helped shape the community.

In chapter 8, we recounted how Chaim Moshe Press had fallen seriously ill shortly after arriving at Mikveh Israel in 1883. He refused to follow the doctor's advice to go back to Russia, and he recovered. He became the community butcher, who sold meat to the farmers on credit – so they could honor the Sabbath even if their finances didn't allow it. Baron Rothschild learned of his generosity and would occasionally reimburse him when the farmers couldn't afford to pay.[187]

Team player. Chaim Moshe Press. His brothers, Kalman, Ẓvi and Shmuel, and his father, Yoel Dov, later joined him in the moshavah.

His wife, Chayeh Rochel, took the lead in organizing the women to form the *bikkur cholim* society for tending to the ill. Whoever was sick for more than a week was taken to the local "hospital" that Chayeh Rochel and her friends established. They cared for their patients with great warmth and efficiently kept notes regarding the type of illness, the stages of its development, and the patient's recovery. They had only basic instruments and accessories, but the care they gave their patients was extraordinary.[188]

Yaakov Laskovsky was one of the officers of the *bikkur cholim* and *chevrah kaddisha* (burial) societies. Physically strong and fearless, he often encountered bands of Arab robbers, who were quite plentiful at the time. He would follow them in hot pursuit and, when he caught up to them, would give them a sound beating.

Litvish cowboy. Yaakov Laskovsky

Zionist ideology stereotyped the eastern European Orthodox Jew as weak, insecure, and submissive. That stereotype (which was accepted even in religious circles!) was a badge of shame that the new generation promised to eradicate. But in attempting to shed this uncomfortable image, the "new and improved" generation shed not only the presumed cowardice

Buried by the Zionist myth. Like Yaakov Laskovsky, Moshe Shmuel Raab was one of the strictly Orthodox *shomrim* (watchmen) who fearlessly defended Petach Tikva in its early years.

of the Diaspora but its religious essence as well.

Laskovsky proved the stereotype wrong. While a profoundly religious Jew, he was a man who would not take guff from anyone. Clearly, his *tallit katan* and yarmulke were no hindrance to standing tall! And he was not alone in his stance. There were many like him in the First Aliyah, though they are ignored by standard history books.

Yechezkel Levin contributed to the *yirat Shamayim* – the God-fearing atmosphere – of Ekron in numerous ways, particularly in his careful attention to preparing for the Sabbath. One Friday, some chicks hatched late in the day, and his wife, Zlata Leah, asked him to hurry and prepare a coop. He refused. "Know this," he said. "Satan provokes Jewish people on the eve of the Sabbath and attempts to lead them into sin so they will not greet the Sabbath Queen properly and, Heaven forbid, might even desecrate the Sabbath."[189] The chicks could wait.

Avraham Yaakov Gellman was the *melamed,* the teacher the farmers brought with them from Russia. Upon his arrival in Palestine, he started a new career as a farmer. He wrote beautifully. One of his most stirring accounts is of Ekron's early trials.

A strange story is told about him. It happened on the very first night the farmers slept in the fields of Ekron after moving out of Aqir. Huddled together in an Arab ruin, everyone had fallen asleep, but Gellman suddenly awoke to the loud, mournful cry of jackals. He was terrified. He had never heard these sounds before and did not know their source.

Knew his priorities. Yechezkel Levin

While his comrades slept, Gellman pulled out a challah, a folk remedy against demons, and waved it over his head, all the while reciting from memory the confessional prayer *Al Cheit,* said on one's deathbed. His friends were awakened by the commotion. When he explained to them what he was doing, they tried unsuccessfully to calm him down. Gellman then retreated into a corner by himself, shivering in fright. The farmers thought their colleague had gone insane. The next day, they asked Avraham Moyal, the Jaffa Jewish leader in charge of the settlement, to take him away. Gellman later returned to Ekron with his wife and family.[190]

Don't cry wolf. A jackal in Israel

Whether the stuff of local legend or the truth, the story illustrates an important aspect of the lives of the pioneers: they faced tremendous psychological pressures. Separated from their loved ones by thousands of miles, cut off from their usual sources of livelihood, and forced to acclimate to an alien environment, they endured incredibly challenging conditions – yet, ultimately, they prevailed.

Spooked. Avraham Yaakov Gellman

Like his colleagues, Moshe Maller had left his wife and children behind and was separated from them for almost two years. Sadly, his wife Chana passed away not long after she arrived in Ekron in 1885. Moshe was then only 36 years old.

Marriage-minded. Moshe Maller

Moshe wanted to remarry immediately. He went to live with his two married children, who shared the same house, and they were not pleased with their father's decision to have another woman replace their dear mother so soon. But Moshe was adamant. He had survived the ordeal of coming to Palestine and all the adversities of creating a new settlement, but the thought of spending the rest of his life alone was too much for him to bear. He wasted no time in contacting a *shadchan* to find him another wife. The matchmaker lost no time either and immediately proposed a match for Moshe – a divorced, childless woman named Bayla. Exactly thirty days after Chana's funeral, "they brought Bayla to him without his ever having seen her before."[191]

The Moshavah Grows

One wintry day during the early period of Ekron's settlement, Chaim Moshe Press went to Jaffa to take care of some personal business. The five-hour journey and inclement weather forced Press to make his way to Mikveh Israel, where he obtained lodging for the night. (Apparently, he was even given his old room, the tool shed!)

Gutsy and good-hearted. Eliyahu Moshe Hershkovitz. His son Yisrael was the first child born in the fledgling settlement.

His roommate for the evening, Eliyahu Moshe Hershkovitz, hailed from Odessa. Hershkovitz was both gutsy and good-hearted, a muscular man with piercing eyes. Press told him about the colony he and his ten colleagues were setting up. By morning, Hershkovitz had decided to cast his lot with them.

Next to join the colony was a carpenter, Aharon Zelig Levitta of Grodno. He had met the farmers while they were training in Mikveh Israel and he was constructing housing at the school. He also worked as a furniture maker. Attracted by their simplicity and industriousness, Levitta became very fond of the farmers and joined the Ekron community shortly after its establishment.

Craftsman. The beautiful Torah ark in Ekron's synagogue – with grapevines adorning its pillars – was crafted in 1886 by Aharon Zelig Levitta.

Shaul Holzner, from Sebastopol, in the Crimea, had arrived in Palestine before the farmers from Pavlovka. He, too, was a student at Mikveh Israel and developed into a proficient agriculturalist. His professional training was welcomed by both the farmers and the Baron's officials as an excellent asset to the enterprise.

Agronomist. Shaul Holzner

Mordechai Neiman was born in the city of Tulcha, in a region that was ruled by Turkey and later ceded to Romania. He came from a well-to-do family, but his father's wealth offered no security when pogroms broke out throughout eastern Europe. The fugitives had two choices: the *goldeneh medinah* of America or the Land of Israel. Neiman chose the latter and enrolled in the Mikveh Israel school to become a farmer. He and his wife

בית משפחת מרדכי נימן
נבנה ב-1883
שופץ ע"י מלכה וצבי נאמן (נימן) בן לוי
בן צבי בן מרדכי נימן ממיסדי המושבה
1999

A different type of *"maskil."* Mordechai Neiman was Ekron's first Chassid. Unlike the *mitnagdim* in Ekron, he enjoyed studying the Zohar. Later in Neiman's life, his home became a meeting place for the town's old-timers where they would learn Torah, chat, and drink tea. He would disparagingly tell his sons: "When I was young, I was considered a *maskil.* You too are *maskilim.* But I was 'enlightened' by Maimonides' *Guide for the Perplexed* and Rabbi Yehuda Halevi's *Kuzari*, while you are 'enlightened' by the books of [the secular Hebrew novelist] Avraham Mapu."

bought land in Rishon Le-Ẓion, but when they discovered Ekron, they felt they would be more at home with the Radomers.

Neiman's arrival in Ekron created a stir, because he was a Chassid while they were Litvaks. (Ironically, he was also different in that he later fought for the modernization of the *cheder* and for the introduction of *chinuch ivri* – nationalistic Jewish education. He had many disagreements with his more conservative colleagues.)

At heart, Neiman was an entrepreneur. He understood farming and how agricultural products could be put to use for both family and business purposes. He agreed with the farmers that the soil of Ekron would produce abundant wheat crops that could be baked into tasty bread. But as a creative businessman, he sought to diversify, so he developed new sources of income from various enterprises.

Shortly after his move into Ekron, Neiman bought two high-quality cows. Next, he went to Sarona, a small Templer colony outside Jaffa, and bought wheat and barley seeds, clovers, and corn, and made enough food for the cows to last an entire year. As a result, the cows were healthy and produced abundant quantities of wholesome milk. The dairy produce was more than enough for his family. He raised chickens as well and developed a fine egg business. In addition, he built a dovecote for birds to be used for food. Neiman's flocks of geese and ducks provided delightful dishes for Friday night dinners. The chickens also provided good food.

True to his belief in diversification, Neiman planted a small

A bird condominium. Dovecote outside the Mazkeret Batya museum

vineyard of 7.2 hectares (1.8 acres). He took good care of it, providing it with fertilizer from his cows and horses, and the vineyard repaid him with a wonderful yield. It was used, like the dairy produce, not for additional income but for his family and the villagers. Everyone could "purchase" a bottle of wine from him for the Sabbath *Kiddush* and *Havdalah* for a penny per bottle. As the buyer would leave, Neiman would say, "Whether you pay me or not, it is all the same to me; I will be rewarded [enough] for these miẓvot."

A man of infinite ideas, Neiman also made grape jams (using three different methods) and stored them in earthenware vessels. The largest grapes were seeded with a hairpin and cooked whole over a low flame. These grapes were placed in glass bowls and reserved as a special dish to serve guests or to be brought to the sick.

No Mr. Meek. Yaakov Gold played an active role in the development of Ekron.

The Neiman household was overflowing with goods of all sorts. Even had Neiman been paid the penny for every bottle of wine, he did not need it. The villagers, who initially poked fun at his diverse activities, soon followed his lead and produced other goods for family use and for income.

Another new arrival was Yaakov Gold, who had founded a Chovevei Ẓion chapter in Iaşi, his hometown in Romania. A feisty character, he gave the Baron's administrators such an earful that he was banished for a time from the settlement.

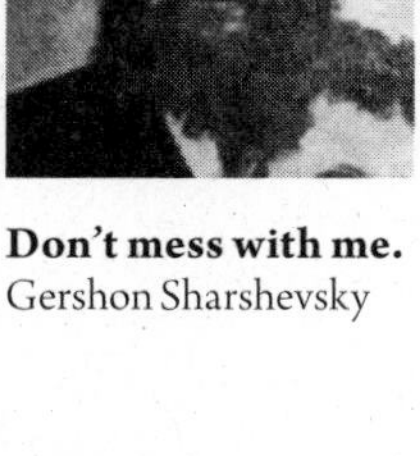

Don't mess with me. Gershon Sharshevsky

Gershon Sharshevsky, the last of the second group to join the settlement, was a tough man who could not be intimidated by anyone. It may well be that his implacable, determined personality was necessary for undertaking the daunting task of creating a pioneer village from scratch.

Jewish Brotherhood and Unity

The feisty pioneers of Ekron/Mazkeret Batya were good neighbors to the other moshavot (colonies), whether or not they happened to share their religious ideals. A dramatic story is told by Dov Ariel, author of *Ha-Moshavah Gedera:*

It happened at the BILU settlement of Gedera. It was Wednesday, October 17, 1888. Three Arab robbers lay in ambush, waiting for one of the workers of Gedera to approach their hiding place. Then they assaulted him and stole his horse. Upon hearing what had happened, the Jewish settlers mounted their horses and gave chase.

About two hours from the moshavah they caught up with the thieves, captured their leader, retrieved their horse, and transported their captive back to the settlement. The Arabs from the nearby village of Qatra assembled; armed with

BILU settlement. Gedera

slings and rifles, they were poised to invade Gedera to rescue their imprisoned comrade. The attack was to commence at midnight.

The Biluim decided they would rather fight to the death than become the objects of their Arab neighbors' scorn. After locking the women in their houses so their screams would not cause distraction, twelve of the men assembled with sticks, stones, and a few rifles.

The brave colonists repelled the first two Arab attacks, but they feared that time was on the side of their adversaries. As the morning light of Friday broke, they sent an SOS to Ekron and Rishon Le-Ẓion for reinforcements.[192]

Twenty young men on horseback came from Rishon Le-Ẓion along with ten Ekronians – *Jews sporting beards and side-locks, all armed and with provisions for the Sabbath,* as that day was the Sabbath eve. All of them were ready for battle and willing to risk their lives for this poor, tiny Jewish settlement, Gedera, which was situated on a hill overlooking [the Arab town of] Yibna.

They all waited on the solitary street of the moshavah. That evening, the Arabs, who had been seen by the light of the moon hiding in the settlement's vineyards, were poised to attack again. At the last moment, the sound of Turkish soldiers from Jaffa galloping toward the settlement scared the Arab attackers off.[193]

The newly expanded nucleus of the moshavah now totaled eighteen families. Their personalities were of all types – quiet, introverted, cooperative, extroverted, aggressive, and even combative. They were hard-working and unassuming people. But there were two red lines that – if crossed – would unite them as one to fight back ferociously: threats to their individual ownership of their farmsteads, and interference in their religious practices. Regarding those two issues, they would let no one – absolutely no one – tell them how to live their lives.

Chapter 15
Everyday Life

Once Ekron was established, the routines of daily life were set in motion. The conventions of nineteenth-century Palestine would seem primitive to many of us today, but the records and memories of the early settlers are uplifting and instructive.

Everyone in Ekron worked hard, yet they were very poor. Chaim Maller, the grandson of founders Yechezkel Levin and Moshe Maller, was an Ekron old-timer who died shortly before the turn of the century. He reminisced with historian Shaul Dagan about how he used to go barefoot around the moshavah as a child – in both summer and winter.[194]

No shoes. Barefoot boy on Ekron/Mazkeret Batya's main street in a picture taken in 1920

Home furnishings were scant. Beds often consisted of two planks covered by straw, and children often had to share these "beds" with their siblings. Blankets often consisted of old coats. Maller remembered shivering throughout the cold nights.[195]

On weekdays, a meal consisted of bread smeared with oil accompanied by a few vegetables and bean or lentil soup. Even with the bare basics, it was possible to be creative. Ẓipporah Maller writes in her memoirs that her father "... used to put little, square pieces of bread in a bowl, pour boiling water on them, season [them] with salt and pepper, and add a teaspoon of oil. We all loved this dish very much. We never saw candy – there was none."[196]

The Sabbath was a treat. They would enjoy a little meat and herring patties for the third meal. But even the traditional braided challah was a luxury that many families could not afford.[197]

Left: **Everyone's mother.** Bayla Maller, daughter of founder Moshe Maller,[198] was known as the "mother of the moshavah." She was a friend to all in their time of joy and celebration and a source of support when tragedy struck. She was the daughter of Moshe's first wife and coincidentally had the same name as her stepmother.

Right: **Golden tongue.** Moshe Leib, husband of Bayla Maller, adopted his wife's name so he could be part of the family "estate" in the fledgling settlement. He had a strong command of both written and spoken Hebrew, and was sought out to lead the prayer services because of his beautiful Hebrew pronunciation and understanding of obscure words and passages.

The Most Precious Commodity – H_2O

The farmers knew that their survival depended on their ability to find and draw water from the earth. After digging to a depth of twenty-eight meters (about ninety-two feet), they struck water. The water was drawn in buckets attached to a rope that was pulled by a horse. The settlers had been promised a mechanical pump, which eventually did arrive from Paris. If the well was the moshavah's "blood supply," then the pump was its heart, the canals its veins, and the gardens and orchards its limbs and organs.

Since fruits and vegetables required intensive irrigation, the pitifully small quantities of water brought up by the buckets were insufficient. A pool with a capacity of 120 cubic meters (31,700 gallons) was constructed next to the well, and from there the water was channeled to the trees and vegetables.

But the pool did more than water lemon trees.

Watering hole. Ekron's Antilia[199] well, renovated in 1994 (the wooden wheel was replaced with one made from steel), is the oldest of its kind in Israel. The Ferris-like wheel had buckets. When the wheel was rotated by horse or mule, the buckets filled with water.

Ferris wheels. Today, the well is a popular setting for weddings.

The pool made village life happier, especially for the youngsters. During the

summer months ... the pool was in use throughout the day: In the mornings before school, during the 10 a.m. recess, at noontime and in the evening. The pool was great ... one could swim underwater and above water. Only one problem interfered with the fun – the girls and boys could not bathe together [for reasons of modesty].

Making a big splash. For the children of Ekron who were either studying in school or helping their parents out in the fields, swimming in the pool was like an oasis in the desert.

A small war between the sexes began as to who could occupy the pool and when – there were constant arguments. The boys usually won, but the girls put up a good fight. Sometimes they managed to get to the pool first.[200]

And what is a proper Jewish community without a *shvitz* (sauna)? The *shvitz* and bathhouse were popular stops for both practical and social reasons:

The houses still lacked plumbing and pipes. Water was brought in by the mules, and each mule could barely carry the amount one would need for *netilat yadayim*. And then the bathhouse was built. It was state-of-the-art, clean, and well equipped. Open for business twice a week (for women on Thursdays and men on Fridays), it boasted an endless supply of hot water, several baths, a heated

Posing for posterity. Members of the community in the fields of Ekron/Mazkeret Batya in 1899. Notice how both children and adults group according to gender. *Snapshot by Isaiah Raflovich*

> *mikveh,* and a sweat room [sauna] – a favorite among the youth and the adults of Ekron, who had enjoyed such rooms in their homeland. ... If you have a shower, a bath, and hot and cold water in your home, you cannot possibly comprehend the immense pleasure people derived from the village bathhouse.[201]

These recreational outlets were an oasis in a community where men, women, and children worked long hours in the fields under the hot Middle Eastern sun.

The Staff of Life

Michla Press, daughter of founder Yaakov Laskovsky, was interviewed by author David Neiman. She was the last surviving member of the first eleven women who settled in the moshavah. She described the process of baking bread.

> I was six years old when I arrived in the Land of Israel with my [family]. Today I am eighty-eight. We disembarked from the ship, spent a month living in a hotel in Jaffa, and then moved to Ekron ....

Right: **Shopping mall.** Jaffa marketplace at the turn of the century

Top: **Centenarian.** Michla Press. When her family decided to leave Palestine for America around 1893, she refused to join them. Her parents hastily arranged her marriage to Shmuel Press, brother of founder Chaim Moshe Press, so she wouldn't have to fend for herself.

> At first, they would bring us our bread from Jaffa; but the bread was inedible – it was either underbaked or burnt! That didn't go on for long, though; two large ovens were soon built on the sides of the road, and we began baking and eating our own bread.[202]

Grist for the mill. Years later, a flour mill was built, which also benefitted Ekron's Arab neighbors. The Old Yishuv in Jerusalem got their *shemurah matzah* flour from Ekron.

David Neiman (son of Mordechai Neiman), in *Mazkeret Batya,* continued where Michla Press left off, describing this important development:

> Initially, their houses here [in Ekron] were not even equipped with kitchens. [So] they built two public ovens, similar to those in their homes back in Pavlovka. The ovens were large, with enough room to bake up to forty loaves at one time. The women baked their bread in pairs, waiting their turn. While some baked only once a week, the connoisseurs would bake twice a week. The bread was well baked, appetizing, and healthy.
>
> Firing up these large ovens was a challenge. To produce a stream of baked goods, the ovens needed to be hot continuously – so hot that all the inner walls would remain red for long periods. But there were no logs or any other fuel sources: Russia had extensive forests, but Palestine didn't. So the Ekron pioneers learned about the thorny burnet – a dwarf shrub, prickly like a wild rose, which grew in the hills near the Arab village of al-Mŭghâr. The men went to the thorn hills wearing

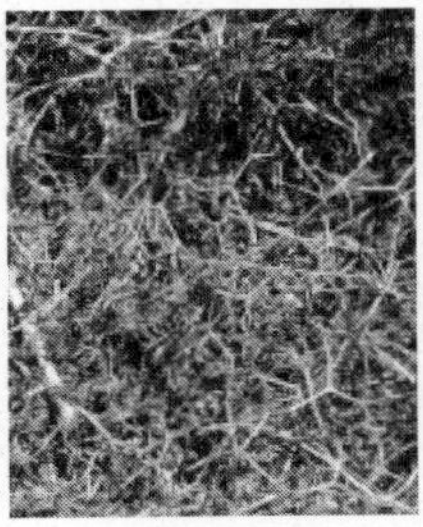

Burning bush. The thorny burnet, or *sirah kozanit* in Hebrew, was used in Ekron as fuel for the bread ovens.

the tall boots they had brought with them from their homelands and their large, straw hats. Whoever has not seen a wagon filled with these thorny plants is missing out on quite an experience. The thorns burned well and produced a strong flame. Within minutes, the oven was glowing and ready for work. The bread was then baked by the heat of these thorns.

The ovens were also used to cook *cholent* [stew] for the Sabbath. Both ovens would be fired up, and all the women would bring their *cholent*. Each woman had an extra-large copper pot. The pots would be inserted into the oven, and its mouth would be plugged with clay. On the following day, the Sabbath, the pots were taken out. The insertion and extraction of the pots required a skillful swiftness, because the pots were at risk of tipping over. The ovens were also used to bake for weddings.[202]

"Bad Air" Days

The Jews in Europe who were following developments in the Holy Land were very concerned about health issues there, especially in the new farming colonies. Newspaper correspondents were aware that their reports on health conditions had the potential to increase *aliyah* from the current trickle or completely shut the valve.

A reporter from the *Chavazelet* newspaper wrote about the health situation in Ekron in 1885-1886:

> The state of health in the colony has been average up to now. The quality of its air[203] is questionable, because it lies in a valley where there are swamps. When the temperature gets very high, it can become dangerous. Thank God, no evil has befallen any of its residents so far – except for two people who have died since its founding. One of them, an elderly man,[204] 76 years old, died in his old age [August 12, 1885], while the other, who was indeed young, died of typhus, which is beginning to take its toll in the larger cities. There is hope that the eucalyptus trees[205] [the farmers] have planted – which they will continue to plant this year – will purify the dirty air and improve the health situation, and every calamity will be distanced from the colony and its residents.[206]

The Doc and the *Feldsher*

Because Yiddish was the common language in early Ekron, the pharmacist was called the *feldsher*.[207] His role was more like that of a doctor's assistant. Because good Jewish doctors did not reside in the colony, but made calls from as far away as Rishon Le-Ẓion or Jaffa, the *feldsher*'s role was crucial. His responsibility was to diagnose symptoms and dispense the proper medications to the best of his ability. Ekron's first *feldsher* was a man named Iẓik, and he was held in great esteem. He never received any formal education, but he learned the craft from his father.

Idealist. Dr. Aharon Mazia

Ekron's first doctor, Aharon Mazia,[208] was no second-class practitioner. Born near Mogilev (in White Russia), he later studied in the famous Mirrer Yeshivah. He then decided to continue his Talmudic studies in the rabbinical seminary of Rabbi Azriel Hildesheimer in Berlin. He began studying engineering in that city but was expelled due to his socialist activism. He completed his studies in Zurich's Polytechnic Institute.

With the outbreak of the Russian pogroms, Mazia heeded the call of the Chovevei Ẓion and decided to move to the Land of Israel. In preparation for his move, he studied medicine, because he heard that people were hesitant about making *aliyah* due to the poor health conditions in the country. After receiving his medical degree from the University of Zurich in 1887, he went to Paris to learn how to treat eye diseases. It was there that he was recommended to Baron Rothschild, who appointed him "doctor of the moshavot" (Petach Tikva, Rishon Le-Ẓion, and Ekron) and sent him to live in Rishon Le-Ẓion. He arrived in Palestine in 1888. Admired and revered by all, Mazia impressed even the Turkish authorities, who commended him on his service and expertise.[209]

A one man show. Chasia (Margolin) Kalmanowitz was Ekron's first professional midwife. No stranger to pangs of childbirth, she came to the moshavah in 1903 with her eight children. Known affectionately as "Bubbe Chaishah," she had a pair of scissors tied to her dress just in case there was an umbilical cord that needed to be cut.

Malaria and trachoma were the two health hazards that plagued all the new settlements, but poor Ekron fared worse than most. Particularly among children, malaria caused considerable suffering, but it wasn't a killer disease as it was in other parts of the world. In Ekron, they used to say, "Purim isn't a *chag*, and malaria isn't a disease" (i.e., Purim isn't a full festival like Passover, and malaria isn't fatal).

In fact, malaria was regarded more or less as a one-day disease. The typical scenario: A child awakes in the morning full of energy, eats breakfast, and runs off to *cheder*. That's at eight o'clock. By nine, he is feeling chills, and his *rebbi* sends him home. By ten o'clock, his temperature rises to 38-39°Celsius (100-102°Fahrenheit.) Another hour goes by, and his temperature now hits 40°C (104°F). That's when his mother begins the standard procedure: She applies moist compresses (which have been soaked in a solution of water and a little vinegar) to his sweating head and body (there was no ice in those early days) and waits for the fever to drop a bit. Then she goes to the moshavah pharmacy. The drug of choice for malaria, quinine,[210] is given only after the patient's temperature goes down. By four o'clock in the afternoon, the child's temperature is just about normal. He gets out of bed and is able to eat, downing a piece of bread dipped in a glass of hot tea. Then he runs outside – slightly weaker and with a bit of a limp, but he's playing with his friends again.

Trachoma caused temporary or permanent blindness. The disease was transmitted by flies, which were quite numerous because of the animals. The barns were close to residences, and as if that were not problematic enough, the disease was transmitted via flies from person to person while people were lined up for treatment at the local pharmacy. More people left the pharmacy infected with trachoma than the number of those who entered.[211]

Another cause of eye disease was the dust from the soil that was kicked up by the winds. Insufficient drinking water was also blamed for eye problems. Eye disease did not cease to be a major issue until the animals were moved farther away from human habitation, more trees were planted, and water flowed plentifully into homes through modern plumbing.[212]

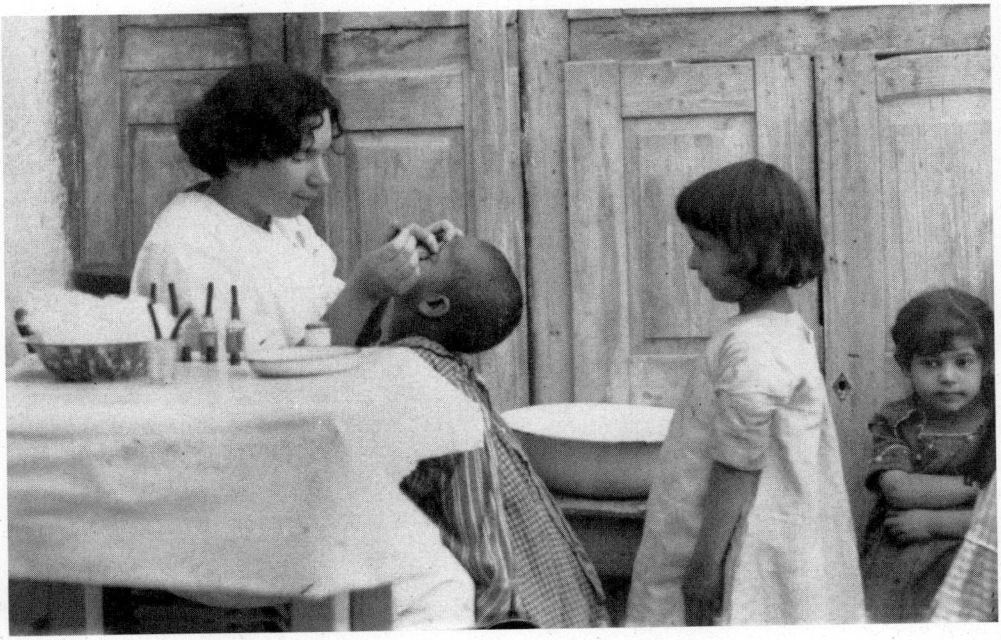

In your eye. Rampant in Palestine, eye diseases were often treated by rubbing a "blue-stone" (copper sulfate) on the infected part of the inner eyelid. Here, children line up in an eye clinic to be examined and treated.

But the general health situation at the very beginning was grave, far worse than portrayed in Neiman's book or by the newspapers. The first colonists were far more likely to die of disease than be killed by Arabs. Avraham Yaakov Gellman summed it up succinctly when he testified before a rabbinic court in Jerusalem in 1893:

> Many difficult and terrible hardships befell us. So many people died – approximately twenty souls. So many men and women became blind to this very day, because the air of this locale was unhealthy. We could barely sleep for a night without evading the malarial fever that struck us. We literally put our lives at risk. Through our efforts, we have improved the air quality of the settlement, but at the cost of the lives of our dear ones and with such unimaginable pain and anguish.[213]

What gave them the strength to face such adversity day after day? To Chaim Maller, the answer was clear: "They coped and managed because they believed that they were *shelichim* fulfilling a holy commandment."[214] In short, they struggled not only for themselves, but for the hopeful message their survival would send to all the Jews of Europe.

Coping with External Threats

When Ekron was first established, the farmers learned the hard way that to the Arabs pinching a few chickens, ducks, or geese from the coop did not fall into the category of theft. The constant poaching was depleting the Jewish-owned flocks, so it was decided that every night two of the villagers would take up guard duty. The farmers had never touched a weapon in their lives. Each guard would take a pitchfork, and that would be his only weapon.

Fortunately, all the village homes were adjacent to each other, and the entire area of the village was no larger than two dunams. The village resembled a small fort and guarding it was relatively easy, but thefts occurred anyway.

One night, two men began their guard duty. One of them was strong, swift, and hot-tempered. Suddenly, the guards noticed someone crawling out from one of the houses. The Arab thief sensed the attention of the guards and fled, and the guards gave chase. The thief ran into a nearby wadi (dry riverbed) but found the guard at his heels, his pitchfork aimed straight ahead. The injured thief was allowed to make his way home.

The next day, the Arab elders of the neighboring town came to ask Ekron's elders for forgiveness. The Arabs promised that no such crime would be repeated. Indeed, for several years, guard duty went on as usual, and no thefts occurred.[214A]

Saved from an Arab Mob

No matter how cordial relations between the Jews of Ekron and their Arab neighbors seemed on the surface, underlying tension always existed, and the farmers were vulnerable to sudden violence. The following story is based on a report in *Chavazelet*:

It was customary for one of the Arab wives from the neighboring village to come to Ekron every Sabbath to milk the animals and attend to other tasks the colonists were not permitted to do on that day. One Sabbath in the spring of 1887, the woman came to do her job as usual. After completing her work in a few homes, she was on her way to another house when she fainted and fell to the ground. Every attempt by the colonists to revive her was futile. She had expired!

When word of her death reached the Arab village, all the Arab farmers, including the relatives of the deceased, hurried to Ekron. When they saw the woman lying on the ground with no signs of life, they became hysterical and accused the Jews of murdering her by giving her a poisonous potion. Some of them screamed for vengeance and began to break into Jewish homes. Others wanted to call the police in Jaffa. No matter how hard they tried, the Jews could not convince the mob that they were innocent.

Noise and confusion followed. One of the colonists thought quickly and grabbed a horse. Taking it out of sight – for he was afraid his fellow Jews might restrain him on account of the Sabbath – he mounted the horse and shot out like a deer to nearby Ramle to find a doctor.

When he soon returned with the doctor, the Arab mob was still screaming and cursing the colonists. The doctor drove them away from the dead woman, then carefully examined her. He diagnosed that she had died on her own and that there was no justification for attacking the Jews. He threatened that if the Arabs didn't listen to him and go home quietly, he would cut her body up into pieces and send them to doctors to verify that his diagnosis was correct. When the *fellahin* heard these words, they quickly lifted the woman's body and brought her back to their village.

When the Arabs had left, the colonists greatly rejoiced, lifting their eyes heavenward and thanking God for saving them from slaughter.[214B]

A Strange New World!

While survival was uppermost in adult minds, the children of Ekron had a greater ability to see the world around them with freshness and curiosity. What was it like for them to see a camel for the first time? Such a weird-looking horse!

They probably didn't realize that the Land of Israel is a major stopover for birds migrating to Africa for the winter from Europe. While most such birds could be found in the northern part of the country, Ekron had more than a few of its own. Some of the new birds they met were the bulbul, the Egyptian vulture, and the partridge. They also saw the hoopoe, whose long, straight beak may have reminded them of the woodpecker.

Top: **Ra-ta-tat!** The hoopoe (in Hebrew, *duchifat*)[215]
Right: **Graceful.** Gazelles were common in the lowland plains before the onset of urbanization.

Wise guy. Barn owl

There was the majesty of the white stork, and there were the sage eyes of the barn owl.

And such unusual plants! The ubiquitous prickly pear cactus was to become the substitute for the picket fences they had back in Russia. The soft, sweet fruit under its prickly covering, the sabra, would one day become the wry moniker for Jews born in Palestine.

But the most jarring creatures for them were the lizards. They

scrambled up and down the walls, darting in and out of sight, delighting some and making others shriek in terror. Not to mention the chameleons and black snakes, which were scary but not poisonous. Children and adults quickly learned to beware of the Palestinian Vipers, whose venom could be deadly.

Above, left to right: **Under the pear tree**. The prickly pear cactus and its Sabra fruit **Climbing the walls.** The gecko **Mousetrap.** The *za'aman shachor* (fire racer) *Left:* **Deadly.** The poisonous *zefa* (Palestinian viper) *Below:* **Sting operation.** Next to the *zefa*, scorpions were the second most dangerous creatures encountered.

The experience of coming to live in this exotic land was spine-tingling and exciting! Eager to be part of this strange new world, they were at first perplexed by everything in it, including the weather. In this place, they wrote home to their friends in Russia, it never snowed in the winter, and it never rained in the summer!

Chapter 16
Between Heaven and Earth

Even to an outside observer, Ekron was bedeviled with physical problems from the very start. Dr. Chaim Chissin, a secular Jew from White Russia, joined the non-Orthodox BILU *aliyah* group in the aftermath of the Russian pogroms and reached Palestine in 1882. Among the first group of pioneers, he worked in Mikveh Israel, Rishon Le-Ẓion, and Gedera. He watched the Ekron experiment with interest and wrote the following practical assessment:

Faster than a speeding sickle. This woodcut appeared in 1893 in the Warsaw annual journal *Achi'asaf*. On the right side of Ekron's Main Street are two grain harvesters crafted by Aharon Zelig Levitta, which revolutionized farming in Palestine.[216]

[In the beginning] a sum total of 2,700 dunams [621 acres] was allotted for the [original] eleven families. That comes out to 250 dunams [62.5 acres] per family – plots that were inadequate, because besides growing wheat the settler had to set aside part of his land for pasture and for growing vegetables. He would therefore need no less than 350 dunams [87.5 acres]. The Ekronians received only two-thirds of their minimal land needs....

Insufficient land was aggravated by the fact that the extended Ekronian households were so large – some of them numbering between ten and eighteen persons....

At the very least, the land should have been apportioned to the original group only. But no! Already in the first year the administration added two more families, and then another five, so that now the families totaled eighteen, each one receiving on average merely 150 dunams (thirty-three acres).

The farmers protested the increase in the number of residents, but the administration answered them "with a smile" that they really had nothing to worry about, because if it became apparent that they were in need of more land, all the [administration] had to do was buy some more. The Baron had as much money as was needed.

This response convinced the settlers. It had been patently clear to them that the Baron would not recoil if asked to outlay additional funds. He would spare nothing on their behalf, as long as they lived up to the hopes that he had for them.

Unfortunately, no matter how much money the Baron had, the administrators would still have been more logical if they had first purchased adequate amounts of land and only then settled more people on it. ... it was clear from the start that there was not a sufficient amount of land available.[216A]

My son the doctor. Chaim Chissin left Palestine in 1887, remained abroad for nearly twenty years, studied medicine in Switzerland, and returned in 1905. He recorded impressions of life in Palestine in his book *Journey through the Promised Land*, which provides invaluable information about life during the First Aliyah period.

With the addition of the seven new families, Yehoshua Ossowetzky, the Baron's administrator overseeing Ekron, did in fact purchase another 1,500 dunams (330 acres) near the Arab village of Nâàneh. But Chissin wasn't impressed:

The first problem was that even with the newly acquired lands there were still only 250 dunams per family – and they needed at least another 100 dunams [twenty-three acres] to make ends meet. The second issue was that it took at least an hour and a half to reach those fields – three hours wasted each day – and since most of the work took place in the winter, the commute in the mud was especially difficult.

The biggest problem was that since the fields were located so far away, it was extremely difficult

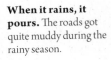

When it rains, it pours. The roads got quite muddy during the rainy season.

to watch over them especially from theft – without spending a lot of money on watchmen. Ossowetzky wanted to solve this by building homes in the new area for the younger couples, but before he could carry out his plans he was transferred to Rishon Le-Ẓion in 1888.[217]

Were the administrators shortsighted, or did they have machinations in mind? It would take a long while for the naïve settlers to find out. In the meantime, the farmers pushed their worries to the back of their minds. Somehow, with the rich earth, the sweat of their brows and God's Providence, they believed their venture would be a success.

Farming on a Higher Plane

Chissin described the farmers as *adukim* – a term used to describe Jews who are very meticulous in their observance of the commandments. Yet he could observe only the outer aspects of their religiosity; he could only guess at the inner spiritual force driving them. As farmers since their youth, they all had been very attached to the soil while still in Russia – how much more so when they began working the soil of the Holy Land. Given the opportunity to observe miẓvot that could be performed only in the Land of Israel, farming took on a dimension of deep spirituality unique to the Jewish traditional worldview. For believers, every agricultural act has a throbbing, mystical energy.

They embodied the ideal of the farmer engaged in holy work described by Rabbi Moshe Sofer,[218] one of the greatest European rabbis and religious leaders of the last 200 years. In his novellae on the Talmud (*Chatam Sofer, Sukkah* 36a) he writes about the unique character of those who work the Land of Israel. His discussion begins with the famous dispute (*Berachot* 35b) between Rabbi Yishmael and Rabbi Shimon bar Yochai of second-century Palestine regarding the propriety of engaging in labor instead of devoting one's full-time efforts to the study of Torah:

> The Rabbis taught: It is written, "And I will bring the rain of your land in its season – the early rain and the latter rain. And you shall gather in your grain, your wine, and your oil" (Deuteronomy 11:14). What does this verse come to teach us? For is it not also written, "[The words of] this book of the Torah shall never cease

[being spoken] from your mouth; you shall meditate on them day and night, in order that you observe to do all that is written in it, for then will you succeed in all your ways, and then will you prosper" (Joshua 1:8)? Should that verse be taken literally [that Torah learning may never be interrupted by mundane affairs]? Therefore the Torah says, "and you shall gather in your grain" – combine an occupation (*derech erez*) along with the study of Torah. This is the opinion of Rabbi Yishmael.

[But] Rabbi Shimon bar Yochai said: If a man plows during plowing time, sows during sowing time, harvests during harvest time, threshes during threshing time, [etc.] what will become of Torah? Therefore, [the answer must be that] when the Jewish people obey God's will, then their work will be performed for them by others. ... But when the Jewish people do not fulfill God's will, then their work must be accomplished by themselves. ...

Abbaye said: Many attempted Rabbi Yishmael's way – and succeeded. Many tried Rabbi Shimon bar Yochai's way – but failed.

Threshing in Ekron/ Mazkeret Batya, 1913. The animals are trampling the wheat to separate the kernels from the stalks.

Opposite page: **Novellae of Rabbi Moshe Sofer on tractate *Sukkah*.** His comments about the sacred nature of farming in Israel start with the bottom line of the right column.

Rabbi Sofer elaborates:

... In my humble opinion, even Rabbi Yishmael applied the verse "... and you shall gather in your grain" only to those living in the Land of Israel (when the majority of the Jewish people is living there). This is so because working the soil in itself is a miẓvah, for one is fulfilling the commandment of *yishuv Ereẓ Yisrael* – settling the Land of Israel – by growing its holy fruit there. It is in regard to this miẓvah that the Torah declares, "and you shall gather in your grain." Therefore, Boaz (although he had many employees) performed the winnowing himself[219] because he was performing a miẓvah. Just as a person cannot claim he is exempt from donning *tefillin* because he is occupied with studying Torah, so too one should not say, "I will not gather my grain because I am learning Torah." And it is possible that with regard to other trades that contribute to the "settling of the world" (*yishuv ha-olam*) – they too would be included in the miẓvah.

A quiet afternoon. Dairy Street (Rechov Ha-Machleiva), later changed to Founders Street. Ekron, 1920

ע״כ בשארי ימים מטביל ביה ונפיק ביה אפי׳ חסרון עד פחות מחציו אינו פוסל ובפרט שישאר כשיעור אתרוג כביצה. אמנם ביו״ט ב׳ דרבנן דמחמרי׳ ככל חומרי י״ט ראשון ובעי לקיחה תמה כמו בי״ט א׳ מ״מ כיון דפליגי בלקיחה תמה ולכמה פוסקים כל שלא חסר כאיסר מקרי לקיחה תמה א״כ יש לסמוך ע״ז בי״ט ב׳ ע״כ בי״ט א׳ פסלי׳ חסר כ״ש וביט״ב עד כאיסר ובשארי ימים עד נקוב למחציתו:

והנה אתרוג המנומר או נקלף ונעשה כמנומר בשנים ושלשה מקומות דמשמע דפסול משום הדר אפי׳ בשארי יומי להפוסלים הדר כל ז׳ מ״מ נ״ל דרוב פעמים ע״י משמוש היד ורוב הנענעים נולדו בו נימורים נימורים וגם נקלף קצת מקומות מהעור העליון הקליפה החיצונה ונעשה מקומות כמנומר ומי יודע אם הוא ממראה האתרוג וכן משמע לעיל ל״ה ע״ב פירש״י ד״ה מפני שמפסידה קליפתה החיצונה נמאסת במשמוש הידים ע״ש וא״א שיהיה כל פעם מראה אתרוג באותו הכתמים והבהרות שנולדו מזיעת הידים נ״ל דהוה הדר כיון שבאו ע״י מצותו זהו הודו והדרו וקצת ראיה לזה מפסחים ס״ה ע״ב שבח הוא לזרעו של אהרן שילכו עד ארכבותיהם בדם ע״ש ובודאי בעלמא כיוצא בזה הוה הקרבהו נא לפחתיך והכא זהו הדרו וה״נ דכוותיה כנלע״ד דרוב פעמים בחוש״מ כבר נעשה כעין מנומר ממשמוש היד ומ״מ כשר וכעין גרדומים דאתו משירי מצוה וכעין מים משירי טהרה ועי׳ לקמן גבי נקיבת העכברים:

אתרוג תפוח סרוח וכו׳. והנה איבעיא לא איפשטא ופסקו לקולא וצ״ע כיון דלא איתפרש שיעור הדר אלא דמסרו הכתוב לחכמים א״כ כל מה שיאמרו חכמים הוא דאורייתא ממש כמו מלאכת חש״מ להפוסקים שהוא דאורייתא אלא שמסרו לחכמים וכל מה שהם אומרים שאסור הוא דאורייתא ולוקים עליו וה״נ דכוותיה וי״ל הכא תלי רחמנא כל מה שנראה לחכמים שזה איננו הדר פסול הוא מדאורייתא בודאי אך מה שחכמים מסופקים אם הוא הדר או לא א״כ עכ״פ אינו נראה בעיניהם שאיננו מהודר שהרי מסופקים בו א״כ שוב אין כאן איסור דאורייתא והדר הוא:

דומה לכושי תנן. שמעתי ממ״ו הפלא״ה זצ״ל בהא דפליגי רשב״י ור׳ ישמעאל ר״פ כיצד מברכין ומסקי׳ הרבה עשו כרשב״י ולא עלתה בידם אמר הוא ז״ל שעשו כרשב״י ולא רשב״י ממש דודאי מי שכוונתו לשם ה׳ הבוחן מחשבותיו ויודע עשתונותיו בודאי יעלה בידו אלא הם עשו כרשב״י נדמו לו ולא בעצם תוכניותם ע״כ לא עלתה בידם ואמר היינו דאמרי הכא אתרוג הכושי היינו הצדיק המשונה במעשיו ככושי המשונה בעורו הוא כשר אך דומה לכושי שרוצה לדמות עצמו לרשב״י זה פסול כי לא עלתה בידו ע״כ דברי הרב ודפח״ח. מכאן ואילך תוספות דברי תלמידו הפעוט כמוני נלע״ד רבי ישמעאל נמי לא אמר מקרא ואספת דגנך אלא בא״י ורוב ישראל שרויין שהעבודה בקרקע גופה מצוה משום יישוב א״י ולהוציא פירותיה הקדושים ועל זה ציותה התורה ואספת דגנך וכועז זורה גורן השעורים הלילה משום מצוה וכאלו תאמר לא אניח תפילין מפני שאני עוסק בתורה ה״נ לא יאמר לא אאסוף דגני מפני עסק התורה ואפשר אפילו שארי אמוניות שיש בהם יישוב העולם הכל בכלל מצוה אבל כשאנו מפוזרים בעו״ה בין או״ה וכל שמרבה העולם יישוב מוסיף עבודת ה׳ חורבן מודה ר״י לרשב״י וע״ז אנו סומכים על ר׳ נהוראי במתני׳ סוף קידושין מניח אני כל אומניות שבעולם ואיני מלמד בני אלא תורה היינו בח״ל וכנ״ל והיינו דמחדש רבא באתרוג הכושי אפי׳ אינו נדמה אלא כושי ממש דהיינו רשב״י וחבריו האמתיים מ״מ הא לן והא להו לבני בבל כשר ולבני א״י פסול דבעי׳ יישוב א״י ע״י ישראל:

אתרוג הכוסר. עי׳ בחידושינו בזה לעיל ל״א ע״ב:

אתרוג שנקבוהו העכברים. להפוסקים דהדר פסול כל ז׳ [לה:] ולקיחה תמה רק ביומא קמא א״כ צע״ג בש״ס דקארי לי מאי קארי ליה מדרב אדר׳ חנינא ומכ״ש דקשה ללישנא בתרא איך אפשר שיהיה הדר נשיכת העכברים ומה בינו לבין שמן של בהכ״נ שנפל עכבר לתוכו פסול משום הקרבהו נא לפחתיך וכבר נתעורר בכל זה בכפ״ת וראיתי בהג״א לפסול אתרוג שהי׳ בו חזזית או שאר פסול וחתכו ממנו אעפ״י שחזר למראה אתרוג מ״מ החסרון הניכר הזה שבא ע״י שהיה פסול מתחלתו נשאר בפסולו ולכאורה י״ל דגם ללישנא בתרא דאמר רב זה הדר רוצה לומר אחר שנחתך ממנו נשיכת העכברים דלא תימא כיון דאתי מכח עכברים פסול קמ״ל וללישנא קמא פריך ש״ס איך אמר רב אין זה הדר הא אפשר לחתוך ממנו וכר״ח דמטביל ביה ומ״ט פוסל רב כל ז׳ ומשני שאני נשיכת עכברים דמאיסי ומשו״ה פסול אף אחר שנחתך ולא קיי״ל הכי אלא כל זמן שנשיכת העכברים בו פסול כל ז׳ ואחר חתיכה מותר בשאר הימים כך היה נלע״ד אלא שלא כ״כ הפוסקים:

ובגדול כדי שיאחז ב׳ בידו א׳. כ׳ הר״ן דעיקר הגירסא הוא שיאחז שניהם בידו א׳ פי׳ האגודה של לולב והאתרוג שניהם בידו א׳ ובירושלמי השיב לו ר׳ יוסי וכי כתיב וכפת תמרים כפת תמרים כתי׳ אפי׳ בשתי ידיו נמי מבואר דלר׳ יוסי נמי אי לוקח שניהם בידו א׳ יוצא ואפשר דעדיף אלא אם לוקחם בשני ידיו נמי שפיר דמי ולפ״ז הא דאמר רבה לקמן ל״ז ע״ב לולב בימין וכו׳ היינו אם רוצה ללוקחם בשתי ידיו יקח הלולב בימין אבל אם ירצה יקחם בידו א׳ וע״כ צ״ע דברי מג״א סי׳ תרנ״א סק״ו. וכ״כ בס׳ א״ר סי׳ תרנ״א סק״י בשם ס׳ אמרכל דעכ״פ יצא בדיעבד אם שניהם ביד א׳. ואולי י״ל הא דפשיטא ליה לרבא לקמן ל״ז ע״ב מין במינו אינו חוצץ וגם הוה לקיחה תמה כשמפסיקים עלי הדס וערבה או עלי לולב בין המינים אעפ״י דהדס וערבה לאו מיני לולב נינהו ולולב לאו מין

"Bringing in the sheaves," 1913. Harvesting – modestly dressed, of course.

But when we are dispersed (on account of our sins) among the gentile nations – and the more we engage in worldly pursuits, the more the Torah is diminished – even Rabbi Yishmael would concede on this point to Rabbi Shimon bar Yochai.[220]

There is little doubt that the farmers believed with all their

Milking this picture for all it's worth. Mazkeret Batya founded Israel's first Jewish-owned dairy cooperative. *Front row (left to right)*: Yiẕchak Sharshevsky, Shmuel Sharshevsky, Alta Sharshevsky (kneeling beside the cow), Noach Skolnick, Ẕipporah Maller (milking), Mordechai Maller, Shoshanna Skolnick, an unidentified young woman, and Moshe Skolnick. *Background:* One Arab worker, Rochel Skolnick (with pigtails, sitting on the wagon), and an unidentified male whose fancy top hat stands out. The warm clothing and the cloudy skies (there is no shade) suggest that the picture was taken in the wintertime. It was taken around 1932. Even then Mazkeret Bayta had a definite religious character.[221]

hearts that even while engaging in the mundane aspects of farming, their "earthy" pursuit contained elements of the spiritual, for they were building up the Jewish settlement of the Land of Israel and paving the way for others to follow.

"A land flowing with milk and honey." The dairy, 1913

Their attitude was apparent to all who visited Ekron,

כפר עקרון. בארץ יהודה
נוסד בשנת תרמ"ה

"Village of Ekron in the Land of Yehuda." An early etching of Ekron. In those days, the region of Yehuda (Judah) referred to Jaffa and the neighboring settlements, from Gedera in the south to Petach Tikva in the north. That included Mazkeret Batya, Nes Ẓiona, Rishon Le-Ẓion and Mikveh Israel.

resulting in several descriptions extolling the climate of pious diligence to their work, their energy, and the buoyant spirit of family enterprise that permeated the settlement.

One of the earliest newspaper accounts appeared in the Jerusalem newspaper *Chavaẓelet:*[222]

> The colonists all excel in their work – they are farmers in the full sense of the word. Their wives and children also perform their duties faithfully. My heart was filled with joy when I went out to the fields and saw how family members all worked together. That included boys and girls from twelve years old and up, harvesting and binding sheaves at the edge of their fields, and all of their field-work was done without employing non-Jewish laborers.[223]

Farming was indeed a family affair, regarded not only as a livelihood but as a privilege.

As early as 1886, the Warsaw journal of Torah and contemporary affairs *Knesset Yisrael*[223A] wrote enthusiastically of the Ekron farmers' success on both physical and spiritual grounds:

> Whoever has seen the wide valley enveloped by fields of amber grain to its rim and surrounded by walls of lush trees planted to guard it and give it an aura of beauty and splendor … whoever can delight at this gloriously uplifting sight, as the wind blows and the stalks sway to and fro, as if whispering their thanks to nature and all

that bestows life upon it ... whoever has seen this can appreciate the charm of the settlement Ekron which stretches out on the plain without a mountain or hill in sight....

We could not believe what we saw, what a delightful scene where God's spirit hovers over it, where entire households go out to their work until evening. We witnessed people, some of whom were beginning to sprout white hairs in their beards, their *payot* and *ẓiẓit* swaying back and forth, marching with their sickles over their shoulders and working with incredible speed and strength; their women assisting them in gathering stalks and bundling sheaves.... And what are the children doing? Some of them gleefully heave the bundles over their shoulders and pile them up in designated places, leaving them to dry in the fields until it is time to gather them into their homes. The rest of the children fly like shadows throughout the valley, tending to their flocks. As the evening approaches, they all return home.

In short – these people have a way of drawing attention to their energetic manner of work, their love of their vocation, to their land, and their expertise in their work.[225]

Perhaps the most glowing contemporary account was penned by Klonymous Ze'ev Wissotzky, a wealthy Jewish activist who established a tea company in Moscow in 1849.[226]

A farmer from the neighboring settlement of Gedera. Notice his cosmopolitan attire – cap and jacket – and statesman-like posture. Dr. Chaim Chissin recognized the difference, writing of the Ekron group: "Finally – to see real farmers in the truest sense of the word. All of them – from children to adults, men and women – were in the fields all day long. They worked with a *bren* – a burning enthusiasm."[224]

"Mr. Tea." Klonymous Ze'ev Wissotzky, an Orthodox activist and financial supporter of Chovevei Ẓion, was a magnanimous philanthropist who donated to causes that ranged from yeshivot (such as those in Volozhin and Telz) to Hebrew literature (such as Achad Ha-Am's periodical *Ha-Shiloach*).

An Orthodox Jew who was active in the Chovevei Ẓion movement, Wissotzky visited Palestine in 1884. In one of his letters, collected and published three years later, he writes about Ekron. He was excited by seeing wheat fields cultivated by Jews in the Holy Land; his impressions are imbued with a religious hue bordering on awe:

> A beauty and trembling grandeur hover over wheat stalks robed in majesty – for they realize that they are the product of sons whose souls yearned to eat of the table of their Father in Heaven, who maintains constant vigilance over this Holy Land from the beginning of the year until its end.
>
> I enjoyed seeing the nice homes, where tranquility and peacefulness prevail. It was here that I came to recognize the glorious tranquility that is the life of the farmers, whose hands faithfully till their land, and whose eyes and hearts are lifted up to their Father in Heaven. It is their hope that He will send them His blessing with holiness and satiate them with wine and oil.[227]

Perhaps to compensate for their feelings of inferiority as farmers, the gentlemen farmers of the other colonies liked to poke fun at the pious Ekronians, depicting them as a country-hick version of the fools of Chelm. For example:

> The Ekronians were unhappy about the large hill separating them from the village of Aqir. They decided one day to do something about it. One night, under the illumination of a full moon, the men picked up their hoes and shovels and made their way to the annoying hill. Before getting their hands dirty, they removed their *kapotes*, which they left on the ground in a pile. After several hours of work, they returned to the place where they had left their *kapotes*. They were gone. The Ekronians were jubilant. "Look how much has been accomplished – we have progressed so rapidly that we can't even see our *kapotes* anymore!"[228]

But everyone knew, as Chaim Chissin himself testified, that when it came to zeal and professionalism, the Ekronian farmers were head and shoulders above the rest.

Chapter 17
Little Lita

The vibrant strength of religious life in Ekron was rooted in the farmers' dedication to the principles on which their lives had been based in Russia. Unlike many of the other pioneers who were also Orthodox, the Ekronians were much more conservative in their attitude regarding the lifestyle and educational institutions of the Diaspora. They did not see Jewish life in the Diaspora as "*galuti*" (reflecting the exile in a demeaning, pejorative sense). To them, the way Jews conducted their lives was just fine: the problem was the gentiles who made their lives miserable. Palestine offered a geographic cure, putting some distance between them and the anti-Semites, with the added dimension of the special sanctity of the Holy Land.

Starting all over. Simchah and Fruma Kalmanowitz and their daughter Bracha

To many of their colleagues in other colonies, the *galut* problem was both internal and external. Some of the negative aspects of Diaspora life had been internalized, and these colonists felt that the land of their forefathers would straighten that out. As a result, they were more open to some of the modern trends and ideas in the air. There was a little less emphasis on preservation and a little more on innovation.[229]

But for the pioneers from Pavlovka, creating "Little Lita" (Lita being the Jewish name for Lithuania) in Palestine was the winning combination. Writing in *Ha-Meliz*, Mordechai Ben Hillel describes a typical evening in Ekron:

> I journeyed [from Be'er Tuvia] and arrived at Ekron as the stars appeared. And what did I see? I beheld a tiny replica of a town in Lithuania. I do not have words to adequately describe the sounds I heard emanating from the windows of the third floor of the big building, the *beit midrash* – sounds so well known and familiar, the sounds of many people studying Torah. I felt like I was really back in Lithuania.

I did not find any administrator, but I did locate the rabbi, while he was poring over a volume of *Tur Yoreh De'ah*. Soon after, the *rebbetzin* brought in two steaming cups of coffee, in the same manner that guests were received in the old country. I left their home and made my way up the steps of the synagogue. [There] I saw nearly all the members of the community sitting around a long table, studying Mishnayot. It was the break between *Minchah* and *Maariv*, and it was not yet harvest time in the country. So the colonists had some control over their time and dedicated set times to Torah study. Everything resembled the way it was done back in Lithuania. My eyes were filled with joy and love as I gazed upon this scene. While this was a common scene in Lithuania, seeing this in a colony in Ereẓ Yisrael arouses a whole different set of emotions.... [230]

Letting the light seep in. Jerusalem, turn of the twentieth century

In his book *Mazkeret Batya*, David Neiman elaborates on the evening studies:

There were two Mishnah study groups. Group *alef* consisted of the more gifted men, who knew which questions to ask and how to answer them. They had spent their youth studying Mishnah; some of them had even studied Talmud, and now their prior learning returned to them. They would sit united around the table, completely absorbed by their learning. There was no electricity at the time, nor were there even kerosene lamps. They used oil lamps and candles; the light that reflected off their excited faces enchanted any who witnessed this sight.

On the other side of the synagogue was another table, at which the "simpler" students studied – group *bet*. With this group, there was no give and take, no discussion. One would read a chapter while the other listened; occasionally they would doze off for a while.... But both classes had one thing in common: this group would complete a tractate, and that group would complete a trac-

משניות
סדר קדשים
עם פירושי הגאונים המפורסמים
רבינו עובדי' מברטנורה · ותוספות יום טוב
כפי שנדפסו עד היום

A farmer's study companion. Cover page of a volume of Mishnah from Ekron/Mazkeret Batya, published circa 1797 in Silesia

tate – and then they would get out the arak (a liquor) and herring and all would fulfill the miẓvah of making a *siyum* while experiencing a spiritual uplift. As the learners were celebrating, the children of the village would join them, filling the synagogue and the *ezrat nashim,* and their joyous sounds could be heard for miles.[231]

Focusing on the lighter side of religious life, Neiman has much to say about that arak, attributing its popularity to the handful of Chassidim who lived there.

… The Chassidim did have one effect on the village: arak. All the Ashkenazim (*mitnagdim*) were agreeable regarding the arak, and so an Ekronian tradition began. Whenever it was a memorial day for one of the deceased, the children of the deceased would come to say *Kaddish* at the synagogue and bring a bottle of arak and some herring. After the prayer, the worshippers would recite the following prayer: "*May the soul transcend and rest in peace in Heaven, among all the righteous.*"

"*Mamesh* [exactly] like in Europe." So reports *Ha-Shiloach* in the excerpt below

There were plenty of miẓvah occasions, *baruch Hashem,* that created an opportunity to down a drink: If [the men] completed

ומצב החיים הרוחנים והצבורים בעקרון הוא ממש כמצבם בערים הקטנות בליטא.
חברה רבות ושונות יש בה: חברה ש״ס חברה משניות, חברה גמ״ח חברה בקור חולים,
חברה קדישא. וכל יושבי המושב הם יראי ה׳ ומדקדקים במצות בקלות כבחמורות

a tractate of Mishnayot – a *siyum* – it was a good reason to finish off several bottles. When someone from the village died, several shot glasses were downed during the last day of the *shivah* and on the last day of the *sheloshim.* If a new child was brought into the world of the Holy One Blessed Be He, that was a fabulous reason to raise a toast; on the *leil ha-Shemirah* ("the wakeful night")[232] and at the *brit* it was so much more so!

"*L'chaim.*" Downing a smoothie in Rishon Le-Ẓion, 1897

Even the animals "contributed" their share of drinking opportunities for the Ekronians: in those days, they had quite a few donkeys, many of which bore their first offspring. When the offspring is born, there is a miẓvah to redeem it with a lamb – and then, of course, another occasion for a *simchah.* The tradition of the Fast of the Firstborn on Passover eve was observed, and what harm could there be if a "regular" Jew partook of the *siyum,* even if he was not a certified firstborn male?[233]

This custom of drinking arak "grabbed them by the throat." Even though they were Litvaks and did not have a *rebbe* (the way Chassidim did, to whom they would direct their toast with a *l'chaim*), they adopted this tradition as if they were.... The habit probably existed back in the old country, but in Ekron the act of drinking arak took on the nature of the sacred.[234]

Communal institutions and societies were formed just as they had existed in Pavlovka:

> The spiritual and communal situation in Ekron is exactly as it was in the small towns of Lithuania. [Ekron] has many and varied societies: the *chevrah Shas* (Talmud study group), *chevrah Mishnayot, chevrah gemach* (free-loan society), *chevrah bikkur cholim* (society for the welfare of the sick), and *chevrah kaddisha* (burial society). All the residents of the settlement are God-fearing people and punctilious in the performance of all the commandments – no matter what their degree of importance.[235]

Bringing in the Vilna *Shas*

When it came to the acquisition of the holy texts that formed the basis of the community's beliefs and way of life, it was a cause for special celebration. Such an event was recorded in an article in *Chavatzelet*[236] written by "One of the participants."

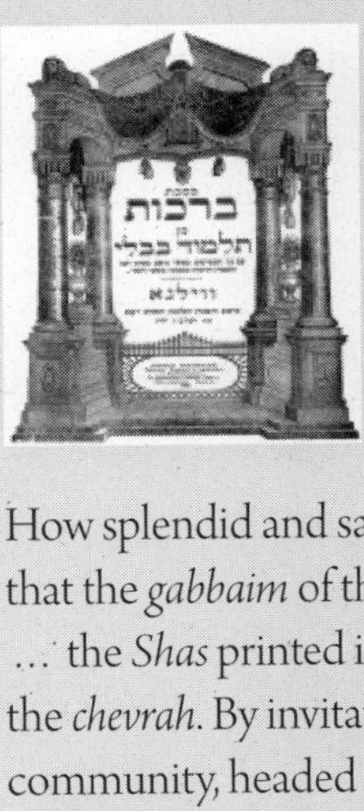

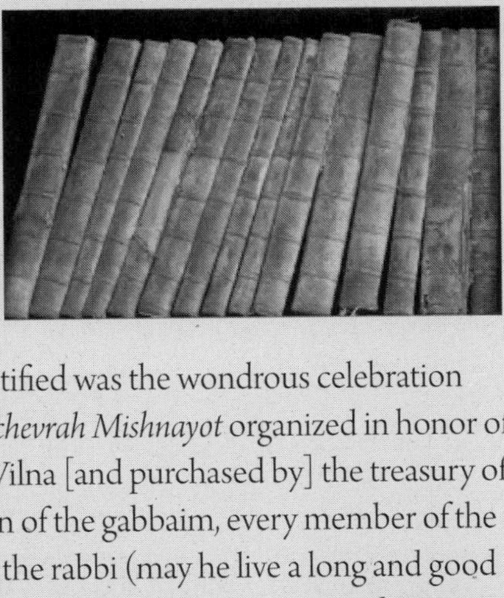

Still in use. *Left:* Title page of the first volume of the Vilna *Shas*
Right: Set of Talmud printed in 5655 (1895), still in the Mazkeret Batya synagogue

> How splendid and sanctified was the wondrous celebration that the *gabbaim* of the *chevrah Mishnayot* organized in honor of … the *Shas* printed in Vilna [and purchased by] the treasury of the *chevrah*. By invitation of the gabbaim, every member of the community, headed by the rabbi (may he live a long and good life), came to the home of Reb Yaakov Arkin on Sunday evening, the 17th of Elul.
>
> Each volume of Talmud was dedicated separately, and each donor personally brought the volume for which he had contributed money into the room. From there, the assembled made their way to the synagogue. Hundreds of candles held by

the children lit up the way, and Jewish songs and melodies were heard from the students and teachers of the Ṭalmud Torah. Music was heard from one of the musicians.

The celebration didn't conclude until after midnight. People returned to their homes in good spirits and were thankful and appreciative of the gabbaim's past and present accomplishments: the writing of a Torah scroll, the Prophets' scroll … and now the acquisition of a complete set of Talmud. They viewed the gabbaim as individuals who would not tire or be weary in strengthening Torah and increasing its glory.

May the Holy One Blessed Be He give them their due reward and bestow blessing and success on all the works of their hands.

Pied Piper. Binyamin Press of Mazkeret Batya was drafted into the Turkish army and ended up as a flutist in the army's band.

The ledgers (*pinkasim*) of the *chevrah bikkur cholim* and *chevrah kaddisha* of Ekron indicate the seriousness of these endeavors, as crystallized in the societies' bylaws:

The chairmen. *Left to right:* Yaakov Laskovsky, Dov Rudovsky, Yaakov Gold

… By secret ballot and majority vote, Reb Yaakov Gold has been elected "first gabbai," and Reb Yaakov Laskovsky and Reb Dov Rudovsky have been elected assistant gabbaim. …

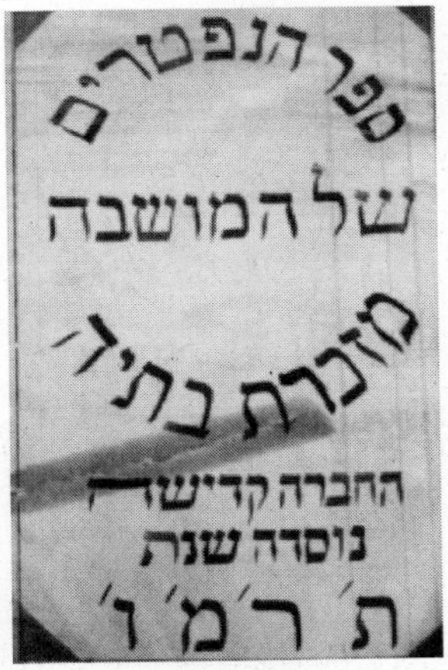

Departures. *Chevrah kaddisha* book of Ekron, 1886

If, Heaven forbid, someone in the community is ill, the gabbai is responsible for sending one or two people to that individual, to tend to him and do whatever is required for his recovery, and to reside there.

The trustees must see to it that those sent to the ill person pray on his behalf, and tend to the sick to the best of their abilities. …

Technicalities of kindness. A book outlining the bylaws of Ekron's *gemach*

The gabbai must send volunteers to the ill based on the lineup of the volunteer roster, without deviating from its order, until the list of volunteers has been completed, after which they start again from the beginning of the roster.

If, Heaven forbid, one of our community passes away, the gabbai is responsible for appointing people to dig a grave and be involved in the needs of the deceased, and do whatever is required for the deceased, as the gabbai sees fit. …

A surviving relative of the deceased must pay the *chevrah*, two francs for [tending to a deceased] child, and five francs for an adult. …

All the above regulations have been unanimously ratified, and in their merit may God bring a complete recovery to all the sick people of Israel … may God wipe away tears from every face, may our Temple be rebuilt speedily in our days, and the Redeemer come to Zion. Amen.

The eve of 23 Tishrei, 5646 [1885], *Ekron*

Seal of approval. Official stamp of Mazkeret Batya/Ekron

People with a heart. Simchah and Mina Kurchevsky. Simchah headed the *hachnasat orchim* society.

Commitment to the mizvah of loaning money to anyone in need took the form of a community *gemach,* a free-loan society. And *hachnasat orchim,* providing lodging for guests and wayfarers, was a high priority. Because families were large and living quarters were relatively small, visitors were accommodated in a building constructed for that purpose.

But the central pillar of their spiritual lives was the synagogue. Their parents before them had begun building a synagogue in Pavlovka even as they were still struggling to make ends meet, for "if there is no Torah, there is no flour" (*Avot* 3:17). So, too, did the people of Ekron place the construction of their synagogue among their first priorities. The *shul* was not only a house of

Ekron's Main Street (today, Rothschild Boulevard). The town's first synagogue, built in 1885, is the three-story building on the left. On both sides of the synagogue are the colony's first buildings, the *kazarmes* used as residences. The street is not paved. (Imagine what it was like in the rainy season!) *Photo by Ben Dov, 1920.*

The house that Rothschild built. This stately and beautiful edifice was built by Rothschild and completed in 1927. Currently, Mazkeret Batya has five synagogues.

prayer, but a place for the learning and teaching of Torah. It was also where the Ekronians would meet for celebrations and where the men gathered to discuss community matters.

A correspondent from the Warsaw journal *Knesset Yisrael* attested to the importance of the synagogue in Ekron:

> ... Filled with illumination from the sun, which penetrates the building through its wide open windows located on all sides. It is the nicest building in the settlement, because it is a house of prayer. It is where the members of the moshavah gather during their rest hours to pour out words of prayer and gratitude to their Benefactor [this time the reference is to God, not the Baron] for bringing them to their inheritance.
>
> ... The Ekronians were religious; every citizen of the village was present for every single prayer. ... even those who were not proficient in the prayers ... would go to the synagogue and at the very least, respond, "Amen!" The workers, who woke up early in the morning, prayed at the crack of dawn; they constituted the first

Deserted. The first synagogue as it appeared after the settlers moved to the new building Rothschild had built for them.

Hachnasat sefer Torah. Transfer of Torah scrolls from the old synagogue to the new one built by Rothschild in Ekron/ Mazkeret Batya circa 1927-1929.

minyan. Their prayers were uttered quickly, but they were expert at them – by the time one had donned a *tallit* and *tefillin*, the other had already completed his prayers and rushed off to work.

The second minyan gathered at sunrise [considered a meritorious practice]; that was the *vatikin* minyan. The second minyan was also composed of workers, but their work was manual work (no cattle); if they were to be slightly late at commencing work for the day, they would not miss much.

There was also a third minyan in the village – the "Seniors' Minyan." Today, they would be called retirees. There were not many elderly in the village at the time; there were barely ten of them to constitute a minyan. They were, of course, in no rush when they prayed. They prayed in the Ashkenazic style; if one or two of them prayed in the Sephardic style, they made sure not to do so loudly, in order not to irritate the others.[237]

A Significant Change in Prayer

Although they continued to pray according to the custom of Ashkenazim, Jewish law mandated that they make one change when they arrived in the Land of Israel. Their *kohanim*, Jewish males who are descendants of the high priest Aaron, were to bless the congregation *every morning* with the Priestly Benediction, *Birkat Kohanim*. This is a beautiful practice, wherein the *kohanim* become a channel to the congregation for God's peace and blessings. But in order to be a conduit for such holiness, one must be in a spiritually uplifted state of happiness, a level deemed

The Rabbis of Mazkeret Batya[238]

Mordechai Leib Rubin
1904-1908

Yaakov Yosef Halevi Dzimitrovsky
1908-1910

Moshe Hameiri Ostrovsky
1911-1919

On the platform. Shlomo Weisberg

inaccessible in Europe except during the Jewish festivals. In the Diaspora, *kohanim* did not perform this ritual even on the Sabbath. In the words of the great Ashkenazic codifier Rabbi Moshe Isserles:[239]

> The custom in all these provinces [i.e., Europe, where the Ashkenazim reside] is that the "raising of the hands" [the Priestly Benediction] takes place only on a festival, because then they are in a joyful state due to the festival. And only someone with a glad heart may bless. That is not true of other days – even the Sabbaths ... for they are preoccupied with thoughts about their livelihoods and their taking off time from work.[240]

This change in the daily prayers helped concretize the farmers' feeling that they were in a higher state of holiness because they were living in the Holy Land. Every day, the village's resident *kohen*, Shlomo Weisberg, would joyfully stride to the front of the *shul* to raise his hands and pronounce the ancient blessing.

aham Eliyahu Altman
0-1948

Avraham Moshe Dovid Hertz
1948-1961

Ẓvi Senderovich
1963-1967

Ephraim Zalmanovitz
1969-

Interference!

An inherent problem in the early days of Ekron was that the deeply religious settlers from White Russia and the semi-assimilated French administrators were often at loggerheads over religious issues. Initially, Ekron was mostly self-administered with minimal assistance from the Baron's administrators. But as time went on, they became much more involved and eventually resided in the settlement. One of them tried to meddle in the way the farmers conducted their prayer services, as we learn from a shocking article in *Ha-Maggid*:

> From Ekron we are informed … that the colony is blooming like a rose, and that the colonists are assiduously applying themselves to their work.… Just recently their synagogue, a very beautiful structure, was completed. To the Benefactor a piece of slander was relayed – that the colonists were taking too much time for their prayers, whether in the evening, morning or afternoon, which is causing them to be idle from their work.[241]

The Baron's boys. "The Baron de Rothschild himself sought to foster a Jewish community in Erez Yisrael that would be faithful to the spirit of the Torah. … The Baron, however, lived in Paris; his agents in Palestine, semi-assimilated devotees of French culture, not only were quite remote from the settlement enterprise but did everything in their power to uproot any respect for religion from among the settlers."[242] Chief administrator Elie Scheid is seated in the center.

To the chagrin of his onsite administrators, the Baron wisely had no interest in tangling with his colonists over religious practices. The article goes on to describe his response to the malicious report:

> The Benefactor has sent a reply to the manager of the moshavah, Mr. Ossowetzky, and ordered him to relay the following to the farmers in his name: "Serve the Lord, our God, with all your hearts' desire, and take as much time with your prayers as you wish – no one may interfere with you."

The administrators' antipathy toward Orthodox religious observance would become even more apparent as the years went by, testing the very fiber of the tiny new settlement. Ultimately, their meddling would create a fissure in the foundation of the religious edifice that the Ekronians were laboring to build, wreaking havoc on future generations.

Chapter 18
The Baron Comes to Town

Friction was building between the administrators and the farmers of the Baron's settlements, and discontent was pervasive. As the settlers began to chafe from their overseers' grip, mini-rebellions were brewing everywhere.

In February 1887, a major revolt against the Baron – or more specifically, against Yehoshua Ossowetzky, his representative – took place in Rishon Le-Ẓion. David Ben-Gurion[243] described the event:

> ... there were many revolts against the management [of the Baron's settlements]. The first was provoked by Yehoshua Ossowetzky.... His mind was warped as a result of his appointment as an all-powerful agent of Rothschild. Michael Halperin, a Rishon Le-Ẓion worker, wanted to publish an article condemning his staff. [When] Ossowetzky heard of this, he told Halperin's landlord to throw out all his belongings – and it was done – Halperin's cot and all his goods and possessions were flung into the street. As soon as the laborers who shared Halperin's lodgings came home and saw this, they asked the landlord to put everything back. The landlord (M. Abramovitz) excused himself, pleading coercion on Ossowetzky's part. About twenty laborers thereupon marched off to Ossowetzky,

Living in the fast lane. Postcard depicting Jewish settlers in Rishon Le-Ẓion

V.I.P. ramp. The Baron, impeccably dressed in a suit and bowtie, and his trademark pith helmet, disembarks from his yacht in Tantura (formerly an Arab village located twenty-four kilometers/fifteen miles south of Haifa). The ramp, decorated with palm branches, was constructed especially for his arrival.

> demanding that he recant. Several farmers joined the procession, for Halperin was well liked and respected by everyone. Seeing the crowd approach, Ossowetzky drew a pistol and fired. No one was hurt, but the settlement seethed with indignation, and when Ossowetzky sent for Turkish soldiers from Jaffa to arrest the "rebels," it rose to fever pitch. [Shmuel Hirsch] was hurriedly summoned from Mikveh Israel and contrived to prevent arrests.
>
> Every single person in the [settlement], man and woman, child and adult, large or small, vine grower or farmhand, assembled in the synagogue.… The [Torah] was taken out of the ark and a solemn Bible oath was taken to expel Ossowetzky and never let him enter Rishon Le-Ẓion again. And so, Ossowetzky was banished.[244]

Three months later, Baron Edmond de Rothschild paid his first visit to Palestine to see the settlements he funded.[245] His tour had the air of a king venturing out of his castle to survey his subjects, and it took him throughout the land, from Jaffa to Jerusalem (where he visited the Western Wall and the Church of the Holy Sepulcher) and then on to Jericho. On the way back, he also visited Rachel's Tomb.[246]

By the 10th of May, the Baron reached Rishon Le-Ẓion and met with the rebels face to face. After spending many hours discussing the conflict with each side, he managed to quell the insurrection – for the time being.

A study in contrasts. *Right:* "The Rothschild Room," former "grand salon" of the Hotel Samuel Bernard, Paris, c. 1750 (now on permanent exhibit in the Israel Museum, Jerusalem). In the 1880s, Baron Edmond de Rothschild acquired the salon. *Page 153:* The spartan sleeping quarters in the moshavah of Gedera, only a few kilometers from Mazkeret Batya. The bed and bureau were made of planks taken from crates, and the "mattress" was a simple linen sack filled with straw. The white pot on the floor by the

bed was in lieu of a bathroom – there was no indoor plumbing. The colonists didn't even have chairs, only stools. What was the Baron thinking when he inspected the settlers' homes in Mazkeret Batya? Although Rothschild contributed nothing to Gedera (the Biluim refused his support on principle), the furnishings of the two colonies were probably quite similar. The Baron donated vast sums for the purchase of land, farm animals and equipment, and the construction of homes, but he left the furnishings to the pioneers themselves.

Like a head of state reviewing his honor guard, he watched as all the farmers of nearby Ekron rode on horseback into Rishon Le-Zion, rifles in hand. They had come determined to bring the Baron and his wife with them to Ekron so that the "royal couple" could assess the results of their toil of the past four years. They also craved the opportunity to express their gratitude to the Baron and to give him the honor and recognition he deserved (and to go to the top with their grievances and requests).

To their dismay, Adelaide Rothschild was not interested. She may have suffered enough after watching her exasperated husband rebuke the farmers in Rishon. But in the end, the Baron acquiesced to go without his wife. He brought along two administrators who were involved with Ekron – Hirsch and Ossowetzky.

When the Baron arrived, he passed through an arch laced with myrtle branches, laurels, and roses, which the farmers had lovingly constructed. Not a single person from the settlement was missing when the Benefactor came calling. They took out the Torah scrolls and wore their Sabbath attire in order to pro-

A hero's welcome. Children and teachers wait for the Baron in Rehovot under a banner constructed in his honor. A similar banner awaited him in Ekron.

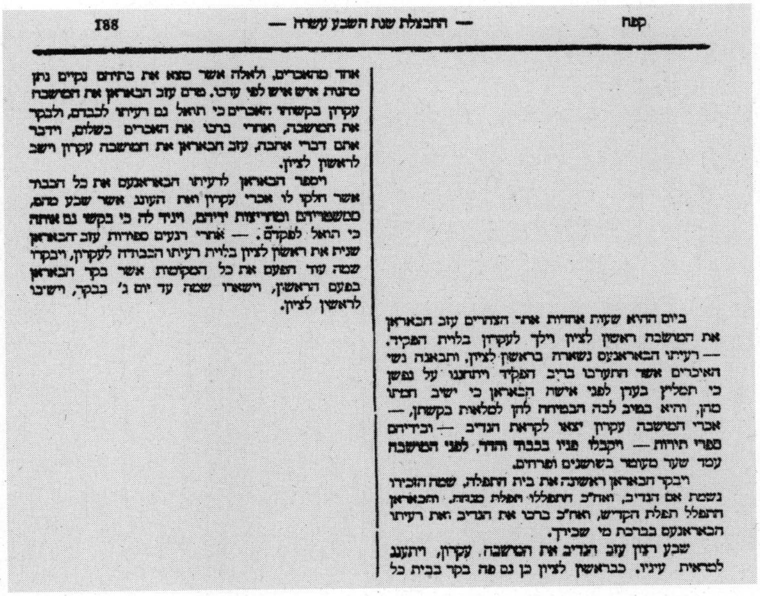

קפח — החבצלת שנת השבע עשרה — 188

ביום ההוא שעות אחדות אחרי הצהרים עזב הבאראן את המושבה ראשון לציון וילך לעקרון בלוית הפקיד. — רעיתו הבאראנעס נשארה בראשון לציון, ותבאנה נשי האיכרים אשר התעדנו בריב הפקיד ויתחננו על נפשן כי תמליץ בעדן לפני אישה הבאראן כי ישיב חמתו מהן, והיא בטוב לבה הבטיחה להן למלאות בקשתן. — אכרי המושבה עקרון יצאו לקראת הנדיב — ובידיהם ספרי תורות — ויקבלו פניו בכבוד והדר, לפני המושבה עמד שער מעוטר בשושנים ופרחים.

ויבקר הבאראן ראשונה את בית התפלה, שמה הזכירו נשמת אם הנדיב, ואח"כ התפללו תפלת מנחה. הבאראן התפלל תפלת הקדיש, ואח"כ ברכו את הנדיב ואת רעיתו הבאראנעס בברכת מי שבירך.

שבע רצון עזב הנדיב את המושבה עקרון, ויתענג למראית עיניו. כבראשון לציון כן גם פה בקר בבית כל אחד מהאכרים, ולאלה אשר מצא את בתיהם נקיים נתן מתנות איש איש לפי ערכו. טרם עזב הבאראן את המושבה עקרון בקשוהו האכרים כי תאל גם רעיתו לבקרם, ולבקר את המושבה, ואחרי ברכו את האכרים בשלום, וידבר אתם דברי אהבה, עזב הבאראן את המושבה עקרון וישב לראשון לציון.

ויספר הבאראן לרעיתו הבאראנעס את כל הכבוד אשר חלקו לו אכרי עקרון ואת העונג אשר שבע מהם, ממשטריהם ומחריצות ידיהם, ויגד לה כי בקשו גם אותה כי תואל לפקדם. — אחרי רגעים ספורות עזב הבאראן שנית את ראשון לציון בלוית רעיתו הכבודה לעקרון, ויבקרו שמה עוד הפעם את כל המקומות אשר בקר הבאראן בפעם הראשון, וישארו שמה עד יום ג' בבקר, וישובו לראשון לציון.

Read all about it! The Baron's visit to Ekron was reported in *Chavazelet.*

vide him with an honor guard suitable for a head of state. The children had been scrubbed clean and were holding flowers, standing in rows facing each other on both sides of the street.

Before Rothschild's entourage reached the "gate of honor," he descended from his carriage and kissed the Torah scroll clutched by one of the farmers. Then he made his way to the synagogue. In the past year, his beloved mother, Batya Rothschild, had passed away. The rabbi said a special memorial prayer for her, followed by Rothschild's recitation of the *Kaddish.*

He then ventured out to the fields and saw them covered with wheat stalks, which gave him tremendous joy. Then he returned to the center of the settlement and "held court" in the administration building, where he listened to the requests of each farmer.

Typical of his patronizing style, the Baron conducted some house inspections to gauge how clean the Russian Jews kept their homes and the farms immediately adjoining them. He found three of them particularly spotless and, like a father, gave the winners a prize. The satisfied Benefactor then "opened his purse" and gave the settlers of Ekron an additional 25,000 francs ($100,000 in today's U.S. currency) for the purchase of additional farm equipment.

His better half. Baroness Adelaide Rothschild was more religiously observant than her husband. It was on her account that the kitchens on the Baron's private yachts were kosher.

Before the Baron departed, the Ekron farmers begged him to come back with his wife. When he returned to Rishon Le-Ẓion, he told his wife about the beautiful reception he'd received in Ekron, his fond impressions, and how much the settlers wanted her to pay them a visit. It took only a few minutes to convince the Baroness, so Rothschild and his wife immediately traveled back to Ekron.[247]

When they arrived at nightfall, the Ekronians were waiting for them with raised torches that lit up the night sky. *Ha-Maggid*[248] reported that the Baron noticed a great difference between Ekron and Rishon Le-Ẓion – especially when it came to the settlers' attitudes. The Ekron settlers were true farmers who loved hard work, yielding excellent results – and they were not in the habit of complaining.

The Baron had reserved a special gift for them, as reported in *Ha-Maggid*:

> The noble Benefactor and his wife were quite pleased with what they saw in Ekron … a community whose people are very industrious and who are genuinely religious Jews who observe *halakhah* with all its stringencies, and this in particular is the great desire of the Baron, and it is what gave him some consolation over the great anguish he experienced in Rishon Le-Ẓion.
>
> He made the following declaration to the people of Ekron: "My dear children, I had a lovely gift in mind for the people of Rishon Le-Ẓion, but in my eyes they do not deserve it. I had

in mind to name that moshavah after my mother, Batya, may her soul rest in Eden, who passed away the last year. But I have changed my mind, because that settlement, whose residents bear much guilt on their shoulders, does not deserve to be named after her.

Therefore, I am bequeathing the name to you, and from now on your community will no longer be called Ekron but Mazkeret Batya."[249]

The Baron left Mazkeret Batya with warm feelings for the colony that now carried his mother's name.[250]

Rothschild's mother and Mazkeret Batya's namesake. Betty (Batya) von Rothschild absorbed the religious atmosphere of her grandparents' home in the Jewish ghetto of Frankfurt. She received both a Jewish education and a secular one. At 19 she married her uncle James de Rothschild and moved to Paris. For the rest of her life, Batya struggled to maintain the religious legacy she brought with her from Frankfurt while adapting to modern Paris. To promote her husband's career, she maintained one of the most elegant salons in the city. Her guests included politicians, painters, artists, musicians, even royalty. To accommodate them, she reluctantly compromised *kashrut*. However, she steadfastly refused to travel or write on the Sabbath and insisted that the family celebrate the Jewish holidays together. She warned her three children against intermarrying and provided them with tutors in Judaism. A devoted philanthropist, Batya supported hospitals, schools, orphanages, hospices, and individuals in need.

The Metamorphosis of Edmond de Rothschild

"A contradiction developed in the man. Chaim Weizmann noticed it the first time he met him. 'Everything about him was in exquisite taste – his clothes, his home – or rather his homes, his furniture, his paintings.… And yet there he was – this aloof immaculate dandy – hip deep in the economics of irrigation, manure and soil rehabilitation.'"[250A]

Chapter 19
Hurricane Alphonse

The Baron was at a crossroads. Although the recent insurrection in Rishon Le-Ẓion was quelled, to Rothschild's way of thinking it was the colonists and not his administrators who were at fault. The Baron trusted and believed in his educated, cultured lieutenants. The unpolished and impoverished "Russians," insubordinate and unreasonable, were taking advantage of his leniency and largesse. He decided that drastic measures had to be taken in order to prevent rebellions from erupting again.

His first step, while still in Palestine, had been to expel the instigators from the colony. Second, he prohibited the colonists from organizing. Third, he created a strong, centralized authority. His orders from Paris would travel down efficiently through the chain of command to his colonies. The implications were far-reaching – he would have to expand his administration in Palestine and give it even greater powers. The Baron, who sincerely wanted to help the colonists, was in effect turning them into subjects and himself into a benevolent dictator.

Rothschild began a search for three men to fill senior executive positions in his administration. One of the résumés he received caught his attention. The man's experience and knowledge seemed quite impressive. He spoke French, Arabic, Turkish, and German, all languages important for dealing with the major players in Palestine. In addition, with his German he could probably communicate with the Yiddish-speaking Russian Jews. His work experience was extensive, as he had represented various French organizations in Alexandria as well as in Constantinople and Smyrna.

Since the Baron was considering him for a supervisory post, logic would have dictated that he ascertain not only whether this man could get the job done, but also how well he got along with people and could win their cooperation. Perhaps the Baron's negative experience in Rishon Le-Ẓion led him to believe that the Russian Jews needed someone who could be tough with them.

It would have made sense for the applicant to have some sort of Jewish education and warm sentiments regarding the Land of Israel and the Jewish effort to settle it. The irony of it all was that Alphonse Bloch, an unmarried businessman from Alsace, was unable to read a word of Hebrew, and he had no interest whatsoever in the Yishuv enterprise.He was just looking for a job.[252]

In 1887, Rothschild appointed Bloch as chief colony administrator for the district of Yehudah (Judah), comprising the settlements around Jaffa, including Rishon Le-Ẓion and Petach Tikva. He was also given jurisdiction over Ekron/Mazkeret Batya.[253]

The singular ability of Alphonse Bloch (also known as Adolph) to brutally quell insurrections and suppress the freedom of his opponents became known with alarming speed. He probably never would have asked Dr. Yisrael Klausner to serve as a character reference. In his work *From Katowice to Basel,* the professor minced no words about the colonists' new boss:

Autocrat. "These are my colonies and I shall do what I like with them."[251]

> He was a tough, brazen man – a man of limited education, contentious, and a liar. Nevertheless, he had tremendous energy. He knew how to instill fear in the hearts of those who were under his authority. He looked at the Russian Jews condescendingly, the farmers of the moshavot in particular. He knew how to find favor with the authorities and how to manipulate [his immediate superior] Elie Scheid, who had a soft, sensitive personality.[254]

Ensconced in Rishon Le-Ẓion, Bloch began to impose his authority. A contemporary writer compared Bloch's entrance on the scene to that of a hurricane.[255] He completed the job the Baron had started, quelling the rebellion by "purging and crushing without mercy … justice and truth and kindred values were immaterial in his eyes."[256]

Under his reign, the farmers' status as proud pioneers changed to that of common laborers receiving daily wages. They were made to sign an agreement in which they formally accepted this new arrangement upon themselves.[257]

Bloch then heaved his authority on Be'er Tuvia, the southernmost settlement of that period, founded by a number of families from Bessarabia.[258] The nucleus of the new settlement consisted of eighteen hapless families who had waited several months in Jaffa for the Rothschild administration to purchase land for them.

He demanded that they sign an agreement similar to the one signed in Rishon Le-Ẓion: they were forced to acknowledge that they had no rights to the land, or any rights to organize, and they had to accept their status as day laborers. The families, who had been pining to settle down, were outraged. When they refused to sign, Bloch cut off their income subsidies and leased their lands to Arab tenants.[259] Most of the immigrants, people of means who had left Europe to build their lives and actualize their dreams, were forced to scatter across the country. They never got a chance to live in their new homes.[260]

Next, Bloch set his sights on Mazkeret Batya.

He had in mind a revolutionary proposal that he had concocted almost as soon as he settled into his new post in Palestine. His idea was that there should be a three-year trial period, during which the administration would gauge whether the farmers had created a viable, self-sufficient enterprise worthy of the Baron's continued support.

The plan was that over the three-year period the farmers were to cultivate their lands according to the directives of the administration, growing and planting only the crops the administrators chose. Bloch's incentive for the settlers to go along with this was that they would receive a guaranteed income, with all their necessities taken care of by the Baron's administrators. Until then, the farmers had lived off their own incomes in addition to some subsidies they received from the administration. They proudly viewed themselves as independent farmers.

Bloch urged the residents of Mazkeret Batya to sign a document declaring that all their possessions belonged to the Baron, and that their status was that of hired laborers who lived on the Baron's lands and were subservient to the authority of his administrators. To the farmers, it seemed that Bloch was taking them back to the Middle Ages and converting them into serfs!

They refused to sign the contract. It was a ruse, they believed, aimed at absolving the Alliance Israélite Universelle of all its previous commitments to them, agreements that had been signed even before they had left Pavlovka for Palestine. Dr. Chaim Chissin recounts:

> The order to sign onto the "clauses" shocked the people of Ekron and they perceived it as an intolerable injustice. In principle, they didn't accept the idea that the Baron had a right to rule over them without limitations. Because it wasn't they who had turned to him with a request to help them settle the land but [on the contrary] it was [his agents] who approached them to emigrate with a promise of providing them [with] a farm and all it entails....
>
> They had trusted the Baron's representatives and left their property and cattle behind in Russia. Now suddenly, after six years of toil, they were instructed to view themselves as hired laborers....[261]

Bloch was taken aback by the farmers' fierce resistance to his plan. Instead of considering their views, he decided to take revenge.

The people of Mazkeret Batya had never shown any signs of rebelliousness against the administrators the way the people of Rishon Le-Ẓion had, so there was no excuse to come down hard on them the way he had with their sister colony. Instead, he decided to fight a war of attrition through faultfinding and by collecting a dossier of petty grievances against them. At the same time, he would turn a blind eye to the farmers' continual requests for money or additional flour rations.

As Passover approached, the farmers found themselves running out of basic supplies. Another three months would go by before they could begin harvesting their crops. They turned to Bloch for assistance. He responded with a flat "no." When they circumvented him by going to Shmuel Hirsch, Bloch added another point of demerit against them. And he was determined to find more.

After some investigation, Bloch discovered that the Ekron farmers were selling some of their wheat off the books, and taking odd jobs (as wagon drivers, for example) – income they neglected to report. Bloch couldn't understand: why would these people need to make money on the side when they were harvesting so much wheat every year? It was obvious to him that they really were, after all, just a bunch of devious *schnorrers* taking advantage of the Baron's generosity.

The French administrator, making a decent salary and living in relatively high style, failed to comprehend the plight of these farmers. Their crops were often meager, never exceeding more than fifty-sixty kilograms (123 pounds) of seed per dunam. So many weeds were interspersed with the stalks of wheat that sorting out the seeds took all the members of each family the entire winter. The prices the farmers received for their crops were low, and they had to employ Arab tenants as additional farm hands, whom they paid with part of the harvest. Finally, the Ottoman tax collectors skimmed off another 10% from their income.[262]

The settlers were constantly complaining that they didn't have enough, while the goal of the administrators, working on behalf of the Baron, was to lead the farmers to self-sufficiency, so they would no longer need their patron's support. Bloch's ardent desire to gain control of their income (and their lives) was not merely a matter of principle. He knew that the Sabbatical year (known in Hebrew as Shemittah) was rapidly approaching. And these settlers, pious fanatics that they were, likely would sit on their hands for an entire year in keeping with the biblical mandate. It was up to him, he decided, to prevent this great damage to the Baron's enterprise.

Chapter 20

Shemittah Enters the Modern Age

For six years you may sow your land and gather in its harvest. *And on the seventh year you shall cease your labors and leave it fallow…* (Exodus 23:10-11)

God spoke to Moses on Mount Sinai, saying, "Speak to the Children of Israel and say to them: When you come into the land that I give you, the land shall observe a Sabbath rest for God. For six years, you may sow your field, and for six years, you may prune your vineyard; and you may gather in its crop. *But the seventh year shall be a complete rest for the land, a Sabbath for God; you shall not sow your field, and you shall not prune your vineyard. You shall not reap the aftergrowth of your harvest, and you shall not pick the grapes you had set aside for yourself; it shall be a year of rest for the land.* The Sabbath produce of the land shall be yours to eat – for you, for your servant, and for your maidservant; and for your laborer and for the resident who dwells with you. And for your animal and for the beast in your land, all its crops shall be for consumption." (Leviticus 25:1-7)

Shemittah, the commandment to leave the land fallow every seventh year, is the centerpiece of the Jewish agricultural laws that are tied to the Land of Israel. The underlying message of the commandment is that the land belongs to God, and that He entrusts its care to the Jews on condition that they follow His Torah. No commandment demonstrates this point more clearly than Shemittah. For nearly 2,000 years of exile, Shemittah was a dormant issue, a body of laws with no practical application. With the return of Jewish farmers to Israel, the Sabbath of the land, the Shemittah year, could once again be observed.

The farmers of Ekron/Mazkeret Batya underwent many ordeals, but none would require more determination and courage than Shemittah. Perhaps Providence had sent them the previous trials as a preparation for the most difficult test they were about to face.

A Change of Heart

Initially, Baron Edmond de Rothschild seemed to support the strict observance of Shemittah. During his visit to Palestine in April and May of 1888, he paid a visit to Rabbi Shmuel Salant, chief rabbi of the Ashkenazic community in

Jerusalem. Among the issues they discussed was the practical observance of Torah law in the Baron's agricultural settlements. Rabbi Salant later reported on his meeting with the Baron:

From Brisk to Jerusalem. Rabbi Yehoshua Leib Diskin. He and Rabbi Yiẓchak Elchanan Spektor were study partners as boys.

> In the midst of this conversation I told the Baron that there are many more laws in the Torah that need to be guarded and observed, such as, ... *terumot* and tithes, and the laws of the Shemittah year. He answered me that he had issued a directive that the colonists must observe all the laws of the Torah and the miẓvot according to the guidelines of the Jerusalem Rabbinate.[263]

By October, however, the Baron apparently changed his mind about Shemittah, and he wanted to know whether Rabbi Salant was ready to change his. As one of his biographers put it, "Edmond thought that idleness for so long a period would ruin most of his young settlements."[264] He sent three of his administrators – Ossowetzky, Bloch, and Vermesser – to ask Rabbi Salant if there was any halakhic solution that would allow working the fields in the Sabbatical year.[265] When Rabbi Salant replied in the negative, they went to the influential sage Rabbi Yehoshua Leib Diskin and were again disappointed.[266] The officials reported to their superiors in Paris that there was no *heter* to be found in Palestine.

Leader of his generation. Rabbi Yiẓchak Elchanan Spektor of Kovno (Kaunas, Lithuania)

The Baron then turned to Ẓaddok Kahn, the chief rabbi of Paris, to find a halakhic solution. Rabbi Kahn turned to one of the leading rabbis of that era, Rabbi Yiẓchak Elchanan Spektor of Kovno, Lithuania. Rabbi Spektor researched the issue and came to the tentative conclusion that the sale of the land to non-Jews would alleviate some of the Shemittah restrictions on the farmers. But he was hesitant to be the sole authority to issue a definitive ruling.

Rabbi Shmuel Mohilever (after some goading from the head of the Vilna branch of Chovevei Ẓion) took a step to encourage Rabbi Spektor. He went to Warsaw and met with two other great rabbinic authorities, Rabbi Yehoshua Trunk of Kutno (the author of *Yeshuot Malko*) and Rabbi Shmuel Zanvil Klapfish, the chief judge of the rabbinical court of Warsaw, to deliberate on finding a halakhic leniency to work the fields during Shemittah.[267] They soon found themselves in disagreement: To what extent did selling the land to gentiles release the land and its produce from the Shemittah laws? Rabbi Trunk believed that the sanctity of the land was inviolate – non-Jewish ownership would remove the sanctity of Shemittah only from its *fruits,* thereby allowing them to be exported.[268] The other rabbis said that selling the land to gentiles would remove the restrictions of Shemittah even from the *land,* thereby permitting Jews to work it. They reached an uneasy compromise – land sold to gentiles could be worked by Jews, but only agricultural labors that were forbidden during Shemittah rabbinically (as opposed to those prohibited by the Torah) could be performed.

Rabbi Yehoshua Trunk of Kutno

Rabbi Shmuel Zanvil Klapfish of Warsaw

Like any compromise, the wording was vague enough to include the opinions of all the rabbis. Meant to help the farmers, this ambiguity would only make things more difficult for them later on.

A few days later, Rabbi Spektor issued his historic decision, which was more restrictive than the ruling made by his colleagues. He, too, allowed selling the land to gentiles, but he permitted only *non-Jewish* laborers to perform labors *rabbinically* prohibited to Jews during Shemittah.[269] This ruling became known as the *Heter Mechirah.*[270] Unfortunately, it also lacked definitiveness and only added to the farmers' confusion.[271]

Nevertheless, Baron Rothschild felt that he finally got what he was seeking. Anxious to maintain the productivity of his nascent farms, he embraced Rabbi Spektor's ruling.

Some historians[272] conjecture that Rothschild had no change of heart at all, that there had been a simple misunderstanding. When the Baron visited Rabbi Salant in Jerusalem, the two men spoke via an interpreter: the rabbi spoke in Yiddish, which was translated into French for the Baron. It is possible that "something got lost in the translation" as the Baron, overwhelmed by the experience, politely nodded without grasping the full implications of the rabbi's words.

To the people of the Old Yishuv, it was unthinkable that the great and magnanimous Baron could have initiated such a turnabout. It was rumored that he had been misled by his scheming anti-religious administrators, who had persuaded him to try to find a legal loophole in order to coerce the religious farmers into working throughout the Shemittah year.[273]

Whatever his motive, the Baron became a staunch advocate of his farmers' working during Shemittah, convinced that not doing so would force him to establish an expansive welfare system in which the settlements would depend entirely on his largesse.

He initially decreed that all farmers in his colonies must rely on the *Heter Mechirah* and work during Shemittah.[274] His stand on the issue led to his vilification in the Jewish press throughout Europe, and his image was greatly tarnished. He had been perceived as a benign and supportive grandfather but was now seen as a ruthless tyrant. To be sure, however, there were those who hailed him as a hero, unwilling to yield to the pressures of perceived religious extremism.

In the Eye of the Storm

Shemittah was not merely a local matter affecting the farmers. The issues surrounding its observance in 1888-1889[275] developed into a controversy that engulfed the entire Jewish world and galvanized many Orthodox European Jews against the *aliyah* movement.[276] They reasoned that since the source of the pressure brought to bear on Rabbi Spektor and other rabbis ultimately derived from the non-Orthodox *maskilim* active in the Chovevei Ẓion movement, the spiritual harm that would inevitably result from that partnership would outweigh the spiritual benefits of living in the Holy Land.[277] The poor farmers of Mazkeret Batya, whose simple dream was to live in the Land of Israel and observe the Torah laws pertaining to the land, were swept into the maelstrom of this struggle. To some extent, the previous Shemittah years of 1874-1875 and 1881-1882 had set the stage for a full-blown battle.

Confusing Precedents

As noted earlier, the French Jewish relief organization Alliance Israélite Universelle established the Mikveh Israel school, the first modern Jewish agricultural school in Palestine. Founded in 1870, the school maintained a synagogue on its premises and believed in promoting Jewish identity. However, it was not focused on observing Jewish law in accordance with traditional Orthodox standards. In the Shemittah year of 1874, Rabbi Eliyahu Guttmacher,[278] Talmudic scholar, mystic, and an early advocate of Jewish settlement in Palestine, complained about the lack of observance of Shemittah in the fields and vineyards of "the Parisian organization." He insisted that Shemittah be observed and warned of the dire consequences of ignoring God's command.[279]

Torah scholar and mystic. Rabbi Eliyahu Guttmacher

But Mikveh Israel was a school, not a settlement, and the questions of what to do about Shemittah as a matter of overall policy concerning Jewish farms were still only theoretical. All that changed, however, with the founding of Petach Tikva in 1878.

Founded by Orthodox Jews from the Old Yishuv, Petach Tikva served as the first test case of Shemittah observance in 1882.[280] A year earlier, Rabbi Moshe Nechemiah Kahanov of Jerusalem had published a practical guide to Shemittah – *Kuntres Sh'nat ha-Sheva* (A Compendium for the Seventh Year).[281] He wrote:

> In our days, many Jews have been privileged to own property in the Holy Land. They have had the merit to work it and to fulfill the special commandments connected to the land. How fortunate are they! And now that the Sabbatical year is approaching, they must be proficient regarding its laws.

Many of these "fortunate ones" were the settlers of Petach Tikva. Yet Rabbi Kahanov, however, was overly optimistic. As it happened, Petach Tikva was located near a malarial swamp close to the source of the Yarkon River. The early settlers suffered so many casualties related to malaria that most of them had to abandon the settlement entirely.[282]

A few diehards persevered and indeed observed the Shemittah laws despite the difficult living conditions.[283] So few

The mother of them all. Chovevei Ẓion Street, Petach Tikva, circa 1900. The colony was known as the "mother of the moshavot."

stayed put in Petach Tikva that there was not much more to lose by being strict about it.[284] They were backed by Rabbi Shmuel Salant, who ruled that no leniencies should be sought.[285] The first real battle over Shemittah was thus pre-empted by the battle with malaria, and malaria won.

The Fateful Shemittah of 1888-1889

Because settlement had taken place in the interim, the upcoming Shemittah of 1888-1889 sparked a passionate debate that would spread throughout the Jewish world. Rabbi Salant again ruled that Shemittah should be observed, and wrote, "... the Jewish farmers already observed Shemittah in 1881-1882 in Petach Tikva, and they did not seek out legal devices to be exempt from it. There is no limit to what God can do to bring about salvation."[286]

Proponents of the *Heter Mechirah* maintained that the chief cause of Petach Tikva's demise was Shemittah, not malaria.[287] Ironically, Eliezer Ben-Yehuda, the editor of the *Ha-Ẓvi* newspaper, had *supported* those who wished to observe Shemittah in 1882, though he was a secular Jew. He believed his support for a religious commandment might influence the ultra-Orthodox community to go along with his views of nationalism.[288] In the

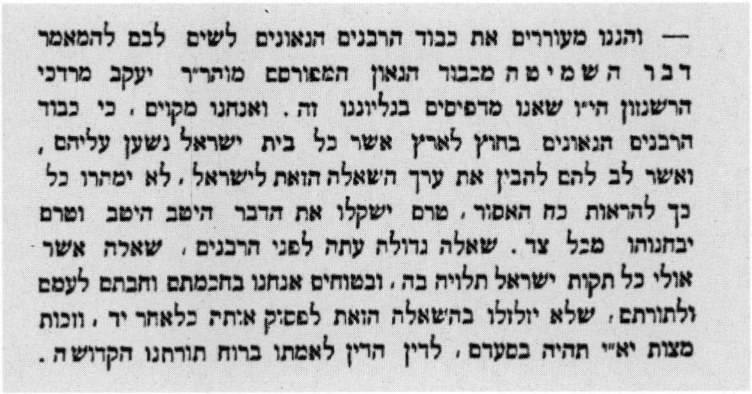

— והננו מעוררים את כבוד הרבנים הגאונים לשים לבם להמאמר
דבר השמיטה מכבוד הגאון המפורסם מוהר״ר יעקב מרדכי
הרשנזון הי״ו שאנו מדפיסים בגליוננו זה. ואנחנו מקוים, כי כבוד
הרבנים הגאונים בחוץ לארץ אשר כל בית ישראל נשען עליהם,
ואשר לב להם להבין את ערך השאלה הזאת לישראל, לא ימהרו כל
כך להראות כח האסור, טרם ישקלו את הדבר היטב וטרם
יבחנוהו מכל צד. שאלה גדולה עתה לפני הרבנים, שאלה אשר
אולי כל תקות ישראל תלויה בה, ובטוחים אנחנו בחכמתם וחבתם לעמם
ולתורתם, שלא יזלזלו בהשאלה הזאת לפסוק אותה כלאחר יד, וזכות
מצות יא״י תהיה בסעדם, לדין הדין לאמתו ברוח תורתנו הקדושה.

A warning. "Weigh the matter very carefully ... because the entire hope of Israel depends upon it ..." – a not-so-subtle hint from Eliezer Ben-Yehuda to the Jerusalem Rabbinate that it should follow the lead of the Diaspora rabbis and allow the farmers to work the fields during Shemittah through use of the *Heter Mechirah*.

Shemittah of 1889, however, he exhorted his readers to support the *Heter Mechirah*.

When it became clear to him that the Jerusalem Rabbinate would pay him no heed, Ben-Yehuda declared Rabbi Salant the chief "enemy of the New Yishuv."[289] In response, the editor of the leading pro-Old Yishuv newspaper accused Ben-Yehuda of being a phony.[290] Acrimonious accusations and counteraccusations swirled throughout Palestine and the Diaspora, and the eyes of the world came to rest on little Mazkeret Batya.

"When in Rome, do as the Romans." Eliezer Ben-Yehuda, an atheist, "... endeavored to maintain the outward appearance of a member of the Jewish community of Jerusalem. He grew his beard, wore long garments, and always walked through the city streets wrapped in his *tallit*" (Ehud Luz, *Parallels Meet*, p. 34). All that ceased when the Jerusalem Rabbinate came out against the *Heter Mechirah*.

Chapter 21 *Crossing the Rubicon*

Autumn 1888. Rosh Hashanah was just around the corner. With the rainy season rapidly approaching, it would soon be time to begin the new cycle of planting the winter crop. The farmers prayed that the upcoming year would be better than the last. The harvest of the past summer had been dismal, reflecting the low amount of rainfall. Adding to these worries, a worldwide influenza epidemic had reached the Holy Land and begun to claim casualties. The people of Mazkeret Batya needed all the help they could get.

They were trapped in the crosshairs of history. The controversy over Rabbi Spektor's *Heter Mechirah* swirled around them – whether or not to circumvent Shemittah was swiftly becoming a practical issue.

Back in Paris, the Baron's men nervously waited to see whether the settlers would work on Shemittah or not. The Baron's close associate Michael Erlanger wrote to Dr. Leon Pinsker, the secular leader of the Chovevei Ẓion movement in Russia:

> I don't know how the colonists will act regarding Shemittah. Six or eight months ago, we [Erlanger and Rabbi Ẓaddok Kahn] wrote to Rabbi Yiẓchak Elchanan Spektor and Rabbi Shmuel Mohilever. After serious deliberation, they ruled that working the soil was permissible if the land didn't belong to Jews. Those [colonists] who want to work may proceed in good conscience. If people still don't want to work, they are free to cease [working], but they will not receive a special subsidy in order to observe Shemittah. The ruling of the rabbis has been publicized and posted in the colonies.[291]

Erlanger gave the impression that a rabbinic *carte blanche* had been given to continue working the fields as in any other year, a misrepresentation of Rabbi Spektor's ruling, which permitted only certain labors by non-Jews. Whether this was deliberate or out of ignorance, or if it was the official policy of the Baron or his own initiative, is difficult to discern.

What was clear to the farmers of Mazkeret Batya was that the Baron would not come to their aid if they chose to observe Shemittah. They knew that to secularists, the Sabbatical year was irrelevant. To Eliezer Ben-Yehuda, Rabbi Salant and his colleagues represented the last obstacle to be removed before the Jewish people could finally be liberated from centuries of superstition and exile. Irreligious settler Dr. Chaim Chissin viewed Shemittah as just another impediment religion imposed on the farmer who wanted to live a "normal" life.[292]

Like farmers all over Palestine who were supported by Baron Rothschild, they debated with one another, sometimes furiously, about which course of action to take. Should they follow the Jerusalem rabbinic authorities who banned any type of work during Shemittah (except for protecting the trees and grapevines from dying)? Or should they rely on Rabbi Yiẓchak Elchanan Spektor's ruling that permitted work on lands sold to non-Jews?[293]

Some farmers pointed to the fact that the land needed a rest in any case. The heated response was that when fields are very large, a farmer can afford to leave a third of them fallow each year, but here in Palestine, farmers have only small plots of land and must sow their entire fields to grow enough crops.

Mazkeret Batya may have looked to other settlers who were meticulous in their observance of Jewish law, such as in Yesud Ha-Ma'alah (in the Hula Valley, to the north) and in Petach Tikva, to see how they were coping with the dilemma.

Unsung hero. David Eisenberg, a founder of Yesud Ha-Ma'alah

Yehoshua Stampfer, one of the strictly Orthodox founders of Petach Tikva, shared how some of his colleagues prepared for the upcoming Shemittah year in a letter he wrote to *Ha-Ẓvi* in January of 1888:

> … In order not to sit [during the Shemittah year] with our hands folded, we are planting many grapevines and fig and date trees this year, for we have explicitly heard from the great *gaon* Naftali Hertz Halevi,[294] the rabbi and *av beit din* of Jaffa, that work done to keep the trees alive is permissible.
>
> Also, many of us have signed contracts with the owners of the surrounding [Arab] villages to allow us to plow their fields for the purpose of growing summer crops, so we will be free to leave our fields fallow in the upcoming season. This is also completely permissible, as the *fellahin* tell us: Only your land is obligated to rest – not you and your animals!

Sole brother. Yehoshua Stampfer made *aliyah* by walking all the way from Hungary to Jerusalem.

> They agree and even praise us for leaving our lands fallow, saying that giving the land of Ummlebis[295] a rest is very necessary, because it has been depleted on account of all the work that has been done with it.
>
> And as far as the *heter* is concerned, I am not ashamed to say that if I were one of those counted amongst the rabbinic decisors of Israel, I would be stringent with regard to the four labors of sowing, harvesting, harvesting grapes, and pruning,[296] which the Torah explicitly prohibits.... [297]

As it turned out, about half the farmers of Petach Tikva did not rely at all on the *Heter Mechirah,* even after receiving a letter from Rabbi Mohilever telling them that the *heter* he'd issued (the *heter* of the three rabbis) permitted them to work.[298] Another twenty-one farmers, who accepted the *heter* of Rabbi Spektor in principle, did not see the prospect of hiring Arabs as economically viable, and they too ceased from work. The rest relied on the *heter.*[299]

The pioneers of Petach Tikva were attacked by the *maskilim* on the pages of *Ha-Meliẓ* and were accused of turning into lazy *schnorrers.* Surprisingly, the secular, Menachem Ussishkin[300] came to their defense and asserted that their motives were purely religious and deserved respect. "They are industrious people who received only a pittance in aid from Chovevei Ẓion and from the Baron – and only for public services."[301]

Grape harvest in Rishon Le-Ẓion, 1911. The Shemittah laws did not have an impact on the vineyards as they did on the field crops (see next page).

Many of the religious farmers of Zikhron Yaakov and Nes Ẓiona (Nachalat Reuven) chose to rely on the *Heter Mechirah* and to work the fields. In Rishon Le-Ẓion, a number of farmers

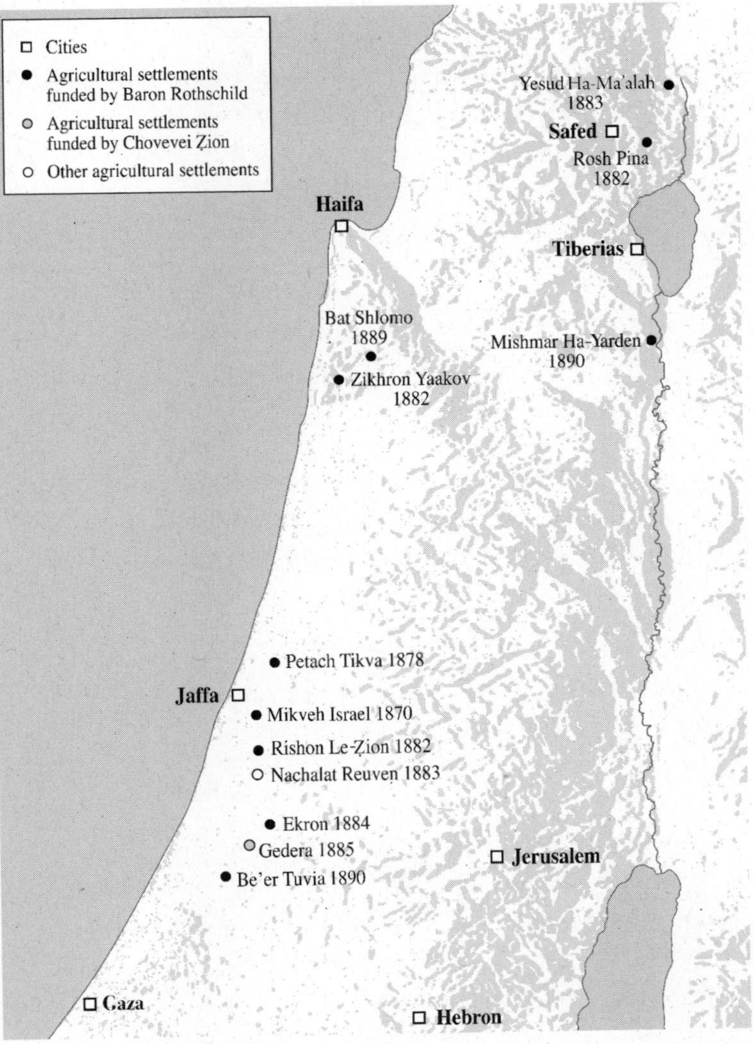

The first twelve. Jewish settlements in Palestine during the Shemittah of 5649 (1889-1890)

were already engaged in grape and wine production and were allowed to tend to the vines in order to keep them alive, even according to the strict rabbinical opinion.[302]

The great surprise was Gedera, the only settlement fully funded by Chovevei Ẓion and the only one manned by non-Orthodox Jews. Ironically, these farmers decided *not* to work the fields during Shemittah. They had been taught by their patron and spiritual mentor, Rabbi Yechiel Michel Pines. He, in turn, had been influenced by his mentor, Rabbi Mordechai Gimpel Yaffe, an "old style" Orthodox rabbi. Pines had developed relationships with the former university students (some of whom were *maskilim* who had been raised in religious homes) and members of the Russian revolutionary movements who became the original settlers of Gedera. Their determination did not last, however. When Leon Pinsker found out about what was going on in Gedera, the mild-mannered gentleman became uncharacteristically enraged, along with other secular leaders. Hounded by the non-religious leadership of Chovevei Ẓion, the Gedera farmers returned to work in the middle of the Shemittah year.[303]

Chaim Chissin contrasted the farmers in Gedera with those of Mazkeret Batya, who had earned his respect:

> … Ekron was different. [Its farmers] were very conscientious about their religious beliefs and from the very start they had to juggle between their physical survival and the demands of their faith.[304]

But even for the fervently religious pioneers of Ekron/Mazkeret Batya, the choice was not clear-cut. Rabbi Shmuel Mohilever was the very man who had initiated the idea of the Mazkeret Batya settlement and had obtained the Baron's funding for it, and he concurred with Rabbi Spektor's ruling permitting work during Shemittah. The pioneers held him in great esteem, as they did Rabbi Spektor, the Lithuanian Torah giant who lived not far away from where they had once resided.

But they had also become very attached to the rabbis of the Old Yishuv who lived in Jerusalem. They were attracted to their piety, learning, and way of thinking. Unlike most of the pioneers of the First Aliyah, the farmers from Pavlovka were hybrids. On the one hand, they were involved in agriculture and development of the Land of Israel. On the other hand, they did not share the nationalistic agenda of the Chovevei Ẓion movement and were not attracted to *Haskalah* thought. They weren't interested in creating a new Jewish society: they were content to recreate the Lithuanian shtetl they had left behind, albeit in the Holy Land, with all its religious requirements.

These settlers pondered the prospect of angering Baron Rothschild, the man who had given them the financial wherewithal to start their new life in the Holy Land. Moreover, Shemittah without the Baron's safety net would be a fearsome endeavor, notwithstanding the Torah's assurance of God's blessing. They had large families to feed and were just barely getting by, even with the added financial support of the Baron.

They also remembered the contract they had signed with Yechiel Brill before they left Pavlovka. Paragraph 11 stated:

> When we settle on the homestead that will be given to us, the officials of the Alliance who are in Mikveh Israel may intervene in our personal affairs only when it comes to matters between man and his fellow man. In matters between man and God, they have no right to intervene and dictate, "This you may do, and this you may not do." We will abide only by the directives of those who are halakhic authorities – and through that we will be successful.

"…And through that we will be successful." Those words still rang true for them. The religious farmer, perhaps more than any other professional, is a partner with God. And his religious freedom is a matter of principle that cannot be compromised. Furthermore, the Jerusalem Rabbinate's declaration was quite clear, as opposed to the ambiguous language of the *heter.*

The farmers of Mazkeret Batya reached their decision just a few days before Rosh Hashanah: they would keep Shemittah as determined by the Jerusalem Rabbinate.[305] The decision was not unanimous, however. Two of the settlers decided they would rely on the *heter* and work that year.[306] The majority understood that it had to establish a united front in order to stand firm against the inevitable pressure it would face. Confronting the two dissenting farmers, the others threatened them with excommunication if they refused to fall in line.[307] The threat worked.

Chapter 22 *The Shemittah Controversy Erupts*

Alphonse Bloch, the Baron's onsite administrator, had lost his first skirmish with the Mazkeret Batya farmers, but he was by no means finished. The new Jewish year had started, and the first battle in the Shemittah war was imminent. Refreshed and energized after spending the Sukkot holiday in Beirut,[308] Bloch was ready to make the first move.

> Knowing the mindset of the people of Ekron and anticipating that he would have to take the necessary means to crush their resistance, Bloch decided to wage a war of attrition. It was the month of September, and the threshing was about to be concluded. Instead of each family keeping the harvest for itself, Bloch wanted to expropriate all the grain from the settlers and put it in the hands of the administration. His intention was to have the power to starve them into submission.[309]

On Friday, September 28, shortly before sunset, the Mazkeret Batya farmers, dressed in their Sabbath finery, were preparing to leave their homes for the synagogue services where they would welcome the Sabbath Queen. The High Holy Days and the Sukkot festival were over. It was *Shabbat Bereishit*, the Sabbath when the annual cycle of reading the Torah begins anew. Instead of welcoming the Queen, they were shocked by the sudden appearance of Alphonse Bloch.

Bloch had the settlers summoned, one by one, male and female, to appear before him.[310] The *Chavaẓelet* newspaper sneered at this behavior, considering it yet another manifestation of his condescending arrogance:

> When it comes to officers and servants, officials and their deputies, and assistants to the assistants, these jobs were all created only to serve the head administrator. Ekron, with its eighteen families, has nineteen officials. Of course, this system is based on sound economics!
>
> The colonists were summoned. When the first one appeared, he asked [Bloch] in all sincerity, "What is your desire, Mr. Manager, sir?"
>
> Bloch: "Bring all your wheat and barley, whatever is piled on your threshing floor, as well as any side income that you have earned in the

marketplace to the administration building. I will then supply you with what you need, commensurate with what you've brought in."

The farmer, not really aware of Bloch's intentions, responded: "Okay, sir. I will follow your order." Then he left.

Then came the second farmer, and Bloch realized he had to be a little more unambiguous about his intentions. So he said to him, "I have decreed that from now on ... whatever income you have earned must be brought to the treasury. I will record everything, and only afterward will I give you what to live on from what you have handed over to me."

This was roughly what he said to each one. Then he declared that he would shortly thereafter send the *jardinière* (agronomist) Mr. Quellin to confiscate the wheat from them. In the meantime, he ordered Boris, the brother of Yehoshua Ossowetzky,[311] to go from house to house and see what wheat was stored there, so the farmers wouldn't be able to conceal anything from them. ...

Before leaving, he also summoned Mr. Levitta [one of the residents of Ekron who received no stipend and had no need for the administration's assistance; he was a skilled worker earning ten francs per day, highly sought after, and very well liked]. Bloch also told him to bring his earnings to the administration and that he would get what he needed to live on from them.

Mr. Levitta replied, "I can't live off the twenty-five-cent daily allowance you are giving the settlers as either a stipend or a loan. My children are accustomed to a higher standard of living. Why should I be a servant when I am making a good living and have no need for any handouts or loans?"

After Bloch applied relentless pressure and succeeded in scaring him, Levitta replied in exasperation, "Okay. I work in Mikveh Israel. This Sunday I will ask Hirsch, the director, his opinion. If he says I should sign on the dotted line (and have to subjugate myself and my children to the administration), then I will."[312]

Bloch left as abruptly as he had arrived, brazenly riding his horse out of the religious community as the Sabbath was about to commence.[313]

As Mr. Bloch left Ekron, the hearts of the colonists sank. Every one of them felt the bone Mr. Bloch had stuck in their throats. The

> people ... sensed that Bloch had laid a trap for them because of their decision not to work during the Sabbatical year, as the rabbis of Jerusalem had decreed, whom they had obeyed as if listening to their own parents.
>
> Bloch had cleverly cornered them with his order. If they took the bait and trusted that he would pay them their wages from the produce they gave him, they would get a rude awakening when they found out that the day they didn't go out to work on the Sabbatical year, they wouldn't have a morsel to eat.
>
> Although Bloch prohibited any unauthorized assembly, the colonists broke the rule and met on that very Sabbath, deciding unanimously that they would not hand over a single kernel of wheat from the granaries, and not a red cent from what they earned elsewhere. What right did he have to do this? Were they indentured servants?
>
> At the conclusion of the Sabbath, Boris Ossowetzky summoned the colonists and asked them whether they were ready to hand over their produce to Mr. Quellin, as Mr. Bloch had ordered.
>
> "Forgive me, my brothers," said Boris Ossowetzky. "It is not my fault that I must force you to accept these harsh decrees, but what can I do? Bloch is being very heavy-handed with me by making me ask you whether you are willing to comply, or whether you will refuse and revolt!"
>
> The colonists all replied in unison that they would neither sign nor give Mr. Bloch a thing.
>
> So Boris quickly mounted his horse to go to Rishon [Le-Ẓion] to inform Mr. Bloch of the colonists' decision, so that he would not send Mr. Quellin to forcibly extract the produce from them and create a nasty quarrel.[314]

Ossowetzky dutifully reported to Bloch the reply of the farmers and warned him they were adamant about their decision. Bloch, who loved confrontation, wasn't taken aback; in fact, he relished Ossowetzky's report. Wasting no time, he rode off to Mazkeret Batya and arrived late Sunday morning.

The details of Bloch's meeting with the farmers are filled in by Dr. Chaim Chissin:

Bloch entered the settlement in a state of rage. In a tone that expressed both harshness and solemnity, he demanded that the settlers explain why they were refusing to fulfill the will of the Baron. Those were loaded words. The Baron was their patron and benefactor – in a sense, a father figure. How could they hurt the man who fed them?

Was Bloch being truthful, or was he concocting this? What did the Baron have to say about this issue, after all? Having no direct contact with the Baron, their only source was Bloch, whom they detested. They couldn't imagine how their benevolent benefactor could come up with such a conniving and scheming proposal. They couldn't be sure, but to them, it was a safe bet to discard the messenger along with the message.

They answered harshness with harshness by telling him that if he really wanted to assist them, then instead of taking away all their produce, the administration should estimate how much grain they had and then deduct that amount from their salaries. However, under no circumstances were they going to give their grain to the administration, having already had one experience with him not too long ago when they'd had nothing to eat, and he'd still refused to give them bread![315]

Failing to frighten the farmers into signing the contract, Bloch proceeded to enlist the aid of the higher-ups in the organization. He contacted Shmuel Hirsch, the regional director in charge of distributing funds to the settlers.

Hirsch called the Mazkeret Batya farmers to his office and tried to portray Bloch as a decent human being with compassion for the downtrodden. According to this dispatch from *Chavaẓelet*, Hirsch tried the "good cop / bad cop" routine on them:

There are many people who believe – this is what Mr. Hirsch was telling them – that the only thing the people of Ekron care about is receiving assistance, even though they have savings on the side. Now I don't believe that, but maybe some of you do have some money saved up? We aren't going to conduct a house-to-house search.

Nevertheless, the Nadiv ["the Benefactor" – Rothschild] won't assist Ekron with another penny. It was Mr. Bloch, a kindhearted and fine man with an understanding of your predicament, who

> worked on winning over the Baron's heart in your favor and sought to ameliorate your pains by taking all your produce and conducting a thorough inventory to clarify, once and for all, that you really aren't making enough to support yourselves. This clarification process will take time – a period of three years. Then, if the director sees that you are not making ends meet, he will give you all the assistance you need.
>
> The colonists replied that they expressed their gratitude to the Nadiv for all the kindness he had bestowed on them. However, they would not accept serfdom under any circumstances. So they each went their way without resolving the issue.[316]

Heroism is the ability to overcome adversity. Two powerful forces were pitted against each other: the force of the settlers' desire to fulfill the will of God, and the iron hand of an administrator determined to subdue them, ostensibly to conform to the will of the Baron. It was a battle of wills that would deeply engage both sides and exhaust their energies.

After the administrators failed to subdue the Mazkeret Batya farmers, they intensified their efforts to force the settlers' hand. They went so far as to offer the settlers what they considered a major concession: agree to work during Shemittah, and you can keep all your income for yourselves. Just go out and *work*.

Bloch decided to bring in the "big guns." Shmuel Hirsch and Emile Franck[317] – the two highest-ranking men in the Baron's hierarchy stationed in Palestine – paid Mazkeret Batya a visit.

Bringing Franck along was noteworthy, for it demonstrated the gravity of the situation in the eyes of the administrators. Ran Aaronsohn, a historian of the First Aliyah, described Franck's special role:

> Unlike Hirsch, who was closely involved in the smallest details of life in the colonies, Franck was able to maintain a distance from the administration, which lent him the aura of a detached, unbiased observer in the eyes of the colonists. Franck was closer to a Supreme Court judge or an arbitrator than an ordinary supervisor.[318]

The farmers' encounter with Franck and Hirsch, which occurred a month after their brush with Bloch, was reported by *Chavaẓelet*:

> Mr. Franck and Mr. Hirsch traveled to Ekron and summoned the colonists. Mr. Franck asked them: Why weren't they going out to work? Why weren't they willing to sign the contract that Bloch had put before them?
>
> The Ekronians responded that in no way would they work during the Sabbatical year, nor would they sign documents that would negate their rights as free human beings.
>
> "So what will come of all this?" Franck asked.
>
> They replied, "If pressuring the poor and oppressing the people of God is what you really want to do, then give us money for travel expenses, and remunerate us for labors performed ... and we will return [to Russia]."[319]

"We will return." Those words speak volumes, for they demonstrate how different the farmers of Mazkeret Batya were from their secular and even religious nationalistic contemporaries: if they couldn't fulfill God's command in Palestine, they would sooner go back to Russia.

When gentle persuasion and outright coercion didn't work, Bloch and the administrators tried a different approach. Since the settlers refused to work the fields because of religion, then the administrators would turn the tables on them and pressure them to work on *religious* grounds. Dr. Chissin offers an account of the dialogue between Bloch and the farmers:

> "By the authority of the Baron, I am ordering you to work the fields this year! If not, the Baron will take everything from you."
>
> "But how can we go out to work after such a serious prohibition was issued by the Jerusalem Rabbinate?"
>
> "I don't recognize such a prohibition! I received a *heter* from the chief rabbis[320] of Russia."
>
> "Where is it?"

Bloch was taken aback by their response. Not only did they not take his word for it, they even had the nerve to demand the original document. In any case, he promised to come up with

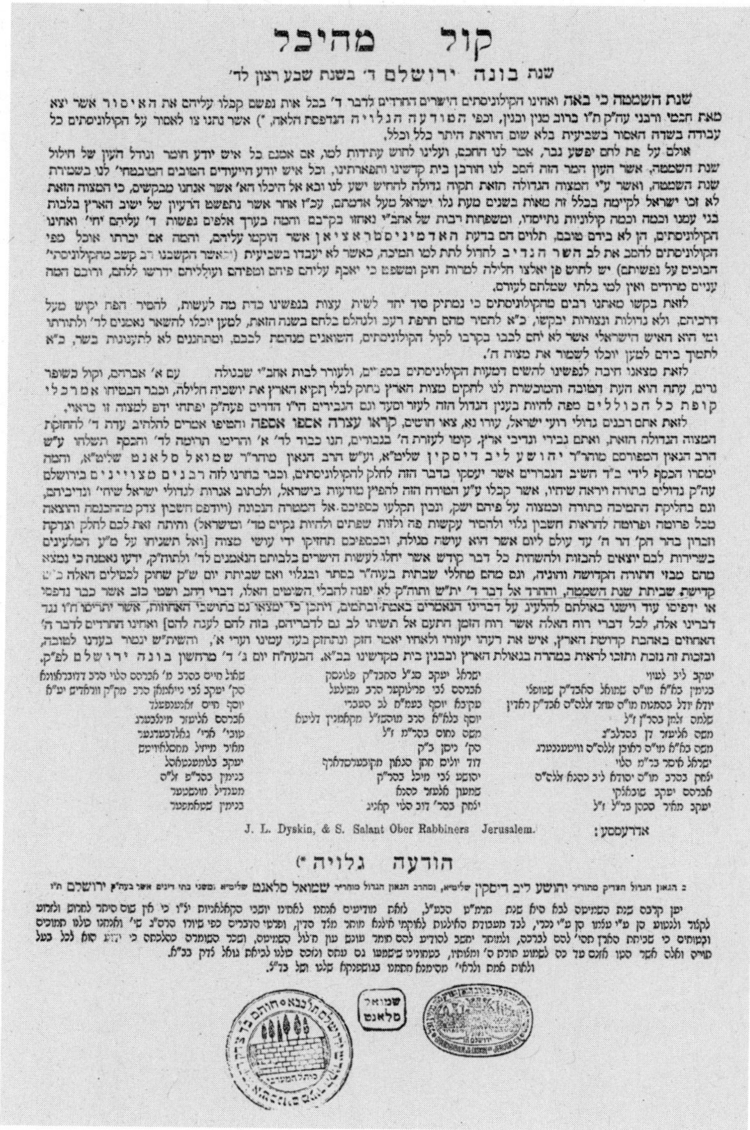
קול מהיכל

שנת בונה ירושלם ד׳ בשנת שבע רצון לד׳

J. L. Dyskin, & S. Salant Ober Rabbiners Jerusalem.

אדרעססע:

הודעה גלויה *)

"A Call from the Palace." A rabbinic appeal for financial aid for the farmers observing Shemittah, with an addendum by Rabbis Salant and Diskin

the document; then he took off.

He immediately dispatched one of his assistants to put pressure on the Jerusalem Rabbinate to rescind the prohibition and issue a *heter* in its place. That naïve presumptuousness turned out to be utterly futile.

At the same time, the Mazkeret Batya farmers sent a delegation of their own to consult with the Jerusalem rabbis concerning the coercive methods employed by the Baron's administrators. The rabbis attributed great significance to the fact that these God-fearing farmers wanted to keep Shemittah despite the pressure. The rabbis told the colonists:

> Our Sages ... permitted flexibility in religious matters depending on the necessities of the times and how it would benefit the nation. However, they taught us a fundamental principle: Those who rule on Jewish law have much latitude, but if an external power attempts to nullify any religious precept through coercion, even if the decree pertains to a matter as insignificant as a shoelace, it must be vehemently opposed.... [321]

Understanding that the settlers needed financial support to sustain them through the Shemittah year, the rabbis promised them a full year's supply of bread if they stuck to their religious principles.[322]

True to their word, thirty of the most prominent Ashkenazic rabbis of Jerusalem issued a proclamation titled "*Kol me-Heichal* – A Call from the Palace" in October of 1888. It appealed to Jews the world over to contribute funds to support the farmers who were valiantly observing Shemittah. The "Palace" referred to the city of Jerusalem, the seat of the Holy Temple. The "Call from the Palace" was a euphemism for the onset of an ideological struggle – a call to arms to defend the traditional religious way of life.[323] (This proclamation may be considered the first shot from the Old Yishuv in a *Kulturkampf* that persists to this day.)

A Call from the Palace (excerpts)

The Shemittah year has arrived, and our brothers, the colonists, who... tremble with all their might at the word of God, have accepted upon themselves THE PROHIBITION that was issued by the Jerusalem Rabbinate... which forbids the colonists to engage in any kind of work in the fields that is prohibited during Shemittah, with no leniencies whatsoever.

... The wise man [Solomon] taught us that for a piece of bread, a man will sin,[324] and we must therefore be concerned about the future....

The idea of farming the Land of Israel has caught on amongst our people, and many colonies have been established ... consisting of over 2,000 people. But their welfare is in the hands of THE ADMINISTRATION that was set up over them.... In the event that [the administrators] persuade the Benefactor to cease funding those who will not work in the Sabbatical year... (as we have heard from those distressed colonists who are pleading for their lives), then we must be concerned lest the colonists violate the laws [of the Torah] as a result of the hunger they and their children are liable to suffer ... for most of these people are very poor, with only their shirts on their backs.

... All they are asking is to remove the specter of the humiliation of hunger and to give them enough bread to eat for this year so they can remain steadfast in their allegiance to God and His Torah....

...We call upon the rabbis to wake up and CONVENE ASSEMBLIES in order to motivate people to support this great mizvah... Please send all contributions to our leaders RABBI YEHOSHUA LEIB DISKIN AND RABBI SHMUEL SALANT, who will give the funds to a select committee that will then distribute the donations to the colonists.

... Don't pay heed to the newspapers that cynically disparage everything that is sacred...amongst their writers are people who denigrate the Torah and its scholars, people who desecrate the Sabbath in secret as well as in public. And if the sanctity of the Sabbath is like a joke in the eyes of these fools, so much more so the sanctity of a whole year of Shemittah....

Signed: J. L. Diskin, & S. Salant, chief rabbis, Jerusalem

The proclamation was publicized in the October 26th (1888) edition of *Chavazelet*.[325]

Quick to respond was Rabbi Samson Raphael Hirsch of Frankfurt-am-Main. Rabbi Hirsch opposed the *heter* to sell the land during Shemittah and issued a proclamation of his own in early Tevet (December) 1888, only several days before he passed away. He affirmed his support for Shemittah observance and appealed for Jews to contribute to the financial welfare of the farmers, promising to publicize the donations.[326] At the end of Tevet, he wrote in his community newspaper, *Yeshurun*:

Famous last words. Rabbi Samson Rafael Hirsch, whose last public appeal was to support Shemittah observance

> I have received the following contributions for the appeal that went out from the *beit din* of Jerusalem on behalf of the God-fearing people who abstain from working their fields during Shemittah: Mr. H. [Rabbi Hirsch was referring to himself] – 20 marks; B. R. – 20 marks; anonymous – 20 marks; anonymous – 10 marks; Theodore Hamburger – 20 marks; O. – 20 marks; Ludwig Rapp – 20 marks. Collection at the annual dinner of the gravediggers of the *chevrah kaddisha* – 138.10 marks. Total: 268.10 marks. Please continue to send in donations.
>
> Rabbi Hirsch[327]

But a strong counter response to the Jerusalem appeal was immediately launched. One of the most inflammatory critiques came from a *maskil* named Mordechai Lubman, who had some very sharp words to say about the Jerusalem sages and the founders of Mazkeret Batya:

> An awesome and fearful storm has begun to demolish and uproot all that we have built with so much toil and travail. Darkness and gloom have covered the skies of the Yishuv, and a fearful adversary has come out of his hiding place with threatening weapons to attack us and eradicate us from the land. Shemittah is the means being used by the shepherds of Israel to scatter their flocks. …
>
> The *Kol me-Heichal* proclamation that was issued by the rabbis of Jerusalem will certainly be read by you – and then you will realize the gall and chutzpah that drips from each and every word. It has the potential to infuriate the Benefactor – which is its whole purpose. For he will spit on the rabbis and all our brothers who repay his kind deeds with insults and curses! When I read this travesty, my blood froze within me, and I was in shock! Such open chutzpah against such a unique man, upon whom the honor of all of Israel is dependent! I couldn't believe that [these rabbis] were capable of being such "impudent dogs."

> And even if we were to assume that the Benefactor in his magnanimous spirit will not pay attention to the barking of these dogs, I am greatly afraid that his patience will run out in bearing the weight of a nation that knows no rest. Behold, the moshavah that was supposed to be a glorious model through its fertility and produce is about to be uprooted,[328] because this past year was a lean one, and they won't be working this year, and in the following year they won't be able to plant wheat, because the rabbis have forbidden any plowing for the following year. [The farmers] will never get support... and inevitably, they will fall. The signs of destruction are already making their appearance.[329]

It is important to point out that there is no mention in the *Kol me-Heichal* proclamation of any criticism of the Baron. There is only one critical reference – against the Baron's *administrators.*

"Cast Your Burdens upon the Lord..."

Meanwhile, the plucky Mazkeret Batya farmers continued to hold out. Dr. Chaim Chissin wrote a blow-by-blow account of another battle with Alphonse Bloch:

> The war of wills continued. Bloch returned to Ekron a few days later. He told them he had obtained a copy of the *heter* and then gave it to one of the colonists to read. After all the colonists took turns reading it, they had a surprise for him: The *heter* turned out to be very limited, allowing fieldwork to be done during Shemittah only by means of non-Jewish laborers! Bloch, who was tightfisted whenever it came to extending monetary assistance and who had insisted that the settlers limit the employment of outside laborers to cut costs, suddenly had the tables turned on him. The settlers reminded him, "...Who knows better than you that if we must employ gentiles, then our profits will be wiped away by our expenses!"
>
> Not to be outflanked, Bloch came back with a quick rejoinder: "I don't know Hebrew," he said, "but according to this copy of the *heter* translated into French, I find no such clause, and I won't budge at all from what appears in the French copy. Therefore, I am warning you: comply and work in the Sabbatical year, and you will benefit from the Baron's largesse. But if you rebel, I will have nothing more to do with you, nor will I ever return to this place."

The Ekronians answered that they would abide not by the Russian rabbis' ruling but rather by the rulings of the Jerusalem rabbis, for three reasons:

1. The administration refused to fulfill the conditions outlined by the *heter* that would allow them to work [during Shemittah].

2. The prohibition [of working during Shemittah] was clear-cut and explicit, while Rabbi Spektor's *heter* was ambiguous and unclear.

3. They ought to follow the Jerusalem rabbis because of Mazkeret Batya's proximity to Jerusalem, rather than the rabbis of Russia, who were far less informed about the local situation.[330]

Bloch was not convinced. There was only one reply he was willing to hear. He immediately ordered all his personnel to leave the settlement – that included his assistant, the doctor,[331] the pharmacist, the teachers, the *shochet*, and others.[332] The Ekronians ended their retort to Bloch with some ringing words that paraphrase a verse from the Bible: "We have cast our burdens upon the Lord, and He will sustain us."[333]

But Bloch was not inspired. The very next day, he posted a notice at the administration headquarters in Rishon Le-Ẓion:

After seeing the ruling of the great Torah sage Rabbi Yiẓchak Elchanan Spektor of Kovno, allowing work [in the Shemittah year], and the letter that this great Torah sage has sent to Rabbi Ẓaddok Kahn of Paris and the Honorable Michael Erlanger, and because these letters have been publicized, and all the colonists are familiar with them, the administration is therefore announcing in the strongest possible terms that all support will cease for any colonist who despite all the above continues to insist that [the colonists] are obligated to abide by the prohibition against working during this Shemittah of the year 5649.

Rishon Le-Ẓion
6 November
2 Kislev 5649[334]

Anyone wishing to see the *heter*
should visit the administration![335]

(Rabbi Spektor did not view reliance on his *heter* as the ideal option and would have certainly supported the farmers.[336] He was likely unaware at that time that his *heter* was being used to coerce people to go against their conscience.)[337]

In addition to the poster in Rishon Le-Ẓion, Bloch sent a messenger to Mazkeret Batya with a message in the name of Mr. Franck, stating that if they refused to work in the Shemittah year, their lands would be transferred to the *fellahin*. The outraged farmers responded that they would fight "till their last drop of blood" against what they felt was a case of blatant extortion.[338]

The battles over Shemittah eroded all good faith between Baron Rothschild and his administrators and the farmers. The emerging lack of trust was expressed in the following incident: Rothschild had purchased the area adjacent to the Arab village of Castina, near Gaza, to expand a new settlement, Be'er Tuvia. To delineate proper boundaries between the settlers and their Arab neighbors, trenches had to be dug around the settlement, where cactus would be planted. Oxen were needed to pull the plows digging the trenches, so the Baron's administrators asked to borrow the Mazkeret Batya farmers' work animals (which were standing idle) rather than purchase new ones. The farmers, fearing this was just another ruse to enfeeble them, refused.

Unsung hero. Leib Abadik, a founder of Zikhron Yaakov

Elie Scheid, originally brought in by Rothschild to bring the colonies of Rosh Pina and Zikhron Yaakov under the aegis of his administration, and now the Baron's chief superintendent of all the colonies, wrote bitterly about this refusal in his memoirs: "All the administration wanted to do was to borrow their animals – which the Baron had purchased on their behalf – in order to dig the trenches in Castina. And they refused. Is this what you call religious piety? Not at all!"[339]

Elsewhere in his writing, he reveals the depth of misunderstanding – and even the contempt the settlers purportedly had for the administrators:

> In the recesses of their hearts, they were convinced that they would no longer need the assistance of the Baron.... They stared condescendingly at his administrators, and when they passed us on the

Memory lane. A sketch of Mazkeret Batya by Elie Scheid in his *Memoirs*

road they acted as if they didn't even recognize who we were, so they wouldn't have to exchange a greeting![340]

The lens through which the Baron viewed his colonists was his team of administrators. Though once the favored child, Mazkeret Batya was beginning to appear cranky and rebellious. The administrators thought the best strategy would be to starve the farmers into submission.

It would not take long. By November 1888, the initial financial assistance to the farmers had dried up, and they were compelled to request a loan from the Va'ad ha-Kollelim in Jerusalem. Despite the fact that this committee supported Shemittah observance in general, the farmers' plea caused considerable dispute. There were many starving Jews with no source of sustenance in Jerusalem; why should funds be allocated to Mazkeret Batya? As reported in *Ha-Ẓefirah*:

> The farmers of Ekron were impoverished and hungry, and some of them came to our Holy City to ask for help, so that they and their wives and children need not continue to suffer from hunger. The great and renowned Torah sage Rabbi Mordechai Gimpel Yaffe, an outstanding individual among the great lovers of Zion, paid a personal visit to the offices of the Va'ad ha-Klali [General Council]

> of Jerusalem and gathered together all the heads of the kollelim, who ... responded to his invitation on Thursday, the 18th of Kislev [November 22,1888]. He outlined to them the profound obligation of supporting these Shemittah-observant farmers, who were withstanding the difficulties of this great test. ...
>
> Then the members of the council debated amongst themselves. Some said it was unthinkable that funds allocated for the destitute, the starving widows and orphans of Jerusalem, be given to those who at least have homes to live in and can support themselves at least six [out of seven] years.
>
> And then there were others who said that it was the duty of the council to help anyone who was faltering, and what difference was there between these and those? Furthermore, [supporting Ekron] would strengthen the Yishuv and its religious life – the reason the council had been established in the first place.
>
> The compromise reached that day was that they would be assisted only by means of loans consisting of a modest sum of 500 francs [$1,000 in today's U.S. currency] which were given to the great rabbinic sage [Rabbi Yaffe] to disburse to those who were faltering. ...[341]

As reported, one of the main sources of moral and spiritual support for the farmers of Mazkeret Batya during those bitter months was Rabbi Mordechai Gimpel Yaffe. He encouraged them to strengthen their resolve not to work the fields – and counseled them not to sign Bloch's contract under any circumstances.[341A]

Chapter 23
A War of Nerves

Four months had passed since the start of the Shemittah year, and the Mazkeret Batya farmers hadn't budged. The Baron's administrators were stymied. These "Ekronim" had to be coerced into submission. The religious newspaper *Chavaẓelet* commented on the latest attempts to manipulate the farmers, adding its customary hyperbolic venom against the administrators:

Yisrael Dov Frumkin. Publisher of *Chavaẓelet,* the voice of the Old Yishuv

> Tevet 5649 [January 1889]
>
> A telegram arrived yesterday from Paris stating that Mr. Bloch was authorized to board up the well in Ekron, depriving the Ekronians and their animals of water to drink, and to shut down the school and send the teachers away. He was also commanded to order the doctor not to treat [the] sick.
>
> [It doesn't take much to guess the source of] this telegram. It fits the [style of] Mr. Scheid, who executes the directives of the Baron and misguides him through his murderous administrators in order to defame [the Baron's] name amongst the Jews and gentiles.[342]

Bloch, who had always seen the Russian pioneers as nothing more than *schnorrers,* was now authorized to force his "lazy" farmers into submission. *Chavaẓelet,* a few days later:

> Ekron:
>
> Last Sunday, 4 Shvat 5649 [January 6, 1889] six members of the settlement were summoned to stand before Mr. Bloch....
>
> Bloch: "I regret that I told you I would be so hard on you and your settlement that nothing would survive. But now I promise you that I will do all in my power to be good to you and to make Ekron the pride of the country. However, [from now on] your

success will be up to you. If you decide to work in the Sabbatical year, I will give you anything you request from me. But if you refuse to work, then I have no choice but to enforce the order to board up the well ... and close the school."

"Do whatever you wish, sir," the colonists all responded. "And we will do whatever is in the power of a Jew – to endure and bear any hardship in order to fulfill the precepts of our holy Torah!"

And then they went on their way.[343]

In February 1889, when the economic situation became very dire, Yaakov Arkin and Chaim Moshe Press left Palestine for a fundraising campaign in the Diaspora on behalf of the settlement.[344] There was some debate as to whether these founders of Ekron would succeed. Rabbi Salant was skeptical. He asked the novice fundraisers, "Why travel all over Europe when all you need to do is make just one stop in Paris and take your case directly to the Baron? Not only that, but your very act of seeking donations will embarrass the Baron and reinforce the public's perception that he is a millionaire miser."

But the farmers rejected his advice.[345]

Arkin and Press were probably unaware of how sensitive the Diaspora Jews were when it came to upsetting Baron Rothschild, or the consequences of taking any actions that would conflict with the Baron's work in the Holy Land. When they visited Alexandria they were hit with articles in the papers that criticized their Shemittah observance as a rebellion against the beneficent Benefactor. Some even claimed that supporting Shemittah observers was tantamount to *siyuah li-dvar aveirah* – abetting a sinful action! The bewildered farmers were essentially told to go home; there was no money for ingrates. After their fiasco in Alexandria, they abandoned the idea of collecting funds abroad.

Brother Versus Brother

Attitudes toward the Shemittah observers were so varied and complicated that even brothers could be divided on the issue. Below is a letter published in the *Ha-Maggid* newspaper and written by Simchah Shulman, a scribe from Safed who was temporarily residing in Egypt when Arkin and Press arrived.

Alexandria, Egypt
22 Adar II, 5649
[March 25, 1889]

Three weeks ago, two emissaries arrived here from Ekron, who were collecting money on behalf of those not working in the Shemittah year. Their next destination was Germany. For travel expenses, they took with them four pounds sterling that was given to them by the people of the moshavah. But the Jews of Egypt are astute, with their "eyes in their heads,"[346] and they responded to them as follows: "The Benefactor, the Baron, under whose auspices are all the settlements in the Holy Land, doesn't need assistance from outsiders. If you refuse to heed his voice, the voice of a merciful father, if you are looking for an excuse to be stringent in order to forbid working in the seventh year (even though the Torah sages have permitted you to work), then you are slackers. And it is not our obligation to help sinners ... you, who are putting yourselves and your children into a difficult situation. ...

With lots of sweat and tears, they managed to collect a small sum of money from our local Ashkenazic and Sephardic brothers – just enough to be able to return to their community.

I also confronted them as to why they didn't have compassion on their own infants and children ... and why they were acting so peculiarly ... by taking actions that embittered their merciful master [Rothschild] ... listening to advice from people who lack any integrity and sincere convictions ... [people] who [really] hate the Yishuv, and whose hatred is what motivates them to befriend you, only to betray you [later] when they are in trouble; and then they will pretend they don't know you. They play games with the lives of these naïve farmers and use them as arrows for their [political] battles.... I warned the two emissaries to return to their jobs and cease from rebellion, but do we have the power to drive out Satan, who prances about in our Holy Land, and can we bring cessation to arguments and quarrels?

Simchah Shulman
Sofer Stam[347]
The Holy City of Safed[348]

In response, Shmuel Shulman (Simchah's brother) wrote the following "open letter":

Safed
Rosh Chodesh Sivan, 5649
[May 31, 1889]

To Yisrael Dov Frumkin, publisher of *Chavaẓelet* in the Holy City of Jerusalem, may it speedily be rebuilt:

My brother Simchah Shulman (who presently resides in Alexandria) published scathing words against our brothers, the people of Ekron in the *Ha-Maggid* newspaper. [He charged that] as a consequence of their refusal to [rely on the *heter*] they wouldn't be able to avoid dependence on outsiders. I was asked whether he got this idea from me.

I want to make it clear that that is not my position. As dear as the members of the other settlements who sought out halakhic leniencies are to me, the members of the settlement of Ekron are even dearer in my eyes, having volunteered at the risk of their lives to fulfill the miẓvah of Shemittah according to its proper *halakhah*, without seeking loopholes....

And who knows [what would have happened] if all our brothers, the members of the settlements, had been together with one mind to desist from work during this Shemittah and let whatever would be be ... Or if all the rabbis and Torah giants of our generation had requested – with one voice – of the great, righteous, and upright Benefactor to relieve the settlers from their work obligations and all the while not to remove his kindness from them – there is no doubt that he would have gladly provided them with all their needs; and the merit of the community would have been his through the fulfillment of this great religious commandment – a commandment whose violation brought about the exile of Israel from its land.

Furthermore, we have been festering with this sin and have not merited fulfilling the commandment [of Shemittah] for over 2,000 years. And even if we take into account the combined total income of the moshavot in the Sabbatical year, what does it all amount to in the eyes of the Benefactor, compared to the large amounts of money he has squandered on the settlements?...

I therefore declare: fortunate is the one who supports our Ekron brothers. And if the sole reason for establishing this settlement was to fulfill this commandment, *dayenu* – that would have been enough! As a token of my sincerity, I am contributing to them the "poor man's offering"[349] of five francs, and it should be sent at my expense, so that I should have a portion, a contribution, and a remembrance of the commandment of Shemittah in the Land of Israel, on the land of Ekron. And may God command that there be a blessing in the produce and in all the works of their hands.

Sincerely,
A Servant of Israel
Shmuel Shulman[350]

Fortunately, there was the Va'ad ha-Shemittah, a committee that collected and disbursed funds to Shemittah observers, especially in Petach Tikva and Mazkeret Batya. In March 1889, the Va'ad ha-Shemittah issued further calls to support the Shemittah observers. Headlined "To the Rescue of Our Colonist Brethren Who Observe the Sabbatical Year," the calls found a receptive audience in the Diaspora, as reported by *Chavaẓelet*:

> When the Holy Land Clerks and Administrators of Amsterdam[351] heard that our farmer brethren, the residents of Ekron, were starving for bread, they quickly issued an order via telegram to one of the bankers here to transfer 500 francs to the Va'ad ha-Shemittah … There is good news from other cities in Europe as well: People of integrity have been aroused to have compassion upon these pure souls and are collecting funds on their behalf, so they can get through the tough times until the harvest of the following year, may it be good.
>
> May God bestow good upon good and instill mercy in the hearts of the rest of our observant brethren to have compassion on our brothers the Ekronians, who are being persecuted for observing the miẓvah of Shemittah properly.[352]

Many prominent individuals responded to the appeal and contributed to the fund, including universally respected Torah sages such as Rabbis Meir Simchah Hakohen of Dvinsk (author of *Ohr Sameach*), Yosef Ber Soloveitchik of Brisk, Yosef Zechariah Stern of Shavil, and Yehuda Aryeh Leib Alter, the rebbe of the Gerrer Chassidim (and author of *Sefat Emet*).[353]

But the monies that poured in were still not enough to feed all the members of these large households, and the Baron's administrators continued to punish the rebels. In early June of 1889, *Chavaẓelet* attested to the deteriorating situation when Eli Scheid toured the Baron's colonies:

> The state of Ekron is precarious. Scheid never bothered to visit [the people there]. Neither would they go to visit him. In one fell swoop, Scheid eliminated every means of support: He didn't pay the *shochet*, he didn't pay the teachers. The doctor no longer makes any calls nor dispenses any medication. …
>
> Scheid was also enraged at the settlers of Petach Tikva because some of them were receiving assistance from the Va'ad ha-Shemittah. Nevertheless, he wasn't half as angry at them as he was at the Ekronians, because he still allowed the teacher to stay and gave the doctor permission to heal.[354]

By the end of the month, the paper recounted yet more sanctions the Mazkeret Batya farmers suffered at the hands of the Baron's administrators:

> Mr. Bloch carried out what Mr. Scheid decreed against Ekron. He deprived them of the French-language teachers, sending them out of the school and packing them off to Rishon Le-Ẓion. [The administrators] also cast out the mules that were turning the wheel for drawing the water [and transferred them] from Ekron to Rishon Le-Ẓion, so the Shemittah observers could not benefit from them. And if these measures would not be enough to chasten them, he was ready to finish them off completely and forcibly banish them from the land (which was earmarked for them, and where they'd toiled with the sweat of their brows) through the intervention of the [Ottoman] government.[355]

Even the secularist Dr. Chaim Chissin was shocked by the treatment of the farmers, whose only crime was remaining steadfast in their religious ideals:

> When Bloch realized the settlers were receiving assistance from the Va'ad ha-Shemittah on a regular basis, he sent the following executive order to Ekron:
>
> 1. Expel one settler.
> 2. Fuse all farming plots together by erasing the boundaries between them.
> 3. Every settler must provide documentation regarding his monetary debts to the Baron.
> 4. All settlers must sign that they are merely hired laborers, that they can be "fired" at any time, and that the land belongs to [Shmuel] Hirsch.
>
> As if that were not enough, they were informed that if they didn't obey these demands, they would be forcibly expelled in fifteen days.... [356]

These decrees didn't surprise the settlers or change their minds.[357] In January 1889, *Ha-Ẓefirah* reported:

> The members of the moshavah of Ekron are steadfast about not working the land in the Shemittah year. In vain do [the administrators] "hold the mountain over their heads,"[358] in vain do they

Chemistry 101. A pharmacy in Zikhron Yaakov. All of the Baron's colonies had pharmacies. The closing of the one in Mazkeret Batya posed a great danger to the public's health – especially that of the children.

attempt to frighten them with severe penalties and threats … the farmers just don't care. Now it was decreed to seal the water cisterns, so they would have no water to drink; also to expel their children from the school and not to let the doctor visit them at all.[359]

The flu that has been wreaking havoc on the world has now spread to the land [of Israel]. The people of Ekron's situation is dreadful and bitter, for they are stranded without a doctor or pharmacy. To their good fortune, Dr. Stein of Jaffa has offered them assistance for free.[360]

Prolific. In 1887, after *Ha-Ẓefirah* had become a daily, editor Nachum Sokolow filled practically every issue. Although *Ha-Ẓefirah* reported very little about what was going on in Palestine prior to 1897, the paper published stories sympathetic to Mazkeret Batya during the Shemittah controversy.

"I Told You So …"

In July 1889, toward the end of the Shemittah year, Eliezer Ben-Yehuda, the rabidly anti-religious editor, wrote:

> This moshavah is like a ghost town. All the numerous appeals of the "Haters of the Yishuv" for people to come to the assistance of the Shemittah observers brought only 4,000 francs [$16,000 in today's U.S. currency] from all over the world – an amount the Benefactor could have appropriated for the settlement in an hour. …
>
> They may have succeeded in destroying Ekron for now and maybe even permanently, but the Yishuv will live on![361]

Paying the Price

The sanctions took their toll. Food stores were depleted, and it was said that the famine was beginning to "claim victims." Nevertheless, the settlers did not buckle under the pressure of the administration. *Ha-Ẓefirah* recounted their sorrowful state in Av (August 1889):

> The situation of the Ekronians is dreadful. There isn't a household in Ekron in which someone isn't sick. In the last two months, about twenty people – men, women, and children – were brought to Jerusalem to convalesce in our clinic that was established for our Ashkenazic brethren, and six or seven sick people are there right at this moment – these in addition to a few sick people who are bedridden in their homes in Ekron, who can't afford to travel to Jerusalem. The doctor stationed in Rishon Le-Ẓion will not pay them a call, because he was forbidden by the administrators to carry out his duties.
>
> The teaching of Torah has ceased because the teachers and *melamdim* have been fired by order of the administration … it makes one heartsick over the little children who are idle because there is no *melamed*. Now [the farmers'] heartbreak worsens, because … the grass has withered, and they don't have the means to buy straw and fodder, and the famine is taking its toll on the animals.

Bloch also began hounding them with legal battles, dragging them to the Ottoman courts for a month and a half:[362]

> In the midst of this awful situation, the administrator continues to torment them and is bringing them to court before the government judges in Jaffa.… Until now the administrators have not won the case, and the judgment keeps being pushed off from week to week. But the situation is dreadful – hunger and sickness within and court battles without – and all this on account of what? Because [the farmers] fulfilled a miẓvah that encompasses many positive and negative precepts with integrity! Let the kindhearted, Torah-observant people among us be sensitive to their brethren in Ekron and swiftly come to their aid. May they have pity on these unfortunate souls and not let them perish from hunger – they, their wives, their children, and their animals.

> That the members of this small settlement in the Land of Israel suffer because they fulfill the dictates of their religion is a blot on the entire Jewish people. It is incumbent on every religious Jew to prevent the desecration of God's Name and offer assistance to these unfortunates, whether a lot or a little. And may those who are merciful be repaid with God's mercy.[363]

News of the famine spread to Europe. An article describing the settlers' suffering and decrying the injustices meted out to them appeared in *Der Israelit* (Mainz, Germany)[364] and was reprinted in *Chavazelet*:

> Charges have reached us from the settlement Ekron that, if substantiated, would cause grief and concern to anyone possessing sensitivity, a sense of justice, and religious tolerance.
>
> The representative of Baron Rothschild in Paris, Mr. Scheid, has used every means at his disposal to force the members of this moshavah to change their minds in spite of their religious convictions. But all his efforts have been futile. These people have suffered pangs of hunger and have borne many sacrifices in order to observe Torah laws according to their inner conscience. And what has Mr. Scheid done? He has called on [the Turkish] government for assistance in forcing the farmers to pay back whatever expenditures the Baron has made on their behalf until now – or to leave their lands.
>
> It is clear that this desecration of God's Name is far from the goals that were envisioned by Baron Rothschild … It is clear that his administrators are misleading him.
>
> We therefore call upon any of our brothers who have contact with the Baron and who have his attention to arouse his concern about the situation in Ekron, which is so sad and aggravating![365]

At the conclusion of the Shemittah year (August 1889), *Chavazelet* surveyed the results of that devastating time and intimated a bleak future:

> You should know, dear readers, that your brothers, the farmers of Ekron, are in deep trouble and facing a great disaster. Together, they, their wives, their little children, and their animals will perish from hunger in the full sense of the word. The pangs of famine

have begun to inflict casualties. Every day we witness many sick people from the moshavah being admitted to our hospitals [in Jerusalem]. The sight of people suffering on account of their faith just tears the heart to pieces.[366]

Chavaẓelet columnist Eliezer Rokeach[367] railed against the inflexibility of the Baron's administrators in regard to the settlers, but he believed that in the end, justice would triumph:

> Our enemies are the Parisians ... their wickedness and sinfulness have been revealed in all its glory by their handing the Ekronians over to the courts for judgment!
>
> ... But Ekron, whose sons never raised a hand against an administrator, who never took the smallest item away from even one of the servants of the servants ... did not sin or commit any wrongdoing other than to refrain from working in the Sabbatical year as proscribed clearly in the Torah. They didn't want to accept any devious and sneaky legal devices concocted by some rabbis to manipulate the Torah.... Behold, for this "crime" they were turned over for judgment!
>
> If Ekron prevails ... (and we have high hopes that our esteemed government[368] will not allow its upright servants to falter) – eternal shame awaits the enemies who have desecrated that which is sacred in our Holy Land. And should Ekron fall, God forbid, then you will be disgraced. For whom did you defeat? A flock of poor families whose whole world consists of their integrity, honesty, and hard work – with streams of sweat flowing from their skin.[369]

To the great distress of the settlers of Mazkeret Batya, it seemed as if even Heaven itself were against them. The low rainfall of the previous year had resulted in a lean harvest. Paradoxically, the rains during the Shemittah year yielded bumper crops for the farmers who had relied on the *heter*. The Jerusalem rabbis had promised God's blessings for those who strove to fulfill the miẓvah of Shemittah, but it appeared that the only people blessed were the Shemittah violators and those who circumvented Shemittah by utilizing the *ḥeter*! Ben-Yehuda was only too happy to point out this irony:

> ...The blessings of the land have had a positive effect on the marketplace. There hasn't been such a decrease in price [for grains] in so many years. A bushel [literally, *se'ah*] of wheat, which even during "cheap" times went for twenty-three gerush, can be sold today for sixteen gerush or less – and the wheat is of very high quality!
>
> In short, this year, the Shemittah year, was a year of bounty and blessing in a most wondrous way for those who tilled the land, just as *Ha-Ẓvi* predicted from the beginning!
>
> And as for the people of Ekron, who have rich and fertile soil – had they worked their lands this year, by the end of this year they could have lived without any outside support. We would have seen one settlement with a high degree of development, and they would be the one group of farmers in all the Land of Israel living by the toil of their hands, without needing any outside assistance![370]

The real McCoy. Mordechai Diskin was one of the fervently Orthodox pioneer farmers of Petach Tikva. He wrote a short monograph of his observations entitled *Divrei Mordechai*. He was related to Rabbi Yehoshua Leib Diskin.

The Old Yishuv drew conclusions very different from Ben-Yehuda's and was enraged at him. In the words of Mordechai Diskin, one of the first farmers of Petach Tikva:

> I shudder and cannot calm myself. Now I understand, in retrospect, what the rabbis of blessed memory meant when they said, "The sinners of Israel do not repent even at the gates of Hell!"
>
> What the publishers of *Ha-Ẓvi* are trying to do by assigning guilt to the rabbis of Jerusalem ... is to create animosity toward the rabbis of Jerusalem and the residents of Mazkeret Batya, and to convince people throughout the world that [Ben-Yehuda] is a "Lover of Zion." ... How is it possible that the *Ha-Ẓvi* newspaper is not ashamed to print, "And perhaps they succeeded in destroying Ekron forever," when they know full well that the writer of those lines is the cause – *he* is Satan![371]

The Jerusalem rabbinate now perceived the Chovevei Ẓion movement as a catalyst for the *destruction* of the nascent Yishuv because of its encouragement of farmers to work during the Shemittah year. These sentiments soon found their way to the pages of *Chavaẓelet*:

> How long will you speak loftily of the idea of Jewish settlement [in Palestine] while your hearts contemplate its destruction, and

the goal of your hatred is to demolish, destroy, forsake, smash, and uproot everything? …

And I will not be in error if I say that anything considered "Jewish" is like thorns in your eyes … and you are looking forward to the day of salvation – the day when Jewish identity will vanish![372]

Chapter 24
Heroes, Fools, or Villains?

During the Shemittah year, the farmers of Mazkeret Batya, who had risked their farms and families to rebuild the Land of Israel in accordance with their understanding of Torah law, had found themselves on the witness stand of world Jewry's opinion. To understand the farmers' dilemma in the context of the passionate climate surrounding them, we should look at the forces that supported, ridiculed, or reviled them.

They were accused of torpedoing the whole settlement effort by thumbing their noses at the Great Benefactor, Baron Rothschild; they were lazy; they were *schnorrers*; they were simpletons; they were turning back the clock and reintroducing a new form of Chalukah – dependence on charity; they were thieves who stole charity money from the widows and orphans of Jerusalem in order to allow themselves the indulgence of observing a stringency that the great Russian rabbis had ruled was unnecessary.

Notable contributor. Rabbi Azriel Hildesheimer, one of the prominent leaders of German neo-Orthodoxy, supported Mazkeret Batya during the Shemittah of 5649 (1888-1889).

But they also had many admirers and financial supporters, some from unexpected quarters. This support included rabbis who ruled *in favor* of the *heter*, such as Rabbis Yisrael Yehoshua Trunk of Kutno and Chaim Eliezer Wachs of Pietrokov.[373]

On the list of contributors to the Shemittah cause that was published in *Chavaẓelet*,[374] other famous names appear as well: Rabbi Azriel Hildesheimer,[375] the dean of the rabbinical seminary in Berlin; and Rabbi Naftali Ẓvi Yehuda Berlin, the *rosh yeshivah* (dean) of Volozhin and one of the heads of the Chovevei Ẓion movement.

Opposite page: **Who's who:** *Chavaẓelet*, 29 Adar 5650 (March 21, 1890), published a list of contributors to the Va'ad ha-Shemittah, which includes quite a few notables from the Jewish world. Rabbis Trunk and Wachs are listed twenty-five lines down in the right-hand column. At the bottom of the right-hand column is Rabbi Azriel Hildesheimer, who contributed 477 marks, while Rabbi Naftali Ẓvi Yehuda Berlin (18 silver rubles) is listed in the left-hand column, seventh from the top.

Beyond financial aid, the farmers' long-time friends bolstered them with moral support when they most needed it. Rabbi Mordechai Gimpel Yaffe, who had played a decisive role in their lives ever since he had inspired them to leave their farms in Pavlovka and settle in Palestine, continued to encourage them in their stand on Shemittah. Regarding this, Rabbi Eliezer Gordon, head of the Telshe Yeshivah[375A] and a contemporary of Rabbi Yaffe, wrote:

> The truth is that in the beginning, even these two colonies [i.e., Ekron and Petach Tikva] did not want to cease from working in

the Sabbatical year, because their hearts told them that doing so would be life-threatening.

However, they couldn't resist acting in accordance with the great Rabbi Mordechai Gimpel, who spoke to them in the name of God, and whose words emanated from a pure soul without any ulterior motives. The fact was that he was well known to all Jewry as a man who cherished the commandment of living in the Land of Israel with all his heart and soul.[376]

55, 219 פראנק.	1199	
ע״י הג״ז 16 מארק.	103	38
ע״י הגז׳ נדבת הישר הצדיק הר״ר שמעון וואלף באראן פאן ראטהשילד 200 מארק, ומקבוצת הר״ר בנימין ראהם 65 מארק.	1952	10
ע״י הגז׳ מהרה״ג הגאבדק״ק ווירצבורג 15 פראנק.	81	30
ע״י הגז׳ בידיעה מעלעגראפית, מקבוצת הרה״ג ר״ב ראהם נ״י 280 פראנק.	1518	10
ע״י הגז׳ מהרה״ג המפורסם אבדק״ק ווירצבורג, ונדבת פלוני 129 פראנק.	693	
מעיר איזאגיצע ע״י הרה״ג מו״ה נתן ארנשטיין שלשה רו״כ.	85	
מהגביר ר׳ נח ליפשיין מוואלקאווסק ע״י הר״ש גדלי׳ 4 רו״כ.	48	
מפלוני אלמוני מווארשא מאה רו״כ בשני פעמים.	1439	15
מהרב הגאון הצדיק המפורסם מו״ה יחיאל שליט״א ראבדק״ק אלכסנדר.	4750	32
מהרב הצדיק ד״ר פלאטא 90 מארק.	580	10
מהרב הגאון מו״ה יעקב דוד הי״ו הגאבדק״ק ווילקאווסק 100 רו״כ. ומבנו של הרב הגאון הרב״נ 8 רו״כ.	1512	
מהרב הגאון הר״ר שמעון הלוי הורוויץ 50 מארק.	331	10
מהרה״ג ר׳ גבריאל פיינבערג 5 לייש.	687	20
מהרב הגאון מו״ה יוסף זכריה נ״י 60 רו״כ.	862	20
מאדעססא 10 רו״כ.	146	30
מהגביר ר׳ עקיבא בערלינווטה 25 פראנק.	136	10
מהר״ר ישראל לעווינשטיין בשני פעמים 60 מארק.	305	10
מקופת קרן ישועה.	172	38
מהרבנים הגאונים הרב הצדיק מו״ה ישראל יהושע שליט״א הגאבדק״ק קוטנא 62 רו״כ, ומחתנו הרב הצדיק מו״ה חיים אלעזר וואקס זצ״ל הגאבדק״ק פיעטערקאב 60 רו״כ.	1635	15
ממאסקווא בשני פעמים	552	10
מהרב הגביר ר׳ משה שור ע״י הר״מ מיזיל 5 רו״כ.	72	
מהר״ר יהושע העשיל העסנער 3 רו״כ.	43	14
מהרה״ג ר׳ שמואל דוד זאלבערג.	2237	16
מר׳ יעקב חיים לעווי בשם אמו 3 לייש.	406	85
מהגביר ר׳ פייביל המכונה פהיליפס תנחום 1 לייש.	135	85
מהורדנא ע״י ר׳ טובי׳ גאלדבערג 6 רו״כ.	72	
מהר״ח בלאך 4 פלורין.	44	60
מהרה״ג ר׳ יו״ט ליפמאן הגאבדק״ק מיר 27 רו״כ.	371	30
מהרה״צ הר״ש מסלאנים 25 רו״כ	337	20
מלונדון ע״י הבאנקיער קאקס 48 פראנק.	251	10
מר׳ משה אהרן זייסמאנן 5 רו״כ.	69	25
מהורדנא ע״י הממונים 49 רו״כ.	679	35
ע״י הרה״ג הר׳ ליב אבדק״ק מינסק 132 רו״כ	1848	
מהרה״ג ר׳ אליקים מ״צ דק״ק הורדנא 2 רו״כ.	28	
מהרה״ג הר׳ אבא יצחק אבד״ק קופציק 5, 50 רו״כ.	73	20
מהרה״ג ר׳ משה סאקאלאווסקי 7 רו״כ.	97	19
ע״י הרה״ג הר׳ יעקב חיים לאנדא 11 רו״כ.	163	7
ע״י הרה״ג המפורסם מו״ה מאיר שמחה הכהן הגאבדק״ק דענעבורג מהגביר ר״ש צבי הורוויץ 5 רו״כ ונדבת עצמו 2 רו״כ.	66	10
מהרה״ג הר׳ יוסף שמואל האמבורגער 1 רו״כ.	13	80
מהרה״ג המפורסם ד״ר הילדעסהיימער נ״י 477 מארק.	3262	
ע״י הרב הגאון אבדק״ס לאדז שליט״א מהרב הגאון הק׳ מו״ה ארי׳ ליב אלטר אבדק״ק גור שליטא 100 רו״כ.	1442	20
ע״י הגז׳ מהרה״ק מיאדמסק מ׳ אברהם ראבינאוויטץ שליט״א 50 רו״כ	432	80
ע״י הגז׳ מקערות בעי״כ בעי״ת לאדז 22 רו״כ.	317	14
מעיר קאוונא ע״י הרה״ג מו״ה דוד וויגאדסקי והר״ר ארי׳ ליב פיקער 84 רו״כ.	1176	
ע״י מו״מ דכולל ווילנא 300 רו״כ.	4200	
מוואלקאוויר ע״י הגז׳ 15 רו״כ.	196	
מהרב הגאון הר״ר נצי״ב מוואלאזין 18 רו״כ.	256	
מקופת הכוללות.	4288	
מר׳ ישמואל ברוך סאנדערס פה 10 פראנק.	54	20
מהרב הגביר ר׳ פנחס ניסינסקי פה 60 פראנק.	327	
מהרב הגביר ר׳ יודל הורוויטץ 20 פראנק.	109	
מהגביר הר׳ שמואל הב לעמבערגער 20 פראנק.	109	
מהגביר הר״ר חיים הירש ליב מהדאק 20 פראנק.	109	
מהגביר הר׳ ארי׳ ליב נוסבוים.	69	
מהגקבין ע״י הר״ח ור״מ מנדיבי עה״ק.	203	20
ע״י הר״מ שעהנבוים.	23	
ע״י הרב הגאון אבדק״ק בריסק שליט״א מפלוני אלמוני.	12	
מהרה״ג ר׳ חיים יעקב נפתלי זילבערבערג מו״צ דק״ק ווארשא ובנו ישיחי׳ 2 רו״כ.	26	
מנדי״ב א׳ מרינא ע״י הר״ר אהרן הורוויטץ 1 רו״כ.	13	
ס״ה.	61,425	11

הוצאה.

נתחלק לבני עקרון כמבואר בפרוטרוט, בחוברת.	4793	35
להם על מצות והוצאת החג, ויין לארבע כוסות.	3344	
על התבן.	3981	15
לטלמרים בעקרון.	1081	
על זריעה.	4594	
להוצאת נסיעתם לחו״ל.	1199	
מה שנשלח לידי הרבנים הרה״ג רמ״צ הי״ו והר״נ הער״ז להלק לחקולוניסתים, קמח, ומזון.	35883	10
לבקו״ח בעד החולאים מעקרון ששכבו שם.	315	
שכר הדפסת מכתבים והחשבון.	671	
לסופרים, נייר ודיו׳	1128	
לשמשים.	353	20
בעד פתיחת החותם.	30	
מעלעגראפען ליפו ולשאר מקומות.	395	
לשלוח מכתבים וקבלות ויתר הו״ק.	2792	
הוצאת נסיעת יפו להעקרונים ולהר״ם.	301	10
הוצאת נסיעת הרבנים יפו לתוך השלום.	200	
ס״ה	60962	10
נשאר	463	1

על הכסף שבא מחודש טבת ולהלן, יבא עד הוספה לחחשבון בקרב הימים אי״ה.

Lover of Erez Yisrael. Rabbi Eliezer Gordon wrote a long letter in July 1889, critiquing the *Heter Mechirah* and the manner in which it came about. He was one of the few leading rabbis who called upon the non-Zionist, fervently Orthodox masses to build a settlement movement that would compete with Chovevei Zion.[377] His calls went unheeded.

Rabbi Yaffe did more than that. In July 1889, toward the end of the Shemittah year, after much ink and venom had been spilled on both sides of the issue, Rabbi Yaffe penned an article titled "*Lo Et La'chashot* (Not a Time to Be Silent),"[378] calling for support for Mazkeret Batya. The rebuttal not only tries to refute all the charges made against the settlers, but is also a spirited defense of the leadership of the Old Yishuv – the Jerusalem Ashkenazic rabbinate.

בעזהשי"ת.

לא עת לחשות

Not a Time to Be Silent. Letter from Rabbi Yaffe defending the Shemittah observers from their detractors.

He writes how distressed he is by the accusations hurled against the Jerusalem Rabbinate – charges that its intent was to sabotage the whole settlement enterprise – and he calls its rabbis "venerable sages, the eyes of the congregation."[379] He then approaches the miẓvah of Shemittah itself and rebuts those who argued in favor of finding a halakhic means to bypass it:

> From the time we were fortunate to know that our people have begun working the Holy Land and tilling its fields, I desired with all my soul to ensure that they fulfill the commandment of Shemittah according to the *halakhah* – after a hiatus of hundreds of years.
>
> ... during the past summer I corresponded with many rabbis, writing that whatever the final determination regarding the halakhic status of Shemittah in the contemporary era – whether it be a Torah requirement or rabbinic ... we are obliged to fulfill it, no matter what, [at least] the *first* Shemittah ... [in order] to "drive the peg firmly into its holy place."
>
> It is incumbent upon us to follow in the footsteps of our ancestors and our rabbis who after returning to the Land of Israel from [the Babylonian] exile accepted upon themselves the commandment of *ma'asrot* – even though they were exempt [from performing it] – and who obligated themselves with an oath to fulfill that commandment as well as Shemittah.[379A]

So there it was: If not now, then when? Rabbi Yaffe clearly felt that if Shemittah was not kept at least the first time, then the wrong kind of precedent would be established, and the miẓvah would be forgotten entirely.

A spirited defense of the Shemittah pioneers and the Jerusalem rabbinate was published by no less a figure than Rabbi Naftali Ẓvi Yehuda Berlin. He wrote two important letters regarding the issue. The first was written in December 1887 to Chovevei Ẓion's secular president, Dr. Leon Pinsker, before the onset of Shemittah, just a few days before Chanukah, which commemorates the victory of the Jewish people over assimilation:

> His Honor should not say that [these Jerusalem] rabbis are [unreasonably] stringent and aren't sensitive [to what is involved] in settling the land and to the pain of those Jews who lack a livelihood. Heaven forbid to say such a thing!
>
> ... His Honor should not make a ruckus and make light

Rabbinical head. Rabbi Naftali Ẓvi Yehuda Berlin, rosh yeshivah of Volozhin and one of the rabbinic leaders of Chovevei Ẓion

when it comes to honoring the sages of Israel, for they are the ones who uphold the nation and Judaism. And were it not for the Torah greats who strengthen [the nation] in every generation, the Jewish people would have already sunk [into oblivion] and been assimilated into the nations of the world, and the name "Israel" would have been forgotten, Heaven forbid.

Rabbi Berlin's analysis of the root causes of anti-Semitism seems chillingly prescient of the anti-Semitism that would engulf the world almost five decades later:

> And every time a generation wants to integrate, to be equal, and to imitate all the gentiles' ways, God instills in the hearts of the nations of the world an intense hatred [in order] to distance the Jews from them – so the Jews will know who they really are.[380]

The second letter was written a little over two weeks before the conclusion of the Shemittah year, in September 1889. It was addressed to Shmuel Yosef Fuenn, chairman of the Chovevei Ẓion branch in Vilna. Fuenn played a decisive role in catalyzing Rabbi Mohilever to issue his *heter*, which paved the way for the *heter* of Rabbi Yiẓchak Elchanan Spektor.

Secular head. Dr. Leon Pinsker, president of Chovevei Ẓion

> I received a letter from Ekron, where they pour out their sorrow to me and ask me to assemble groups for their salvation and welfare. And although I share their pain, I have reflected on this and decided that it is not my place …
>
> Nevertheless I want to arouse within His Honor sympathy for these destitute people, and not to wrongly accuse them of sins they never committed.
>
> For they followed the will of the Torah *geonim* of Jerusalem as written in *Sanhedrin* 88b, "It is incumbent to go to the *beit din* that is nearest to the city one resides in." And the *beit din* in Jerusalem is certainly not inferior to a *beit din* in the Diaspora.

Now the past is over, thank God, and the Sabbatical year is about to conclude. May God grant us that in the upcoming Shemittah we will see everyone upholding the sanctity of the land in all its details, *which is the basis of our existence in our Holy Land.*

But now we must not forget the men who risked everything to guard the sanctity of the land.

And I don't have to spell out to a wise man like you (may there be more like you in Israel!) that observing Shemittah is our pride, and the pride of all Israel and the Torah, and this will elicit God's good will in the upcoming days,[381] may they be good, in which we desire to elicit God's good will with all the utterances of our lips.[382] And may God lengthen your days and years and grant you the merit to see the good of Israel and the Holy Land.[383]

An interesting defense of the Mazkeret Batya farmers came from an anonymous writer, whose letter appeared on page one of *Ha-Meliẓ* (22 Tevet 5649/December 26, 1888), just when the situation was rapidly deteriorating in Ekron. The letter, titled "In Defense of the Colonists," was signed with the strange pseudonym *Ha'mishtamet,* which could mean shirker, slacker, or evader. In any case, the root of the Hebrew word is *sh/m/t,* which is the same as the root of Shemittah. The letter sums up the accusations and then explains, in a very practical, down-to-earth way, why the colonists of Mazkeret Batya chose not to work on Shemittah:

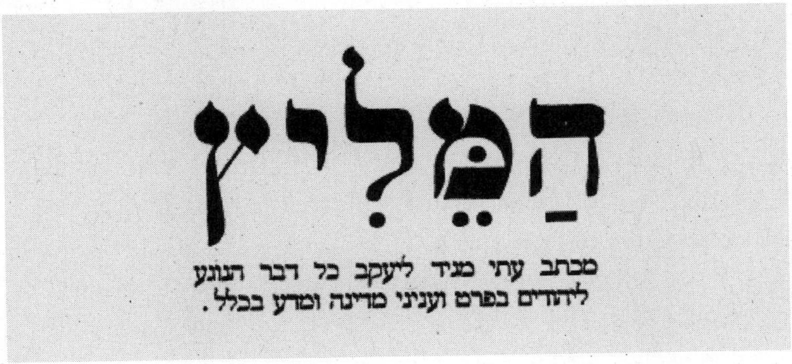

In Defense of the Colonists

The newspapers have been full of analysis and explanations as to why some colonists chose not to work this year, in opposition to the *heter* of the great rabbis of the Diaspora. Some say it was due to sloth, while others say it was their way of expressing their bitterness to their administrators. And so on. In any case, Chovevei Ẓion argued that the reason they rebelled against the great rabbis of the Diaspora [to be stringent instead of lenient] was due to presumptuousness.

However, the colonists are really innocent of the charges leveled by Chovevei Ẓion. According to the reports that have reached me, there was another reason [for their decision], which the rabbis who were lenient could not have foreseen, as in any case when we are dealing with a new set of circumstances.

The colonists are simple people; they are not great Torah scholars or *poskim*. They don't know to what extent work on Shemittah is forbidden or permitted. All they could do was rely on what the rabbis told them.

They couldn't rely on the *pilpul* of *Ha-Ẓvi*, nor on the reports of *Ha-Meliẓ* nor on the directives of the Sephardic rabbis. Because you don't determine Jewish law from a newspaper, and Ashkenazim don't ask Sephardim questions on *halakhah* (because, to our sorrow, our Torah has turned into two – one for each of these two groups – and that which is permissible for one is completely forbidden for the other). (See p. 435.)

It is understandable that once the Jerusalem rabbinate forbade working in the Sabbatical year, the colonists could not even consider the option of working before they got a clear-cut *heter* from the *geonim* of the Diaspora – with their signatures affixed to it – that work is permitted this year, so that "the humble may eat and be satiated" (Psalms 22:27). If that had indeed been the case, then any person who decided to be stringent for himself would have been a fool and worthy of rebuke.

Additionally, this *heter* needed to be received in time for the farmers to make the necessary preparations for work, such as hoeing, weeding, and fertilizing in their proper times.

But while the Jerusalem rabbis came out very clearly forbidding work, the rabbis of the Diaspora did not come out with an equally clear voice permitting it. Sorrowfully, the power of those who forbid was more definitive than the power of those who permit. The *gaon* of Kovno, who even in his youth would flee from quarrels, was taken aback by the charges leveled against him by the rabbis of Jerusalem regarding the *heter* that he promised the Benefactor, and he tried to dilute the *heter* without breaking his promise to the Benefactor, by permitting work [only] through a gentile.

Regarding a *heter* like that, the colonists were justified in saying: "Keep your favors to yourself" – for what will the poor farmer be left with if he has to pay hired hands for a whole year?

The rest of those rabbis who issued a *heter* also never bothered sending their rulings affixed with their signatures. According to what I have heard, all they did was request that a certain individual write to the colonists, informing them that work was permitted for them. I am told that the letter was written in soft, amorphous language that included [little more than] a blessing of assurance that the colonists need not worry about transgressing the prohibition of working during Shemittah.

So the colonists' interest in relying on the *heter* was gone. On one side were the Jerusalem rabbis who forcefully declared that work during Shemittah was forbidden. On the other side was a "private citizen" [i.e., Rabbi Mohilever] who spoke hesitantly, in ambiguous terms.

In addition to all this, the great and well-known *gaon* Rabbi Gimpel Yaffe arrived in the Holy Land just before Rosh Hashanah and sided with the stringent opinion. This *gaon* set up his residence in Yahud [Petach Tikva], and he is the rabbi of Mr. [Yechiel Michel] Pines … and the Ekronians were under [Rabbi Yaffe's] authority when they were still back in Russia.

Now when the people of Petach Tikva,[384] the director of Gedera [Pines], and the people of Ekron heard that the rabbi of their [former] town forbade working during Shemittah, and not a single one of these farmers had in hand a signed *heter* that was clearly and unambiguously worded – they all decided not to work this year.

I ask you, fellow Jews – I ask those of you who support the Benefactor – who is to blame here?

The Other Side of the Story

Who, indeed, was to blame? We heard what was being said about the farmers by people who supported their action, but what was being reported to the Baron?

Defiance. Ingratitude. Laziness. As reports regarding the farmers' opposition to the *heter* streamed into his office in Paris, the Baron grew increasingly exasperated and enraged at his beneficiaries.

Mr. Medallions.
Elie Scheid

Elie Scheid's memoirs reflect Rothschild's administrators' perspective on the Shemittah issue, an attitude that undoubtedly influenced the Baron. Note Scheid's interpretation of events as well as the motives of the Mazkeret Batya farmers:

> The Shemittah year arrived in 1888/89. The rabbis of Russia held as one man[385] that because the settlers were in dire straits, they were permitted to work under certain conditions.
>
> The Jerusalem rabbinate was opposed [to the *heter*] for various reasons. One of [its] stranger considerations was that the Baron was rich enough to feed all the settlers.[386]
>
> The [farmers] in all the moshavot worked,[387] except for the Ekronians – who were conceited enough to think of themselves as holier than all the other colonists. They earnestly accepted upon themselves the ruling of the Jerusalem rabbis – because they preferred idleness. Two of the [Ekron] settlers followed the rulings of the Russian rabbis – really to spite the Jerusalem rabbinate. In any case, it is hard to fathom how difficult the settlers made the lives of these two dissenters – all because that they weren't willing to be part of a united front.
>
> The *adukim* [fervently Orthodox] supported the Ekronians. If such fervency is sincere, then it deserves respect. Jews who come from Russia and Romania to live and die in the Holy Land are without doubt more religious than the average [western] European Jew. That is obvious. But such is not the case when it comes to the Ekronians. For if their motives were truly "for the sake of Heaven," there are grounds for exonerating them; there is no justification for invalidating another's religious beliefs.
>
> But they were just interested in material gains … as I will now prove. …

Shemittah commenced on Rosh Hashanah [September] 1888 and concluded on Rosh Hashanah 1889. The threshing was completed in the month of August. The [Ottoman] government collected its taxes, and the settlers gathered in the remaining harvest. They had, more or less, enough to support themselves for the rest of the year.[388] All that was left for them to do was to take a walk, or simply sit with their hands folded and wait for events to unfold. There was no way of knowing what the Baron would eventually decide by the Rosh Hashanah of 1889. By then, they would have no means of support for the upcoming year. They could only hope that the Baron would take their strict religiosity into consideration and his financial assistance would be a substitute for the crops they did not gather.

[But] immediately after the end of the Jewish holiday season, they started with their shenanigans. One Jerusalem newspaper published an article claiming that the Baron – by refusing to provide them with financial assistance because they had been insistent on observing Shemittah – was in effect allowing them to starve. This article was dispatched to all the fervently Orthodox Jews of Europe, and it found an attentive audience there. In any case, [the farmers] obtained financial support because the Jerusalem rabbis sent letters of appeal on their behalf.

The settlers were very careful not to mention that each and every one of them had gathered enough crops to last them just about throughout the year. They chuckled amongst themselves over the naïveté of their fellow Orthodox Jews. *In the recesses of their hearts, they were convinced that they wouldn't need the Baron anymore....*[389, 390]

The Baron Speaks Out

Scheid undoubtedly conveyed these perceptions to Rothschild, fueling the Baron's feelings of hurt and anger. Rothschild expressed his deepest emotions to one of his closest advisors, Rabbi Ẓaddok Kahn. Although the Baron always communicated in French, he dictated this particular letter to his secretary in German, and the German words were written out in Hebrew characters, for the Baron's intention was that the letter should eventually reach Rabbi Shmuel Mohilever. The Baron wanted to be sure that the rabbi could read it for himself. The Baron correctly assumed that after Rabbi Kahn finished reading the letter, he would add a few words of his own and forward it to Rabbi Mohilever.

What sparked the Baron's outpouring was a letter he had just received from Rabbi Shmuel Mohilever, who asked the Baron to forgive the Ekronians. The outraged Benefactor spared no words, and his letter exposes the huge gulf of misunderstanding between the two sides.

Royal rage. The Baron believed that Rabbi Mohilever had deceived him.

September 15, 1889
Paris
To: Herr Ober Rabbiner [Chief Rabbi], Ẓaddok Kahn

I hasten to reply to your letter that you did me the favor of writing on the third of this month. I do not wish to leave unanswered a letter from a person such as you, whom I respect so deeply. Had I not wished to avoid causing you unpleasantness when I described the condition of Ekron, I would have completely ignored Rabbi Shmuel's request.

I cannot tell you how astonished I was upon reading Rabbi Shmuel's letter. My astonishment was even greater when I learned that the letters I had addressed to him through Mr. Scheid remain unanswered. It was his duty not only to answer those letters, but also to take action on the matter. Chief Rabbi, allow me to retrace a little history.

No doubt, you recall that in 1883 you introduced me to Rabbi Shmuel Mohilever, who pleaded with me that I take under my wing numerous unfortunate Jewish farmers who could not remain in Russia and desired to settle in Palestine. I pointed out to him at that time that the enterprise would encounter great difficulties, even dangers. Nevertheless, I granted his request and, to show that the Jews could make good farmers, I told him he could send to Palestine ten individuals who were capable farmers, and then we could see what was to be done later.

What did Rabbi Shmuel do? He selected not ten persons, but eleven *families* with two hundred members. So I was deceived by Rabbi Shmuel. I could have complained against him, but I said nothing, though the situation became worse due to the Turkish laws. I exerted my utmost efforts to secure land for these families and also to obtain permission to build dwellings. Finally, all difficulties were overcome. I purchased a huge tract of 2660 dunams [612 acres] for them in Ekron. As they claimed this was insufficient, I purchased an additional 2,000 dunams in Niavi [Nâàneh].

Instead of erecting, as is customary, houses consisting of two rooms and a kitchen, I built them houses of four rooms, and I had barns built adjoining their houses. Two years ago when I visited them, I allowed myself to be misled by them. They showed me that the houses were still too small and asked me to make additional rooms out of the barns. I granted their wishes. How have they reacted toward me? Not one word of recognition or satisfaction. Not one of them, after five years, has come to tell me that he can earn his own livelihood, which they should have been able to do, for I know they have the means. But no! They prefer to tell lies, these pious people. They have but one purpose: to extort as much money as possible from me.

The Shemittah year has now arrived. I understand and admire all religious outlooks. I would never have entertained the notion of acting against [the farmers'] religious principles, but the Shemittah year is just a pretext for them not to work. For there are things they are permitted to do, things that were permitted by the most pious rabbis who lived in the days when Palestine was a Jewish land. Now [their] case is different. They simply don't want to work. I sensed the rebellion that was beginning. I therefore had Mohilever informed about it. What has this rabbi done – he who is responsible for this? He has not even replied, not one word. In addition to this, I am represented in the newspapers as being an oppressor who wants to force these people to transgress the laws of the Torah, and the colonists in the meantime exploit the opportunity by collecting alms all over Europe.

Has Rabbi Mohilever done anything about it all this time? Nothing! *He is to blame for everything, because I did everything based on his pleading.* He says nothing, and through his silence, he strengthens the rebellion. He ignores the letters that have been written to him. It seems that he seeks to shirk all responsibility, and meanwhile the agitation grows.

Since every year [the colonists] claim that they are dying of hunger, and this year even more so than under normal circumstances, I wanted to know how long their resources would last and asked them for an accounting, which they refused to make. The oxen, not working, nevertheless had to eat. I demanded that during the Shemittah year the oxen, which belonged to me, be used for making roads and hauling water for the colonists in Castina (Be'er Tuvia), as they have no well. This, too, they refused.

One of the colonists even laid a hand on one of my representatives. Instead of expelling him from the colony, he was, on the contrary, encouraged and abetted to do so again.

At the same time, these Jews have forgotten one of the first principles of our religion, namely, the duty of every Jew to honor the memory of his parents. Thus, they prevented a colonist from saying the *Kaddish* prayer, because he wanted to obey the halakhic ruling of Rabbi Yiẓchak Elchanan of Kovno. These are the very same people being portrayed to me as pious!

None of them has yet asked to be forgiven. Still Rabbi Shmuel wants me to forget everything. In my eyes, Rabbi Shmuel's word is no longer worth anything, and I can no longer consider his requests. I will now have to use my own judgment in this matter. The longer this lasts, the harsher my attitude toward them will be. Chief Rabbi, do you know what I think? I will tell you the truth. These colonists of Ekron want to take the land and houses away from me and then scoff at me. This will never happen. Let Rabbi Shmuel know that I will send the colonists of Ekron and all their families back to him and then we will see what he does with them. Other than travel expenses, I will not give them a cent.

In the pleasant anticipation of seeing you again soon,

Edmond de R.[391]

Rabbi Kahn certainly must have found the letter unsettling. Before forwarding it to Rabbi Mohilever, he attached a personal note of his own:

To my friend, the illustrious, great sage … Rabbi Shmuel Mohilever:

I received the enclosed letter from Baron Edmond de Rothschild, and to my distress I did not find what I was hoping for, because in it he says some very harsh words in his rage. The settlers of Ekron

> have disgusted him, and if they don't ask forgiveness soon and change their course, I can't predict what will happen. May God cancel any evil decree against Israel.[392]

Apparently, the Baron had written to Rabbi Mohilever repeatedly. Why *didn't* the rabbi issue even a single reply to all the letters? An answer to this question is provided by his grandson, Dr. Yosef Mohilever, and casts Rabbi Mohilever in a starkly self-sacrificing, heroic light:

In his younger years. Dr. Yosef Mohilever[393] (his doctorates were in agronomy, philosophy, and pedagogy, besides his rabbinic ordination) studied Torah from his grandfather, Rabbi Shmuel Mohilever. When Rabbi Shmuel Mohilever could not attend the First Zionist Congress due to poor health, he sent his grandson Yosef to represent him and to read a letter of greetings to the delegates.

> The *gaon* Rabbi Shmuel Mohilever had no peace of mind at that time. How many times had he tried to sway the Ekronians with his numerous letters and telegrams, to no avail, all while this major conflict was taking place in Ekron!
>
> During those confusing times, Rabbi Mohilever received many letters from Baron Rothschild asking him to intervene in the matter and to exert some influence on the Ekronians. The *gaon* ... even wanted to make a trip to the Land of Israel for that purpose, but due to illness he was forbidden by his doctors to undertake such a journey. Then he reflected: if he replied to the Baron and told the Baron how things really stood – that is, that he had done everything in his power but hadn't succeeded – the Baron would certainly be even more incensed at the Ekronians, and his wrath would spell catastrophe for them as well as for the entire settlement enterprise.
>
> Therefore, he decided not to reply to the Baron at all. And even though this would arouse the Great Benefactor's anger against *him*, it would at least succeed in diverting it from the Ekronians. Because this silence would appear as an admission that he, not the Ekronians, was guilty – [as though] he didn't want to influence them.[394]

Although the Mazkeret Batya farmers did not heed Rabbi Mohilever's lenient halakhic ruling, and they never replied to *his* numerous letters to them, he shielded them and was willing to suffer the humiliation and rejection of the great Baron Rothschild, so long as he believed he was capable of protecting them.

Despite the venom and recriminations in the Baron's letter to Rabbi Mohilever, the rabbi saw the bright side of its historical

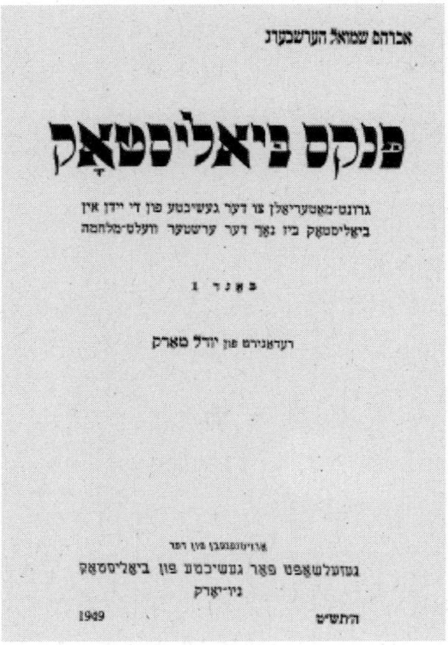
אברהם שמואל הערשבערג

פנקס ביאליסטאָק

גרונט-מאַטעריאַלן צו דער געשיכטע פון די יידן אין
ביאַליסטאָק ביז נאָך דער ערשטער וועלט-מלחמה

באַנד 1

רעדאַגירט פון יודל מארק

ארויסגעגעבן פון דער
געזעלשאַפט פאַר געשיכטע פון ביאַליסטאָק
ניו-יאָרק

1949 התש"ט

Pinkas Bialystok. Title page. A *pinkas* is the official record book of the Jewish community.

portent, as we see from the author of the *Chronicle of Bialystok* (translated from the original Yiddish):

> When Rabbi Shmuel Mohilever showed me the letter from Baron Rothschild, he told me he would request that this letter be placed beneath his head when he passed away, because it proves that he was the first person who inspired the Baron with the ideal of settling Ereẓ Yisrael – that through his meeting with him, the Baron became actively involved.[395]

Chapter 25
The Noose Tightens

Even before the Shemittah year drew to a close, the Mazkeret Batya farmers knew that the cold winter was looming. They had no seeds to plant and no money to buy any. Bloch hoped that the farmers, crushed by their impoverished situation, would become desperate enough to succumb to his demands.

But he was foiled at the last minute. Chaim Moshe Press went to an Arab in Ramle and purchased, for 250 Napoleons on credit, one hundred sacks of wheat kernels! He promptly distributed them to the rest of the farmers.[396]

According to Dr. Chissin's account, it was the Va'ad ha-Shemittah that saved the day. In September 1889, it contributed wheat kernels for the purpose of sowing the fields for the upcoming winter season.[397] Chissin recorded (perhaps with some satisfaction) Bloch's reaction:

> Bloch was infuriated. Now the settlers would plow and sow their fields easily, the winter days would pass, then the wheat would ripen, and then they would need the Baron's administrator [Bloch] even less. He was angry that a rabbi [Mordechai Gimpel Yaffe] had gone to the rabbis [of the Va'ad]. He protested the action taken by the Va'ad, branding [its members] meddlers – but they completely ignored him. This time Bloch was convinced that he had the lower hand, and that was only because of the rabbis – whom he had always despised, and for whom he had no respect at all. He realized that these rabbis were not people who didn't know how to respond. They held the power to overcome *him* – the terror of the settlements![398]

The farmers had won their battles with Bloch. They had persevered and observed Shemittah as interpreted by the rabbis in Jerusalem. But they had paid a heavy price – in poverty, illness, and the loss of the good will of the Benefactor.

Rabbi Mohilever – who had borne the brunt of the Baron's displeasure – had foreseen that the crisis in relations between Mazkeret Batya and the Baron's administration would not be over after the Shemittah year. He feared that Bloch (and the Baron) would not settle for anything less than the farmers' total capitulation. That meant that they would have to sign on to the "clauses" already signed by the settlers of the other colonies funded by Rothschild – effectively turning them into day laborers.

Emboldened by their year-long defiance of the Baron's administrators, the Mazkeret Batya settlers were not ready to give in to pressure. They had already triumphed over one injustice that threatened their religious freedom. They would not succumb to what they considered another unreasonable demand, a breach of contract that would deny them their human dignity.

Moderate *maskil*. Shmuel Yosef Fuenn. He was the bridge between Chovevei Ẓion's Orthodox rabbis and its more radical elements.

Anticipating their attitude, Rabbi Mohilever had sent word to Shmuel Yosef Fuenn (chairman of the Chovevei Ẓion of Vilna) to convene an emergency meeting of Chovevei Ẓion to discuss this matter. He wrote to Fuenn: "It seems quite possible that the colony will completely crumble.... And if that is true, the whole edifice of Chovevei Ẓion in Russia will go up in flames, God forbid. For this matter alone, we are obliged to convene a meeting and think of ways of reducing the conflict."[399]

In mid-August 1889, Chovevei Ẓion met in Vilna and decided to send a letter to Mazkeret Batya, urging the farmers to sign an agreement with the Baron's administrators and accept his full authority:

> We believe it is the right thing for you to take our advice and sign onto the stipulations of the Baron's administrators. We are confident that no evil will befall you from this.... We are advising you for your own good.... If there are some conditions that may be hard for you to accept at the beginning, remember that "the Land of Israel is acquired through tribulations" [*Berachot* 5a], as the saying of the Rabbis, of blessed memory, goes. We are confident that if you are receptive to the words of the Baron and his administrators, then he will be very good to you.... [400]

Radical *maskil*. Moshe Leib Lilienblum. The *kippah* came off, but the beard remained.

The letter was transcribed by Moshe Leib Lilienblum, the secretary and one of the driving secular spirits behind the Chovevei Ẓion movement. He had been an ardent opponent of resting the land during Shemittah, which certainly did not endear him to the Mazkeret Batya farmers.

He attached a memorandum instructing Yechiel Michel Pines, the representative of Chovevei Ẓion in Palestine, to warn the farmers of the urgency of the situation. Pines was also asked to assure them that Chovevei Ẓion back in Russia would do everything in its power to improve their relationship with the Baron, but that the farmers would have to do their part.

Although Pines spoke to them, his heart wasn't really in it. He may have seen this as a "Catch-22" situation, for this action may have saved Mazkeret Batya in the short term but would likely ruin it in the long run. As he confided in a letter:

A complex man. Yechiel Michel Pines was a student of Rabbi Mordechai Gimpel Yaffe and the brother-in-law of Rabbi David Friedman ("the Karliner"). Pines was a rabbi, a lover of the Land of Israel, a representative of Chovevei Ẓion, an early ideologue of religious Zionism, a patron of the BILU in Palestine (and of Jewish outreach to the secular Biluim) and active in the revival of the Hebrew language. (He coined two Hebrew words related to clocks and created many others.) He established the first Jewish factory in modern Palestine, which manufactured bricks and rafters. He fought everyone: the conservative religious elements of the Old Yishuv on account of his educational reforms (he was excommunicated by Rabbi Yehoshua Leib Diskin); the radical *maskilim*, because they were anti-religious; and the Chovevei Ẓion over the Shemittah issue.

> … And I am not just theorizing but [telling you] that we have seen with our own eyes how acceptance of these terms has ruined places like Rishon Le-Ẓion, Zikhron Yaakov, and Castina. Once they sign on that they are hired workers, they *see* themselves as hired hands. In the beginning, each colonist viewed his homestead as most precious and worked hard to improve it with all his might. He was working for his own home. Day and night he did not rest, for he was concerned about his property. And even if he received assistance from the Baron, he kept pondering how to rid himself of this "miserable bread,"[401] and he would attempt with all his might to achieve economic independence.
>
> But now? Woe! My heart is broken, but I cannot deny the truth. All the colonists – even the best amongst them – have become so demoralized.… They now go out to work to fulfill their minimum obligations and receive their salary. And this is what they are saying: "We won't be keeping it [the harvest], so why work hard?"
>
> … The bottom line is that this new policy which the Baron's administrators have adopted and have convinced him to go along

> with has had a corrupting influence on all aspects – and ruined morale.[402]

Although the settlers of Mazkeret Batya received Pines cordially, they remained adamantly opposed to signing away their farms.

It was around this time, toward the end of the Shemittah year, that Elie Scheid visited all the Baron's colonies in Palestine, except Mazkeret Batya. His comments on the place, forwarded to the Baron, were scathing:

> The Benefactor takes pride and pleasure in all his colonies, because a spirit of peace and tranquility pervades them all. . . .
>
> But the Ekronians are the rotten apple . . . they are stiff-necked in their refusal to agree to the clauses that were presented to them on behalf of their sponsor, who desires their good and happiness, because a hidden hand is behind all that is agitating them.[403]
>
> [I decided] . . . to avoid them altogether, because they were so wrong for listening to the [outside] agitators and not complying with the *heter* to work that was issued by the great halakhic authorities of the generation. They are guilty of ruining the colony.[404]

"Outside agitators" was obviously a reference to the rabbis of the Old Yishuv. Over the year, the Mazkeret Batya pioneers had earned the respect of other fervently Orthodox farmers, but their hostile situation with the Baron was seen as a poignant tragedy. Mordechai Diskin, the Orthodox activist from Petach Tikva, took it upon himself to go to Scheid and try to mend his relationship with Mazkeret Batya. Scheid's reaction was shocking. Diskin wrote:

> Mr. Scheid didn't even bother asking me what I'd come for; he just started talking . . . and when he finished talking, I began telling him about the Ekronians and about making peace. He immediately metamorphosed into a different person and started raging, saying that he would expel all the Ekronians and replace them with capable young men. Then, in his wrath, he brazenly told me that he didn't need any mediators and didn't want to talk anymore. And here I could sense the depth of his animosity.[405]

In the meantime, rumors that the Baron was about to make a decision to expel the Ekronians for insubordination were getting louder and more widespread. In terror, Rabbi Mohilever wrote to Michael Erlanger in Paris. Erlanger sent him a reply on September 4, 1889, telling him that the rumors were unfounded. He said that the Baron had no intention of throwing the farmers out of Palestine. Not only that, but…

> … even though they rebelled against him (and they also rebelled against His Honor [i.e., Rabbi Mohilever], because they rejected his halakhic ruling in favor of the others), and even though they opposed everything he said and didn't listen to him, he has decided not to punish them at all.[406]

Erlanger's appraisal was that there was still time to mend the rift between the farmers and the Baron if they were willing to comply with his conditions. Erlanger expressed the sentiments prevalent in Chovevei Ẓion circles at the time – that the Jerusalem rabbis hated the whole agricultural Yishuv enterprise and were trying to destroy it with their strict halakhic rulings. No matter what happened to the families of Mazkeret Batya, there were plenty of families waiting to take their place and accept the administrators' conditions. Erlanger ended his letter with these words:

> We should address our pleas not to the Baron, but to them [the farmers]. May it be their desire that they open their eyes, do their daily work, and pay no attention to senseless words.[407]

The farmers ignored all entreaties to sign away their farms. Two months later, in exasperation, Erlanger sounded a more ominous note. He wrote:

> … if they continue to act callously with the Benefactor – who knows what [the Baron] will command concerning them? He has the power to expel them from there and cast them elsewhere whenever he pleases.[408]

Erlanger reiterated that the only reason the Baron hadn't already done so was due to his incredible forbearance, which had been considerably weakened throughout the dispute. He threatened that his patience might soon run out.

The writer Mordechai Ben Hillel, who visited Palestine in the beginning of October 1889, disagreed sharply with Erlanger and company's negative perception of the settlers of Mazkeret Batya. But neither did he endorse Rabbi Mohilever's dire predictions.

> I am worried sick that something bad will happen to the people of Ekron.... When you look at the faces of these farmers, you see that they are plain people, plain Jews and simple farmers, with no wile or hubris. Their appearance just inspires goodhearted people to like them and feel compassion for them.
>
> But whoever predicts that "Ekron will be uprooted" is mistaken. The settlement of Ekron will never disappear! And even if the Baron distances some troublemakers from the [settlement], there is no danger to Ekron, because better people are always in the wings to take their place. Even the [anti-*heter*] Jerusalemites now realize that they went too far and are making efforts to turn the hearts of the farmers back toward the Baron. The Baron, too, is distressed about his beloved colony and will forgive them....[409]

The complicated legacy of Mazkeret Batya's stand would fuel controversy over the Shemittah issue for generations to come. To some, the farmers' suffering was a beacon of enduring faith and determination to fulfill a mizvah at any cost; to others, it was all the more reason to seek practical applications of Jewish law that would preserve the spirit of the law without extreme hardship. And the tensions between the religious settlers and the Baron's secular administrators would continue – a forerunner and symbol of the ongoing struggle between the spiritual successors of the Old Yishuv and New Yishuv to this day.

Chapter 26

The Land and People Rest from Controversy

The protracted struggle between the Baron's administrators and the farmers of Mazkeret Batya had taken its toll on both sides. The farmers and their families were in dire straits, suffering from tremendous poverty, and had lost all means of supporting themselves. They were under constant threat of being either expelled or sued in the Ottoman courts.

The Baron's men, especially Alphonse Bloch, were stymied and burned out. Although Bloch was a master at manipulation and demagoguery, his skills were no match for the dogged determination of the farmers to adhere to their religious principles. Manipulation works well when the interests of one's opponent are rooted in selfish pursuits, but the farmers' ideals were rooted in something far greater. Bloch and Scheid had no experience dealing with people who had such deep religious faith and convictions; they failed to understand them.

To both men's genuine surprise, threats and punitive measures had failed to "persuade" the farmers to buckle. The two options remaining were either to give in to the farmers and lose face, or to use all their power to drive them off the land through the Ottoman legal system. On the other hand, expelling the farmers from Palestine would only further sully the already tarnished image of their boss as a ruthless tyrant.

The rabbis also wanted to find a way to break through the impasse. They feared that the colony's deteriorating relationship with the Benefactor was reaching the breaking point. So they initiated their own peace overtures. Rabbi Yaffe asked Rabbi Diskin to write a letter to Rabbi Spektor requesting that he plead with the Baron to be merciful toward the people of Ekron.[410]

Searching for an honorable exit from the conflict, Bloch put out his own feelers as well. He turned to Rabbi Shmuel Salant, a man he had despised, and made an appointment to see him on November 18, 1889.

The meeting between the two was reported in *Ha-Maggid*.[411] Rabbi Salant was almost 73 years old. He had been living in Palestine since 1841, about forty-eight years. Bloch had been in the country for only a year.

Rabbi Salant greeted his guest warmly and inquired about the welfare of the Baron. Bloch informed Rabbi Salant that

Symbol of the Old Yishuv. Rabbi Shmuel Salant was honored by the Israel Postal Authority for his decades of untiring work and leadership on behalf of Jerusalem and the Yishuv.

the Baron was ready to forgive the people of Ekron for the sins they had committed against him if they would only repent of their wrong ways, stop being so stubborn, and obey the orders of his administrators. The Baron's generosity was also contingent on the expulsion of Mazkeret Batya's chief agitator, Yaakov Gold.[412]

Bloch wanted to break their resistance, and he wanted Rabbi Salant to do the dirty work for him. Apparently, Rabbi Salant felt it was in the best interests of the farmers to comply.

After their fateful meeting, Rabbi Salant wrote a letter to Rabbi Naftali Hertz Halevi of Jaffa and to Rabbi Yaffe, two men the farmers admired and trusted. He wrote that he had heard from "reliable sources" that now was the opportune time to mend the rift between the moshavah and the Baron. He assured them that the Baron was willing to forgive the farmers if they would cease raising money from the outside and look solely to his generosity for all their necessities. Moreover, Rabbi Salant insisted that they had to accept the authority of the Baron's administrators. He told the rabbis:

> I have been told that either a majority or minority [of the farmers] have made up their minds to go down to the fields of the Baron and sow there without his permission. I therefore request of you to order them not to commit any wrongdoing, and not to do anything without the authorization of the Baron, because those fields belong to him. And because [the Baron] wants with all his heart to bestow kindness justly and properly, we must use all possible means to make peace [between the two sides].
>
> This great mizvah to broker the peace falls upon you, because both of you live near the farmers and the administrators. And although I have heard that the farmers have taken a solemn oath between them [not to betray one another], you have the necessary [halakhic] mandate to nullify any form of oath or prohibition that they have placed upon themselves.
>
> If, God forbid, the Ekronians stubbornly resist this opportunity, then I will remind them that it is regretful that they ignored the advice I gave them in my home last year not to ask for handouts from everyone and not to request charity monies that were

> designated for the destitute of Jerusalem. It is through these actions that they have angered the Baron. What I advised them was to send the right people to Paris to beseech the Baron to allow them to observe the Sabbatical year and not to pay attention to arrogant purveyors of falsehoods who wish to uproot the serious commandment of Shemittah. I further told them that I would try to get funding for their travel expenditures from the Kolel ha-Perushim. I was confident that the Baron would willingly receive them and would support them without requiring them to work in the Sabbatical year. I told them this many times, but they weren't willing to listen, and now they are suffering [the consequences].[413]

The next paragraph addressed the farmers, instructing them not to feel sorry for themselves because of their new status, but to realize how fortunate they were – if they would only compare their situation to that of the typical Jew of the Old Yishuv:

> And, therefore, don't harden your hearts like [the ancient Israelites] at Meribah.[414] Rather, have forbearance, and see how beneficial serenity is, and appreciate how satisfying it is to work the land.[415]
>
> And I know that thousands of people among the residents of Jerusalem would consider [the farmers] very fortunate because [of the dignity and privilege] of eating bread that comes from the toil of their hands, for which they themselves yearn. But what can they do? For there is neither labor nor employment. If only there would

Learning the art of earning. Fervently Orthodox young men learn tailoring at the Diskin Orphan Home in Jerusalem (early twentieth century). The orphanage was established by Rabbi Yehoshua Leib Diskin as an alternative to the orphanages set up by Christian missionary groups.

be jobs for the residents of Jerusalem, they would surely work with joy and happiness.[416]

Rabbi Salant next turned to the Va'ad ha-Shemittah. The farmers of Mazkeret Batya and their families had survived in part because of the committee's activities.[417] In his letter to its leaders, the rabbi urged them to persuade the farmers to make peace with the Baron.

Me'ah She'arim's spiritual leader. Rabbi Shaul Chaim Halevi Horowitz

Jerusalem
25 Cheshvan 5650
[November 19, 1889]

To the Honorable Rabbis Shaul Chaim Halevi [Horowitz],[418] Shlomo Zalman Baharan,[419] and Chaim Sonnenfeld:[420]

Shalom!
In my opinion, it is right and urgent that we put an end to all the quarrels among the Ekronians, so that they may eat the bread obtained through the toil of their own hands with honor and dignity. I am therefore asking you to travel to Ekron and from there [take the farmers with you] to Mikveh Israel. (For I hear the Baron's colonial administrators are getting together there. Rabbis Mordechai Gimpel Yaffe and Naftali Hertz Halevi will also be there.)

Then you should speak to the Ekronians in my name, and try to impress upon them the good will of the Baron. Try to influence the administrators to look upon them with kindness and to give them the honor that upright farmers who till the soil deserve.

May God help the three of you succeed in bringing this matter to a favorable conclusion.

Your friend,
Shmuel Salant[421]

David Baumgarten, the *Ha-Maggid* correspondent who dispatched the report regarding this letter, believed that the resolution of this dispute not only was vital for the survival of Mazkeret Batya/Ekron, but also had major implications for the success of the settlement enterprise as a whole.[422] Baumgarten surmised that many farmers throughout the Baron's settle-

Like two heads of state. Rabbi Yosef Chaim Sonnenfeld (center) escorts Thomas Masaryk (later to become the first president of the democratic Czech Republic) during his visit to Jerusalem in 1927. From the time he arrived in Palestine until his death in 1932, Rabbi Sonnenfeld never left the Old City of Jerusalem for more than thirty days at a time.

ments were uneasy with his policies and were at one stage or another in the process of rebellion. All eyes were on the settlers of Ekron. They alone had defied the Baron regarding Shemittah, had survived that difficult episode, and were now struggling with a gripe that many other colonies shared – the issue of self-determination.

The settlers of Mazkeret Batya realized that it was not in their long-term interest to remain in a protracted war with the Baron. Furthermore, their allies, the rabbis who had urged them not to work during the Sabbatical year, were now earnestly attempting to make peace between them and the Baron. They decided to come to terms with the administrators.

It was big news when the two sides finally reached a truce. Michael Erlanger wasted no time confirming the good tidings to Rothschild:

> I have good news to announce to His Honor. We have been informed by the director of Rishon Le-Ẓion that the people of Mazkeret Batya have ceased their revolt and [have agreed] to again

come under the patronage of the Baron based on the conditions he has stipulated to them for their own benefit.

... They see that even the sages of Jerusalem have turned their backs on them upon recognizing their incorrectness. Let us hope that they will better their ways from now on and succeed in all their endeavors, God willing.[423]

Ha-Maggid eagerly reported the agreement:

Hope and Peace for the Ekronians!

I am happy to report that they have finally succeeded, praise God, in making peace, [a peace] of justice and integrity, based on the details hammered out between the administrators and the Ekronians. [The text of the agreement] was sent to His Honor, the Baron, via telegraph. His Honor's reply arrived three days later; he concurred with everything. The Baron was also pleased that his request that the troublesome Gold family be expelled was also carried out. And he [in turn] acceded to the Ekronians' wishes to continue to sow their fields with wheat without having to plant vineyards.

Based on these points, all the people of Ekron have returned to their work in the fields, to harrow and seed, and their support will be restored to what it was before without any decrease. ... [424]

Historic irony. Across the street from the museum in Mazkeret Batya still stands the residence of the Gold family. Inscribed on a plaque are these words (in Hebrew): *By the sweat of their brows, they ate bread.* The Golds left behind their descendants and house, but Alphonse Bloch is long gone, without a trace.

Behind the scenes, one of those who played a role in the reconciliation was a Chovevei Ẓion activist by the name of Yiẓchak Leib Goldberg (1860-1935). In an audience with Baron Rothschild, Goldberg attempted to portray the Mazkeret Batya settlers in a more favorable light.

Two years later, when Goldberg paid a visit to Mazkeret Batya, his secret advocacy on behalf of the moshavah was revealed by the *melamed,* Avraham Yaakov Gellman:

Gellman stopped by the door, turned toward those gathered, and said, "*Rabbosai*! I am self-imposed by an oath of silence regarding two important matters that affect our settlement. But now, I can no longer restrain myself and remain silent. First of all, thanks to this man, Mr. Goldberg of Vilna, and his money, we have this pharmacy. Second, after the Shemittah, when, due to our commitment to observe this mizvah, destruction befell us, so we were compelled even to sell our work animals and barely had a morsel of bread left, it was this man, Mr. Goldberg, who went to the Baron and restored the Baron's compassion on us."

Peacemaker and philanthropist. Yizchak Leib Goldberg. From 1878 till 1914, he worked tirelessly in Vilna for the rebuilding of Palestine. Historian Shimon Dubnov described Goldberg as one of the few who "said little but did a great deal."[426]

Goldberg didn't know how to react. How had the *melamed* found out? After all, everything had been done discreetly, with the explicit request that his identity not be leaked. No one applauded, but Messrs. Arkin, Rudovsky, Maller, Skolnick, and others shook his hand. Till his last days [Goldberg] could never forget the expressions on their faces.[425]

The peace that ensued, however, turned out to be only a cease-fire. Mazkeret Batya had one more battle to fight, a battle it could win only through surrendering.

The Triumph and Tragedy of Mazkeret Batya's Shemittah

> The settlers of Mazkeret Batya were made of unique material, combining great love for the Land of Israel, fear of Heaven, and an unyielding determination to settle the land. It is difficult to find any parallel to them anywhere else in the country. Their decision to stand firm even when their struggle seemed all but lost is truly astonishing.[1]

Shemittah, by itself an immense undertaking, took on gargantuan proportions for the pioneers of Mazkeret Batya. These

[1] Mordechai Naor, *Sefer le-Mazkeret: Mazkeret Batya-Ekron – Me'ah ha-Shanim ha-Rishonot* (Jerusalem: Ben-Zvi Press, 2010), p. 322.

newcomers carried the additional burdens of having to adapt to an alien environment and its diseases such as malaria and trachoma. Having never borne arms in Russia, they had to take up rifles – and risk their lives – in order to defend their property from their Arab neighbors and rescue their (secular) brothers in Gedera. With Shemittah, in addition to loss of income, the colonists were hounded in the Ottoman courts and threatened with expulsion. Eventually they suffered from hunger and malnutrition and reportedly even starved to death.[2]

Rothschild's rabbi, Ẓaddok Kahn. *Photo by Atelier Nadar, circa 1904.*

Perhaps the only person who could have swayed the Baron in favor of the Ekronians was Rabbi Ẓaddok Kahn. The son of a peddler, Rabbi Kahn had risen to become the chief rabbi of France. Greatly respected by the Baron, the rabbi could have defended the colonists on religious grounds (though it was he who had sought and obtained the famous *Heter Mechirah* from Rabbi Yiẓchak Elchanan Spektor).

Rabbi Kahn faced a terrible dilemma. He was fully aware of the Ekronians' anguish, as all the reports from Palestine and the various functionaries came his way. Far from insensitive, he was always helping destitute east European Jews and even fought the Jewish establishment to absorb more refugees into the French community. He wasn't afraid to stand up for what he believed in either, courageously supporting Chovevei Ẓion even as French Jewish leaders attacked him and French Jews feared accusations of dual loyalty. But the piety of the Ekron

[2] Twenty-four years later, when another debate over Shemittah was raging in the Holy Land, Rabbi Avraham Yiẓchak Kook wrote to Rabbi David Willowsky (Ridbaz) of the sacrifices of these first Shemittah pioneers: "... when the rabbis ... succeeded in convincing the settlers of Ekron not to release their lands [from the obligations of Shemittah], I later saw a letter written by these same rabbis appealing for support because there were cases of people actually dying from hunger [in Ekron]." Rabbi Avraham Yiẓchak Hakohen Kook, *Iggrot ha-Re'aya* (Jerusalem: Mossad Harav Kook, 1962), vol. 2, letter 555, p. 190.

farmers clashed with Rabbi Kahn's own outlook – which he imparted to French Jewry – that Judaism needn't hinder a normative lifestyle and could be integrated into modern life. Shemittah would also be used by opponents of colonization of Palestine as another proof why colonization was impractical. The rabbi was in an unenviable position.

Considering all the difficulties the Ekronians had already endured prior to Shemittah, their desire to observe this commandment without any leniencies makes one marvel. These farmers didn't just grudgingly accept Shemittah, they *longed* for it. Their religious sentiments resembled those of the Ashkenazic rabbis in Jerusalem:

> They paid no heed to those who called for searching for leniencies through various stratagems in order to exempt themselves from this commandment. For this Divine commandment in particular encapsulates both the uniqueness of the Jewish people and the holiness of the land, and we have been yearning to fulfill this precept from the very day the Jewish people was exiled from its land.[3]

Furthermore, the Ekronians and some of the Jerusalem rabbis didn't see Shemittah as a stringency to be observed at the expense of settling the land. On the contrary, they viewed it as an integral part of a dynamic process that would strengthen the colonies. In stark contrast, their opponents regarded Shemittah as an obstacle.

As the Shemittah controversy raged, the voices of doom predicted the early demise of Mazkeret Batya. "עקרון תיעקר" – "Ekron will be uprooted!" they cried. One year of not working the land would destroy the young settlement's infrastructure, and its recovery would be painfully slow, if at all. Moreover, it was claimed, a year of idleness would make the settlers lazy and even more desirous of sponging off the Baron rather than making it on their own. Alarm bells were sounded by Eliezer

[3] Rabbi Shlomo Zalman Auerbach, *Ma'adanei Erez, Shvi'it* (Jerusalem: Ozrot Shlomo, 5768), introduction.

Ben-Yehuda in *Ha-Ẓvi,* by Chovevei Ẓion, and by Baron Rothschild's administrators.

While Shemittah did set the colonists back regarding their debt payments to the Baron, in every other respect the naysayers were wrong. The Ekronians made a quite a comeback.[4]

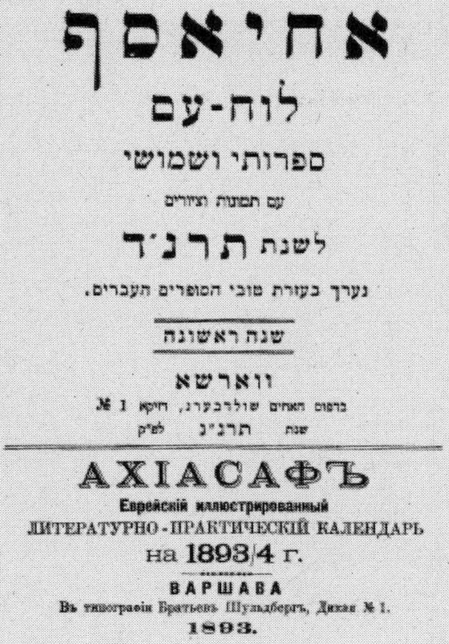
אחיאסף
לוח-עם
ספרותי ושמושי
עם תמונות וציורים
לשנת תרנ״ד
נערך בעזרת טובי הסופרים העברים.
שנה ראשונה
ווארשא
בדפוס האחים שולדבערג, דיקא № 1
שנת תרנ״ג לפ״ק

АХІАСАФЪ
Еврейскій иллюстрированный
ЛИТЕРАТУРНО-ПРАКТИЧЕСКІЙ КАЛЕНДАРЬ
на 1893/4 г.
ВАРШАВА
Въ типографіи Братьевъ Шульдбергъ, Дикая № 1.
1893.

Literary almanac. Title page of the first edition of *Achi'asaf,* for the years 1893-1894.

One senses Mazkeret Batya's buoyancy and independence in the pages of the *Achi'asaf* Hebrew almanac. In its first edition, published in 1893-1894, a mere four years after Shemittah, the yearbook said of the farmers:

> By now the Ekronians *could have been on their own* – for they are the best Jewish farmers [in Palestine] – if not for the bad blood between them and the administrators....
>
> The Ekronians *want to remove themselves from the yoke of the administrators* and their meddling in their affairs, especially regarding [the administrators'] great expenditures, which ultimately will cost [the Ekronians]. Therefore they say: We

[4] There are several possible explanations for this comeback: (1) Shemittah caused relatively little damage, because the moshavah was still in its infancy. (2) The colonists believed in their cause and mission. (3) They were fiercely independent and took responsibility for themselves. (4) They loved farming; it was their passion.

don't want you, your trusteeship, *your support,* or your tree plantings. Let's calculate exactly how much we owe [the Baron] and divide it according to a set number of years, and *we'll gladly pay you on an annual basis ...*

This year the colonists sowed even more than in previous years, for they sowed twenty-five dunams of winter wheat and 1,500 dunams of summer wheat. They also heavily fertilized their fields. *It seems that their quarrel with the administrators energized them even more.* The wheat yield was high – enough to supply all the colonists' needs for a year.[5]

Tragically, and paradoxically, the very administrators who declared Shemittah an unnecessary religious stringency that the settlers had no right to take upon themselves at the Baron's expense were willing to waste much more of his money just to break them.[6]

In insisting on the feasibility of full Shemittah observance, the colonists were way ahead of their time.

The following Shemittah was another story.[7]

---

5 *Achi'asaf* 1 (5654/1893-1894), pp. 145-146. Emphasis added.

6 See chapter 29 for Achad Ha-Am's blistering critique of the administrators as well as chief administrator Elie Scheid's frank admission to him. As noted there, to teach the "ungrateful" farmers to appreciate their Benefactor, they were given stipends based on the size of their households rather than on their output, though this move destroyed their incentive to work.

7 Yehuda Grazovsky-Gur reported in *Ha-Shiloach* that in 5656 (1895-1896) the summer wheat was sown by Arabs, which required a leniency regarding Shemittah, and most of the farmers were employed in the Baron's orchards and received regular stipends. See Naor, p. 123. One must take into consideration that the same Jerusalem rabbis who had forbidden any leniencies during the previous Shemittah were more permissive for that of 5656. To understand why, see Yechiel Michel Tucazinsky, *Sefer ha-Shemittah* (Jerusalem: Mossad Harav Kook, 5766), p. 60. Another factor is that the Ekronians' fighting spirit was broken following the orchards controversy (discussed in chapters 27-29).

Chapter 27
The Battle of the Orchards

Although the farmers and the Baron were seemingly reconciled, their problems with his administrators were not over. Alphonse Bloch had determined from the Shemittah debacle that he *must* wrest total control of the land from them. Only a few months after the dust settled, he initiated a war of even greater intensity. It would be Bloch's last conflict with the people of Mazkeret Batya.

A number of contemporary accounts have been written about this highly publicized and well-documented conflict, which became known as "The Battle of the Orchards." A detailed account is found in Dr. Chaim Chissin's book *Journey through the Promised Land*:

> Peace finally reigned. But it was easy to foresee that the tranquility wouldn't last for long. Bloch was never going to forgive the settlers for his defeat, and it was just a matter of time before the conflagration would reignite. The earlier events had all impacted on the administrators so that after Shemittah, when they returned to the moshavah, their perception of the Ekronians was negative. The aura and grace with which they had originally perceived the Ekronians and the respect they had for their exceptional farming skills were gone....
>
> In May 1890, when Scheid came for his yearly tour of the moshavot, he summoned the Ekronians and informed them that the Baron had concluded that field crops [wheat and other grains] alone were not a sufficient source of income. He therefore wanted them to switch to orchards – the only viable income option that would also enable them to gradually pay off their debts [to the Baron].
>
> Scheid's words had great significance. What he was trying to say was that seven years of experience in Ekron had proven that growing grains in Palestine was not profitable. As far as the administration was concerned, it had done its best; the settlers were given sufficiently large plots of good land for each farm [and by now should have become financially independent]. Yet the settlers still insisted on getting their yearly subsidies.
>
> The farmers countered that they hadn't been provided with enough land to turn a profit and that the administration simply

> didn't give them credence. But as the administrators saw things, this was a bottomless pit, and even after additional land purchases there would still not be enough money generated for the people to live on.
>
> Unfortunately, the problem was not grain. It was the administration, which retarded the settlement's growth at every stage. [The administrators] should never have accepted new settlers when the existing amount of land was insufficient for the current number of farmers. And if they were going to accept more people, then they needed to purchase more land.[427]

While historian Ran Aaronsohn maintains that the Baron's motives may have been purely economic, because citrus and other fruit orchards were in fact much more profitable than growing grains, Chissin perhaps reflected the sentiments of his contemporaries: the administrators' desire to change the economies to orchards was intended for their *own* benefit. He is explicit in his charges:

> When an economy is based on field crops, the incompetence of these managers is readily apparent at each harvest. However, when an economy is based on vines or any other kind of fruit trees, it is possible to get away with mismanagement through wasting money, stupidity, and gross incompetence, because the mistakes are concealed over time, and it takes years before they are exposed.
>
> For example, would it be such a disaster if plum trees didn't work out? Not at all – just plant strawberries or even almond trees! If winemaking didn't succeed, then make cognac or raisins. The advantage of orchards is that if you don't succeed, you can try again – and the final accounting can be pushed off to a later date. No matter how stupid they were, the [administrators] could put on an appearance of competence.
>
> The Baron's decision to convert the economy of Ekron to orchards was truly aggravating for the settlers. As lovers of the plow, accustomed from their youth to the cycle of plowing, seeding, harvesting, and threshing, they felt it was too late for them to change from a vocation to which they had devoted their entire lives to a completely new one. They could not deny that

the orchard industry looked quite promising. Nevertheless, they knew that growing grains also brought in a respectable income, if they could only get sufficient land for that. Furthermore, to start an orchard meant starting all over again after having spent seven years [establishing their grain business]. It meant having to accept assistance all over again for years to come and to get entangled with new debts to the Baron.

But what worried the settlers the most was the sneaking suspicion that concomitant with the establishment of the orchards, the administration would slowly and systematically take their land away from them [by designating more and more area for orchards], [eventually] forcing them to turn into laborers.

So in 1890, the quarrels between Ekron and the Baron's men returned with a vengeance, with the administrators' using unbelievably drastic and even cruel means to discourage the settlers from any attachment to their land and from growing wheat – those very [things] that the Jewish people today sees as its salvation.

Knowing that the "orchard plan" was not liked by the Ekronians and was liable to arouse their fierce opposition, the wily Bloch was going to use his time-tested strategy of wearing out the enemy through attrition.

In the winter of 1890, the administration set up a nursery for a new orchard in an area previously used for growing vegetables. They then assembled the settlers and informed them that because they were living in overcrowded conditions, giving rise to various diseases, the administration wished to move the young families from the congested center and provide them with separate housing. This would be done only on condition that these younger farmers would be willing to work in the Baron's orchard.

"And who will till the fields?" the settlers asked.

"You can hand over the fields to the Arabs, or not even bother seeding them at all. The Baron has no need for your wheat; he wants you to become proficient in tending orchards."

The settlers wished to avoid argument as much as possible and therefore agreed to work in the orchard. The administration was ecstatic. This was a clear sign that the settlers were being weaned off the plow. The field crops began to wane.[428]

The friction became explosive the following year. The administrators introduced secular studies in the school of the moshavah, and the farmers attacked them for it. In another development, the administration stopped handing out monthly stipends and started to pay only for work it specifically had requested, a system already in place in Petach Tikva and Yesud Ha-Ma'alah.[428A] The new system effectively killed individual initiative.

Chissin documented the administrators' ongoing campaign to control every inch of Mazkeret Batya:

> In 1891 [the administrators] began the process of preparing the soil for the new orchards. Steam-driven plows were brought in for making furrows in the ground to a depth of about sixty centimeters [two feet].
>
> With the approach of winter in 1892, the settlers requested from the administration mulberry and almond saplings, so that each farmer could plant them in his individual farm.
>
> In response, Mr. [Avraham] Brill [no relation to Yechiel Brill], Ekron's manager and agronomist, candidly told them that the Baron wanted the orchards to be worked communally, and that only afterward would they be parceled out to the individual farmers. Bloch was interested in setting up the same system he had established in Petach Tikva, whereby the settlers worked the orchards as day laborers.
>
> The drawbacks of such an approach were obvious. The settlers didn't believe the orchards would eventually be transferred to them. Moreover, they understood that there is a big difference in attitude between a hired hand and one who is self-employed. The latter, because he is working for himself, will invest energy and initiative far beyond what any employee will put forth.
>
> But that's not what suited Bloch's spirit: it is much easier to tyrannize hired hands.
>
> Then Brill sent hired laborers into the areas that belonged to the settlers, to dig holes for planting saplings. The farmers were enraged. They saw this act of the administration as the implementation of what they realized was its true intent and goal all along – to turn them into common laborers.[429]

Under Ottoman law, not only was a tree planted by an individual on a piece of land proof of ownership, it *established* ownership. By planting trees on the farmers' plots, the administration was claiming their land, driving the last nail into the coffin of private enterprise. Chissin wrote of the ensuing battle:

> The people of Ekron were tied to their land with every fiber of their being; they were connected to it and saw it as part of their very essence and flesh, as an acquisition that could never be nullified. They couldn't even bear the thought that the Baron had any right to do with that land as he pleased. They were ready to do anything asked of them – to work in the Baron's orchard and even forgo growing field crops – but the very idea that there was a scheme to take over their land was unbearable to them. So when the administration sent in its workers, the Ekronians drove them away.
>
> Brill ran off to Rishon Le-Ẓion to report to his boss, Mr. Bloch, what had happened. Bloch told him to tell them "in the name of the Baron" not to interfere with the workers. But the Ekronians paid absolutely no heed to these words, [and six of them openly rebelled] and planted the trees themselves – each person in his private plot.
>
> This time Bloch used the same weapon previously used by the settlers: the support of the rabbis. He asked Rabbi Naftali Hertz Halevi, the rabbi of Jaffa, to adjudicate between him and the settlers and to order them to stop the tree planting until the issue was resolved. The settlers replied that they couldn't stop because the tree planting season would soon be over and they would lose an entire year. Rabbi Hertz asked them to temporarily halt the planting, but they wouldn't obey him. Then Bloch turned to the Jerusalem rabbinate.... [430]

The settlers pondered Bloch's remarkable maneuver. It must have been shocking to them that a man who, until now, had openly detested the rabbis was turning to them for help. They decided to take him up on his proposal to have rabbis adjudicate the case. Because so much was at stake, it was agreed by both sides that four rabbis – one from Jaffa and three from Jerusalem – would sit on the panel.[431] The fate of the farmers was now in the hands of a rabbinical court.

ג) באה״ק.

ירושלים, ט״ז שבט. — בין אכרי „עקרון״ ובית הפקידות פרץ סכסוך בגלל אשר העקרונים נטעו עצי שקדים על אדמת „נעניא״ מבלי קחת ע״ז רשות מאת פקידם ה׳ בלאך. ה׳ בלאך הזמינם לדין לפני הרב דיפו, אך הם לא התרצו לדון לפני הרב מיפו כי אם לפני רבני ירושלים. ה׳ בלאך התרצה להם, וישלח את ה׳ ת. גאלדבערג לבקש את רבני ירושלים כי ישפטו בין האכרים ובית הפקידות. כבוד הרבנים לא יכלו בעצמם ללכת ליפו, ויבחרו בכבוד הרבנים הג׳ הר׳ שאול חיים הורוויץ הי״ו והר׳ חיים זאנענפעלד הי״ו והר׳ שלמה זלמן בהר״ן הי״ו, להסר את הסכסוכים, וחפץ הרבנים הנ״ז הצליח בידם והשיבו את השלום על מקומו.

It's war! The fight was reported in *Ha-Meliz*.

Chapter 28
On Trial

The farmers' rabbi. Rabbi Naftali Hertz Halevi (1852-1902), originally from Bialystok, was appointed the rabbi of Jaffa by the leadership of the Old Yishuv in 1886. His jurisdiction extended to the moshavot in the area, which included Ekron and Rishon Le-Zion. Engraved on his gravestone are the words "He dedicated his life to placing the establishment of the moshavot on a Torah footing."
(ומסר נפשו להעמיד ישוב המושבות על דרך התורה.)

"The Battle of the Orchards" moved from the countryside to a rabbinical court in Jaffa. The four rabbis charged with judging the case according to Torah law were Rabbi Naftali Hertz Halevi of Jaffa and Rabbis Shaul Chaim Halevi Horowitz, Shlomo Zalman Baharan, and Yosef Chaim Sonnenfeld of Jerusalem.

The transcript of the arguments presented by both sides is on file in the Central Zionist Archives in Jerusalem.[432] It is invaluable not only as a source of the details of the proceedings, but because it sheds a fascinating light on the mindset of the settlers as they experienced their difficult beginnings in Palestine. On the witness stand, they had the opportunity to reminisce, but they also had to confront the charges of the Baron against them. Let's listen in as the trial proceeds.

Testimony of Mr. Bloch

[presented in a mixture of German and Hebrew]

Three years ago, the colonists were taken in [by the administration in Palestine] as hired laborers. During their first year, they were allowed to till the land as they had done before. They were satisfied with this arrangement.

In the second year, I asked the Baron to do them a favor and allow them to continue to work under the same conditions. Afterward, Mr. Scheid arrived and promised the Ekronians that he would give them tree saplings to plant and that he would improve their living conditions.

The administration sent Mr. Brill to Ekron to take care of the planting of the saplings. While Brill was preparing the ground for the saplings, the Ekronians were silent. However, as soon as Brill started making holes in the ground [to insert the saplings], the Ekronians insisted that they do the planting themselves.

[Bloch goes on to describe the unfolding of events more or less as described above by Chaim Chissin. We skip to his final arguments.]

... Honorable rabbis! I have three complaints. The first is that the farmers didn't obey the [previous] order of the rabbis [to desist from planting the saplings]. The second is that the Ekronians knew full well the Turkish laws that state that one acquires land ownership through the planting of trees. Third, [the farmers] embezzled

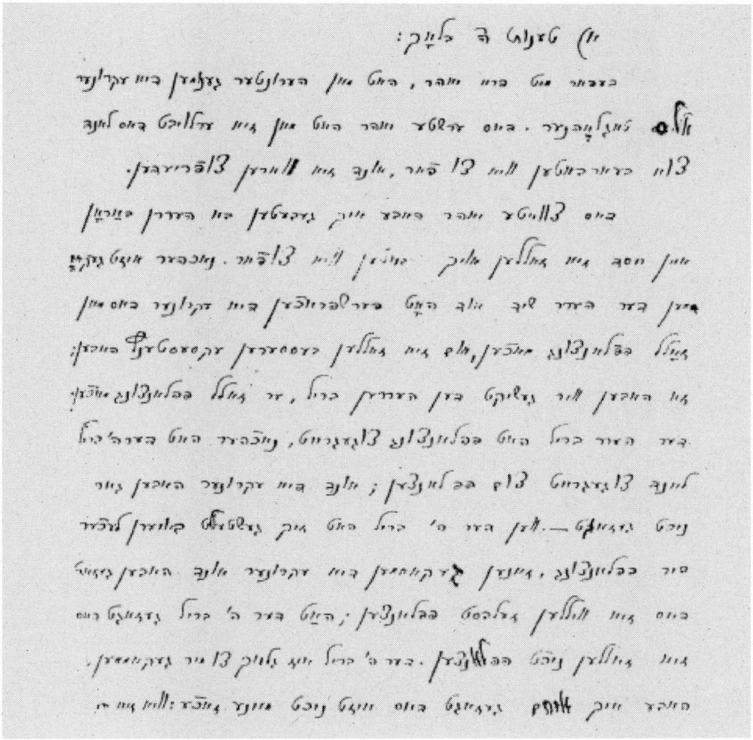

I want justice! Transcript of Adolph (Alphonse) Bloch's arguments before the Jerusalem *Beit Din*, presented in German.

the land of the Baron for themselves. These are the three charges that I present to the rabbis. I request [that the settlers] be punished to the full extent of the laws of the Torah, without any compromise, and [I further request] that you make the sentence for Mr. Neiman especially severe, because he was the instigator of the six Ekronian offenders. I also request that the court demand that the Ekronians return the land to the Baron in the same condition as they received it, and that all expenses [incurred to restore the land] should come out of their own pockets.

It is my wish that the Baron will see me vindicated according to the laws of the Torah.[433]

A summation of the administration's arguments against the settlers appeared in *Ha-Meliẓ*.

The main point of the administration's contention is as follows: As long as the colonists do not repay their debts [to the Baron], their status is only that of day laborers. They therefore do not have the power to determine policy in administrative matters.[434]

The transcript continues with the points made by the farmers:

Testimony of Mr. Neiman

… Mr. Mordechai Neiman [who was on the colonists' side] arose and asked the following question: "Mr. Bloch says that he wants to be exonerated before the Baron – [but] we aren't suing Bloch for anything!"

Rabbi Naftali Hertz Halevi then interjected that he had in his possession a letter from Mr. Bloch, in the name of the Baron, requesting that this case be brought to the court. Furthermore, Mr. Bloch had presented to him four telegrams – two from the Baron and two from Mr. Scheid – with the same request. Neiman proceeded to present his case:

> Bloch contends that the Ekronians are merely day laborers: Does it make sense that the Baron would bring in families from faraway lands, having them leave their property and all they possess, just to become hired hands? …
>
> And here is another indication that we aren't hired hands: Six years ago, I started a vineyard that I planted myself [without any assistance from the administration], and every year I have been benefitting from it. Does that sound like a hired laborer?
>
> Regarding Mr. Bloch's statement that after Shemittah we would become salaried employees, the following is our response: Prior to Shemittah, Mr. Scheid came to us and told us the following: "If you want, you have the right not to work during the Shemittah year, but realize that you will not receive any support or assistance from the Benefactor during that time!" Our reply was that our job was to abide by the guidelines of the rabbis.
>
> A few weeks later, Mr. Bloch came with Mr. Franck from Beirut and demanded that we do work in Shemittah ourselves [instead of Arab laborers].[435] However, we did not want to violate *halakhah*. Now, how is it possible that we are hired workers? How could we have hired outside Arab workers to work for us?

Testimony of Aharon Zelig Levitta

When Mr. Ossowetzky was our administrator, and he saw that the land we had been given was full of thorns and all kinds of weeds and wild growth, he ordered each one of us to clean out his portion and rid the land of the thistles. I spent twelve Napoleons of my own money to accomplish this; so too, each one of us cleared his land of the thistles. Mr. Ossowetzky informed the Baron of this ... and the Baron was pleased.

Each of us also built a barn, planted grapevines, and fertilized his field in the manner of someone who is working for himself, without being ordered to do so. I ask, is that behavior typical of hired laborers?

Testimony of Yaakov Laskovsky

When I arrived here with my brother-in-law, it turned out that we weren't able to get along, because we were arguing all the time. So we went to the administrator, and he told us that he didn't meddle in the colonists' private affairs. Then we went to Mr. Hirsch at Mikveh Israel, who said, "You can't just throw [your brother-in-law] out of the house. You must make peace with him." We returned to our house, and I was ready to apportion to him a third of my plot, [on condition that] he would [move and] live in his own house, but the arguments between us persisted. I wrote Mr. Scheid, saying, "I brought my brother-in-law with [the understanding] that he would help me in my work, not divide the plot with me."

Mr. Scheid replied as follows: "In this colony there are no hired hands, no helpers, and no servants. Every man works for himself and maintains his own property."

Then Ephraim Skolnick presented a summary of the odyssey of the farmers, from the time they met with Yechiel Brill in Pavlovka until they found a suitable place for the colony.

Testimony of Ephraim Skolnick

After Yaakov Arkin and I had inspected the property, and we liked it, we came to Mr. Hirsch with this question: How will our settling in this place unfold? We have abandoned our land [in Russia] without bringing any money, and we are dependent on the promises that have been made to us.

Hirsch told us explicitly, "You should be very clear about this: The land and all that is needed for it will be given to you as an outright grant [literally, "gift"] because the Baron doesn't need your money. [He asks only] that if you are successful, you provide assistance to other Jewish [immigrant] brothers of ours who are in dire straits."

They apportioned the land of Ekron to each family according to the number of members in each. Then Mr. Hirsch, Avraham Moyal, and Mr. Benschimol (who is now an administrator in Zikhron Yaakov) drew lots, and thus they divided the land among all the families, each one taking its portion. Then they drew up a plan [i.e., map] and in each lot inscribed the name of the owner of the lot for the record. Boundaries were demarcated between the plots of land to serve as guideposts for each family. Then we commenced working our land, and we constructed housing, all in the manner of people working on their own behalf.

Eloquent. Avraham Yaakov Gellman and his wife

Testimony of Avraham Yaakov Gellman

Avraham Yaakov Gellman (the *melamed*-turned-farmer) next told the story of the settlement of farmers in Palestine and how they were treated. No one described their pain and suffering more eloquently:

In the contract dealing with our resettlement in the Land of Israel, which was also authorized and validated by the *beit din* of Rozhinoy, the following conditions were stipulated: We would be settled in Mikveh Israel – a place where homes were already constructed, vineyards had been planted, and wells had been dug – because it was close to Jaffa, enabling us to sell our milk, eggs, and vegetables in the city, so we would be able to make a good profit from our work.

We would not have undertaken the trip had we been presented with just vague promises. In the end, however, they didn't give us the lands of Mikveh Israel, because Mr. Hirsch said that the property wasn't really theirs; it was leased for their use for only one hundred years, after which it would revert to the government. He told us to look for land that would belong to us and our children for posterity. We pleaded with Mr. Hirsch to assist us, but he wasn't of much help, until they finally bought the lands of Ekron for us.

When we settled in Ekron [where travel time to Jaffa is over six hours], we were saddled with additional expenditures for our community and we were lacking in many of the amenities we would have received had we stayed in Jaffa, the site originally designated for us.

For two years, we had neither homes nor vineyards …

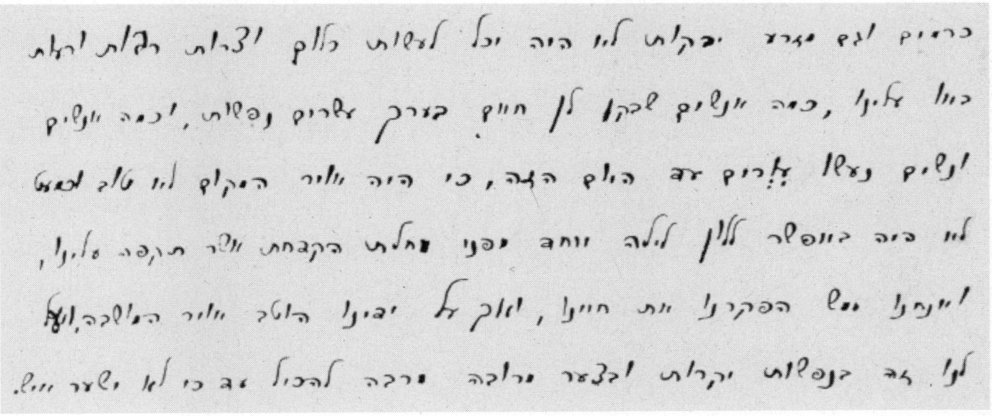

Many difficult and terrible hardships befell us. So many people died – approximately twenty souls. So many men and women became blind to this very day, because the air of this locale was unhealthy. We could barely sleep for a night without evading the malarial fever that struck us. We literally put our lives at risk. Through our efforts, we have improved the air quality of the settlement, but at the cost of the lives of our dear ones and with such unimaginable pain and anguish.

"So many became blind to this very day." Written testimony of Avraham Yaakov Gellman to the rabbinical court in 1893

Dark clouds. At the height of the orchards controversy, news of Michael Erlanger's passing at the end of 1892 brought the colony to a standstill as it mourned the Baron's right-hand man.

> Therefore, we argue that we are not at all obligated to bear the cumbersome and extra costs that our settling in this particular locale has forced upon us, as opposed to what we would have expended had we stayed in Mikveh Israel.
>
> The bottom line is this: The fields, homes, animals, and plowing equipment were given to us as an outright gift by Mr. Hirsch, according to the previously mentioned contract of obligations drawn up by Rabbi Mordechai Gimpel [Yaffe] of Rozhinoy and Mr. Yechiel Brill.
>
> With regard to Mr. Bloch's assertion that we didn't heed the directive of the rabbis and went ahead and planted almond trees, it has already been mentioned by Mr. Neiman that we were compelled to rush, because in just another eight or ten days it would have been too late in the season to plant [them] … and in any case, we planted them prior to the ruling of the rabbis; only because we were hoeing the earth subsequent to the planting did it [falsely] appear to Mr. Brill that we were still involved with the planting of the saplings.

The rabbinical court deliberated on the litigants' arguments and evidence for about six weeks. Tension mounted in the moshavah as the projected date of the final verdict approached. Although it was getting close to Purim, normally a time of festivities, the atmosphere was somber. *Ha-Meliẓ* reported:

> Last Monday, the colonists of Ekron decreed a fast day, and they recited the prayers for Yom Kippur Katan as well as Selichot. They prayed that God would lead them to a victorious judgment.[436]

A Landmark Decision

The verdict was handed down on 21 Shvat 5653 (February 7, 1893). The ruling, which was so fateful for the settlers, went quickly to the heart of the matter:

> It appears to us that the main argument revolves around the question: Was the land given to the settlers as an outright gift from the Benefactor once they had proven themselves? …

The rabbinical judges had asked the settlers for proof that the Baron had actually given them the land as a gift. Unfortunately, the evidence backing the farmers' claim was somewhat flimsy, as it was based on essentially one argument:

> ... that they left their [secure] situation and status – abandoning their inheritance in Russia, where they had made a living by their sweat and toil – and came to secure themselves in the Holy Land. They left not by order of the Benefactor but based on a promise that they had heard – that he was willing to support their working the soil of the Holy Land until they were self-sufficient. ... Then they would pay back [the Benefactor], a little at a time, all the money that had been laid out for them. The goal was to set the stage for other colonies and widen the scope of Jewish settlement in the land.

The rabbinical court then set forth policy guidelines regarding the authority of the administrators and the authority of the farmers. When it came to spiritual and religious issues:

> ... it was the Benefactor's desire from the very start to demonstrate to the world the Jewish people's capability of observing even the minutiae of Torah laws without interfering with living normal lives. On the contrary, the practice of Torah and *derech ereẓ* is the basis of the Jewish people's pride and uniqueness, as our people have demonstrated in the past. Therefore, with regard to any religious matter – whether it pertains to the education of the children, *kashrut,* and other halakhic matters – they are to follow the practice of their ancestors without any interference [from the administration].

With regard to worldly issues, however:

> ... it is self-evident that any matter concerning activities that affect the well-being of the colony and the facilitation of its expansion is the business of the administrators acting on behalf of the Benefactor. Since it is their job to have the [colonists'] best interests at heart. ... the settlers must appreciate that fact [and comply]. This way, the Yishuv will succeed in expanding, and the farmers will fulfill the will of the Benefactor.
>
> ... the general operating principle is that [the farmers are not to interfere with any mundane] matters regarding the moshavah,

such as what to plant or seed, etc., or payment schedules [which are decided by the administration]. … Anyone whose actions contribute to the disintegration of the settlement may be expelled after a review [by the *beit din*] of the matter. [437]

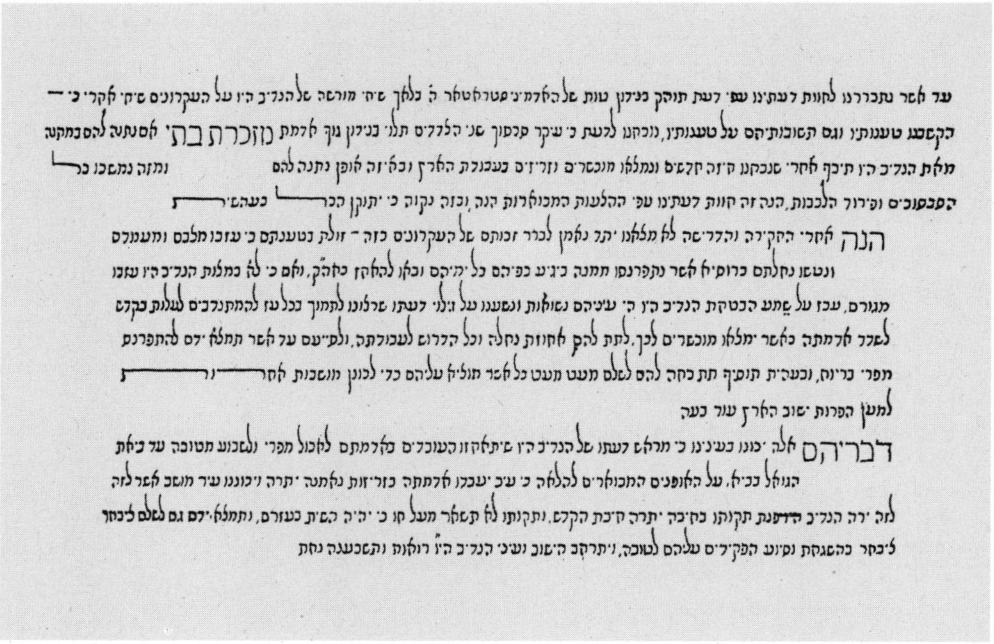

The verdict is in. Excerpt from a page of the *beit din*'s verdict regarding the orchard controversy. In the second paragraph, the judges question the farmers' assertion that they would have never left their established farms in White Russia to come to Palestine to work merely as hired laborers, and that it was their understanding that Rothschild had given them title to the land.

The farmers' greatest nightmare was now realized. Their closest ally, the Jerusalem rabbinate, ruled that the land was not really theirs until they paid the Baron in full for all expenses accrued to him, something that might take decades to accomplish. In the meantime, they would be at the mercy of the Baron's administrators. [437A]

The court ruled in favor of the administrators regarding the saplings planted by the farmers on their plots and ordered that they be uprooted. For the *beit din*, the uprooting was not a simple halakhic matter, however, since it might have impinged on the mizvah of settling the Land of Israel. The court decided to take into consideration the administration's claim that the planting had upset the Ottoman government.[438] If the plantings would weaken the legal status of the Yishuv, then uprooting was really in effect a form of *strengthening* the settlement of the land. And to lessen the possible halakhic prohibitions of uprooting fruit trees, it was preferable to have the uprooting performed by non-Jews.

The court ruling affected the entire relationship between the farmers and the administration forevermore. The press published the verdict, stirring up heated opinions in all sectors. The secular *maskil* writer and social critic Achad Ha-Am[439] viewed the action of the *beit din* as no less than a betrayal:

> Even the great rabbis of Jerusalem supported the administration, and at the administration's request they went to Ekron to persuade the colonists to submit to their masters. When the [rabbis] additionally suggested that the superintendent of the colonies also come to Ekron to speak to the farmers, the superintendent ordered his lieutenant to relay the message to them [that he could not come, because] he was ill. But he whispered to his lieutenant that he was actually distressed

The bottom line. The conclusion of the verdict, signed by the rabbinical judges. The bottom signature is that of Rabbi Yosef Chaim Sonnenfeld.

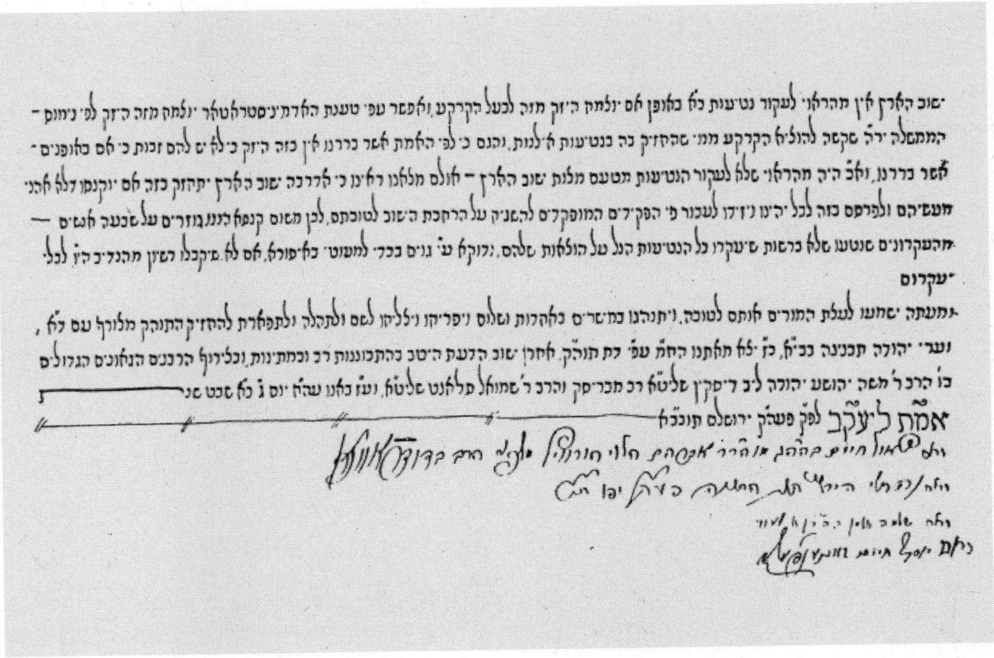

> that the rabbis had succeeded in calming the farmers' spirits. He would have preferred that they not succeed, thus enabling him to implement drastic disciplinary measures on the moshavah.[440]

On the other hand, the religious Zionist Yechiel Michel Pines viewed the verdict in a positive light, because the farmers had been given the opportunity to implement Torah law:

> The Ekronians won a huge victory, because now their fate was in the hands of a *beit din,* which weighs its words on the scales of justice, as opposed to their being prey to the whims of the administrators, who base their judgments on what happens to feel right to them. If the Ekronians had not been foolish, they would have known how to appreciate this victory, and they wouldn't have been so arrogant as to ruin it on account of their stubbornness. To our dismay, we must concede that they lost their senses by thinking that through their sheer determination they would be able to continue stubbornly resisting even the rabbis.[441]

The court sent Mr. Bloch a copy of its ruling accompanied by a letter requesting that he show compassion toward the farmers and "manage them in a gentle manner and not throw someone out as soon as he commits an offense."[442]

Coming to Blows

Despite the pleas of the rabbis, the farmers' relationship with the administration was still raw, as they were especially afraid of the blurring of boundaries between the individual plots of land. They invited the judges to pay them a visit. When they arrived, the farmers laid out all their arguments and concerns. The judges then saw a need to add a proviso that the borders between family plots had to stay where they were.[443] But that was not enough to mollify the settlers. Pines wrote:

> ... the Ekronians refused to fulfill the directive of the administration and said, "We came here to be free and not to be slaves. The land is ours, and we will work it as we see fit."[444]

Moreover, they defied the *beit din* and adamantly refused to have the trees uprooted.

Although Bloch was asked by the court to deal kindly with the settlers, his reaction to the their intransigence was nothing short of rage. He sent Mr. Gross, his second in command, to quell the uprising. Over the course of February 1893, Bloch sent Gross a number of letters revealing both the desperation of the farmers and Bloch's reaction to their outright rebellion:

Rishon Le-Ẓion
12 February 1893

Dear Mr. Gross,

This morning I sent Mr. Brill a copy of the verdict, which is to be posted on the administration building [in Mazkeret Batya].

For now, we are asking just one thing from the rebels – remove the trees. ... And the trees will be removed, even if we have to employ force. If you think [the farmers] won't obey, first give them a warning by posting another notice on the administration building. Then grab as many Arabs as you can find to pull out the trees. ... Make sure you have the upper hand. *If the rebels oppose your efforts or if they try to attack you, you can come to blows and sic your famous dogs on them. ...*[445]

Emissaries of Chovevei Ẓion and others attempted to persuade the farmers to relent, to no avail. But when the rabbinical judges made another trip to Mazkeret Batya, their pleadings did succeed and the farmers finally uprooted the trees in dispute. But there would be no happy ending to the story.

The administration demanded that the settlers temporarily remove the border posts demarcating the individual properties before plowing would commence, so the vineyards could be planted without hindrance, after which the farmers could return the markers. But the colonists were afraid that the wily Bloch was up to his old tricks. Two families, Laskovsky and Levitta,[445A] defied Bloch's demand and encouraged the other colonists to follow their lead.

Bloch wanted to expel them, but all the farmers rushed to their defense. He wanted the two families to stand trial in a *beit din,* but they refused. He responded by denying them all public services, just as he had decreed during the Shemittah year.[446]

Bloch's goal was to crush the colonists once and for all. He waited for an offense that would provide him with an appropriate pretext. He got his chance a few months later, in August 1893.

A year earlier, Yehoshua Rubinstein had been evicted from the moshavah. (Rubinstein was one of the founders of Ekron.) Either on his own initiative or through the influence of some of the younger hotheads in Mazkeret Batya, the expellee returned one day to his former house (which had been turned into a pharmacy), broke down the door, and unceremoniously expelled the current tenant, the pharmacist.

Like a tornado hit it. Avraham Brill lived on the second floor of the administration building, until he moved into a private home 1895. The building now houses Eran Shamir Village Museum, Mazkeret Batya.

Brill then asked the older settlers to evict this man from the community. Chaim Chissin reported:

> It was clear that the settlers should have carried out this justified request. It made sense in light of their very own strong stance regarding their rights to their lands and their view [of themselves] as the true owners of the moshavah. That meant that they had a responsibility to impose order and not to allow dispossession of someone's home. But their hatred of the administration was so great that even the old timers lost their senses. They told Brill: "We didn't tell him to come here, so we're not going to make him leave. That's your business. Take care of it in the way at which you fellows are so adept."[447]

Brill then contacted Bloch, who summoned the police to evict the squatter.

The very sight of the Turkish policemen elicited indescribable rage. All the townspeople took to the streets, prepared for anything. Although they could sense a tragedy in the making, they didn't care – they were in total despair, with not even a glimmer of hope on the horizon.

Smiling for the camera. Turkish officers

The police tried to arrest [the Rubinsteins],[447A] but they resisted. The old-timers, with tears in their eyes, begged the young people not to mix in. When one of the policemen hit [Mrs. Rubinstein], the outraged women of the moshavah hit the policeman back. That was the defining moment. Then a few of the young people entered the fray and jumped on the policeman, and a desperate battle ensued.

Some people barged into the administration building where Brill lived and began to smash glasses, vessels, furniture, and whatever else they could get their hands on. Brill, shocked and disoriented, fled to Rishon Le-Ẓion with the rest of the colony's administrators in tow.

[The policeman escaped, and a few hours later he reappeared on the 5th of August with fifteen colleagues.] The residents, who

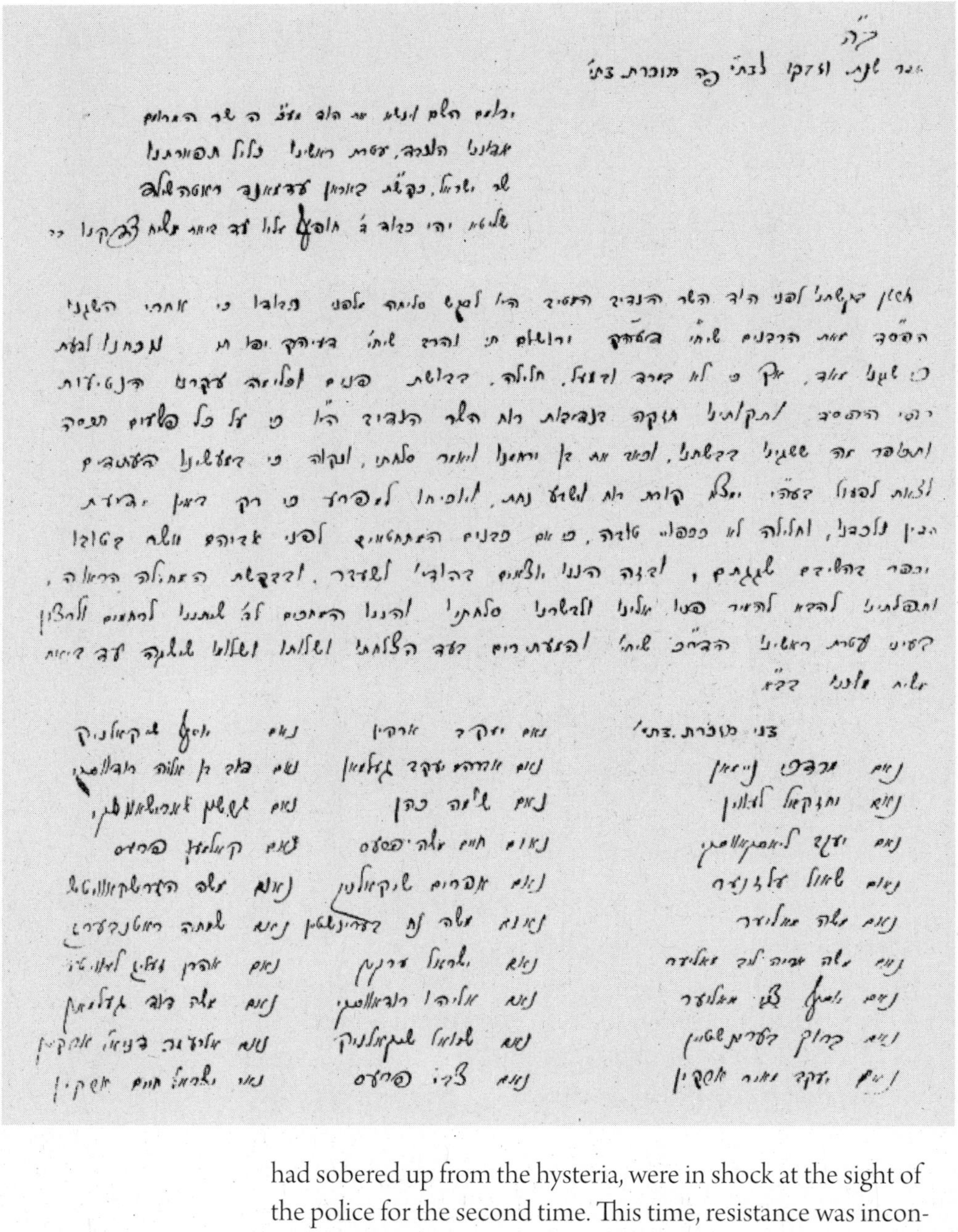

had sobered up from the hysteria, were in shock at the sight of the police for the second time. This time, resistance was inconceivable. The police conducted a week-long investigation, and [eight] of the settlers were arrested [including Mr. Rubinstein and one woman] on charges of attacking an on-duty policeman. The [eight] were taken to the prison attached to the governor's residence in Jaffa.

Bloch was ecstatic. He had been waiting for some time for the settlers to give him the excuse he needed. Now he was ready to ensnare them in his net while giving the impression that he was merely standing on the sidelines.

The settlers struggled to release their comrades from the Jaffa prison but didn't have a clue how to do so. There was only one option left: [to beg forgiveness from Baron Rothschild and to] turn to Alphonse Bloch. Bloch was ready to intervene and get the prisoners released on condition that all the settlers would affix their signatures to the following agreement, his infamous "clauses":

- The settlers relinquish all claims to private property on the moshavah.
- They must obey all orders from the administration.
- The administration reserves the right to evict from the settlement any person it deems fit, and the evicted has no right to appeal.
- Four of the settlers [Laskovsky, Levitta, Gellman, and Rubinstein] and their families are to be evicted from the settlement immediately.

They signed the agreement. The prisoners were released.

At the end of October, after an absence of nearly three months, Brill returned to Mazkeret Batya with some other administrators. The pharmacy and school were reopened, and everything returned to "normal."[448]

Dr. Mordechai Naor points out in his book *Sefer le-Mazkeret*, that Baron Rothschild was keenly aware of what was going on, and even telegraphed Bloch not to make any compromises and to immediately expel the Levitta and Laskovsky families.

The remaining colonists grieved over the loss of their comrades. The absence of Aharon Zelig Levitta, the skilled carpenter who had crafted their beautiful Torah ark, hurt them the most. He had developed harvesters that greatly assisted the farmers. But when these implements fell into disrepair, Levitta wasn't around anymore to fix them. The economy of the moshavah suffered on account of this.[448A]

Opposite page: **We're sorry.** Copy of a letter sent by twenty-nine colonists (the original bears their signatures), apologizing to Baron Rothschild. In the letter they wrote:
נוכחנו לדעת כי שגינו
מאד... וכאב את בן ירחמנו
ויאמר סלחתי.
"We realize now that we made a terrible mistake. [Please pardon us] the way a father pardons his son and says, 'I forgive you.'"

Sons of the founders with the Turks in better days. Left to right: Yisrael Chaim Arkin, Shmuel Skolnick, Yechezkel Levin (founder), Ẓvi Skolnick, Yosef Maller, Eliezer Daniel Arkin, Yisrael Ẓvi Holzner

It was over. Five years of strife between the farmers of Mazkeret Batya and the Baron's administration had finally ended. They had lost more than their pride, more than their land. The peace that ensued marked the beginning of decline and spiritual ruin.

Chapter 29
Broken Spirits

The farmers of Mazkeret Batya had prevailed in the difficult Shemittah controversy, but the decision of the rabbinical court and its aftermath left them feeling defeated. No longer did they believe that they were masters of their own destinies. Their fighting spirit was broken.

Alphonse Bloch had finally won his war. He decided to take leave of Palestine; his job there was done. He exited from the stage of history barely leaving a trace. The Museum of Rishon Le-Ẓion possesses a journal marking the centennial since the founding of the town; it is a thick volume with scores of documents and photographs, including a section on the Baron's administrators. But Alphonse Bloch's picture is nowhere to be found.

There is no picture of him in the Museum of the First Aliyah in Zikhron Yaakov either, or in any of the historical journals of that period, even when the focus was on the Baron's administrators. It is odd that a photo of the man who played such an important role in the development of the New Yishuv should be missing from all the history books. Perhaps he never posed for a picture or allowed his picture to be taken. Perhaps his photographs were purposely removed after he was gone.

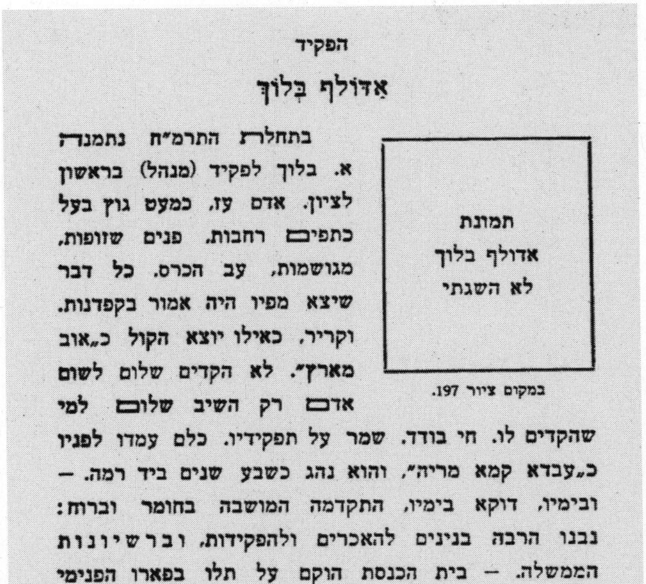
הפקיד

אֲדוֹלְף בְּלוֹךְ

בתחלת התרמ"ח נתמנה א. בלוך לפקיד (מנהל) בראשון לציון. אדם עז, כמעט גוץ בעל כתפים רחבות, פנים שזופות, מגושמות, עב הכרס. כל דבר שיצא מפיו היה אמור בקפדנות. וקריר, כאילו יוצא הקול כ„אוב מארץ". לא הקדים שלום לשום אדם רק השיב שלום למי שהקדים לו. חי בודד. שמר על תפקידיו. כלם עמדו לפניו כ„עבדא קמא מריה", והוא נהג כשבע שנים ביד רמה. — ובימיו, דוקא בימיו, התקדמה המושבה בחומר וברוח: נבנו הרבה בנינים להאכרים ולהפקידות, וברשיונות הממשלה. — בית הכנסת הוקם על תלו בפארו הפנימי והחיצוני. — היקבים הגדולים שאין דוגמתם בכל המזרח, תחתיים, שניים ושלישיים. — כרו באר חדשה. — נוסד בית־הספר העברי־עברי הראשון בעולם. —

תמונת
אדולף בלוך
לא השגתי

במקום ציור 197.

The missing head. The official history of Rishon Le-Ẓion, written by David Yudelevich, contains numerous photographs. Curiously, not a single photo exists of Alphonse Bloch.

Bloch and his image were gone, but the scars he inflicted remained for a long time.

The devastating psychological effects of the farmers' capitulation to the administrators were portrayed by Achad Ha-Am in his article "Ha-Yishuv ve-Apitropsav" (The Yishuv and Its Guardians).[449] He wrote a blistering critique of what he had witnessed on his tours of Palestine. To him, Mazkeret Batya symbolized all that was wrong with the way the Baron, though well meaning, ran his colonies. In chapter 2 of his monograph, he gives an overview of the history of Ekron and asks a painful question: Was the whole venture worthwhile?

Critic. Asher Hirsch Ginsberg (Achad Ha-Am), shown above during one of his visits to Palestine, made a quick stop at Mazkeret Batya on July 13, 1893.

> ...What exactly are the [Ekronians] doing here, and what benefit is derived from their living here? There is no easy answer to this question.
>
> ... All the fruit trees that were planted have hardly been a success, and what paltry profits they will bring in aren't even worth considering – except for the olive trees, where it is still too early to tell, and which currently are not producing any income at all.... [In the meantime] each farmer "lives under his trees"[450] – and is getting financial allowances [twelve francs a month per person, and thirty per horse].
>
> In order that they not get bored, because they have nothing to do, they "entertain themselves" with some work by sowing a little bit of wheat and barley between the trees. All the work they do covers only a fraction of their expenses, because the land they sow is small in quantity and poor in quality on account of the trees that were planted, which have depleted it of nutrients.
>
> But so what? The farmers don't have to worry at all about their income – that's the job of the administration.... Whether the farmers do well or not doesn't make any difference in the end, because the administration will compensate each person up to the amount of allowance that it has already predetermined, which is calculated according to the number of members of each household.
>
> And this is the way these people have lived here, almost twenty years now, with the administration in charge of them, taking over 100,000 francs [$400,000 in today's U.S. currency] out of the Benefactor's pocket every year, an amount that would suffice to support at least three communities like Ekron without [the farmers' doing any work] and [without any need for an] administration. Had all this money somehow been distributed just to the farmers of Ekron, they would have become rich enough by now to have been able to repay the Benefactor a sizable amount of their debt.

... In 1893, when I was returning to Europe from the Land of Israel, I happened to be on the boat with the superintendent of all the Benefactor's administrators at that time [Elie Scheid]. When I shared with him how bizarre the method of "improvement" of Ekron seemed to me, he candidly told me that they had to do what they did, because as long as the farmers had even a little bit of independent income without any help from the administration, it would have been impossible to control them.

... Had these [administrators] gone mad? Why would they prefer to spend hundreds of thousands [of francs] over many years and to turn hard-working, industrious people into idlers and *schnorrers*? ... No – they hadn't gone insane, and what they did was logical and thought out according to the logic of guardianship: The farmers are "coarse" people who don't know how to appreciate their benefactors and don't obey them properly.

Therefore, some new "improvement" needed to be invented to deprive the farmers over the course of many years of any capability of rejecting the "kindnesses" of the guardians or of living without their support for even an hour. Then they wouldn't be able to disrupt the order of things, and all would be peaceful.

Unfortunately, these "coarse" farmers realized what the true intent [of the administrators] was and resisted them with all their might. That's when the days of disturbances and rebellion came to Ekron ... but finally, predictably, the stronger side prevailed. They forcefully quelled the rebellion and threw the rebel leaders out of the colony, and those who remained were forced to surrender and no longer interfered with the good efforts of the guardians to "improve" the settlement.

In the ten years since the "improvements" ... it has cost the Benefactor at least one million francs [$4 million in today's U.S. currency]. And yet they will have to start all over again. That is the unanimous opinion of the farmers, and they happen to be right. ...

Achad Ha-Am didn't spare the farmers his sharp tongue either:

One has to admit that even if in the beginning the farmers had no choice but to remain silent, little by little, they got used to their situation and started to willingly acquiesce. The people of Ekron are not heroes. They are just average, plain people, and a plain

> person is liable to make peace with baseness and laziness, as when it is forced upon a person over a long period, and his needs are taken care of, so he need not worry.

Achad Ha-Am didn't see the people of Mazkeret Batya as heroes. He looked only at the result of their situation after the many years of strife. He did not take into account the large families, the religious principles by which they lived, the sacrifice of abandoning their family inheritances in Russia, and all the hardships the Ekron/Mazkeret Batya farmers and their families endured. He never denied that they had gone through a grueling ordeal, yet he did not see that their confronting the challenges made them into heroes.

Broken in spirit, and even blamed for their own defeatist attitude by writers such as Achad Ha-Am, the farmers despaired of their future and that of their children. Their new mindset and weakened resistance rendered them less likely to fight the secularist innovations in education introduced by the administrators. Though outraged initially, the pious farmers from Pavlovka watched helplessly as their children's devotion to living a religious life guided by the Torah was uprooted and discarded in the name of progress.

The Secularization of Mazkeret Batya

Although Baron Rothschild was not personally observant, he did believe in the concept of the holiness of the Land of Israel, and he wanted the Jewish settlers of that land to observe its religious precepts. His vision called for rehabilitation of the persecuted Jews of the Diaspora through a spiritual renaissance in the Land of Israel. He believed that engaging in productive, honorable trades – especially agriculture – while living in the land of their forefathers would create a healthy milieu that would have a positive effect on their observance of the Torah. Rothschild's rescue program for Russian Jewry was based on religion, not nationalism. He invested large amounts of funds to ensure that every colony under his control would have a synagogue, a *mikveh,* a community rabbi, and a *shochet.*

However, the attitude of his administrators toward Orthodox Judaism ranged from ambivalence to outright hostility. Products of French secular culture, they undermined the Baron's wishes right under his nose.

Almost from the outset, there was a major clash between the religious settlers and the Baron's administrators concerning education. When they arrived from Russia, inculcating their children with Torah and love and fear of God was the farmers' *raison d'être*. To that end, they established a traditional Talmud Torah. The Baron's administrators, however, saw it as their task to guide the educational system of the moshavot toward the goal of converting every *cheder* into a modern school.[451]

The gap between the worldview of the parents and the teachers in the modern schools set up by the administrators in Rothschild's colonies is aptly portrayed by the writer Moshe Rinot:

A new generation emerges.
Top: Leah and Yisrael Hershkovitz
Bottom: (Right to left) Zelda, Moshe, and Malka Press

> Indeed, there were many parents who did not have a favorable view of the increasing secularization, and the minimal amount of religious education provided by the teachers in the schools in the settlements did not assuage them. They believed that the task of a school was not merely to teach *about* the mizvot, but to instill in the students the *desire*

Generation gap. Right to left, seated: Yisrael Hershkovitz, his wife, and Yisrael Arkin

The Torah as a way of life. First day of school for a child, wrapped in a *tallit*, in a traditional *cheder*. Talmud Torah Etz Chaim, Old City of Jerusalem, circa 1925. The veteran *melamed*, holding up the letter *aleph*, is R. Eliyahu Salomon. *Details of this photograph courtesy of R. Ẓvi Aryeh Tucazinsky, current principal of Etz Chaim.*

to fulfill them. The teacher was there not just to teach the prayers, but to pray together with the students in the school, and to join the prayer services in the settlement's synagogue. They saw coeducation as a breach of traditional values and the conduct of the teachers as too non-observant.

The teachers countered that the function of the school was to teach the children the subjects that the parents desired, but instilling the religious values of fulfillment of miẓvot and prayer in the home or the synagogue was the job of the parents and the extended family.[452]

The study of Tanach [Bible] eventually edged out the study of Talmud, and "Bible stories" replaced the traditional study of

> *Chumash* [the Five Books of Moses]. It was not long before a secular atmosphere pervaded the schools. As a result, a new Hebrew generation arose in the moshavot, which was detached from its religious Torah sources.[453]

This trend accelerated during the Second Aliyah, when a large wave of nationalistic *maskilim* arrived in Palestine.

For the reader with religious sensibilities, it is heart-rending that the Baron's very own administrators were destroying the spiritual pillars for which the settlers of Mazkeret Batya were ready to give their lives. One example is that of Avraham Brill, the administrator of Mazkeret Batya, who went so far as to banish the *melamed* and his students from the synagogue. For a time, the moshavah had no official Talmud Torah. Eventually word of what had occurred got back to Paris. The Baron became infuriated when he heard what Brill had done. He castigated Eli Scheid (who oversaw Brill) and ordered him to reopen the *cheder.*[454]

David Neiman (son of founder Mordechai Neiman), a product of the modern school, describes with fondness what it was like and points out the struggle between the parents and the educational system:

Tanach as an academic subject. Bible class in a secular high school

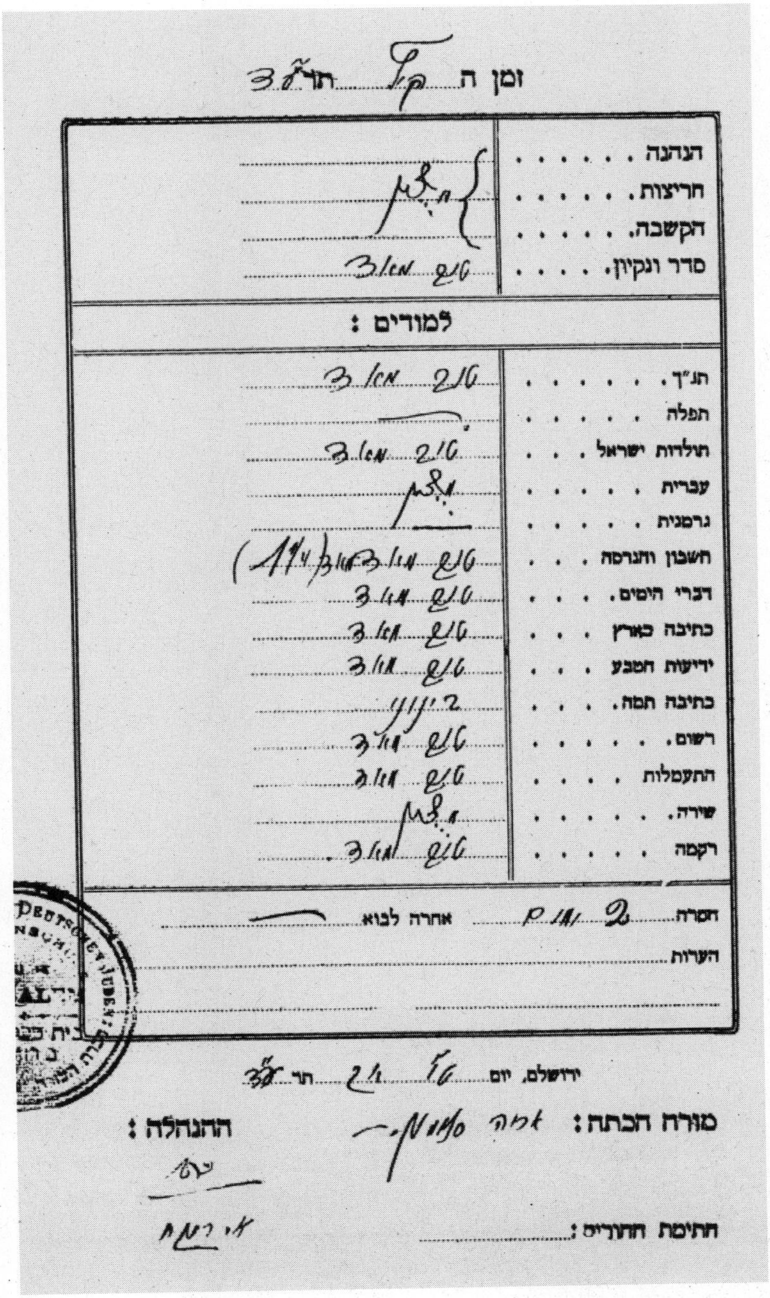

זמן ה.......... תר...

הנהגה	
חריצות.	
הקשבה.	
סדר ונקיון.	
למודים :	
תנ"ך.	
תפלה	
תולדות ישראל . . .	
עברית	
גרמנית	
חשבון והנדסה . . .	
דברי הימים. . . .	
כתיבה בארץ . . .	
ידיעות הטבע . . .	
כתיבה תמה. . . .	
רשום.	
התעמלות	
שירה.	
רקמה	

הסרה.......... אחרה לבוא..........

הערות..........

ירושלם, יום.......... תר..........

מורה הכתה: .... ההנהלה :

חתימת ההורים:..........

Making the grade. Report card from Mazkeret Batya's school in 1915. The only religious subjects were Bible and prayer. By this time, many of the children of Mazkeret Batya were no longer Orthodox.

The school had four classrooms. The rooms were spacious; they each had many windows, which provided plenty of light. The walls were covered with maps and the scientific table of the elements, and inkwells were nailed to the desks to keep the children from tipping them over. The teacher sat near a small platform; the school had a very cozy atmosphere. Notebooks with nice covers had been donated from France, one for each student. There were three teachers in the school: one who taught Hebrew and general education, a rabbi for religious studies, and a French teacher. The Ekronians did not agree to let the boys and girls study together. They also objected that the language of instruction was Hebrew.

Because they wanted their children to be educated just as they had been, they took their boys out of the school. Only two boys remained in the school in the big classroom – two boys and six girls. The children did well in school in all their studies, aside from French. The teachers were totally dedicated to the children, providing them with assistance during their spare time and their vacations. They spent much time with them in order to accustom them to speaking in Hebrew. They tried to instill a love of the country, the people, and the language in their hearts. The teachers would occasionally take the children to one of the nearby villages on a field trip, waving a blue and white flag as they walked and singing national marches. Of course, the children who had been forced to

The competition. Class picture from the modern school

Under the table. Scene from a traditional *cheder*. The *cheder* in Mazkeret Batya was underfunded and poorly staffed, while the modern school was well funded by the Baron's administrators and staffed by well-trained teachers.

leave the school and sent to study with the rabbi lost out on both ends. The rabbis were always changing, and the children were constantly in and out of school.[455]

It is easy to read between the lines and understand the contrasts Neiman is portraying. We read about desks with inkwells and maps and scientific tables vs. the chaos that seemed to reign in the *cheder*. Pandemonium is not a natural by-product of traditionalism but the result of an underqualified *rebbi* or *melamed*. For the graduates of the modern schools, their teachers were the greatest gift Ekron had ever given them.

Furthermore, for these teachers, teaching was not merely a job but a calling, a mission. They were incredibly devoted to the students, and they succeeded in winning over their hearts and spirits. The teachers played a major role in the secularization process.

The school wasn't entirely secular, for it offered a token amount of religious education. But it was pervaded by a nationalistic, modern, and "progressive" atmosphere – in those days, "modernity" and secularism were a package deal. Religion was seen as clashing with science and social progress. The net result was a weakening of religious faith among the students.

Jewish Olympics. Ekron/Mazkeret Batya's contingent at the Maccabiah games (see "Ekron" in the banner)

Scout's honor. Mazkeret Batya scout troop

There were many other secular influences too: sports and athletic leagues, with their colorful banners, competitions, and parades; the youth organizations and their uniforms, outings, and activities; and the Jewish self-defense organizations. Those who refused to join must have felt they were really missing out. The wave of the future was passing over them.

The beleaguered state of the religious community in Palestine at that time is reminiscent of the situation in the Galician Chassidic communities between the two world wars. They were virtually defenseless against the inroads of modern philosophies and movements that were successfully infiltrating them.[456]

The Baron's lieutenants also tried manipulating the parents into sending their children to the modern school through economic pressure,[457] by offering monetary allowances for each child who attended. The farmers, with their huge families, were always struggling financially and found the financial inducement seductive.

The secularization of Mazkeret Batya did not take place overnight; it took two generations. The *maskilim* in Palestine were able to accomplish in as little as twenty to thirty years what the Christian world could not do in 1,000 years – disengage the Jewish people from its religious faith.

In March 1908, a mere twenty-four years since the founding of Ekron, when Avraham Yiẓchak Hakohen Kook, the chief rabbi of Jaffa, was asked by Rabbi Yiẓchak Izak Halevi[458] which of the settlements needed assistance in bolstering its religious education, he responded:

> … There is nothing to decide here, because *all* the moshavot desperately need assistance. The influence of the modern schools is wrecking and destroying the Land of Israel.[459]

The Old Yishuv counterattacked the *Haskalah* with its own initiative. In 1903, Rabbi Zerach Braverman founded the Shomrei Torah (Guardians of Torah) organization whose goal was to establish traditional *chadarim* on the moshavot.

Initially, the effort was quite successful, for the organization created a curriculum that adapted slightly to modernity in order to counter the competition: along with the regular fare of Talmudic studies, there was some Hebrew (grammar and writing) and arithmetic.[460]

Mazkeret Batya residents were enthusiastic about Shomrei Torah and were among the first to request that the organization

Guardians of the Torah. Letterheads in Hebrew and in German of the Shomrei Torah organization.

Hats and jackets, please. Rabbi Avraham Yiẓchak Hakohen Kook delivering a lecture in his yeshivah in the 1920s. The sage sitting to Rabbi Kook's left, on the other side of the ark, is Rabbi Yaakov Moshe Charlop, the rabbi of the Shaarei Chesed neighborhood and community.

establish a Talmud Torah in their community. But they were bitterly disappointed by the organization's lackadaisical response, as can be seen by this letter to Shomrei Torah, which was published in *Chavaẓelet*:

> Our moshavah was the first to actively support your efforts to establish schools in all the moshavot, to teach Jewish children Torah, fear of God, and *derech ereẓ*. The fathers are groaning that they cannot properly educate their young due to great pressure and inadequate resources. Thank God, you have succeeded in challenging the haters of Torah ... But our community – which was the first to support you – was the last to receive assistance from you. If you delay any longer, the voice of Esau will be heard instead of the voice of Jacob....
>
> So the responsibility of educating the children falls upon you, the members of this holy organization, and not on the parents, who are working in the fields from morning to night. You will have to give a reckoning in the future regarding your negligence toward

our children, if you do not fulfill your obligation to install expert and talented *melamdim* under good supervision.

[signed] In the name of all the fathers, "One of the Fathers"[461]

Counterattack. Rabbi Zerach Braverman

Good publicity and some friendly pressure never hurt, as can be seen by this follow-up article in *Chavaẓelet.* Based on what the organization eventually did for the community, it seems that Shomrei Torah did not take Ekron seriously enough.

Ekron: The Shomrei Torah organization sent us two *melamdim* to enable us to stand up to our adversaries. One man is around 80 years old. May God lengthen his days and preserve his strength, because his workload is great, and he has to eat his meals each day in the home of someone else, [the meals representing part of] his salary....

And the other is a young man straight out of yeshivah. Perhaps he is a scholar, but he is not a teacher. These are the soldiers fighting the battle to break into the fortified city!

[signed] An Ekronian[462]

Though Shomrei Torah's teachers were lackluster, the desperate parents of Mazkeret Batya preferred them over the modern school, as can be seen by the lament of Yaakov Chazanov, a member of the secularist BILU organization:

We see that in some of the moshavot the modern schools are crumbling ... while the Jerusalem-based Shomrei Torah Talmud Torahs are flourishing and being built on the ruins of the modern schools. For example, Rishon Le-Ẓion had a solid school and now it has deteriorated to the point that it was not worth the effort to re-establish it, and the modern school in Ekron is completely destroyed.[463]

Shoestring budget. Rabbi Dr. Moshe Auerbach

But eventually Shomrei Torah ran out of money. The Orthodox community of Frankfurt sent Rabbi Dr. Moshe Auerbach to lead the organization; but without the necessary funding, his best efforts were in vain.

The *melamed*'s lowly social status and meager salary, his lack of formal pedagogic training, and the *cheder*'s other deficiencies were no match for the modern schools. By the eve of the First World War, the battle for the souls of the youth had been lost. Mazkeret Batya's Talmud Torah, like those of most of the other moshavot, had closed its doors.[464]

About forty years after the founding of Ekron, the new generation felt confident enough to desecrate the Sabbath publicly. The wave of the future – secularism and "Enlightenment" – had swept over the Land of Israel, as it had in Europe.[465] Some excerpts from a poem ("All by Myself") written by a contemporary observer in 1902 lament:

> The *ruach* (wind; spirit) carried them aloft
> The Light swept them all away…
> I was left behind, all alone,
> And the *Shechinah* too.
> Its broken right wing
> Trembled over my head.
> My heart discerned hers –
> It was trembling over me,
> Over her son, her only one…
> The wind carried them aloft
> They all took off.
> And only I remained. Alone – all alone.[466]

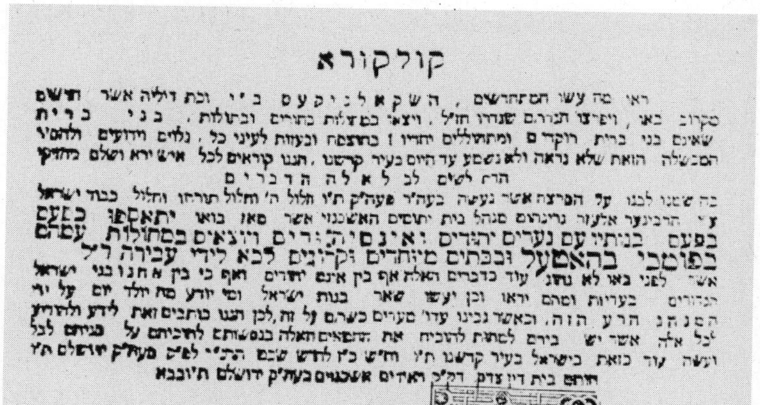
קולקורא

בפעם בבתיהם עם נערים יהודים ואינם יהודים ויוצאים בבתולות עמהם
בפומבי בהאמעל ובבתים מיוחדים ומרקדים לבא לידי עבירה ר״ל

חותם בית דין צדק דק״ק האדים אשכנזים בעה״ק ירושלם תובב״א

קול־קורא נגד ריקודים מעורבים של בנים ובנות. שנת תרנ״ד

Changing winds. A poster in Jerusalem denouncing mixed dancing (1895)

Chapter 30
End of a Generation

What became of the principal players in our story? Baron Edmond de Rothschild and Rabbi Shmuel Mohilever had labored to lay the groundwork for bringing the Jewish exiles back to their homeland and were mutually responsible for the founding of Mazkeret Batya. So dedicated were they to these ideals that even death could not sever their connection to the Holy Land.

Coming Full Circle

On November 2, 1934 (24 Cheshvan 5695), Edmond (Binyamin) de Rothschild was laid to rest at Père-Lachaise, the largest and most prestigious cemetery in Paris.

The Benefactor was gone. He had lived for eighty-nine years and between 1882 and 1899 had spent what is estimated to be about $100 million,[467] helping the Jewish downtrodden from eastern Europe to take root in the Holy Land and pave the way for others who would follow.

"King of Israel." Baron Rothschild devoted fifty-two years of his life to rebuilding the Land of Israel. His death coincided with the seventeenth anniversary of the Balfour Declaration.

Although he was blind for the last ten years of his life, Rothschild retained his sharp wit and was emotionally expressive almost till the end. As a genial and eccentric old man, he would entertain visitors by cracking cherry pits between his teeth.[468]

On the day of his funeral, the entire Yishuv came to a standstill to pay homage to its patron. He had done it all – from founding and/or funding most of the settlements of the First Aliyah to introducing the cash crops of bananas and grapefruits and establishing the Holy Land's wine industry. Emotions ran high in the Great Synagogue of Tel Aviv, where such notables as Chief Rabbi Avraham Yiẓchak Hakohen Kook, the British high commissioner of Palestine, and leaders of the Yishuv were present.

***Kaddish* for their father.** Paris, 1934. *Right to left*: Maurice Edmond Charles de Rothschild (1881-1957), James Armand de Rothschild (1878-1957), and Yisrael Levi, chief rabbi of France.

Only a few months later, Edmond's life partner, his wife Adelaide, was laid to rest at his side.

Though Rothschild was buried in Paris, his heart had always been in Palestine.[468A] In his will, he requested that he be reinterred "inside a rock" in the Holy Land. Less than two years later, after his son and daughter-in-law had conducted an extensive search for a suitable location, they found the right place for their father's last interment: Um el Alaq, a magnificent site situated on a hill overlooking the blue Mediterranean on one side and the plains of Samaria on the other, had a large enough rock from which to carve out an underground crypt. Today the place is known as Ramat Ha-Nadiv, located between Zikhron Yaakov, just to its north (named after Edmond's father, Jacob Rothschild), and the lovely town of Binyamina (which he named after himself).[469]

In 1954, twenty years after Rothschild's death,[470] his remains, along with those of Adelaide, were taken by an Israeli frigate from Marseille to Haifa. Once in Haifa, the coffins were greeted by a nineteen-gun salute. Thousands of people lined the road as the procession made its way south to Ramat Ha-Nadiv.

Coming home. The Israeli frigate carrying the remains of Rothschild and his wife approaches the Haifa dock.

Following the biers was a procession of settlers paying homage to the Baron, each with a bag of earth from every colony he had founded and supported.[471]

Paying homage. Representatives of communities funded by Rothschild brought bags of soil to be used for his reburial in Israel.

The Avi Ha-Yishuv, the patriarch of the nascent Jewish community in the Land of Israel, was buried in a man-made cave, just as the Jewish Patriarchs were interred in the Cave of Machpela in Hebron. His son, James, recited the *Kaddish* at his parents' graves. Three years later, he too passed away.[472]

Although Rothschild laid the physical groundwork for later Zionist settlement activity, his sense of identity often clashed with that of many of the secular Zionists. In 1925, for instance, when debating the pros and cons of retaining Talmudic instruction in Palestine's schools, Chaim Kalvarisky (one of his colony managers) lobbied for a secular, freethinking curriculum. Rothschild retorted:

> Monsieur Kalvarisky, I know you well and I have known your ideas for a long time now. The difference between you and me is that you, Monsieur, are a national Jew and I, I am a Jewish Jew.[473]

Rabbi Shmuel Mohilever: From Bialystok to Mazkeret Batya

Although Rabbi Shmuel Mohilever had always encouraged others to live in the Land of Israel, he did not set foot there until 1890 (the year following Shemittah), eight years before he passed away. Despite flagging health, Rabbi Shmuel led the first official delegation of Chovevei Ẓion to the Holy Land. When he arrived in Jerusalem, he was received with great honor by all sectors of Jewry. At the request of Rabbi Shmuel Salant, he gave the Sabbath sermon at the Churvah Synagogue in the Old City.

He trekked to nearly every new settlement, and the sight of Jews striking roots in the Land of Israel filled him with ecstasy.

Uneasy alliance. Rare picture of Rabbi Mohilever taken at a national convention of Chovevei Ẓion. Rabbi Mohilever is seated fourth from the left. Fifth from left is Leon Pinsker, the secular president of Chovevei Ẓion, followed by Rabbi David Friedman, one of the greatest Talmudists of that era. He later switched sides and joined the anti-Zionist camp.

In the settlement of Yahud, adjacent to Petach Tikva, Rabbi Shmuel caught up with a dear old friend and "comrade in arms," Rabbi Mordechai Gimpel Yaffe. Though the two rabbis had sharply differed regarding the *Heter Mechirah*, they were bonded by a shared sense of values. After meeting with Yaffe, the venerable sage claimed that he'd gotten a taste of the World to Come:

> [Rabbi Mohilever] saw how [Rabbi Yaffe] was strolling, together with his students, between the rows of trees in the olive groves of Yahud, inhaling the pure, fresh air and experiencing the splendor of nature in our Holy Land.
>
> When he observed this, he said, "If anyone wants to get a taste of the World to Come, he should travel to Yahud and observe the

world of Rabbi Mordechai Gimpel Yaffe. It is a world where there is no hatred and no jealousy. It is just a place where the righteous sit and enjoy the Divine Presence."[474]

Rabbi Mohilever was too sick to attend the First Zionist Congress, organized by Theodor Herzl in 1897, but he sent a message via his grandson to be read there. Knowing that his words would be heard by a predominantly non-religious audience, he made one point very clear:

תורתנו, שהיא מקור חיינו, צריכה להיות יסוד תחייתנו בארץ אבותינו.

"Our Torah, which is the source of our lives, must be the basis of our renewal in the land of our forefathers."

A large assemblage. Funeral procession of Rabbi Shmuel Mohilever in Bialystok

His words remained merely a slogan. They did not succeed in becoming a guiding principle in the Zionist movement.

He passed away in June 1898 and was buried in Bialystok. But his story didn't end there. In August 1990, the rabbi of Mazkeret Batya, Ephraim Zalmanovitz, had an intriguing idea. He had just read an article in the *Ha-Ẓofeh* newspaper about an Israeli, Shmuel Sultz, who had grown up in Bialystok and claimed he could locate the grave of Rabbi Shmuel Mohilever. The paper said that on a recent visit to Bialystok:

> [Sultz] had ascended the hill where the graves were situated but encountered total devastation. All the gravestones had been smashed by hooligans. Nevertheless, he is convinced that with a lot of effort, the grave of Rabbi Mohilever could be discovered.[475]

When Rabbi Zalmanovitz saw Achiezer Arkin during prayer services in Mazkeret Batya's central synagogue, he excitedly told him about the article and opined that it was better that Rabbi Mohilever's remains be reinterred in Mazkeret Batya, the community he had helped establish with Baron Rothschild, than stay in the ruins of a desecrated cemetery in Poland. The rabbi suggested that the first step would be to obtain the Mohilever family's permission to reinter the remains.

Arkin was enthusiastic about the idea and started to search for members of the Mohilever family living in Israel. It didn't take long to discover Aryeh Leib Mohilever living in Jerusalem. Arkin called and made an appointment to meet him.

He was introduced to a man in his eighties, a great-grandson of Rabbi Shmuel Mohilever. Upon hearing the idea of reinterring his great-grandfather, Mohilever became very animated. He told Arkin that he would contact his brother, a retired architect who lived in Ramat Gan, so the family could issue the necessary authorization to allow for the transfer of their ancestor's remains.

Word of this project reached David Begun, a resident of Haifa. He wrote a letter to the head of the town council of Mazkeret Batya, saying that he had done some professional restoration work at the Bialystok Jewish cemetery and had pinpointed the location of Rabbi Mohilever's grave! He would be willing to join in the effort to reinter the rabbi's remains in Mazkeret Batya.

Pilgrimage. Boys from the religious Zionist youth group Ha-Shomer Ha-Dati, made a pilgrimage to the grave of Rabbi Mohilever in Bialystok in June 1929.

Paying their last respects. Rabbi Moshe Ẓvi Neriah (standing, second from left) eulogizing Rabbi Mohilever at his reinterment in Mazkeret Batya, followed by Rabbi Yisrael Meir Lau (then chief rabbi of Tel Aviv), Rabbi Mordechai Eliyahu, *zt"l*, Israel's Sephardic Chief Rabbi, and Minister of Education Zevulun Hammer, *z"l*. Also present were Ashkenazi Chief Rabbi Avraham Shapira, *zt"l*, descendants of the founders of Mazkeret Batya, members of the *Hashomer Haẓair* Kibbutz Gan Shmuel (which was named after Rabbi Mohilever), Rabbi Chaim Druckman, and Dov Shilansky, speaker of the Knesset.

A meeting was set up in Tel Aviv, attended by a number of people, including the head of Mazkeret Batya's local council, Arkin, Sultz, Rabbi Zalmanovitz, Begun, and David Spiegel, the head of a *chevrah kaddisha* from Bnei Brak who was experienced in the transfer of remains from the Diaspora to Israel.

Begun brought with him pictures he had taken of Mohilever's *ohel* (tomb). These would later serve as the basis for the replicate in Mazkeret Batya.

It was decided at that meeting to start work on the project before the onset of the winter rains and snow. Careful not to arouse the attention of the Polish authorities, an inconspicuous delegation was sent to Bialystok. All the delegates told the Polish government was that they wanted to transfer someone's remains. The significance of the person involved, "who passed away long ago, in 1898," was kept secret.

Last stop. *Ohel* of Rabbi Mohilever in Mazkeret Batya – a replica of his tomb in Bialystok

Rabbi Mohilever's remains were flown to Israel on Thursday, November 7, 1991. His first burial had been in Bialystok on 19 Sivan, 5658 (June 9, 1898); his second burial was in Mazkeret Batya on Sunday, 3 Kislev, 5752 (November 10, 1991). Although Arabs are typically employed to dig graves in Israel, the organizers decided that in deference to Rabbi Mohilever, Jewish hands would prepare the grave. Achiezer Arkin's brother received the privilege.

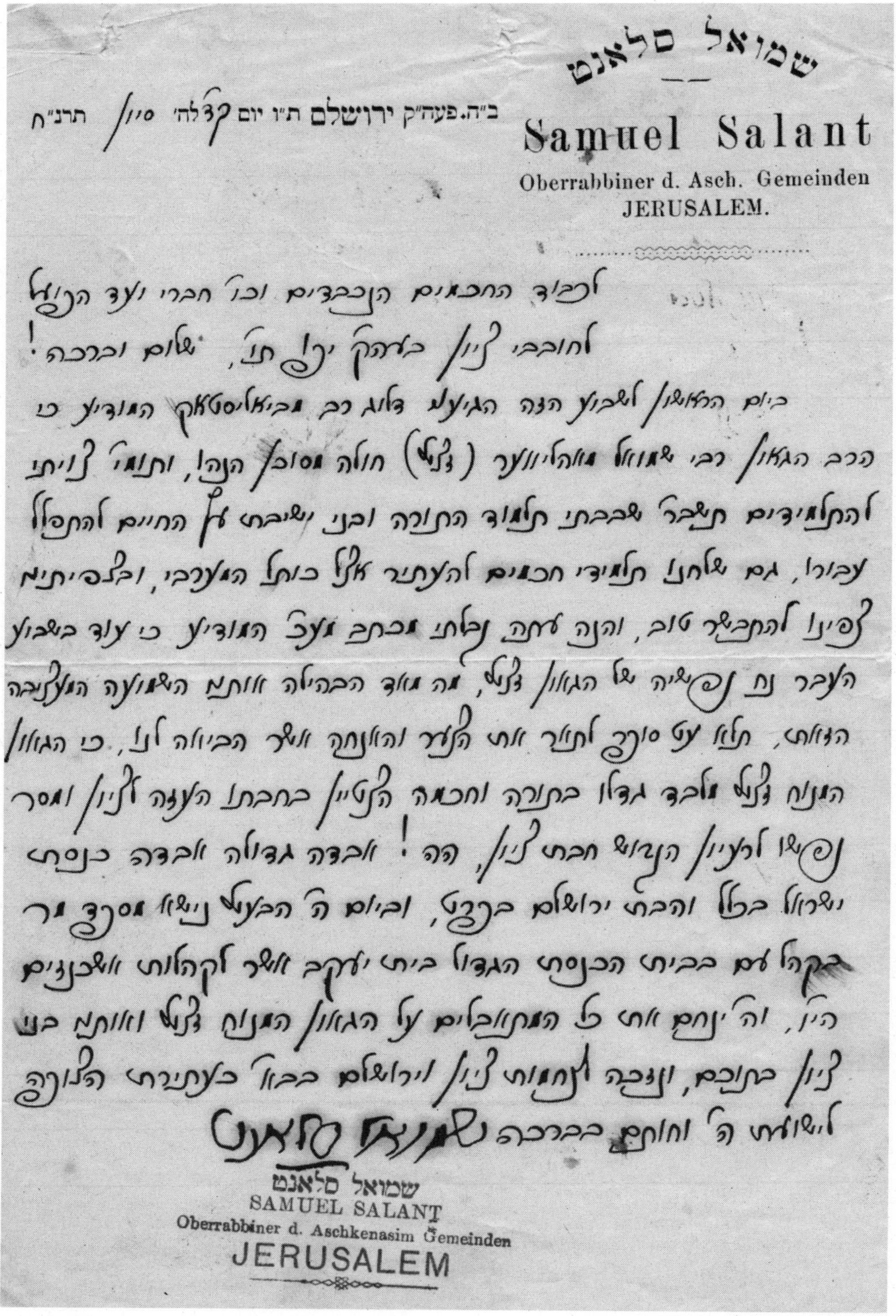

שמואל סלאנט

Samuel Salant

Oberrabbiner d. Asch. Gemeinden

JERUSALEM.

ב"ה. פעה"ק ירושלם ת"ו יום ב' לה' סיון תרנ"ח

לכבוד החכמים הנכבדים וכו' חברי ועד הפ"צ

לחובבי ציון בפעה"ק ירו' ת"ו, שלום וברכה!

ביום הראשון לשבוע הזה הגיענו דבר מביאליסטאק המודיע כי
הרב הגאון רבי שמואל מוהליווער (זצ"ל) חולה מסוכן הנהו, ותומי צויתי
להתלמידים המופלגים שבבתי תלמוד התורה ובני ישיבות על החיים להתפלל
עבורו, גם שלחנו תלמידי חכמים להעתיר אצל כותל המערבי, ובצפיתינו
צפינו להתבשר טוב, והנה עתה נתקבל מכתב מעיר המודיע כי עוד בשבוע
העבר נח נפשיה של הגאון זצ"ל, מה מאוד הבהילה אותנו השמועה המעציבה
הזאת, הלא על סופר לתאר את הצער והאנחה אשר הביאה לנו, כי הגאון
המנוח זצ"ל מלבד גדלו בתורה וחכמה הצטיין בחבתו העזה לציון ומסר
נפשו לרעיון הקדוש חבת ציון, הה! אבדה גדולה אבדה כנסת
ישראל בכלל והבת ירושלם בפרט, וביום ה' הבעל"ט נעשה מספד מר
בקהל עם בבית הכנסת הגדול בית יעקב אשר לקהלות אשכנזים
הי"ו, וה' ינחם את כל המתאבלים על הגאון המנוח זצ"ל ואותנו בני
ציון בתוככם, ונזכה לנחמות ציון וירושלם בבוא' [illegible]
לישועת ה' וחותם בברכה שמואל סלאנט

שמואל סלאנט
SAMUEL SALANT
Oberrabbiner d. Aschkenasim Gemeinden
JERUSALEM

Present to pay their respects at the reinterment were chief rabbis Mordechai Eliyahu and Avraham Shapira as well as members of Israel's parliament.

Zevulun Hammer, then minister of education, pointed out the poignancy of the event in that it was Rabbi Mohilever who had given the famous and stirring speech at the first Chovevei Ẓion conference in Katowice in 1894. At the time, he'd compared the return of the Jews to their land and their spiritual renaissance there to the prophet Ezekiel's vision of the Valley of the Dry Bones.

In that address, Rabbi Mohilever called upon the Chovevei Ẓion activists to seek official permission from the Ottomans to permit the Jews to settle in Palestine. He called for the combination of Torah and vocational education to enable Jews to learn and engage in productive trades. He even spoke of a Jewish sovereign entity in Palestine that he dreamt would become a home to eight million Jews – all before Herzl.

Opposite page: **Condolences.** "The depressing news [of his passing] frightened us.... Besides his greatness in Torah and wisdom, he excelled in his love of Zion...." Letter of condolence from Rabbi Shmuel Salant to Chovevei Ẓion regarding Rabbi Mohilever's death, dated 24 Sivan 5658 (June 14, 1898)

Rabbi Shmuel Salant

It was Monday, the eve of Rosh Chodesh Elul, 5669 (August 16, 1909). During the entire afternoon and evening, a crowd of people gathered in and around the house, waiting anxiously for reports concerning the health of the rabbi. The dreadful news was finally announced – it was over. Rabbi Shmuel Salant was ninety-three years old and had served as the Ashkenazic chief rabbi of Jerusalem for nearly seventy years.

Talmudic genius, halakhic authority, teacher, rabbi, mediator, fundraiser, ambassador at large, builder of institutions and neighborhoods, marriage counselor, community organizer, disciplinarian, and social worker, Rabbi Salant was genuinely beloved by a vast population. In the words of his grandson Nathan Salant: "The news spread like lightning and had an indescribable effect upon the city. Men cried. Women fainted. The scene was terrible."

The deceased requested in his will that no public eulogies be given for him, that his body not be brought into the synagogue, and that there be no delay regarding the burial. If he died at night, the funeral should not wait until morning.

אבל כבד בירושלים!

The Committee of the general Jewish hospital MISGAB-LADACH express you his great sorrow for the great misfortune of the decease of the chief Rabbi SAMUEL SALANT the 16th, August 1909

משגב לדך בתוככי ירושלם ת״ו

מוהר״ר שמואל סלאנט זיע״א

ביום ב׳ ער״ח אלול התרס״ט.

Adresse: Rabbi Isaac Aschkenasi and Committee of „Misgab-Ladach" in Jerusalem (Palestine).

Above: **It's over.** Public announcement of the death of Rabbi Salant.

ספר

זכרון

רבינו שמואל סלאנט

שהי׳ שבעים שנה ראש הרבנים

בעיה״ק ירושלים תובב״א

נתן נטע סלאנט

Remembering *zayde*. Details of Rabbi Salant's funeral in this chapter were culled from *Sefer Zikhron Rabbeinu Shmuel Salant*, written in Yiddish and English by his grandson Nathan Salant, published in 1920.

The rabbis honored all of his last wishes, with the exception of having the funeral at night. They thought the crowd would be entirely too large, and it would be a dangerous undertaking.

The funeral began the next morning at 7 a.m. The streets around the house were mobbed with an estimated 40,000 people, and 10,000 escorted the bier all the way to the cemetery on the Mount of Olives.

Very short addresses were given by the leading Ashkenazic and Sephardic rabbis in Jerusalem. Apologizing for their brevity, they explained that they were only fulfilling the wish of the departed forbidding eulogies. Representatives of all the foreign consuls in the city, and the Ottoman mayor of Jerusalem came to pay their last respects. Turkish soldiers in full uniform escorted the body to the cemetery. It was a fitting tribute to a man who was popular among Jews and non-Jews alike.

His impact on the landmark Shemittah battles had been considerable. It will be recalled that the farmers of Mazkeret Batya held him in such high regard that when they had to decide whether to heed the man who paid their bills (their financial backer and patron, Baron Rothschild) or the man who guided their conscience (their spiritual mentor from Jerusalem, Rabbi Shmuel Salant), the rabbi won out.

There were those who found Rabbi Salant's position unfathomable. It seemed all the more unusual for a pragmatic moderate who excelled at uniting the fractious *kollelim* and divisions within Jerusalem's Ashkenazic community, one who was so ingenious at finding halakhic solutions to ease the economic burdens of city's poor, and to whom building the Yishuv in the Land of Israel was so dear.

Perhaps an understanding of Rabbi Salant's mindset and aspirations can help us appreciate the feelings and attitudes of the Mazkeret Batya pioneers who followed him, even after their Shemittah ordeal was over.

Shemittah Observance as a Mechanism for Blessing and Security

Rabbi Salant left behind no written records of his deliberations, shedding no light on how he came to his decision. His great-grandson, Rabbi Nisan Aharon Tucazinsky, told this author (in April 2010) that there is also no oral history in the Salant family regarding the matter. He suggested that perhaps the best clue could be found in what was written by his father, Rabbi Yechiel Michel Tucazinsky in his book *Sefer ha-Shemittah*.

In section 2 (chapter 3) of the book, he asks why Rabbi Salant was more lenient in the Shemittah of 5656 (1895-1896) than he was in 5649 (1888-1889):

> In 5656 … even some of the rabbis who forbade [relying on the *heter*] now began to look into ways to find a leniency. The strength of their argument to be strict was based on the following consideration: By prohibiting the farmers from relying on the *Heter Mechirah*, the commandment of Shemittah would be fulfilled in all its details, the past sins of transgressing earlier Shemittot would be atoned for … and as a result the [Divine] blessing would be bestowed upon the Land of Israel and the Jewish

Looking back. Rabbi Yechiel Michel Tucazinsky, author of *Sefer ha-Shemittah* (published in 1951), received his rabbinic ordination from Rabbi Shmuel Salant and was married to his granddaughter. A notable *posek* in his own right, he wrote a number of important works on the laws of mourning (*Gesher ha-Chaim*) and on the Jewish calendar.

> people – drawing us nearer to the hoped-for destiny [very possibly intimating the ultimate Redemption]:
>
> ועל ידי זה תקוים הברכה להארץ ולישראל ונתקרב לייעוד המקווה.
>
> Alas, the experience [of the Shemittah of 1889] showed that few farmers were able to withstand the test. The majority of the colonists did not even heed the rabbis' call to observe Shemittah fully, but instead relied on the *heter*. Therefore the great rabbis who previously had been stringent were now concerned about the possible ruin of the settlement enterprise. (For by not facing the test [of Shemittah] the blessing would not be fulfilled.) Furthermore, the rabbis were concerned that if they did not find a means of circumventing Shemittah, the farmers [due to laxity] would stumble and cause others to stumble by transgressing the prohibitions of working the land during Shemittah and benefitting from its [sanctified] fruits.

Rabbi Tucazinsky's words are illuminating. In effect, he is saying that Rabbi Salant and the Jerusalem rabbis wanted to compel the colonists to observe Shemittah because they believed it would result in prosperity and ultimately the sanctification of God's Name. Though only a small percentage of Jews lived in the Land of Israel in 1889, Rabbi Salant was convinced that the ancient promises of the Torah would be fulfilled as they were in Biblical times, as long as the farmers were in full observance of Shemittah – and that its observance might even bring the Redemption closer.[476]

> *If you perform My decrees,*
> *And observe My ordinances and perform them,*
> *Then you will live upon the land in security.* (Leviticus 25:18)
> *I will grant your rains in their seasons,*
> *And the land shall yield its produce,*
> *And the trees of the field their fruit.*
> *Your threshing shall overtake your vintage,*
> *And your vintage will extend until the next threshing....* (Leviticus 26:4-5)
> *I will walk among you, and I will be a God to you,*
> *And you will be a nation to Me.* (Leviticus 26:12)

A historic opportunity to renew God's special covenant with the Jewish people and its land was at hand. But Baron Rothschild and a majority of the colonists would have no part of it. A disappointed Rabbi Salant very reluctantly agreed (orally) to a limited *Heter Mechirah* according to the guidelines established by Rabbis Yehoshua Leib Diskin and Naftali Hertz Halevi for the Shemittah of 1896.

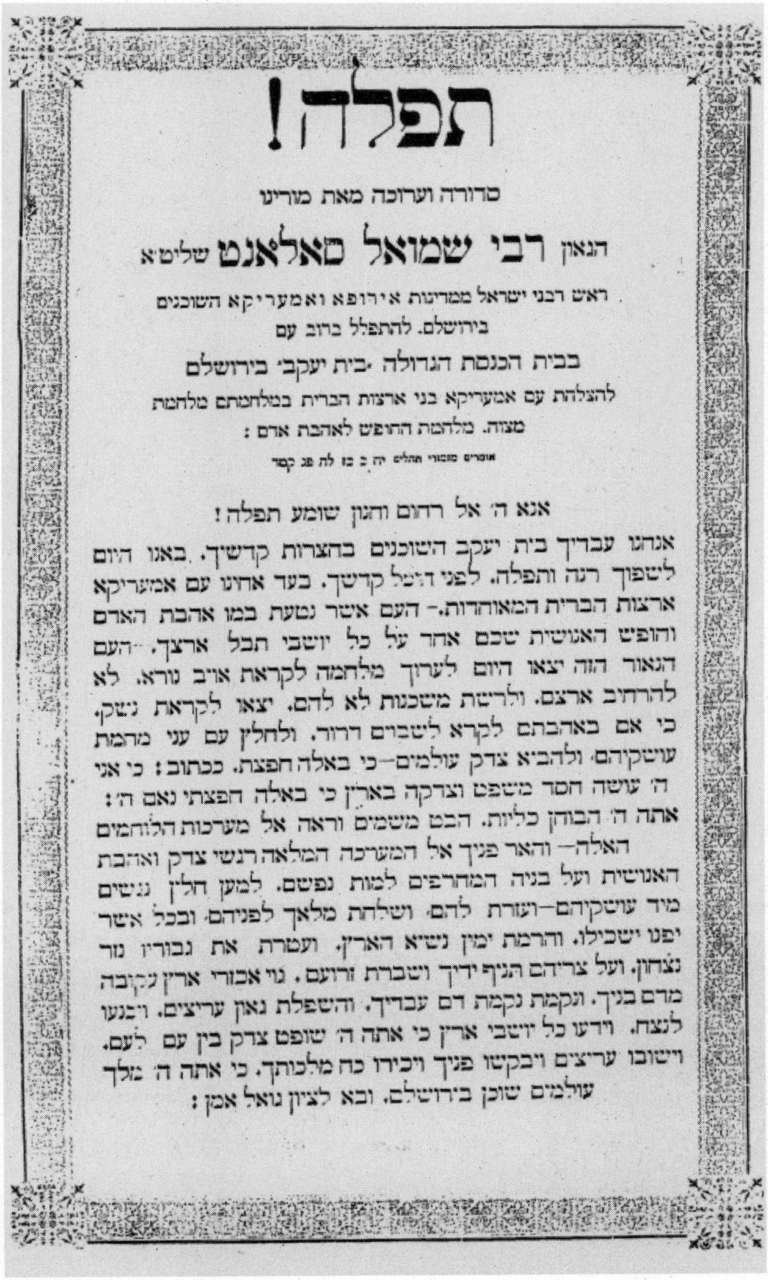

תפלה!

סדורה וערוכה מאת מורינו

הגאון **רבי שמואל סאלאנט** שליט״א

ראש רבני ישראל ממדינות אירופא ואמעריקא השוכנים
בירושלם. להתפלל ברוב עם
בבית הכנסת הגדולה ״בית יעקב״ בירושלם
להצלחת עם אמעריקא בני ארצות הברית במלחמתם מלחמת
מצוה. מלחמת החופש לאהבת אדם:

אומרים מזמורי תהלים יח כ כו לה פג קמד

אנא ה׳ אל רחום וחנון שומע תפלה!

אנחנו עבדיך בית יעקב השוכנים בחצרות קדשך. באנו היום
לשפוך רנה ותפלה. לפני היכל קדשך. בעד אחינו עם אמעריקא
ארצות הברית המאוחדות.– העם אשר נטעת במו אהבת האדם
והופש האנושית שכם אחד על כל יושבי תבל ארצך.–העם
הנאור הזה יצאו היום לערוך מלחמה לקראת אויב נורא. לא
להרחיב ארצם. ולרשת משכנות לא להם. יצאו לקראת נשק.
כי אם באהבתם לקרא לשבוים דרור. ולחלץ עם עני מרמת
עושקיהם. ולהביא צדק עולמים—כי באלה חפצת. ככתוב: כי אני
ה׳ עשה חסד משפט וצדקה בארץ כי באלה חפצתי נאם ה׳:
אתה ה׳ הבוחן כליות. הבט משמים וראה אל מערכות הלוחמים
האלה— והאר פניך אל המערכה המלאה רגשי צדק ואהבת
האנושית ועל בניה המחרפים למות נפשם. למען חלץ נגשים
מיד עושקיהם—ועזרת להם. ושלחת מלאך לפניהם. ובכל אשר
יפנו ישכילו. והרמת ימין נשיא הארץ. ועטרת את גבוריו נזר
נצחון. ועל צריהם הניף ידיך ושברת זרועם. גוי אכזרי ארץ נקובה
מרם בניך. ונקמת נקמת דם עבדיך. והשפלת גאון עריצים. ויבנעו
לנצח. וידעו כל יושבי ארץ כי אתה ה׳ שופט צדק בין עם לעם.
וישובו עריצים ויבקשו פניך ויכירו כח מלכותך. כי אתה ה׳ מלך
עולמים שוכן בירושלם. ובא לציון גואל אמן:

Rooting for the Yankees. "For the success of America, the people of the United States ... in their war for freedom and the love of mankind. . . ." An inspiring prayer composed by Rabbi Shmuel Salant for the victory of the United States Army in the Spanish-American War. It was recited in the Churvah Synagogue (then known as Beit Yaakov) in Jerusalem in 1898.

Perhaps the most fascinating description of Rabbi Salant was penned by a non-Jew (who made his living by exposing the faults in people and the injustices in societies). The November 1909 issue of *Pearson's Magazine* featured an article by the journalist James Creelman, who interviewed and photographed Rabbi Shmuel Salant only fifteen days before he passed away. Creelman made a stop in Jerusalem while investigating the alleged massacre of 30,000 Christians by Muslims in Asia Minor. Although he had a tendency to dramatize, it is clear that the journalist was genuinely impressed by Rabbi Salant.

The following excerpt from Creelman's long article "The Turk, the Christian, and the Holy Sepulchre" focuses on his interview with the aged rabbi. If anyone entertained doubts about Rabbi Salant's sense of compassion based on his firm opposition to the *Heter Mechirah*, he may think twice after reading this fascinating tribute to a rabbi of the "old school":

A flair for drama. James Creelman was a journalist-advocate who traveled extensively to find stories and was unafraid of great risk. He was considered one of the premier reporters of his day.

> It was my privilege to see and talk with Samuel Salant, the venerable and saintly grand rabbi of Jerusalem. This remarkable man, perhaps the most exalted and revered figure in all Israel, died since this article was begun a few weeks ago. He was ninety-five years old and was grand rabbi of Jerusalem for nearly seventy years. There was another grand rabbi, recognized by the Turkish government and supported by the Sephardim [sic] Jews , but the great body of the Jews in Jerusalem, particularly the Russian, Roumanian, and German Jews – the Ashkenazim – acknowledged only Samuel Salant, the gentlest, most learned, and most beloved Jew in Jerusalem since Israel was scattered and trodden underfoot in the ghettoes of Europe.
>
> Pushing through crowds of porters, donkeys, camels, and peddlers, and descending the narrow Street of David, I found the grand rabbi in a small, second-story sitting room beside a weather-worn synagogue and school.
>
> He was a small, thin man with snow-white

hair and a scanty beard. On his head was a flat-brimmed hat of black velvet, and a long, silk gown of reddish brown, with black stripes, clung in folds about his body. His shrunken face was wizened and puckered. His gray eyes were almost blind. His voice was thin and whispering. He sat by a table covered with red-patterned cloth, and an old-fashioned clock ticked loudly overhead.

Before this appealing figure, majestically old and pathetically weak, stood a group of bearded men in quaint, Orientalized European clothes, with corkscrew curls hanging before their ears. Words can hardly express the tender reverence with which they looked upon their aged rabbi.

The grand rabbi's hands were small and so thin that the light seemed to shine through them. Taking my hands in his, he clung to me like a child. His shriveled, white face, down with the meager hair hung on either side, was lit with a smile of welcome, and his dim eyes looked wistfully into space.

Beside him sat his grandson, who was also a grandfather. His great-great-grandchildren were in the courtyard outside, from which came the sound of laughing, romping Jewish schoolchildren.

When he heard some of the story of the massacre of thirty thousand Christians in Adana, the grand rabbi seemed to be deeply troubled.

"It was dreadful," he said. "I sent a hundred francs to the Christian relief committee as soon as I heard of it. It was not much, but it was all I could spare, for I am a poor man. I hope that noth-

"Honorable *Mentschen.*" Table of contents of *Pearson's Magazine*, November 1909, in which Creelman's piece about Rabbi Salant appeared. *Pearson's Magazine* specialized in literature and political discussion. (It published H. G. Wells' *The War of the Worlds* from April to December 1897.) Creelman's article was originally published in the October 24, 1909, issue of the *New York Times*, with a picture of the funeral procession for Rabbi Salant on the Mount of Olives.

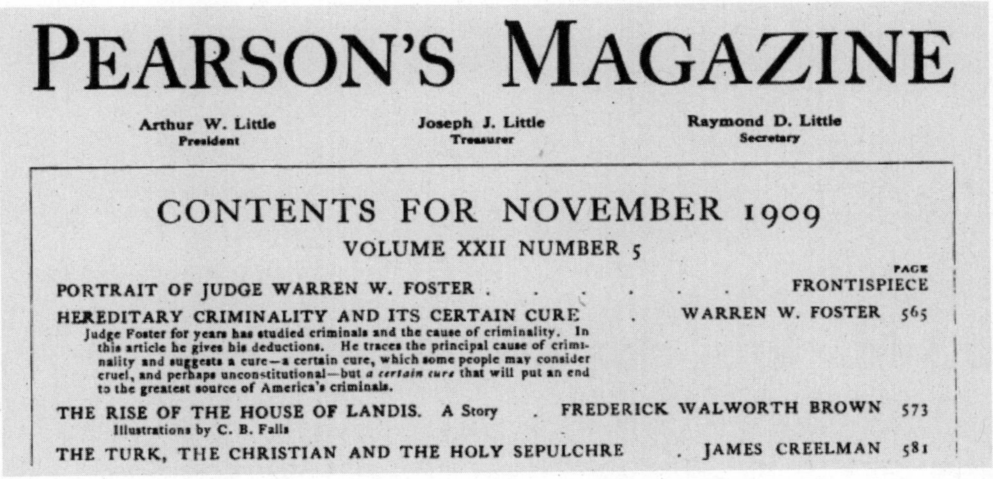

PEARSON'S MAGAZINE

Arthur W. Little, President — Joseph J. Little, Treasurer — Raymond D. Little, Secretary

CONTENTS FOR NOVEMBER 1909

VOLUME XXII NUMBER 5

His last photograph. The caption for this picture in *Pearson's Magazine* reads, "Samuel Salant, grand rabbi of Jerusalem for nearly seventy years. This remarkable photograph, made for *Pearson's Magazine* in July, a few days before his death, is the only portrait for which the grand rabbi ever sat. He was ninety-five years old and had great-great-grandchildren living – the most venerable and beloved figure in all Israel."

ing like that will ever occur again in the world."

I asked him about the movement to establish a Jewish nation. [Note: The First Zionist Congress had taken place in Basel, Switzerland in 1897.] "The Jews should return to Palestine," he said. "That is the best thing for them. There never was a better time in history for Jews to return to their own land. Palestine is now ready for its own people. When I came to Jerusalem it took four weeks to make a journey that can be made in four days now. It is wonderful, wonderful!

"Whether the Jews are to find their future in Palestine or Mesopotamia God only knows. No one can foretell the will of God. We are all in His hands."

He raised one hand as though almost in benediction and lifted his face upward. "Our forefather Abraham used to live in Mesopotamia, which the Bible calls Arham Naharim [sic]. God Almighty said to him, 'Go out of Mesopotamia, and go into a land which I will show you.' That land was Palestine.

"I know what they say about colonizing Jews. But tell our people in America not to forget their poor brethren here. A king was walking in the night, and no one knew him to be the king, save one who recognized his face and put a light in the window in order that he might find his way. And the king said, 'Why not come out into the street with the lamp and go before me, that I may see where I go?' So why not give us light in Palestine, where we are?"

I can recall conversations with many distinguished religious leaders – with Leo XIII in the Vatican; with the Archbishop of Canterbury in Lambeth Palace; with the Sheik-Ul-Islam in Constantinople; with Pobiedonostseff, the thin-lipped procurator of the Holy Synod, in St. Petersburg; with cardinals, archbishops, and patriarchs of many faiths – even with a great, rumbling, mysterious Mahatma from the Himalayas. But I cannot remember anything more impressive than the face of the grand rabbi of Jerusalem.

Rabbi Mordechai Gimpel Yaffe

"Although Rabbi Mordechai Gimpel Yaffe was one of the towering Jewish figures of his era with few who could be called his peers, contemporary historians do not appreciate the man's greatness."[477]

No figure had a greater impact on the Ekron pioneers than Rabbi Mordechai Gimpel Yaffe. It was he who persuaded them to make *aliyah* and fully observe Shemittah in defiance of Rothschild's administrators. Rabbi Yaffe believed with all his heart that no matter what the final halakhic status of Shemittah would be, at least one Shemittah should be observed in its entirety. Regardless of the rabbi's stand on Shemittah, no one could accuse him of being an opponent of colonizing and rebuilding the Land of Israel. He was, after all, one of the founders of Chovevei Ẓion and one of its greatest advocates.

Rabbi Mordechai Gimpel Yaffe was a paradox. He was avant-garde when it came to settling the Land of Israel, being one of the first to head Rabbi Ẓvi Hirsch Kalischer's revolutionary call to colonize the land. On 21 Sivan 5643 (June 26, 1883) Rabbi Yaffe was chosen to be one of the six rabbinical members of the steering committee (along with Rabbi Shmuel Mohilever) to establish a national Chovevei Ẓion movement. Yet his inner piety seemed to echo an epoch long gone:

והיה תמיד מתאבל על ירושלים ומתאנח עליה מאין הפוגות.
בלילה היה בוכה על חורבנה בתיקון חצות בקול בכי קורע לב ונפש.

He was constantly mourning over Jerusalem and sighing over it without letup. At night, he would wail over its destruction at *tikkun chaẓot* with a cry that would pierce one's heart and soul.[478]

Mourning over Jerusalem. Rabbi Mordechai Gimpel Yaffe

Rabbi Yaffe never returned an insult – if it was directed

against him personally.[478A] But when it came to matters that affected Torah observance or the community at large, he was fearless. He was also a consummate scholar who with his meager salary amassed a personal library of over 4,000 books. After his passing, it was discovered that he had written glosses in every one of them. He was a prolific author as well. Unfortunately, few of his writings have survived.

Practicing what he preached, he made *aliyah* himself in 1888, retiring after being in the rabbinate for forty years. At a time of life when his colleagues eased up a bit, he undertook the difficult and exhausting move to Palestine – along with his entire library.

But there is more. Upon his arrival he again demonstrated his profound love for rebuilding the Land of Israel by choosing to live in the agricultural community of Yahud, shunning offers of a rabbinical position in Jerusalem. For three years he taught a select group of Torah scholars. Tragically, his new life in the land of his dreams was cut short by malaria.

He was eulogized in Lithuania by Yerucham Fishel Pines, who worked with him on many projects back in Rozhinoy. He was buried on 25 Cheshvan 5652 (November 26, 1891).[478B] Engraved on his tombstone, located in the Segulah cemetery of Petach Tikva, are the following words:

And from there [Yahud]
his light shone forth
to illuminate the settlements
and teach their children
the way of God
through the commandments
connected to the land
and through resting from work
in the Shemittah year.

Moving testament. Gravestone of Rabbi Mordechai Gimpel Yaffe

The Pioneers of Mazkeret Batya

"They Never Called Themselves Zionists..."

A visit to the cemetery of Mazkeret Batya reveals but a fraction of the story of its founders. The grave markers of its earliest residents are uniquely tube-shaped, appearing like coffins only partially submerged in the ground. The words engraved on them barely tell us about the lives of the men and women who trekked from Russia to a homeland they had never seen.

The question has been asked: Were they the first Zionists? To this, Chaim Maller, grandson of founder Moshe Maller, responds:

> Our forefathers, upon their immigration to the Land of Israel ... never stated that they were Zionists.
>
> ... They said that whoever fulfills the commandments of our religion piously and faithfully, and first and foremost the commandment of settling the Land of Israel, is a Zionist, since the passage "And may our eyes behold Your return to Zion in compassion" is repeated in the morning, afternoon, and evening prayers. What is Zionism if not the fulfillment of this commandment?"[479]

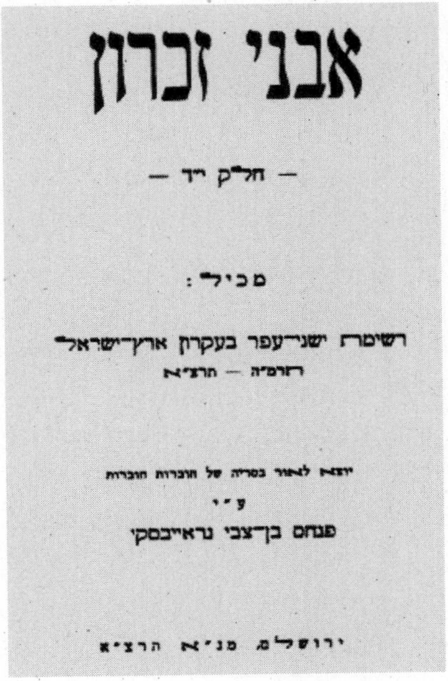
אבני זכרון
— חל"ק י"ד —
מכיל:
רשימת ישני־עפר בקרקע ארץ־ישראל
תרמ"ה — תרצ"א
ע"י
פנחס בן־צבי גראייבסקי
ירושלם סנ"א תרצ"א

Book of the deceased. According to *Avnei Zikaron*, the community of Mazkeret Batya lost thirty-seven children between 1885 and 1931, an indication of the severe hardships the families endured.

First to go. Avraham Mordechai Levin, father of founder Yechezkel Levin, was the first settler to pass away in Mazkeret Batya. It was considered a great merit to be buried in the Holy Land.

Gravestone of Ẓvi Arkin. "Here lies R' Ẓvi, son of Avraham Shlomo, of blessed memory, who died on Friday, Sabbath eve, on 1 Elul [5]651 [September 4, 1891]."

Let us see what became of some of the early founders of the moshavah.

Ẓvi Arkin, a lifelong "man of the soil," died of sunstroke while hauling limestone to build a home for his family so the Arkins could move out of the crowded *kazarme* they were living in.[480] He was only forty years old and had lived nearly nine years in the Land of Israel; he felt blessed to have observed all the special commandments pertaining to the Holy Land, including Shemittah.

His many descendants live all over Israel. Two of his great-grandsons, Yisrael Chaim Arkin and Amihud Arkin (both, at this writing, in their seventies), carry his "farming genes" and are still working the fields of Mazkeret Batya. (See Amihud's moving story in "A Son of Mazkeret Batya Honors His Past," in the next chapter.) Another great-grandson, Achiezer, recorded for posterity his great-grandfather's courage and fear of God in the book *Nachshonei ha-Shemittah* (*The Shemittah Pioneers*) and produced a short movie about the founders' struggles. Ẓvi Arkin has a number of descendants who have returned to Orthodox Judaism.

Yaakov Arkin passed away twenty-nine years after his brother, Ẓvi. He had arrived

Below: **Gravestone of Yaakov Arkin.** "Here lies the distinguished rabbi, leader of the pioneers, and founder of the settlement in the moshavah Ekron – Yaakov, son of Avraham Shlomo Arkin, from the city of Rozhinoy. He died at a ripe old age in the month of Nisan, in the year [5]680 [1920]." *Bottom right:* **Near his father.** Arkin's father is buried right behind him.

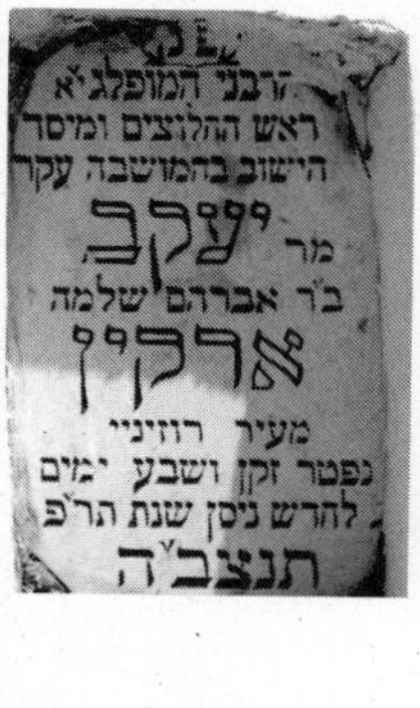

All in the family. A rare picture of Yaakov Laskovsky (far left), one of the founding members of Mazkeret Batya. Standing to his right are his daughter and his wife, both in modest attire. To the right of Mrs. Laskovsky is another daughter, dressed in considerably different garb (in the original, unretouched photo, she is sleeveless), with her husband standing stiffly erect for the camera. Unlike his pious father-in-law, he holds his hat in his hand and faces the photographer bare-headed. The split in religious standards is recorded for posterity, yet it appears that the family unit is still intact.

in Ekron a few days before Chanukah in 1883, lived an intense and hard-working life there. Humility and piety shone from his face.

Yaakov Laskovsky was one of the *gabbaim* of the *bikkur cholim* and *chevrah kaddisha* societies. An article in *Bustenai* (Orchard), published by the Union of Farmers in the Land of Israel, said of Laskovsky:

> [He] excelled in his youth in his strength and courage. He often encountered bands of [Arab] robbers, who were quite plentiful in his time. But he managed to make them flee and even gave them the good beating they deserved.[480A]

As a result of his fighting the Baron's administrators on behalf of the farmers' rights, he was expelled from the moshavah. He moved with his family to Denver, Colorado. Determined not to be buried in America, he returned as an elderly man to Palestine, where he spent the last years of his life. Laskovsky willed a large sum of money to the Diskin Orphan Home in Jerusalem. He passed away at the age of 86.

Chana Maller (Moshe Maller's first wife) is buried in Mazkeret Batya, and her gravestone bears her name, the date of her passing, and the words "The Chaste Woman." She left behind three children: Yosef Ẓvi was a member of the committee that oversaw the settlement, and he was the point man between it and the Turkish authorities. He was also in charge of the settlement's dairy cooperative, and he married Ẓipporah. She was one of the few settlers of Mazkeret Batya who put into writing some reminiscences of the moshavah's early years. Maller's second son, Yehoshua, married Shaina Riva; and her daughter, Esther, married Shlomo Skolnick.

Gravestone of Moshe Maller. "The honorable elderly gentleman. Died on Hoshana Rabbah, 21 Tishrei 5667 [October 10, 1906]."

Moshe Maller married his second wife, Bayla, after Chana's demise. They were married thirty-three years, until she passed away. Maller remained a widower for the remaining twenty-four years of his life.[481] He is buried next to Bayla in the Mazkeret Batya cemetery.

Golden hands. Gravestone of Shlomo Weisberg, the resident *kohen*, who lived to the ripe old age of 85. He passed away on 17 Tishrei 5709 (October 20, 1948).

Shlomo Weisberg's job every morning was to convey the wish that God bestow His blessings on the Jewish people. Beginning with the material and physical aspects of life, the blessings reach their crescendo with the prayer for inner peace. Considering all the turmoil the pioneers went through, such a blessing was a necessity for their survival.

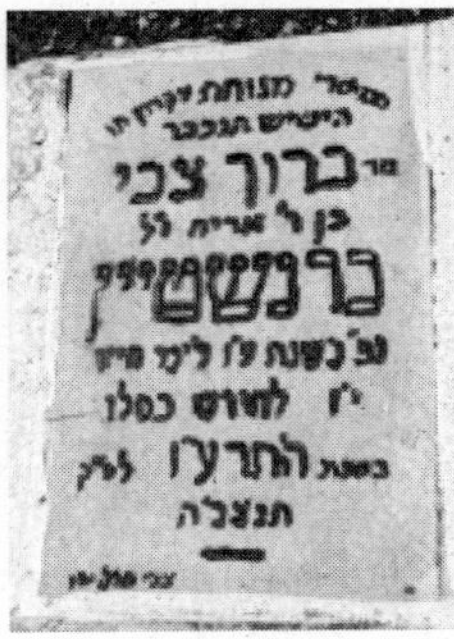

Left: **In defense of his country.** Yoav Shacham Bernstein is buried near his grandfather, founder Baruch Ẓvi Bernstein. He was killed in a battle against terrorists near Hebron on 30 Cheshvan 5727 (November 13, 1966). *Right:* **Gravestone of founder Baruch Ẓvi Bernstein.** He passed away in Kislev 5676 (1915).

Weisberg, the *kohen* who was zealous in his observance of the Torah and the commandment of Shemittah, brings to mind another zealous *kohen* from the distant past: Phinehas [Pinchas], grandson of the high priest Aaron, who slew the Jewish prince Zimri along with his consort, the Midianite princess Cozbi. God granted him "My covenant of peace" (Numbers 25:11). The medieval Italian biblical commentator Rabbi Ovadiah Seforno elaborates, "I will grant [Pinchas] peace i.e., reprieve from the angel of death." Weisberg died at the ripe old age of 85 and was one of only two founders who lived all the way through the founding of the State of Israel.

Baruch Ẓvi Bernstein married off all his daughters to carpenters, because he believed that carpentry was a holy vocation, an integral part of building the land. He passed away at age 77.

Mordechai Neiman was a man of apparent contradictions: he was a Chassid with a penchant for Jewish philosophy, an intellectual and a creative entrepreneur, an advocate of *chinuch ivri* and a religious conservative. He blended all of these disparate traits into one beautiful mixture of truth and compassion. His descendants had the following carved on his gravestone: "Here rests

A unique personality. Gravestone of Mordechai Neiman

in peace a God-fearing man, filled with great religious fervor, love of his people, his Torah, and his land, Mordechai, son of Ẓvi Neiman. One of the first pioneers to make *aliyah* during the last exile, who came to rebuild the ruins of the Land of Israel. He merited being one of the builders of the moshavah of Mazkeret Batya, which also goes by its old name, Ekron. He passed away on the holy Sabbath, on the eve of Rosh Chodesh Kislev, 5670 [November 13, 1909], at the age of 83."

Chaim Moshe Press: In the March 14, 1934 edition, dedicated to the fiftieth anniversary of Ekron's founding, *Bustenai* wrote:

From cover to cover. Chaim Moshe Press enjoying a newspaper

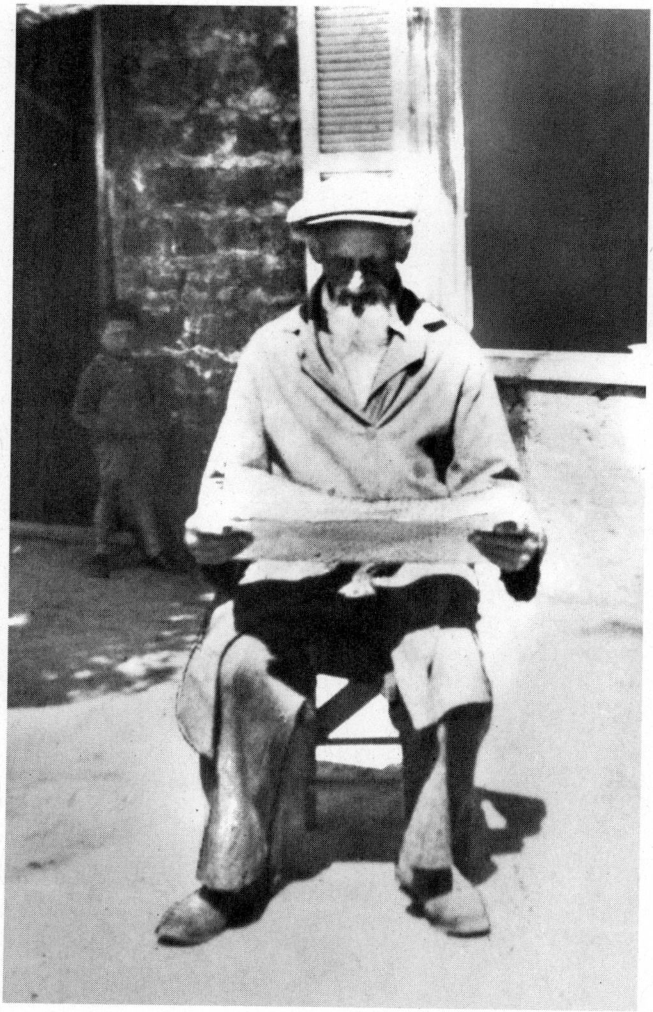

... [Mr. Press], who today is ninety years old, has not lost his vigor. [He] ... is not bound to a wheelchair. He has physical activities that he enjoys – like chopping wood. His mind is alert. Not only is he not depressed, but he has a passion – current events and newspapers. He devours them with gusto. But most of all, he can look out on a growing community that he started with his own bare hands. He can look back on his life as a simple farmer in an obscure hamlet in White Russia, who was suddenly presented with a challenge that he felt was possibly his life's calling, and he did not hesitate to meet that challenge. Now he can look back at all the trials and difficulties he endured and have the satisfaction of realizing that through his small, individual decision, he made history by paving the way for other Russian Jews to make their new home in the Land of Israel.[481A]

Etched in stone. The gravestone reads: *Chaim Moshe Press, son of Yoel Dov. One of the first pioneers of the Yishuv and one of the founders of the moshavah of Ekron. He got along well with people; he was hospitable and merited a long life. He passed away on 24 Kislev 5709 [December 31, 1948] at the age of 101.*

Though he had taken sick when he arrived in Palestine, he outlived his companions by many years[482] and was the only founder to *celebrate* the establishment of the State of Israel, a source of joy in the last year of his long life. His grandson, Aryeh Press, lives nearby in Rehovot and often takes people on tours of Mazkeret Batya. When Aryeh was young, it was his privilege to escort his grandfather to *shul* every Friday night – a pleasure he performed every week until he was thirteen years old, when his *zayde* passed away.

A proud grandson. Aryeh Press, a frequent visitor to the Mazkeret Batya museum, stands next to a drawing of his beloved grandfather.

Parting Words

Walking in hushed silence past the tombstones of Mazkeret Batya, one gets a sense of the greatness that simple people can achieve when fate calls out to them at a crucial juncture in history. Their spirits seem to hover overhead. One strains to hear them as they whisper to one another.

The graves, huddled together, are reminiscent of their lives: while surrounded by magnificent fields, their huge families were crammed inside their *kazarmes*. Diagrams of large family trees adorn the walls of the museum of Mazkeret Batya, and there are many descendants scattered throughout the land.

What would these God-fearing people have to say about the results of all their blood, sweat, and tears? No doubt, the tears would have a bittersweet taste. These pioneers established a beachhead in the Promised Land, and their success beckoned thousands more to follow. No doubt, they would have been proud of their descendants who became soldiers, businessmen, and professionals.

But what about their innermost desire – to transplant the Torah they knew and practiced in the old country to the Promised Land? How did they feel when they saw their grandchildren swept away by modern trends right here in the Holy Land?

During their lifetimes, they saw their land and independence torn from them by the Baron. They saw how his anti-religious administrators and secular *maskilim* succeeded in alienating their grandchildren from their most cherished beliefs. And it seemed that they were powerless to overcome the forces that would overwhelm them. In their day, they may have wondered: why did God bring them here? Was it worth all the effort?

Today, we are the beneficiaries of their steadfast faith, whether or not we are descended from them, whether or not we are farmers, whether or not we live in Israel. With the perspective of decades upon decades of growth and change, every Jew may finally ask: what spiritual legacy did the pioneers of Mazkeret Batya leave behind?

Ode to a Vanishing Breed

The periodical *Ha-Shiloach* was full of praise for the farmers of Ekron. Below is a sample from 1897 by Yehudah Grazovsky-Gur (whose pseudonym was מד״ד), a *chinuch ivri* teacher in Mazkeret Batya who was married to Rachel Neiman, daughter of founder Mordechai Neiman. It provides a fitting final tribute to the pioneers mentioned in this book.

הַשִּׁלֹחַ

מכתב־עתי חדשי

למדע, לספרות ולעניני החיים.

המוציא:
קלונימס זאב ויסאצקי.

העורך:
אשר גינצברג.

כרך א.

(חוברת א—ו).

חשון–אדר ב׳ תרנ״ז.

עקרון. לו היה לי לדבר על עקרון לפני שבע או שמונה שנים, כי אז החלותי
בשפת בעל־ההשקפות הנזכר: „אין מושבה אחת אשר כה ינעם לנו לדבר על אדותה
כעל אדות הכפר עקרון“. כי באמת היא היתה המושבה היחידה שראויה היתה לשם כפר,
ויושביה היו היחידים שיכלנו לקראם אכרים במובן האמתי של המלה הזאת. אמנם גם
היום לא נמצא בה את „העירוניות“ במדה שהיא נמצאת ביתר המושבות, אבל כפר ממש,
כמו שהיתה לפנים, איננה עוד. היו ימים שאכר עקרוני רעה כל הלילה את בקרו, ובבקר
השכם, אך עלה השחר, לקח לו פת לחם יבש וילך לחרוש את שדהו; היו ימים שכל
בני עקרון, אנשים ונשים יחדו, יצאו השדה לקצור ולאסוף את תבואתם; היו ימים שבעקרון
לא נראתה „מגבעת“ על ראש אשה ונערה; היו ימים שהכירו הכל את האכר העקרוני
בבגדיו הפשוטים בתכלית הפשטות, בנעליו הגסים ובכובעו הישן והמעוך. אולם הימים
האלה עוד אינם, ואך זכרונם נשאר, כמים עברו.

The genuine article. Article from *Ha-Shiloach* praising the people of Mazkeret Batya. *Bottom:* Translated excerpts.

Ekron's residents are the only ones we could refer to as farmers in the truest sense of the word. Even nowadays you don't find there that kind of "cosmopolitanism" that exists in the other moshavot … There was a time when an Ekron farmer tended his cattle nearly all night, then arose in the wee hours

"Recognizable by his old and crumpled hat."
Yechezkel Levin

of the morning, grabbed a crust of bread, and went off to plow his field. There was a time when all the people of Ekron – men, women, and children – would go out to the fields together to harvest and gather in their crops. There was a time when a brimmed hat was never seen resting on any woman's or young lady's head in Ekron. There was a time when everyone could recognize a farmer from Ekron just by his extremely simple attire, his coarse shoes, and his old and crumpled hat. But those days are gone. ...[482A]

Chapter 31

The Living Legacy of Mazkeret Batya

What legacy did the pious farmers of Mazkeret Batya leave us? Was all their suffering to uphold their religious principles in vain?

We cannot draw a clear line of cause and effect between the spiritual acts of the Mazkeret Batya farmers and their impact over time. Yet the majority of today's agricultural communities whose policy is not to rely on the *Heter Mechirah* are located within a twenty-minute drive from Mazkeret Batya. In the Sorek Valley, traveling westward along Route 3, you will find the Poalei Agudah settlements of Yesodot (one of those rare *Chareidi* agricultural *yishuvim* in Israel, and probably what Mazkeret Batya would have looked like today, had it not gone secular), Beit Chilkiah, Chafetz Chaim, and Bnei Re'em. These are places where the legacy of Mazkeret Batya lives on. (See appendix VII.)

Rooted in the Holy Land. Thirty years ago, Yehuda Deutsch and his family made *aliyah* and were the first Americans to be accepted as members of the *moshav* Yesodot. He asked to be assigned to the vineyards because of the numerous religious commandments attached to their upkeep. Deutsch is pictured pruning the vines in preparation for the Shemittah of 5768 (2007-2008).

But it's not just about Shemittah.

The legacy of these early pioneers lives on in the beautiful Eran Shamir Village Museum of Mazkeret Batya. In one of my conversations with Daphna Shimshoni, the museum's director, I asked her, "You are so emotionally involved and committed to this museum. I see you put your heart and soul into it. But what kind of connection do you, as a secular Israeli, have with the strictly Orthodox farmers that this museum memorializes?"

Her answer was illuminating. "The vast majority of the visitors to the museum are secular people. I want them to meet face to face with *people who had values.* What I want this museum to impart to them is that we grow up today without really being fully conscious of who we are, what we are all about, and what we are living for. We lack awareness. These farmers were aware!

They knew what was meaningful to them, and that sense of meaning, that awareness, was precious enough for them to pay a heavy price to maintain their ideals. For them it was Shemittah. For our visitors, it may be something else. But at least they should walk out and ask themselves, 'Who am I? What is really important to me?'"

One final point:

All that we have today – the farms, the infrastructure, and the people who make up Israel – would not be here were it not for the trailblazers who arrived in the last decades of the nineteenth century, for they proved to the skeptics that the Land of Israel could indeed become a homeland for the Jewish people. It was the people of Mazkeret Batya and the other colonies of that First Aliyah era who paved the way for everything that followed.

I researched Mazkeret Batya's story for almost five years. Its people and land, its successes and failures, have touched me deeply. As I pieced together this poignant history, I reflected sadly that only three Shemittah cycles later, only three farmers on the entire moshavah of Mazkeret Batya were willing to observe the miẓvah for which their forefathers had nearly sacrificed their lives.

Then I met Amihud Arkin, great-grandson of founder Ẓvi Arkin, who still lives in Mazkeret Batya. Speaking to him, I began to realize that the strength and spirit of the early founders re-emerges in mysterious ways. This is Amihud's story, written when I met him in 2008.

A Son of Mazkeret Batya Honors His Past

When I first met 72-year-old Amihud Arkin, I was struck by what a big and brawny guy he was. Despite his tank-like build, weather-beaten, tough-as-leather skin, and hands with the gripping strength of a pit bull, I could immediately see he had a friendly and gentle soul. No early retirement (or any retirement) for him: he still gets up at 5:30 every morning, and after prayer services in the synagogue (built by Baron Rothschild) he's off to the fields. He is truly an *ish sadeh*, a man of the field.

When Amihud was twelve years old, the British turned away

Horsing around. Amihud Arkin in his younger days

a ship named *Exodus,* filled with refugees and Holocaust survivors. The world was outraged. His brother, Eliezer Moshe, volunteered to take part in a retaliatory raid against a British radar station. He lost his life.[483] A few months later, Amihud read the *haftarah* at his bar mizvah as his father stood beside him on the *bimah,* crying profusely.

The family tragedy brought Amihud prematurely to a vocation that has since been his life and soul. By the time he turned fourteen, he started working on the family farm. He was desperately needed, especially in the absence of his soldier brother who had perished.

His older brother. Eliezer Moshe Arkin. (See note 483.)

Mesirut nefesh (self-sacrifice) is a hallmark of the Arkin family. Over the years, Amihud became aware of the family history: how his great-grandfather had defied Baron Rothschild to keep the mizvah of Shemittah in 5649 (1888-1889) despite severe consequences; and how his grandfather Yisrael Chaim had been one of three Mazkeret Batya farmers who steadfastly refrained from working the land during the Shemittah of 5670 (1909-1910). At the time, the remaining farmers of Mazkeret Batya complained that the threesome was wrong in not relying on Rabbi Kook's *heter.* Yisrael Chaim Arkin and his two comrades published an open letter in *Chavazelet,* publicizing what Rabbi Kook had personally told them:

Three farmers observe Shemittah. Open letter published in *Chavazelet* with Rabbi Kook's answer to the three farmers who wanted to observe Shemittah. (Continuation on opposite page.)

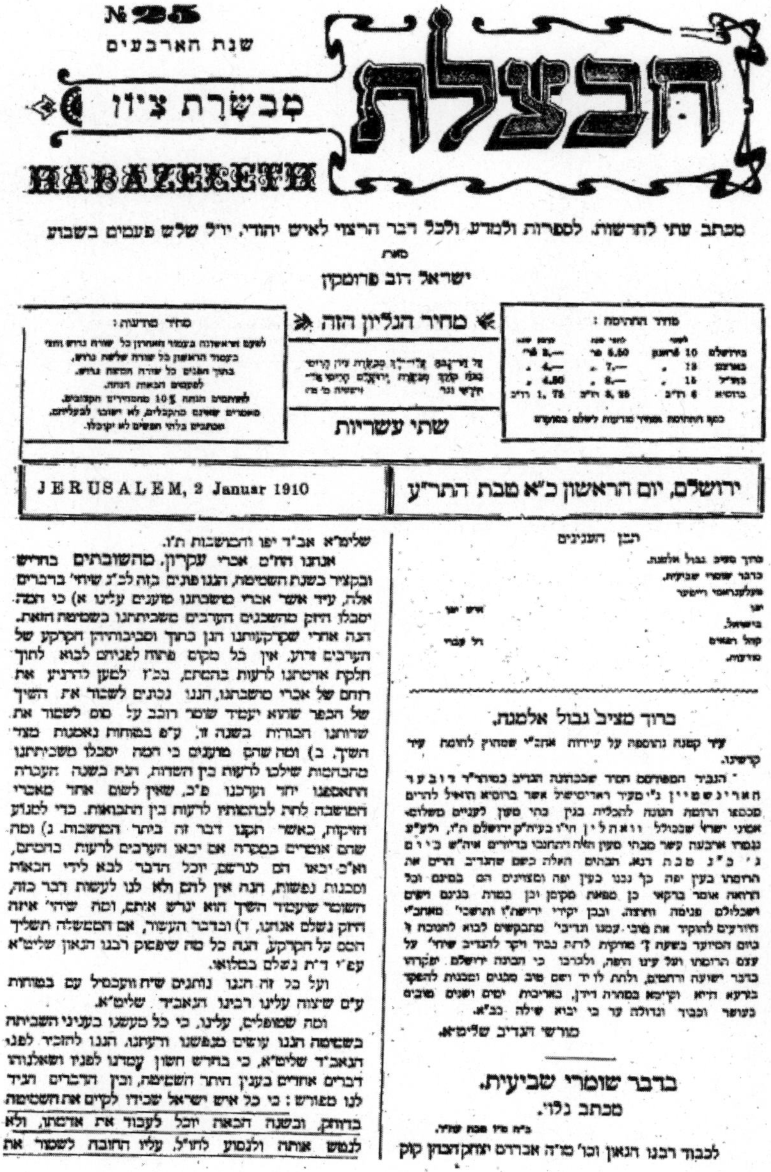

№ 25
שנת הארבעים

חבצלת
מבשרת ציון
HABAZELETH

מכתב עתי לחדשות, לספרות ולמדע, ולכל דבר הרצוי לאיש יהודי, יו״ל שלש פעמים בשבוע
מאת
ישראל דוב פרומקין

מחיר הגליון הזה
שתי עשריות

JERUSALEM, 2 Januar 1910 | ירושלים, יום הראשון כ״א טבת התר״ע

ברוך מציב גבול אלמנה.

עיר קטנה נתוספה על עיירות אחב״י שמחוץ לחומת עיר קדשנו.

הנגיד המפורסם חסיד שבכהונה הנדיב כמוהר״ר דוב בער חארינשטיין נ״י מעיר ראדיסישל אשר ברוסיא הואיל להרים מכספו תרומה הגונה להבליה בנין בתי מעון לעניים משלומי אמוני ישראל שבכולל וואהלין הי״ו בעיה״ק ירושלם ת״ו, ולע״ע נגמרו ארבעה עשר בתי מעון האלה ויתחנכו בדירות אי״ה ביום ג׳ כ״ג טבת דנא. הבתים האלה כשם שהנדיב הרים את תרומתו בעין יפה כך נבנו בעין יפה ומצוינים הם בפנים וכל הרואה אומר ברקאי כן ספאת מקמן יבן בנות בנינם ויפים ישכלולם פנימה וחוצה. ובכן יקירי ירושלם ת״ו ותושבי׳ מאחב״י הודעים להוקיר את פעלי עמנו הנדיבי׳ מתבקשים לבוא לחנוכה ביום המיועד בשעה ד׳ מזרחית לתת כבוד ויקר להנדיב שיחי׳ על עצם תרומתו ועל עינו היפה, ולברכו כי הבונה ירושלם יפקדהו בדבר ישועה ורחמים, ולתת לו יד ושם טוב מבנים ומבנות להאקי בארעא היא וקיימא במהרה דידן, באריכות ימים ושנים טובים בעושר ובכבוד וגדולה עד כי יבוא שילה בב״א.

מוקירי הנדיב שליט״א.

ברבר שומרי שביעית.
מכתב גלוי.

ב״ה כ״ו טבת שעה״ר.

לכבוד רבנו הגאון וכו׳ מו״ה אברהם יצחק הכהן קוק שליט״א אב״ד יפו והמושבות ת״ו.

אנחנו הח״מ אכרי עקרון, מהשובתים בחריש ובקציר בשנת השמיטה, הננו פונים בזה לכ״ג שיחי׳ בדברים אלה, ע״ד אשר אכרי מושבתנו טוענים עלינו א) כי הבהמה יסבלו היזק מהשכנים הערבים משביתתנו בשמיטה הזאת. הנה אחרי שקרקעותינו הנן בתוך ומסביבותיהן הקרקע של הערבים זרוע, אין כל מקום פתוח לצאנם לבוא לתוך חלקת אדמתנו לרעות בהמתם, בכ״ז למען להרגיע את רוחם של אכרי מושבתנו, הננו נכונים לשכור את השיך של הכפר שהוא יעמיד שומר רוכב על סוס לשמור את שדותינו הבורות בשנה זו, ע״פ בטוחות נאמנות מצד השיך. ב) ומה שהם טוענים כי הבהמה יסבלו משביתתנו מהבהמות שלנו לרעות בין השדות, הנה בשנה העברה התאספנו יחד וערכנו פ״כ, שאין לשום אחד מאכרי המושבה לתת לבהמותיו לרעות בין התבואות. כדי למנוע היזקות, כאשר תקנו דבר זה ביתר המושבות. ג) ומה שהם אומרים במקרה אם יבאו הערבים לרעות בהמתם, וא״כ יבאו הם לגרשם, יוכל הדבר לבוא לידי הכאות וסכנות נפשות, הנה אין להם ולא לנו לעשות דבר כזה, השומר שיעמיד השיך הוא יגרש אותם, ומה שיהי׳ איזה היזק נשלם אנחנו, ד) ובדבר העשור, אם הממשלה תשליך המס על הקרקע, הנה כל מה שיפסוק רבנו הגאון שליט״א עפ״י ד״ת נשלם בשלמות.

ועל כל זה הננו נותנים שיח ועכסול עם בטוחות ע״פ שיצוה עלינו רבינו הגאב״ד שליט״א.

ומה שטופלים עלינו, כי כל מעשנו בעניני השביתה בשמיטה הננו עושים מנפשנו ודעתנו, הננו להזכיר לפני הגאב״ד שליט״א, כי בחדש חשון עמדנו לפניו ושאלנוהו דברים אחדים בענין היתר השמיטה, ובין הדברים הגיד לנו מפורש: כי כל איש ישראל שבידו לקיים את השמיטה כהלכה, ובשנה הבאה יוכל לעבוד את אדמתו, ולא לנטוש אותה ולנסוע לחו״ל, עליו החובה לשמור את

Any Jew who is capable of observing the miẓvah of Shemittah in spite of the difficulties, and in the year following Shemittah will be able to return to working his fields without needing to abandon them and leave the country, has an obligation to fulfill the miẓvah of Shemittah in accordance with all its laws.[484]

When Amihud's father, Zalman Mendel, took over the reins

אברהם יצחק הכהן קוק
A. I. KUCK
GRAND RABBIN de JAFFA
et Colonies
יפו והמושבות

השמיטה כהלכה, וזה יהי' זכות גדול לכלל האומה!
ובשמענו את דבריו הק' שדבר בחום נפש הסכמנו
בנפשנו להיות בשובתי השמיטה, ושאלנו את מרן הגאב"ד
אם פקידי המושבות יצערנו ע"ז ע"ז השיב הגאב"ד:
„כי בעת שעשה את המכירה ע"י פראנק פסק עמו
בפירוש. אם ימצאו אכרים שישבתו בשמיטה אל נא
יפגע בהם! והוספנו לשאול! אם יש ביכולת האכרים
האחרים לעכב בנו, ויענה לנו: כי אין להם כל צדקה
להפריע בעדנו ממצוה גדולה כזאת, שאין לשער
רוממותה, ומרוב שמחתו ועליצות נפשו הטהורה והקדושה
הביע לנו ברכה בכתב, וכי יעזרנו השי"ת בכל אשר
נפנה, ונזכה לקיים את כל המצות התלויות בארץ. אך
למען השלום שלא תפרע חננו נותנים את כל הבטוחות
הנ"ל שלא יסבול שום אחד ע"י שנקיים את מצות השמיטה
כמצוה עלינו, ונקוה להשי"ת כי בשמיטה הבאה יהי' כל
ישראל בשובתי שמיטה בלי שום הפקעה.

שלמה וויסבערג
ישראל חיים ארקין
ישראל ארקין.

Supportive of Shemittah observers who wanted to be stringent and not rely on his *heter*. A young Rabbi Kook, when he was the rabbi of Jaffa

of the family farm, he made the decision to rely on the *Heter Mechirah*, as did Amihud.

But one morning Amihud woke up and decided that in the Shemittah year of 5768 (2007-2008), he was not going to work the fields. This decision was not based on his being seventy-two years of age. As mentioned earlier, he is as strong as an ox, works the same hours as he did when he was in his twenties, and loves every minute of it.

He simply decided to preserve the living legacy of his family. To actualize his intention, Amihud went to the offices of Keren Ha-Shvi'it (see page 356) in Komemiyut (near Kiryat Gat) and signed the following declaration:

> I, the undersigned, Amihud Arkin, fifth-generation resident and farmer of the moshavah of Mazkeret Batya, hereby declare that agriculture is my sole means of support. Below is a detailed list of all tracts of land, excluding vineyards, where I cultivate crops. It is my stated intention to have them lie fallow in the Shemittah year of 5768.[485]

"My other car is a Porsche." Amihud Arkin standing beside his tractor in a fallow field. Behind him is the green field of another farmer, whose land is not "resting." In the background is Mazkeret Batya.

I asked Amihud what made him do it. His reply (in Hebrew): *"Lehachazir atarah le-yoshnah"* – to restore the crown to its former glory.

But his decision came with a price – a test of *mesirut nefesh* reminiscent of his grandfather's.

• The hundreds of dunams of land that he cultivates are not his own but are leased from the Israel Lands Administration. The only way he can ensure that he will continue to cultivate them after Shemittah is by maintaining the lease payments – at 120 shekels per dunam.

• Just before he made his decision regarding Shemittah, Amihud had purchased a new tractor. He approached the tractor company and requested that it freeze the contract, so he wouldn't have to pay out money for a whole year while his tractor sat in the garage. His request was denied.

• Amihud feared he would lose a worker who had been at his side for years. If he let him go, there would be no guarantee that he would come back after a year. Losing someone you have worked with for years, and finding the right man to replace him as your assistant, is no easy task. So he took it upon himself to be on the constant lookout for temporary outside employment for his worker, so he would never leave him.[485A]

But the greatest sacrifice of all – for Amihud, that is – was giving up a vocation that nourishes his soul, for an entire year. He loves to run his hands through the growing stalks of wheat in his fields and tend to his vineyards. He has loved farming for fifty-eight years. And he let go of that as well.

He would still have some work to do in the vineyards. During Shemittah, the vineyards were under the jurisdiction of a *beit din,*

A family tradition. Ẓvi Arkin's great-grandson next to a sign that reads, "Here we observe Shemittah!" Unlike his neighbors, Amihud waited until after the Shemittah year to sow wheat. The delayed rains that year came when the wheat stalks in the fields of the other farmers were withering, but the timing was perfect for Arkin. His wheat stood at least two feet taller than that of his colleagues, though he sowed much later.

and were called *oẓar beit din* (see glossary). He was put in charge of running it, compensated only for the labor costs. He could not earn any profit, since the grapes were technically ownerless. Arab laborers were hired to prune the vines and be involved in the harvesting – all under his supervision. And Amihud, in turn, was instructed by a rabbinical advisor from the Shemittah organization regarding exactly what kinds of labors the Arabs were permitted to perform.

I asked Amihud what his farmer colleagues had to say about his decision. In a tone that would make his ancestors proud, he casually replied, "They think I am *meshuga*. And I really don't care."

A Personal Note

I have tried to convey to the reader the heroism and self-sacrifice of the founding members of Mazkeret Batya. This included their pioneering spirit in leaving the old country in order to colonize the Holy Land and forge a path for other Jews who were fleeing persecution. One aspect of their courage and integrity was their following their conscience and observing the laws of Shemittah fully without relying on any leniencies such as the *Heter Mechirah*. The reader may get the mistaken impression that this book is one more tome that is

Revered by all. Posters like this one featuring a picture of Rabbi Yizchak Elchanan Spektor side by side with the Gaon of Vilna were found in homes throughout Lithuania.

taking sides in the polemic that rages to this day regarding the *Heter Mechirah*. I want to state that that is not my intention at all. By no means do I seek to denigrate those who employ the *Heter Mechirah*. Shemittah is very complicated, and the issues involved are way over my head, so I have no opinion as to which side deserves more credence.[1]

---

[1] I had the privilege of interviewing Rabbi Aharon Goldberg, son of Rabbi Zalman Nechemiah Goldberg and grandson of Rabbi Shlomo Zalman Auerbach, *zt"l*, in his home in Jerusalem on December 16, 2007. Rabbi Goldberg has edited some of his famous grandfather's works, including the second edition of *Minchat Shlomo*. When I asked him about his grandfather's position regarding Shemittah and the *Heter Mechirah*, he recounted the following incidents, which he personally witnessed:

After spending several hours with a group of rabbis from the Poalei Agudah movement, who had consulted him about how to observe Shemittah without resorting to the *Heter Mechirah*, Rabbi Auerbach was visited by rabbis from Ha-Poel Ha-Mizrachi, whom he instructed in the proper utilization of the *heter*. (He himself did not rely on the *heter*.)

My intent in publicizing those farmers who do not rely on the *heter* is to pay tribute to the Mazkeret Batya pioneers. My goal is to demonstrate that their sacrifices were not in vain, and that they laid the groundwork not only with regard to helping establish the Yishuv, but in forging a path for those who wanted to observe the commandment of Shemittah in the fullest sense – according to the letter of *halakhah* as well as its spirit. May the deeds of the founders inspire all people to live a life of integrity and have the courage to follow their conscience.

Rabbi Goldberg added that Rabbi Yisrael Meir Lau, Israel's former chief rabbi, consulted Rabbi Auerbach as well: "Rabbi Lau never asked him, 'Should I use the *Heter Mechirah*?' He asked, '*How* should I use the *Heter Mechirah*?' And my grandfather understood that the question behind the question was 'What can we do for the masses (המון עם), the average Israeli who isn't concerned and can't be bothered with the strictures of Shemittah? We who are religious [and observe Shemittah] will do okay, but what about the rest?' He cared about them too. He believed that something needed to be done on their behalf."

Afterword

The contemplation of things as they are,
without error or confusion,
without substitution or imposture,
is in itself a nobler thing
than a whole harvest of invention.
Francis Bacon

Idealists or Opportunists: Why Did They Follow Yechiel Brill to Palestine?

Why did the farmers of Pavlovka heed Yechiel Brill's call to follow him to Palestine? In this book, I have adopted the position of Achiezer Arkin:

> They had come to Palestine imbued with the mission of planting Torah – more than any other crop – in its stubborn soil. (p. 2)
>
> They were keenly aware that their establishment of a model colony could pave the way for other European and Russian Jews to make their new homes in Palestine rather than in America. It was their love of Klal Yisrael (the Jewish people) and their love of Ereẓ Yisrael (the Land of Israel) that drove them.... (p. 7)
>
> Although Brill described many of their qualifications, he did not state why the farmers wanted to give up their prosperous farms in Russia – farms that had been painstakingly established by their parents a generation earlier – to embark on the treacherous venture in Palestine .... [They] were devout and pious Jews who prayed three times a day ... they took the prayer "Let our eyes behold Your return to Zion in mercy" to heart. Their love of the Land of Israel and their desire to fulfill the agricultural miẓvot motivated them to take up the challenge. (p. 27)

But others disagree. Dr. Yerakh Tzur, editor of the website of the Eran Shamir Village Museum, Mazkeret Batya, recommended that I revise the passages quoted above. Otherwise, he claimed, this book would be just another hagiography, idealizing its protagonists.

According to Tzur, the plain, unvarnished truth, stripped of all sentimentality, is that the farmers were fleeing economic hardship and anti-Semitism. Period.

Tzur believes that the other First Aliyah pioneers – who came to Palestine on their own initiative, with or without a sponsor – were the true idealists. They were determined to build

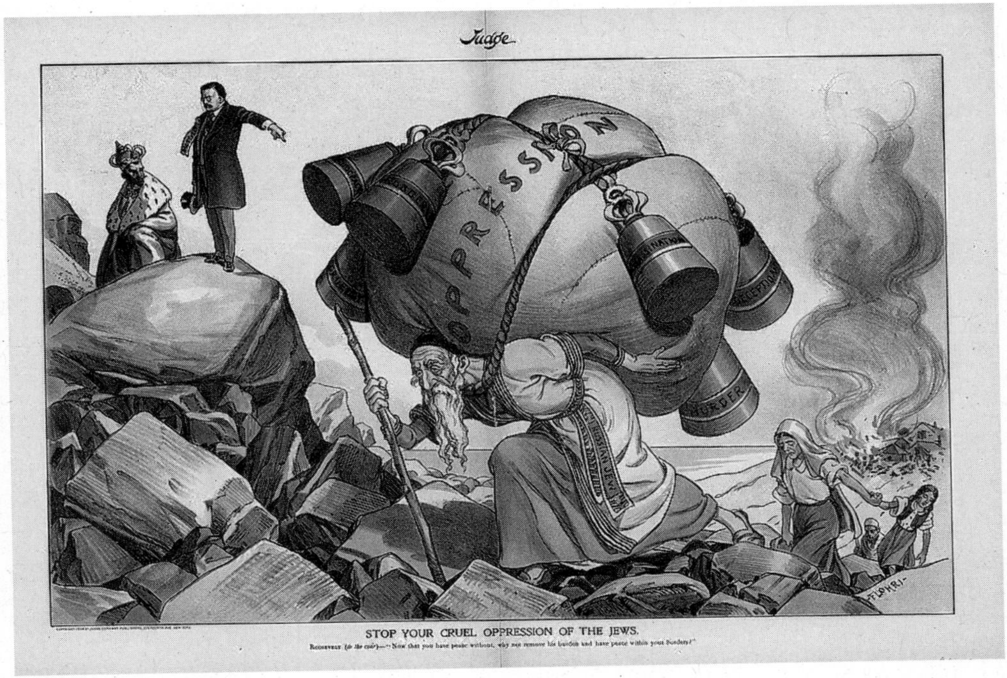

Save Czarist Jewry. Political cartoon from 1905 shows an aged man labeled "Russian Jew" carrying a large bundle labeled "Oppression" on his back. Hanging from the bundle are weights labeled "Autocracy," "Robbery," "Cruelty," "Assassination," "Deception," and "Murder." In the background, on the right, a Jewish community burns, and in the upper left corner, Theodore Roosevelt speaks to the Emperor of Russia, Nicholas II, "Now that you have peace without, why not remove his burden and have peace within your borders?"

a society based on traditional Jewish values and nationalism. In contrast, the Pavlovka farmers came only after Rothschild's offer and with no social vision, just a desire to escape Pavlovka's crushing poverty. Yisrael Chaim Arkin, Achiezer Arkin's older brother, told me, "I think Tzur's understanding of their motives is closer to the truth than that of my brother. I visited Pavlovka myself. I can tell you how primitive the place is. You can imagine how bad it was 120 years ago. They probably were only too happy to get out." (Nevertheless, he finds it exemplary that, because of their religious values, they preferred the Holy Land over the United States, despite the vast difference between the two destinations.)

Tzur and Yisrael Chaim Arkin suspect that Achiezer Arkin and other descendants of the Pavlovka pioneers (especially the religious descendants) are projecting their own ideals and values onto their ancestors, thereby exaggerating their merits.

But Achiezer Arkin feels passionately that the Pavlovkans were true idealists with a burning desire to settle the Land of Israel. For them, the Baron's proposal was like a lightning bolt in a pitch-black sky, a dream come true.

Their tenacity in the face of disease and other suffering, and their starvation on account of their strict observance of Shemittah (which they could have avoided by relying on the *heter*), points to people seeking more than just the good life.

Dr. Mordechai Naor, author of *Sefer Le-Mazkeret,* a history of Mazkeret Batya, inclines toward Achiezer Arkin's point of view. The fact that the farmers left on such short notice, with no safety net, suggests more than mere opportunism. Skepticism regarding their idealism, he told me, reflects the post-Zionism in vogue in Israeli academic circles, which discredits the stature, motivations, and ethical values of Israel's founders and even of their forerunners.

Family portrait. Seated: Shmuel and Sarah Skolnick; Standing: their son, Leib

The skeptics would counter that the farmers' commitment to Shemittah and to the commandments connected to the land wasn't necessarily *why* they wanted to settle there, but something they took upon themselves (along with obeying the Jerusalem rabbis) once they arrived.

Their recruiter, Rabbi Mordechai Gimpel Yaffe, was a founder of Chovevei Ẓion. Envisioning the mass immigration of Russian Jews to Palestine, perhaps he exhorted the Pavlovkans to lead the way. The farmers greatly respected him and presumably found his message inspiring. But it may not have been their primary motive.

Yechiel Brill had a vision as well. He abandoned both his family and his newspaper for months to make his mark on history. But he never told us what those who went with him were thinking.

Neither did they. And with over 120 years between us, we will never know.

So were the Pavlovka farmers idealists or opportunists? Perhaps the truth is somewhere in between. Perhaps prior to Brill's choosing them, they indeed had no ideology. Given the opportunity to settle the Land of Israel, however, they were excited about fulfilling this commandment – and creating a better life for themselves and their children. And that commitment gave them the strength to survive.

Even the cynics concede that the Pavlovka farmers were courageous, hardworking pioneers steadfast in their religious beliefs. Whatever else they may or may not have been, these trailblazers deserve our respect and admiration.

Appendix I
A Farmer's Work Is Never Done

Farming is not just about seeding a field, sitting back in the rocking chair, and whistling until harvest time. It is intensive labor that lasts throughout the year. In order to gain appreciation for our pioneering farmers, we have selected excerpts from a kind of "Farmer's Almanac" that was published in *Ha-Shiloach* (volume 2: Nisan-Elul 5657 [1897], p. 460) and lists the farming chores for each month of the year by type of agriculture (field crops, vineyards, orchards, vegetable gardens, citrus groves). Since the Ekronians considered themselves wheat farmers, we have listed the responsibilities that come under the heading of "field crops."

> ***November***: The first plowing following the first rains (*yoreh*); sowing barley and legumes (for fodder).
>
> ***December***: Sowing barley in clayish soil; sowing wheat, potatoes, and beets; plowing the field in preparation for the corn planting.
>
> ***January***: Sowing wheat; the first plowing for the summer crops (which will be watermelons and sesame).
>
> ***February***: The second and third plowing for the summer crops (including melons and squash).
>
> ***March***: Planting corn; harvesting grasses, barley and clover (which are used for animal feed); plowing for the summer crops.

April: Planting corn, watermelons; harvesting barley and legumes.

May: Barley harvest; beginning of wheat harvest; sowing sesame.

June: Wheat and sorghum harvest; gathering in the potatoes; the last plowing (for growing watermelons, melons, and squash).

July: Threshing the wheat and barley.

August: Threshing; gathering in the sesame and watermelons.

September: Threshing the sesame.

October: If the rains come early, then the winter fieldwork is advanced (from November to October).

Keep in mind that they did not have herbicides. The farmers were constantly hoeing for months to keep the weeds from choking the plants. After the threshing, all members of the family were busy for weeks on end separating the chaff from the kernels. After the grain was organized into piles, the farmers watched as their income shrank before their eyes. First the Ottoman tax collectors came and took their 10%. Then the workers came and took their share. Finally, other creditors came for payment. There were times when the farmer, after all his hard work, had nothing to bring home for his own family.

Getting hitched.
Plowing in Petach Tikva

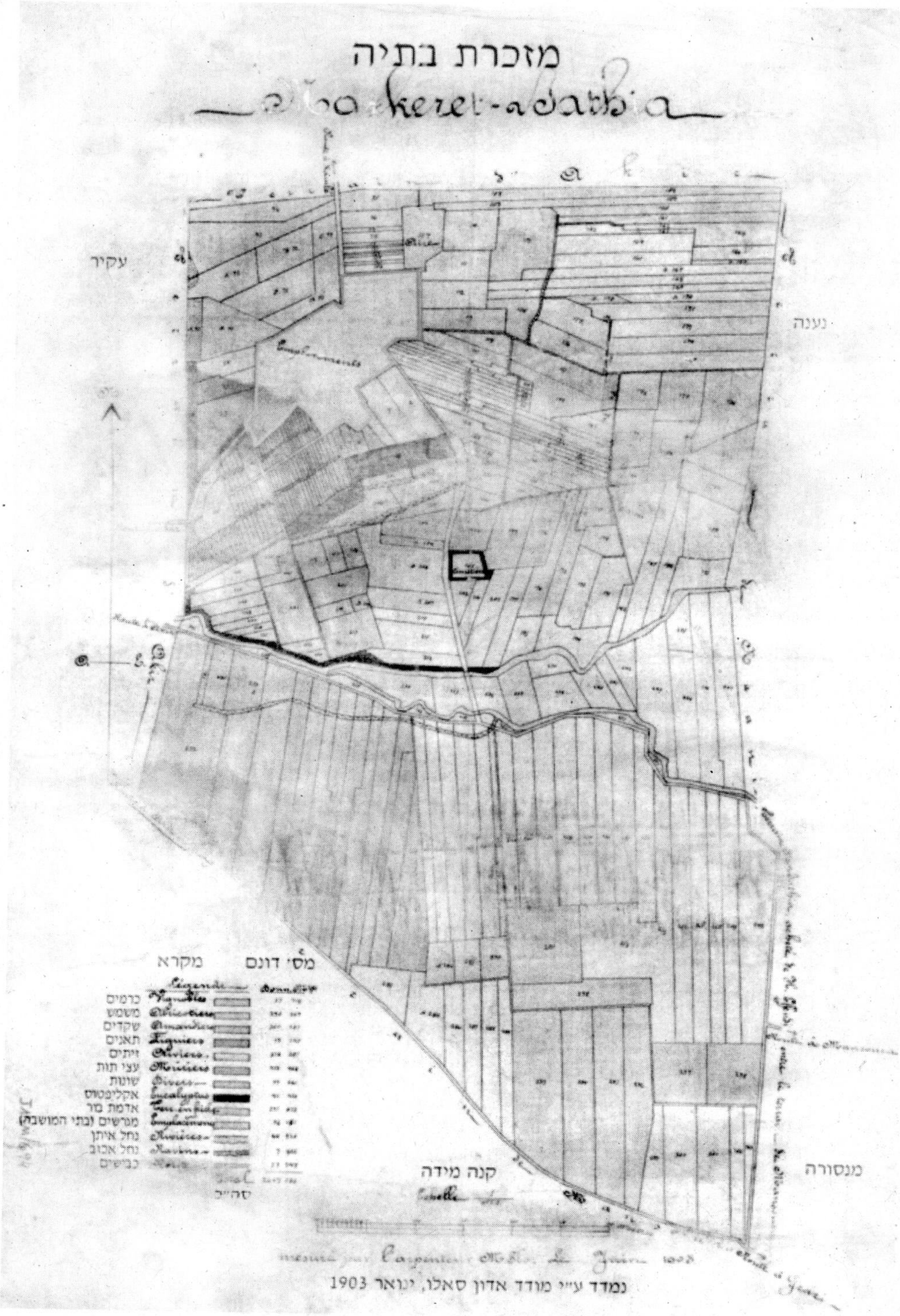
מזכרת בתיה
עקיר
נענה
מקרא
מס' דונם
כרמים
משמש
שקדים
תאנים
זיתים
עצי תות
שונות
אקליפטוס
אדמת בור
מגרשים (בתי המושבה)
נחל איתן
נחל אכזב
כבישים
סה"כ
קנה מידה
מנסורה
נמדד ע"י מודד אדון סאלו, ינואר 1903

Twenty Years of Toil Followed by Hard Times

This 1903 map of Ekron/Mazkeret Batya shows the layout of its fields. Written in French and Hebrew, the map legend, from top to bottom, reads: Vineyards, apricots, figs, olives, mulberry trees, miscellaneous, eucalyptus, uncultivated land, plots and houses of the moshavah, Nachal Eitan, Nachal Achziv, roads.

Yet there's "A time to plant and a time to uproot the planted" (Ecclesiastes 3:2), as evident from the following comments on this list (based on an essay by Yisrael Chaim Arkin that appeared in *Sefer le-Mazkeret*, pp. 319-340):

> *Mulberry trees*: A certain type of moth lays eggs that produce silkworms that feed on mulberry leaves. The worms then build cocoons. It is from these cocoons that silk threads are made. Baron Rothschild established a factory for producing silk threads in Rosh Pina. Mazkeret Batya was one of several settlements that bred silkworms for this facility. When the factory closed in 1905, the mulberry trees of Ekron were uprooted.
>
> *Apricots*: [The farmers] used to dry and crush the apricots and make them into "apricot leather" for export. This – which is a type of fruit roll-up – lasts a long time without refrigeration. Unfortunately, that enterprise also failed.
>
> *Almonds*: Meant for export, like just about everything else they produced. That also failed.
>
> *Grapes*: Vineyards were planted for wine production. Unfortunately, they were hit by phylloxera – pale yellow, sap-sucking insects that feed on the roots of grapevines, eventually deforming them and cutting off the flow of nutrients to the vine. After this occurred, in 1898-1899, Mazkeret Batya's vineyard industry basically came to an end.
>
> *Olive trees*: A large number of trees were forcibly uprooted and confiscated by the Turks to be used as fuel for their steam locomotives during the First World War.

But Mazkeret Batya made a comeback. At the beginning of the twentieth century, with the establishment of Jewish neighborhoods in Jaffa and the beginning of Tel Aviv, there arose a Jewish domestic market for fresh eggs, fruits, and vegetables. Mazkeret Batya also developed a thriving dairy industry that supplied the new Jewish neighborhoods with fresh milk. Until the start of World War II, the farmers had a strong market in Europe for their *etrogim*. They also sold wheat, onions, beets, tomatoes, and cucumbers.

Opposite page: **"A time to plant and a time to uproot the planted."** Map of orchards in Ekron/Mazkeret Batya, 1903.

Appendix II

How Did Shtetl Jews Become Farmers?

Pavlovka was a tiny hamlet in White Russia, home to Jewish farmers. How and why did Russian Jews turn to agriculture?

While farming was never a major Jewish occupation in eastern Europe, there were still quite a few Jews who made a living off the land. Russian anti-Semitic legislation starting at the turn of the nineteenth century brought about the expulsion of many Jews from lands they once owned and farmed. The peasants had complained to the czarist government about unfair Jewish competition. As a result, the Jews were forced out of the countryside and had to settle in towns and cities.[486]

In 1827, Czar Nicholas I legislated an annual conscription quota on Jewish males ages twelve through twenty-five, requiring them to serve in the Russian army for twenty-five years. He demanded ten recruits for every 1,000 inhabitants.[487]

Army service almost guaranteed the death knell for Jewish practice for anyone unfortunate enough to be drafted – child or adult. An absence of twenty-five years from family and synagogue, without kosher food, prayer books, or permission to observe Jewish rituals and holidays, was more than enough time to eradicate Jewish identity and commitment. For religious Jews, this was a decree to be avoided at all costs, the greatest nightmare a Jewish parent could imagine. The fear of child conscription into the dreaded Cantonist Battalions loomed large for many decades.

Ironically, the czarist regime occasionally zigzagged in its policies. Prompted by the complaints of gentile business owners about the success of their Jewish competitors, the government would, on rare instances, encourage the Jews to leave behind the pursuit of business and become more "productive," i.e., allow Jews to settle on farmland and establish agricultural colonies.[488] One such instance occurred in 1850, when Czar Nicholas I made some farmland available in White Russia. At that time, new farmland in White Russia was scarce.

This particular offer was especially attractive, for the Jews who accepted it would be exempt from the dreaded conscription for twenty-five years. Two agricultural settlements were established, one on each side of Rozhinoy, in the district of Grodno. One of them, Constantinova, named after Czar Nicholas' older brother,[489] was founded by fifteen families.[490] Pavlovka, the other settlement – named after Pavel (Paul), the czar's father – was also established by fifteen families, with another fifteen joining the following year.

It must have seemed like a miracle to these Jews to be offered land by the Russian government. But it was only after interminable delays and endless bureaucratic haggling with the regime that they were finally given their piece of land – and nothing else. With no background in agriculture, and no technical or monetary assistance from the government, they needed an even greater miracle to succeed.

There were eight long years of hardship and grinding poverty before they were finally able to establish themselves firmly. In the end, they triumphed over their initial ignorance of agriculture, the hunger, the harsh climate, the indifference of their Jewish neighbors in Rozhinoy, and their own government, which had left them totally dependent upon their own devices and meager resources.

The Founding of Pavlovka

The following articles about Pavlovka appeared in *Ha-Meliz*[491] in 1861 and 1862, respectively. The jargon is rich in references to the Bible and rabbinic literature, typical of the Hebrew newspapers of that era.

If you are a Tanach buff, you might enjoy the challenge of identifying the Biblical verses from which much of the stylistic paraphrasing was adapted. Because a literal, word-for-word translation makes for very awkward and heavy reading, I have taken the liberty of making some stylistic and structural changes.

One can detect a lot of dry humor between the lines. The editors and writers were operating under the thumb of the government censors.

Jews Who Work the Land

by Yosef Staravolsky[492]

Part I

... It has now been ten years since we thirty families have converged on [Pavlovka]. Most of us hail from [the town of] Mishnikova, in the Bialystok district. Each one of us was drawn [to Pavlovka] from our respective former residences by the cords of freedom that were tossed to us by Czar Nikolai, of blessed memory. In his public manifesto he proclaimed that anyone of Jewish stock and called "Israel"[493] who dwelled in the state of Russia would have [the males of] his household rewarded with an exemption from military service for twenty-five consecutive years ... [if they fulfilled the following requirements]:

One: They were willing to travel [to their new inheritance] at their own expense (and not at the expense of the czar's treasury). *Two:* All future outlays for construction would come out of their own pockets. *Three:* All agricultural implements would be purchased with their own money (without any assistance from the czar's treasury). *Four:* They had decided to support themselves through the toil of their hands rather than

Battle of Stoczek, 1831. The Russian army's crushing of the November Revolution eventually paved the way for the creation of Pavlovka.

making a living from the anarchic world of business, which is based on falsehood. *Five:* They have elected to leave the land of [their previous domicile] ... and establish their farming community on a plot of land adjacent to Rozhinoy. (This land formerly belonged to the estate of the famed Sapieha [family][494] which bequeathed[494A] its properties to the czar's treasury, may he be exalted, after it sided with the [Polish] rebels in the year 1831.)[495]

From the very outset, we suffered, because we ran out of money even before the project got off the ground, for in order to find the time we needed to beseech the local officials to carry out the intentions of the exalted government, we were forced to take leave of our work for six months.

We were so joyful when we finally saw our yearnings fulfilled a half a year later, when the bureaucrat nonchalantly pulled out the necessary documents (which we grabbed with both hands), and we took [them] right away to ... the government official in Slonim, so he would show us the land that had been designated for us as an inheritance by the exalted government. After we were shown our land, we departed from our communities with songs and hymns and settled in the valley where we have been privileged to establish our new residence.

However, immediately upon our arrival, and over the course of the first year, we had no means of supporting ourselves.[495A] The little money we had left was spent on food for our households. [We didn't have any income in the meantime, because] we were busy trying to make the government offer materialize [by dealing with all the bureaucracy], forcing us to expend [money] on travel expenses.

There was no one to turn to.... So we turned to God and hoped for His salvation.... On Him we cast our burdens,[496] so He would rejuvenate us (as long as the breath of life was still within us). We raised our hands[497] and hearts up [in prayer] to our Father in heaven, begging that He bring bountiful blessing upon our land, from which we draw our livelihood and provide food for our households.

It was our sense of hope that eased our sorrow and travail and enabled us to commence working the land with a joyful heart – even though we weren't proficient in farming. We toiled so hard at that time, with so little to show for it! Our start was very difficult, because we came here during a period of famine. For the next six consecutive years, we never had enough to eat, because the drought devoured the toil of our hands. Even if we sowed much, we gathered in very little. We were looking forward to abundance, and behold, there was paucity! Then God looked upon us from on high and from His abode,[498] and He took notice over our affliction and toil,[499] and He remembered us with years of satiation and blessing and success from the work of our hands.[500]

However, although we were not lacking in bread because of the good will of the One "Who satiates the hungry," suddenly a southern wind brought the disease of pestilence upon our animals, and in one month we were bereft of whatever the arrows of famine had spared us.

Imagine to yourselves, my brothers and friends! People like ourselves, who came from a different land to a place where no one knew us or our birthplace. Therefore no one felt obliged to extricate us! We could only rely on God. But to bystanders, it appeared as if God had abandoned us, as if we were a people whom He had abandoned – because He'd brought pestilence and famine upon us. So what was there for people to say? Based on the "evidence," they could justifiably argue that we were unworthy. That's because people judge based on what they see – for "a man sees through his eyes."[501] Why should they befriend us if God had estranged Himself from us, and if we had been forced to move so far from our hometowns? How could we justify ourselves before them if God's hand had hurt us?

But we are no more sinful than the rest of humanity ... It was our decision to bear the suffering with a positive attitude. We tilted our shoulders to bear the yoke[502] of our sorrows the whole seven years from the time we arrived. But in the eighth year, God began to "enlarge our borders"[503] with animals, [bountiful] crop yields, and the construction of all the buildings we needed – all through the toil of our hands and the help of our Father in heaven. And from that time onward, we have been happy and praise the Lord's Name and bless the exalted government in whose mind God put the thought that it should be good to us and allow us to settle in the land of our sojourning and satisfy our souls' thirst.[504] ... We can only thank God and pray for the welfare of the exalted government.[505]

Part II[506]

Five years after we'd begun assessing whether we had taken the right path before God and fulfilled our obligations commensurate with the good hand of God that was upon us, we realized that what we lacked was someone who could serve as a rabbi, spiritual guide, and preacher; who could teach us the path to God and strengthen us in those areas where we were weak and deficient; and who would be a source of pride in the *beit midrash* we'd built during the first five years with the toil of our hands and the contributions of the residents of our village. We'd received no outside assistance.... Neither did we reach out for help from the well-known, wealthy brothers, the sons of the deceased magnate Aryeh Leib Pines.

Thirty-two years after its founding, when this agricultural settlement was well established and the hardships of the past were stories to be told to the children, three men – a rabbi, a community activist, and a journalist – would appear with a bold proposal. Thanks to the financial resources of one of the richest men in the world, the lives of the children of those who had founded Pavlovka would be changed forever.

Appendix III

Reliving History: Letter from Rabbi Mordechai Gimpel Yaffe to His Son-in-Law and Daughter

There were many forces acting on the pioneers of Mazkeret Batya with regard to the upcoming Shemittah of 5749/1889: The rabbis of the Old Yishuv were on one side, and Rabbi Yiẓchak Elchanan Spektor, Rabbi Mohilever, Baron Rothschild and his administrators, and Chovevei Ẓion on the other. Fear of poverty and of angering their benefactor, the Baron, versus fear of violating *halakhah*. Rabbi Mordechai Gimpel Yaffe was a key player in the Shemittah controversy. He was the determining factor in their decision, because he was in the field. No matter how great the stature of Rabbi Spektor, the farmers relied even more on Rabbi Yaffe's judgment, because he was there, and the farmers knew that he truly understood their situation.

Shortly after finishing the manuscript for this book, I was fortunate to meet Rabbi Raphael Reichman, the distinguished *rosh yeshivah* of Yeshivas Me'ah She'arim, in Jerusalem, who had in his possession a letter from Rabbi Yaffe to his son-in-law, Rabbi Yosef Zechariah Stern, and to his daughter. Rabbi Reichman graciously permitted me to scan the letter for this book, so it could be shared with the wider reading public.[507]

Rabbi Yosef Zechariah Stern. A prolific Torah scholar, he authored over forty books.

The letter was written seven months after Rabbi Yaffe settled in the Holy Land. In his letter he claims that had he not personally intervened, Mazkeret Batya and Petach Tikva would have "uprooted everything" and not observed Shemittah at all. (ותודה לאל כי עלה בידי לחזק ענין השמיטה בשני הקאלאנעם האלו, שהם בקשו לעקור את הכל.)

He writes that anybody with integrity, even the more "modern" rabbis, was in favor of being stringent with regard to Shemittah. (ויראה כי גם דעתו ודעת כל הישרים אף ממשכילים להחמיר.)

He also asserts that Rabbi Spektor's *heter* was of little consequence except in enabling those who would violate *halakhah*. (ושגגה יצאה מהם לפרוץ גדרים היכא דשכיחי עבדים המתפרצים)

To make it easier to read Rabbi Yaffe's cursive handwriting, a typed version follows the original, and the numerous abbreviations have been spelled out in brackets. The last few lines of the letter, addressed to his daughter and written in Yiddish, have been translated into English.

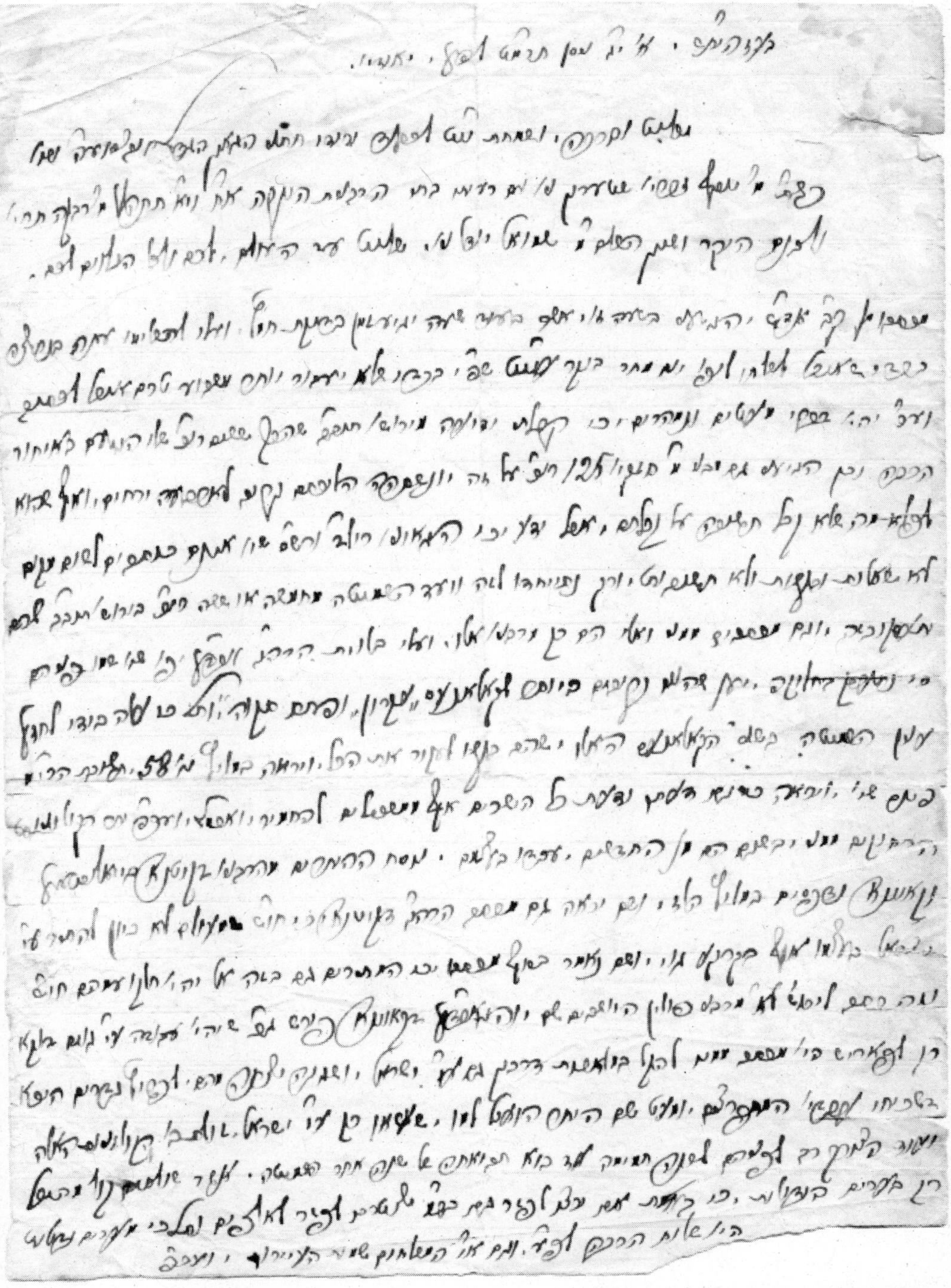

From a father-in-law to his son-in-law.
Side one of letter

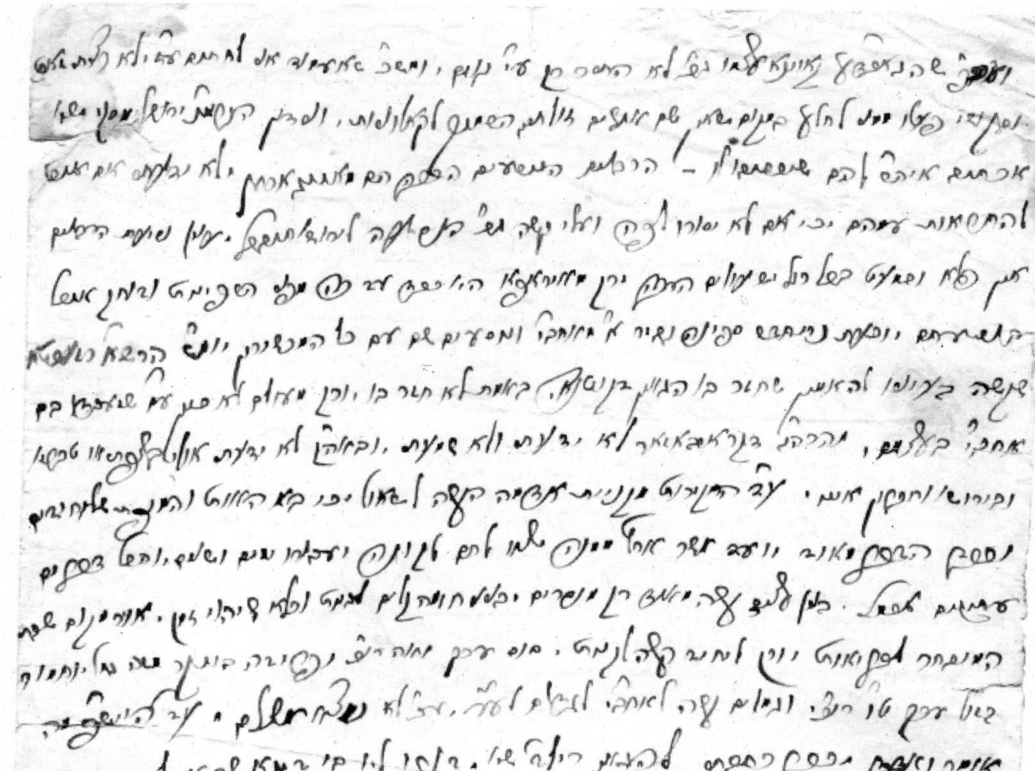

From a father-in-law to his son-in-law.
Side two of letter

בעוזהית"ש [בעזרת השם יתברך], א' י"ג ניסן תרמ"ט[1] לפ"ק [לפרט קטן[2]], יאודי' [יאודיה[3]].

שלום וברכה ושמחת יו"ט [יום טוב] לכבוד ידידי חתני הגאון הגדול חו"ב [חזק ואמץ בתורה] סוע"ה [סיני ועוקר הרים] וכו' כש"ת [כבוד שם תפארתו] מ' [מר] יוסף זכרי' שטערין[4] נ"י [נרו יאיר] עם רעיתו בתי הרבנית היקרה א"ח [אשת חיל] וי"א [ויראת אלקים] תתהלל מ' [מרת] רבקה תחי' ולבנם היקר ושנון השלם יודל נ"י, שלום עד העולם לכם ולכל הנלוים לכם.

מכתבו מן כ"ב אד"ש [אדר שני] הגיעני בשעה זו, אשר בעוד שעה יגיע זמן בדיקת חמץ, ועלי להשלימו עתה בנחיצה בכדי שאוכל לשלחו ליפו יום מחר בוקר עיו"ט [ערב יום טוב] ש"פ [של פסח], בכדי שלא יעבור יותר משבוע טרם אוכל לכתוב, וע"כ [ועל כן] יהי' דברי מעטים ונמהרים, כי קבלתי ידיעה מירוש' [מירושלים] תוב"ב [תבנה ותכנן במהרה בימינו] שהסך ששים רו"כ [רובל כסף] שלו הגיעם באיחור הרבה, וכן הגיעני גם מבני מ' חזקי' 125 רו"כ על זה, ונשתהה הליכתם קרוב לארבעה ירחים, ואף שהוא לפלא מה שלא קבל תשובה על קבלתם, אבל ידע, כי הגאוני' [הגאונים] ריל"ד [רבי יהושע ליב דיסקין] ורש"ם [ורבי שמואל סלנט] שי' [שיחיו] אינם כותבים לשום מקום לא שאלות ובקשות ולא תשובות, רק נתייחדו לזה וועד השמיטה מחמשה או ששה רמ"כ [ראשי מתיבתא וכוללים (?)] בירוש' תוב"ב שהם יתעסקו בזה, וגם מכתבים ממני ואלי הם רק מרבני' [מרבנים] אלו, ועלי בלוית הרה"ג [הרב הגאון] אבד"ק [אב בית דין קהילת] יפו שי' [שיחיה] שמו פניהם כי נתעסק בחלוקה, יען שהננו קרובים ביותר לקאלאנעם עקרון ופתח תקוה, ות"ל [ותודה לאל] כי עלה בידי לחזק ענין השמיטה בשני הקאלאנעם האלו, שהם בקשו לעקור את הכל, ויראה במליץ[5] נו' [נומר] 58 תשובת הרי"מ [הרב יחיאל מיכל] פינס שי', ויראה כי גם דעתו ודעת כל הישרים אף ממשכילים להחמיר, ואכמ"ל [ואין כאן מה להאריך], ועכ"פ [ועל כל פנים] יתר הקולוניות הרחוקים ממני, בשגם הן מן החדשים, עבדו בעצמם.

נוסח ההתירים מהרבני' [מהרבנים] דקוטנא, ביאלוסטאק וקאוונא נדפסים במליץ הלז, ושם יראה גם מכתב הרה"ג דקוטנא כי חו"ש [חס ושלום] שמעולם

---

[1] April 14, 1889.

[2] The Hebrew year has been written abbreviated from 5649 to 649.

[3] That is, Yahud (יהוד), a satellite community of Petach Tikva, where Rabbi Yaffe was residing. Petach Tikva was founded in 1878. Three years later (during Shemittah), most of the residents had to abandon the settlement due to malaria. They resettled next to the Arab village of al-Yahudiyya.

[4] Rabbi Yosef Zechariah Stern (1831-1903) was the son-in law of Rabbi Yaffe. A great Torah scholar, he answered queries from all over the world. He was an avid supporter of settling the Land of Israel and of the Chibbat Ẓion movement. Like his father-in-law, he opposed the *Heter Mechirah*.

[5] The newspaper *Ha-Meliẓ*.

לא כיון להתיר ע"י ישראל בעצמו אף בקרקע גוי, ושם נאמר בסוף מכתבו, כי המתירים גם בזה אל יהי' חלקו עמהם חו"ש, וזה כתב לירוש' לא' [לאחד מרבני פולין היושבים שם, והגאבד"ק [והגאון אב בית דין קהילה] דקאוונא פירש ג"כ [גם כן] שיהי' עבודה ע"י [על ידי] גוים דוקא, רק לפאריש הי' מכתב ממנו להקל במלאכות דרבנן גם ע"י ישראל, ושגגה יצאה מהם לפרוץ גדרים היכא דשכיחי עבדי' [עבדים] המתפרצים, ומעט שם היתר הועיל למו, שעשהו ע"י ישראל, זולת ב' הקולניות האלה, ועוד הצורך רב לפניהם לשנה תמימה עד בוא תבואתה של שנה אחר שמיטה, אשר שולחים קול מהיכל רק בערים הגדולות, כי באמת אם ירצו לפזר גם בכ"מ [בכל מקום] יצטרכו לפזר לאלפים, ות"ל [ותדע לך] כי מערים גדולות הי', שילוח הרבה לפ"ע [לפי ענין?] וגם א"י [אינם יודעים] המשלחים שמות העיירות, ועכ"פ [ועל כל פנים] שהגאבד"ק [שהגאון אב בית דין קהילת] קאוונא עצמו ג"כ לא התיר רק ע"י גוים , ומש"כ [ומה שכתב/שכתבתי] שאעמוד אני לחתום ע"ז [על זה], לא רציתי זאת, ובקושי פעלו ממני לחלק במקום שאין שם אנשים זולתינו הסמוך לקולניות, ונידון הגרמ"נ [הגאון רבי משה נחום] ירושלימסקי[6] ש"י אכתוב איה"ש [אם ירצה השם] להם שיכתבו לו.

הרבנים הנוסעים הרבה הם מאוננארן, לא ידעתי אם אוכל להתראות עמהם, כי הם לא יסורו לפה, ועלי קשה גם כן הנסיעה לירוש' תוב"ב. ענין נסיעת הרבנים אין פלא , וכמעט בכל רגל יש עולים הרבה, ורק מאיראפא היה כבד עד כה מפני הספינות ודוחק אוכל בנסיעתם, וכעת נתחדש ספינה גביר אחד מאחב"י [מאחינו בני ישראל] ונוסעים שם עם כל המכשירים.

ומ"ש [ומה שאמר] הרש"א רזעכטא[7] שקשה בעיניו להאמין שחזר בו הגאון מקוטנא, באמת לא חזר בו, רק מעולם לא כיון ע"מ [על מנת] שיעבדו בם אחב"י בעצמם.

מהרה"ג [מורנו הרב הגאון] דקראסבאזאר[8] לא ידעתי ולא שמעתי, ובאה"ק [ובארץ הקודש] לא ידעתי, אולי בצפת או טברי' [טבריה], ובירוש' וחברון אינו.

ע"ד [על דעת] החקירות מקניית אדמה הקשה לשאול, כי בא האות

---

[6] Moshe Nachum Yerushalimski, the rabbi of Kayelitz (קיעלץ), was one of the great Torah scholars of Poland. (See Y. M. Stern, *Gedolei ha-Dorot*, vol. 3, p. 944.) He was an avid collector. His collections consisted of 7,000 letters of correspondence (which contained many Torah novellae) as well as 2,400 postcards from the years 1872-1914. His collections can be accessed online at *www.schocken-jts.org.il/library4.htm.*

[7] Perhaps Rezekne (Rezhitsa in Russian), a city in Latvia (*Encyclopedia Judaica* [Jerusalem, 1971], vol. 14, p. 140).

[8] He was referring to Rabbi Chaim Chizkiyahu Medini (1833-1905), the author of the halakhic encyclopedia *Sdei Chemed*. Rabbi Medini was born in Jerusalem. He was the chief rabbi of Krasbazar (or Kraso-bazar), a city in the Crimea, from 1866-1899. He then returned to Palestine and lived in Hebron.

והמופת של יחידים יכבד הדבר מאד, ועד אשר ארץ ממנה יצא לחם לקונה יעברו ימים ושנים, והכל דברים עתיקים, אכמ"ל. בנין עצים קשה מאד רק מנסרים, בניני חומה קלים לבנות ובלא שיהוי זמן, אויר מקום שבת המובחר לבריאות, ורק ליחיד קשה לקנות. סום ערך מאה רו"כ ופרידה ביוקר מזה גמל וחמור בזול ערך ט"ו רו"כ, וגמלים קשה לאחב"י לגדלם לע"ע [לעת עתה], ע"כ [על כן] לא נמצא אצלם.

ע"ד [על דבר] הייש"פ [היין של פסח] מה אומר ואדבר, כמו כתבתי להגאון ריל"ד שי' דקרו לי' בי דינא שריא, להתיר דברים שנהגו בהם איסור, ובדור פרוץ כזה, דור מה רמו עיניות ואשר אמרתי ראי' [ראיה] מגמ' [מגמרא] לא אזכור, ואם אמרתי הוא בחסיסי היכא דשכיחי עבדי, שהגר"א [שהגאון רבינו אליהו] ז"ל [זכרונו לברכה] ציין מקור מזה.

ושלום כנפשו ונפש חותנו לעד דושו"ט [דורש שלומו וטובתו] כה"י [כל היום] מברכו בשמחת יו"ט.

מרדכי גימפל

טייערע טאכטער לעבין, איך האב גיהאט גרוים עג"נ [עגמת נפש] פון דיין גיזונטהייט. דער עוויינגער זאל דיר צו שיקען די גאנצע רפואה אין גאנצין, און אויך ליכטיקייט אין די אויגין.

בעט פאר דיר דיין פאטער,

מרדכי גימפל [9]

My dear, beloved daughter,

I was very distressed regarding your medical situation. May the Almighty grant you a complete recovery and restore the glow in your eyes.

The one who is praying for you, your father,

Mordechai Gimpel

---

[9] My thanks to Rabbi Lipa Rabinowitz of Shaarei Chesed, Jerusalem, for translating this section from Yiddish to English.

Appendix IV

A Gem from Ireland: The Letters of A. S. Hovsha

In 1892 a young bachelor from the city of Limerick wrote two letters to S. A. Hirsch, Esq., the head of Chovevei Ẓion in England. In the first, he expressed interest in traveling to Palestine:

> ... Reffering [sic] to the 10 or 12 young men you are going to send [,] as I think of going my self to Palestine in the soon future I wish to propose myself. – After hearing from you that the above mentioned numbers has not being filled up yet, and that there is no objection [,] I should give you all the particulars about myself.
>
> I am Sir
> Respectfully yours,
> A.S. Hovsha

We can surmise that his application was accepted, because in the second letter, he requested assistance regarding his upcoming visit to Palestine:

> 12 Wellesley Place
> Limerick Oct. 17th 1892
>
> Dear Sir,
> ... I am going in December to Palestine. You would greatly oblige me in giving an advice whether I should naturalize or not as I find it very bothersome would I be left in Jaffa not beeing [sic] a Naturalized English subject and therefore having no pass. I am a bachelor and go by my self only – and also what route am I to take and can you recomend [sic] me a Shipping Co or Firm where I can purchase my ticket.
>
> Respectfully yours,
> A. S. Hovsha

After reaching Palestine, Hovsha worked in Baron Rothschild's orchards in Ekron in the midst of the Orchard Controversy. After two months there, he sent a letter dated 2 Sivan 5653 (May 17, 1893) to Chovevei Ẓion in London, reporting on what he'd observed there.

Although pages 4 and 7 are missing, the letter offers a fascinating glimpse of life in Ekron and the struggle between the settlers and the administrators. Some excerpts:

> It is believed abroad that the Baron's Colonists are the happiest, but I find not the slightest foundation in this but in the reverse. . . .
>
> I learned in England to respect order and discipline, to follow a Leader and obey him blindly. I therefore tried my best to justify the doings of the administration but must admit I failed . . . I not only could not find patriotism or philanthropy amongst the respected Baron's administrators, but could neither find an English gentleman . . . .

A street in Ekron/ Mazkeret Batya. Date unknown.

The Central Zionist Archives

List of files of the archive

of

***Hovevei Zion* Association in England**

A2

Jerusalem. January 2005

Catalogue of the Chovevei Ẓion Association in England archive. It was transferred from the Jewish National and University Library to the Central Zionist Archives in 1936.

Ecron the 2nd Sivon 5653

Dear Sir.

After my staying here now
this over two months and learning
all about our Colonists and working
brethern, can I now fulfil my
promise to your wish when in
London on my Journey to this our Holly
Land, I therefor begin:
I came in to Jaffa without any
trouble, there was no more Jews on
Board the french Steamer „Niger",
but all French and English people
I was taken for one of them
and was never asked a passport...
Same day I got a Colonists car for
Ecron and how happy was I to
see our farming brethern settled
in this beautiful Colony, two-storied
stone houses form a fine broad
Street, in front of them stand

"Fulfilling his promise." Page 1 of A. S. Hovsha's letter to Chovevei Ẓion Association in England, file A2/132-13

2

Giant-like big trees spreading thier leafs of delightful smell over the vegetables surrounded with flowers; all houses are kept very clean you would hardly belive our Brethern of the small towns of Russia to keep such order and cleanliness although thier dress and habits are same as have been there. Ecron is recond to be the most Religious of Colonies and not without reason—

The fields are sowed with mostly all wheat; this year is, thank God a very good year, every Chavovi Zion member would no doubt be satisfied, and every leader of mentioned Association would find his hard toil not fruitless or hopeless and would say: [illegible] [illegible]! Only for the war between the collonist's and Administration if [illegible] — this bear of

"Ekron is reckoned to be the most religious of colonies."
Page 2, file A2/132-14

3

Battle undermines our only hope of restoring our wandering Nation to a resting place and happy peacefulness.— It is belived abroad that the Baron's Colonist's are the happiest, but I find not the slightest foundation f in this but in reverse...
I refrain from all devided parties, you can judge by my ability to establish a Branch to your respected Chovevi Zion Association amongst the two parties in Limerick, I Learned in England to respect order and discipline, to follow a Leader and obey him blindly I therefor tried my best to Justify the doings of the Administrators but must admit I failed... I not only could not find patriotism, or philanthropy amongst the respected Baron's administrators, but could neither find an English Gentleman

"Neither patriots nor philanthropists."
Page 3, file A2/132-15

5

us the other half an hour, and hope we shall be pardoned for only half praying לגרוש, but I regret the English manners and equalness of classes.- I tell you this incident as a specimen the colonists beeing dealt with thus: They had a general vegetable garden for patatoes and such like, this was taken away by the administration and for exsample my host sowed patatoes on his land nearest to the colony and paid 10 Franc to a man to watch them at night- still one third has been stolen out of ground, and same happend nearly to every one, this garden beeing no more for all on one place where 3 or 4 watchmen could have it secure, the arabs are so daring a nights disturbance is not too seldom, when the Bell is rung, young men seated on horses, ~~[illegible]~~ pistols in hands

"[With] pistols in hands."
Page 5, file A2/132-16

6

And are hunting after them.—
There had been enough of fightingabout
the plantation question, the Administration
found plantation to pay best and
said to have all Lands planted
as one garden the colonists to work
as slaves and be paid daily so that
they could live upon and the fruit
when ever it will come to pay the
Baron untill all is paid and then
it will be devided to them again,
the colonists said that they want
to plant themselves and could do
so ~~with~~ 10% of the administrations
expense and if they got loans they
would repay or if otherwise they
will never be able to pay and will
allways have to remain daily
labourers. And so it would be.—
the Administration meant to do thier
work by force and the colonists resisted,

"The colonists want to plant themselves."
Page 6, file A2/132-17

Appendix V

Pavlovka and Aqir: A Tale of Two Bitter Endings

Pavlovka was a Jewish hamlet in White Russia, while Aqir was an Arab village in Palestine. They seem so far apart, yet both were inextricably tied to Mazkeret Batya. They had another thing in common – a tragic end.

By 1885, the last of the original eleven families who would establish Ekron/Mazkeret Batya had left tiny Pavlovka. What did the villagers who were left behind feel toward their neighbors who had departed for the Holy Land? Envy? Pity?

As news trickled in about the farmers' wars with the Baron, and their succumbing to fatal malaria and blinding trachoma, many Pavlovkans may have shaken their heads and even patted themselves on the back for staying put.

Grim forebodings. Rosh Hashanah postcard sent in 1932 by Zev Feldman of Pavlovka to his relatives in Mazkeret Batya. In the center is a chicken used for *kapparot*, a ritual performed during the Holy Days. Feldman, his wife, Pesha Leah, and their three children perished in the Holocaust.

Little Pavlovka changed hands several times over the next decades. As a result of the Polish-Russian War, it became part of Poland in 1921. In September 1939, weeks after the signing of the Molotov-Ribbentrop Pact, it was swallowed up by Russia, which nationalized its farms.

In June 1941, the German army invaded the Soviet Union. Mobile killing units known as Einsatzgruppen – composed primarily of SS and German police personnel – followed on the heels of the Wehrmacht.

> [Their objective was the liquidation of] ... those perceived to be racial or political enemies found behind German combat lines in the occupied Soviet Union ... wherever the Einsatzgruppen went, they shot Jewish men, women, and children without regard for age or sex, and buried them in mass graves. ... The Einsatzgruppen ... were composed of four battalion-sized operational groups.[508]

Einsatzgruppe B, starting from Warsaw, swept across White Russia and massacred Jews in Grodno, Minsk, Brest-Litovsk,

Slonim, Gomel, and Mogilev. On November 2, 1942, it entered Pavlovka.

> [The Jewish villagers] ... were marched or transported by truck to an execution site, where trenches had been prepared. In some cases, the captive victims had to dig their own graves. After the victims had handed over their valuables and undressed, men, women, and children were shot, either "military-style," standing before the open trench, or lying face down in the prepared pit, in a manner that came to be known irreverently as "sardine packing."[509]

In one day, they were all gone.

Many of the victims shared family names with the pioneers of Mazkeret Batya and were probably relatives: Levin, Rubinstein, Maller, Bernstein, Laskovsky, Press, and Sharshevsky.

יד זכרון
לקדושי פבלובה הי״ד
מושבת האם של מקימי וראשוני מזכרת בתיה
אשר נספו בשואה, ביום כ״ב חשון תש״ג (2.11.1942)
ח. נ. צ. ב. ה.

Yizkor. Plaque memorializing the Pavlovka victims of the Holocaust

The memory of these martyrs is preserved on a memorial plaque in Mazkeret Batya's cemetery, near the graves of the *landsmen* who founded the moshavah.

The End of Aqir – A Tale of Conflicting Narratives

In chapter 11, we learned that the settlement of Ekron was established on land that had been purchased from the Arab village of Aqir. For several weeks, the pioneers of Mazkeret Batya lived in Aqir itself, and their Arab hosts treated them well. Today, all that remains of the original Aqir are two dilapidated mud houses in the center of the Israeli town of Kiryat Ekron.

What happened to Aqir's residents? It depends on whom you ask. There are two versions of the story, reflecting the divide between the Israeli political Left and Right. But first, a brief introduction.

Changing of the guard. New immigrants cleaning up the rubble in the abandoned Arab village of Aqir. If the Arabs had won the war, it would have meant the end of Jewish Mazkeret Batya.

All that's left. One of two original Arab mud houses of Aqir that remain today.

On October 21, 2004, the Israel Defense Forces assassinated Adnan al Ghoul, a senior Hamas operative in the Gaza Strip. With word of his death, many Israelis breathed more easily, for al Ghoul had been involved in several deadly terrorist attacks within Israel, including at Dizengoff Center in Tel Aviv and in Beit Lid.

As I write these words, the southern town of Sderot, near the Gaza Strip, has been bearing the brunt of thousands of homemade Palestinian rockets, another achievement al Ghoul could add to his "résumé," as he has been called "the father of the Kassam." All this, however, is just a small part of the story, because the Hamas terrorist had roots that went back to Aqir, poignantly symbolizing the tragedy of the conflict between the Jews and Palestinian Arabs.

Journalist Tsur Shezaf wrote the following story, dated October 22, 2004:

It turns out that many years earlier, during the Arab riots of 1936, al Ghoul's grandfather, the *mukhtar* (village head) of Aqir, defended the Jews of neighboring Mazkeret Batya with his own body. In the old days, there was a marvelous friendship that existed between the family of al Ghoul and the Jews. This friendship took a sharp turn in 1948.

... Aqir's relationship with neighboring Ekron (Mazkeret Batya) was renowned. The relationship was solidified even further between the two village leaders: Mr. Skolnick, grandson of Ephraim Skolnick, one of the original eleven founding fathers of the moshavah then numbering about 100 souls, and al Ghoul, grandfather of Adnan al Ghoul and the *mukhtar* of Aqir, a town of about 2,500 inhabitants back in 1948.

As a sign of the special relationship between the villages, the two "*mukhtars*," who were not that young back in the 1930s, exchanged their walking canes. Skolnick's cane went to al Ghoul, and al Ghoul's stick was now used by Skolnick.

The bloody clashes, also known as the Arab Revolt, broke out in 1936. Grandpa al Ghoul took the walking stick he had gotten from Skolnick and sat himself down in the village center by the main road leading to Jewish Mazkeret Batya. He put the cane down by his side and placed his hunting rifle on his lap, announcing to all in the village that if anyone amongst them had in mind to go and hurt the Jews he would first have to reckon with him.

Ekron and Aqir sailed through three years of the Arab Revolt and bloody clashes without a single hair falling or a single home being damaged.

... On May 4, 1948, Battalion 52 of Brigade 5 (Givati) reached Aqir and informed the residents of Aqir that they would have to evacuate the village and go south, in the direction of Gaza. Grandpa Ghoul took the cane given to him by Skolnick and made his way to Ekron.

"Now it's your turn to defend us," he told Skolnick. Skolnick took the cane of Ghoul and went to the Givati officers' tent standing not far from Mazkeret Batya. He related to them how the men of Aqir had been good neighbors, what Grandpa Ghoul had done at the inception of the disturbances, and how he had kept Aqir and Ekron out of the conflict at a time when Givat Brenner and Nââneh were being attacked.

> The officers were unmoved, attaching no significance to the fact that the village was friendly. No, there was nothing to be done, they had to be expelled.
>
> Skolnick returned to Aqir and announced there was nothing he could do, since the orders were coming from the top echelons.
>
> The people of Aqir loaded up as much as they could and traveled east to Isdud,[510] south to Majdal, and finally to Gaza, setting themselves up ultimately in Wadi Aza.
>
> Had [Adnan] Mahmoud al Ghoul, the man who engineered and directed so many terrorist attacks, ever heard the story of the cane? It is reasonable to assume that he had not only heard about it, but that the cane can be found today in one of the refugee camps situated in Wadi Aza, in the neighborhood of those who were expelled from Aqir.[511]
>
> I heard this story from Professor Skolnick of Cabri,[512] grandson of the Jewish "*mukhtar*" of Ekron/Mazkeret Batya, who passed away two and a half months ago. All that's left is for me is to quote Chanoch Levin's[513] words: "We succeeded – awfully."[514]

How true is this account? Before drawing any conclusions based on Shezaf's telling of the story, we should consider a different perspective, offered by Chaim Eliezer Arkin. He was a fourteen-year-old living in Mazkeret Batya in 1947.[515]

> At that time, Aqir had 4,000 residents, while Mazkeret Batya's Jewish population consisted of 400 souls. Were relations warm and cordial between us and Aqir in 1947? I would prefer to term them "functional."
>
> Now the only way you could travel from Mazkeret Batya to the main highway was via Aqir. And they did allow Jews to travel through the village.
>
> By 1947, some tension began to build between the two communities. A pre-military training group for teens had been formed in Aqir, very similar to the Jewish Gadna groups. In addition, an Iraqi [army] detachment had arrived in town. Nevertheless, the situation, although a bit tenser, had not basically changed.
>
> Between November 29, 1947 [the date the U.N. voted to partition Palestine into two states: one Jewish and one Arab], and May 15, 1948 [the date of the declaration of the State of Israel], ... they

put up a roadblock at the entrance of the village, declaring their intention to inspect whoever was passing through.

One day, a Jewish truck driver asked if he could pass through and was granted permission. After [entering], his truck was stopped, and he was forced out. He was murdered, and his truck was burnt.

The Givati brigade launched its first attack on the village in retaliation for the murder of the truck driver. They wanted to convey the message "Don't mess with the Jews." I don't remember there being any Arab casualties, and I don't believe the Givati's original intent in the attack was to scare the residents of Aqir into fleeing.

As a result of that attack, 90% of the inhabitants fled the village. Some of them fled south to Gaza, while others fled east toward the village of Nââneh and then beyond.

The 10% who remained were clustered in the village center. The [Jewish military] commander in charge of Mazkeret Batya as well as the regional commander went to Aqir and told [the residents] that there had been an order from the higher echelons that they all had to leave. [The IDF] didn't want these few remaining Arabs to stay.

What do I think about Shezaf's story of the two "*mukhtars*"? I don't know. It is possible. [But] I remember Skolnick as just a regular fellow, not a leader of Mazkeret Batya. I want to emphasize that it was only the last 10% remaining in Aqir who were forced out.

These two accounts are a stark reminder that "history" is never purely objective. Even with the best intentions, details and emphases are tailored to create a particular impression, and the reader would do well to regard all histories – including this one of Mazkeret Batya – as a blend of fact, legend, conjecture, and the author's perspective.

Appendix VI

Just as good health cannot be maintained without the presence of a doctor for the physical body, the spiritual health of a place can be maintained only where there is a resident doctor of the spirit.

– a Mazkeret Batya resident, quoted in *Chavaẓelet*[2]

Ekron's First Rabbis[1]

From the very start, the pious farmers of Mazkeret Batya insisted that a rabbi guide them. As Michael Erlanger wrote to Shmuel Hirsch in a letter dated May 2, 1884:

> They are requesting a rabbi and a *shochet* – basically, someone who can provide for their religious needs, answer questions in Jewish law, etc. I thought they already had such a person, but apparently not. It shouldn't be hard to find someone like that in the Land of Israel. But he has to be right for the job – not lazy – and he will work together with the others. This request will not displease Mr. de Rothschild.[3]

Rothschild responded positively, and Mazkeret Batya became the first moshavah in the southern region (as opposed to the Galilee) to have a full-time rabbi.

Such rabbis' influence extended far beyond the synagogue. They were involved in community life from cradle to grave. Many were *mohalim,* and all conducted weddings according to Jewish law. And all chickens and cattle were brought to the rabbi for ritual slaughter.

As spiritual leaders of agricultural communities, these rabbis had to know *halakhot* unfamiliar to many of their urban counterparts. Even if they knew the Jewish agricultural laws in theory, the rabbis of the moshavot had to go out into the fields with the farmers and learn firsthand, especially about *kilayim*[4] and *orlah.*[5]

---

[1] I am indebted to Yael Arkin, great-great-granddaughter of Mazkeret Batya founder Ẓvi Arkin, author of "Beit ha-Knesset be-Mazkeret Batya ke-Meshakef et Chayyei ha-Ruach ba-Moshavah" (Michlelet Yaakov Herzog, 5770 [2009]). I am also grateful to Chaim Dzimitrovsky, grandnephew of Yaakov Yosef Halevi Dzimitrovsky, Ekron's fifth rabbi, for source material.

[2] "Ekron," *Chavaẓelet,* 4 Tammuz 5664/June 17 (1904).

[3] Shmuel Yavne'elli, ed., *Sefer ha-Ẓionut,* vol. 2, *Tekufat Chibbat Ẓion,* book II (Tel Aviv: Mossad Bialik, 1944), p. 249

[4] *Kilayim* is the crossbreeding of seeds or animals, which is prohibited. See Leviticus 19:19 and Deuteronomy 22:9-11.

[5] *Orlah* (lit. "uncircumcised") refers to a tree's first three years of fruit, from

The rabbis also had to answer questions regarding milking on the Sabbath.

And of course, they had to master the laws of Shemittah. Ironically, there was no rabbi in Mazkeret Batya when the farmers observed their first Sabbatical year, in 5649 (1889-1890). They had to rely on the rabbis of Jerusalem.

For some rabbis, their stint in Mazkeret Batya led to more prominent positions in Jerusalem.

None of Mazkeret Batya's first five rabbis lasted more than five years, and one of them stayed only two years. One reason was financial. Initially, Baron Rothschild paid their salaries. But in 1900, when he handed the reins over to the Jewish Colonization Association, the moshavah became responsible for funding, making the rabbis' income precarious. Furthermore, Ekron's younger generation had less respect for Torah scholars than their parents had. Rabbi Avraham Yiẓchak Hakohen Kook, who as rabbi of Jaffa also oversaw the southern moshavot, received complaints of disrespect toward the rabbis. As he wrote:

> Jaffa
> 16 Shvat 5667 [January 31, 1907]
>
> To my esteemed friends, the residents of Ekron, and to their leaders, the honorable governing board, shalom and blessings!
>
> ... I am dismayed to hear that people on the moshavah had the temerity to denigrate your esteemed rabbi [Rabbi Mordechai Leib Rubin]. One of them even tore up an announcement from the rabbi. As if that were not enough, [this resident] uttered words not worth repeating. When I became aware of this, I was distraught. I cried out, "What has become of us! How could such an upright community as Ekron, in the Holy Land, disgrace a venerable Torah scholar?!"[6]

---

which it is forbidden to benefit. See Leviticus 19:23-25.

[6] R. Avraham Yiẓchak Hakohen Kook, *Iggrot ha-Re'ayah* (Jerusalem: Mossad Harav Kook, 1962), letter 57.

The First Five

Simchah Bunim Halevi Ossowetzky (1884-1888)

Ossowetzky was the father of two of Baron Rothschild's colony administrators – Boris and Yehoshua Ossowetzky. Though Rabbi Ossowetzky was a Chassid, his flock was composed mainly of "dyed in the wool" Litvaks. As an avid supporter of Jews settling the Land of Israel, he loved his congregants. He eventually moved to Zikhron Yaakov (where his son was in charge) and is buried there.

From Chicago to Ekron. Baruch Chomah

Baruch Chomah (1890-1895)

Chomah (originally Choimah) was born in Kovno in 1859. He held a pulpit in Chicago before making *aliyah* and becoming the rabbi of tiny, rural Ekron. (In 1891, his father, who had adopted the surname Werner, was appointed spiritual leader of the Machzikei Hadat congregation in London.)

Chomah was a dynamic speaker and active in strengthening traditional Jewish education.[7] In 1892, he led the eulogies in the moshavah for Michael Erlanger, the Baron's right-hand man in Paris.[8] Chomah later moved to Jerusalem, where he dedicated himself to scholarship.[9]

A true lover of the Land of Israel, Chomah spent his last years in Rishon Le-Ẓion, tending his vineyards. He passed away in Rishon in 1920.

Moshe Meir Aharon Halevi (1896-1903)

Little is known about this rabbi. He taught Talmud daily in the community's synagogue. After leaving Mazkeret Batya, he corresponded regularly with Rabbi Kook, by then the rabbi of Jaffa, on matters of *halakhah*.

---

[7] David Tidhar, ed., *Encyclopedia le-Chaluẓei ha-Yishuv u-Vonav* (Tel Aviv, 1947), vol. 11, p. 3794 (*www.tidhar.tourolib.org/tidhar/view/11/3794*).

[8] Mordechai Naor, *Sefer le-Mazkeret - Mazkeret Batya - Ekron – 100 ha-Shanim ha-Rishonot* (Jerusalem : Ben-Zvi Press, 2010), p. 136.

[9] Chomah's works include *Makor Baruch* (Jerusalem: Y. D. Frumkin, 5664 [1904], on prayer; *Chomat Aish-Dat* (St. Louis: Manchester Printing Co., 5687 [1927]), on the transmission of the Oral Law; and *Ktav Beit Yisrael* (Jerusalem: Agudat Talmud Torah, 5663[1903]) (*www.hebrewbooks.org/32828*), on the reestablishment of the Sanhedrin in modern times. See Bernard Homa (Chomah's nephew), *A Fortress in Anglo-Jewry: The Story of the Machzike Hadath* (London: Shapiro, Valentine & Co., 5713 [1953], p. 23 (*www.israel613.com/books/MACHZIKE_DAT_LONDON-E.pdf*).

Mordechai Leib Rubin (1904-1908)

Only twenty years after Ekron's founding, secularization had crept up on the moshavot. In response, the rabbis in Jerusalem established religious schools there and sent qualified rabbis[10] such as Mordechai Rubin, then only thirty-three but already a Torah scholar of great stature.

A great Torah scholar. Mordechai Leib Rubin

Rabbi Rubin's constituents were very strict about Jewish agricultural laws. One of their questions concerned growing vetch[11] alongside oats. This practice preserved vetch after heavy rains, but was it *kilayim*?

The farmers consulted Rabbi Rubin, and he asked them to take him out into the fields. The farmer who led him explained that not everyone grew these species together, and those who were stringent were upset with those who were "sinning" with *kilayim*. Rubin shot back, "I have come out here to learn about *kilayim*, not about sins and sinners." In the end, he permitted the combination.[12]

Rabbi Rubin was so admired that in 1904-1905, a "year of blessing" for the moshavah, the residents attributed their good fortune to his presence.[13]

Yet gentle and refined Rubin was mistreated by some.[14] Another account has it that the pious and erudite rabbi's talents

---

[10] See "The Secularization of Mazkeret Batya," in chapter 29.

[11] Bakyah (בקיה) in Hebrew. A legume cultivated for forage and soil improvement.

[12] Naor, *Sefer le-Mazkeret,* p. 160.

[13] Ibid.

[14] R. Kook, *Iggrot ha-Re'ayah,* letter 57.

עקרון.

יום א׳ כ״ב סיון.

הן נודע בשערים כי העיר ה׳ את רוח רבני ירושלים, וע״י השתדלות והתעוררות הרה״ג ר׳ זרח ראובן בראוערמאן הי״ו ההאגדו לאגדה אחת אשר בשם „שומרי תורה" תקרא, ואשר כ׳ מאורינו הגדולים הגרש״ס והג׳ האדר״ת שליט״א עומדים בראשה ומטרתה היא ליסד בתי ת״ת בכל המושבות אשר יתנהלו עפ״י המצוינים שביראה שבירושלים, ואשר יוכלו לשאת עליהן את חותם תכנית היהדות בכל פרטיה, ובתים כאלה כבר יסדו (אם אמנם ברוב עמל) במושבה „פתח תקוה", ובמושבתנו מזכרת בתיה היא עקרון, (וכנשמע ידם נטויה לכונן בתים כאלה גם ביתר המושבות).

וזאת שנית שמו להם לקו בכל מושבה רב מוסמך מבני הישיבות שבירושלים, לנהל את העדה בענינים שבין אדם לחבירו, ולמקום, בכלל, ולהשגיח על בתי הת״ת בפרט, ואשר החסרון הזה מורגש היה מאד במושבות, כידוע לכל בקי במצב הישוב בעבר והוה, ונחוץ היה מאד למנות את החסרון הזה, כי שופטים ושוטרים תתן לך „בכל" שעריך כתיב, לא רק בערי הפלך והמחוז. ידעתי כי יתלוצצו עלי הלצים בשמעם את דברי אלה, אבל יגידו הם מה שיחפוצו, ואנחנו על כרחינו צריכים להודות כי כשם שאין מצב הבריאות יכול להתקיים בשום מקום מבלי המצא בו רופא גשמי, כן אין מצב הרוחני של כל מקום יכול להתקים מבלי המצא בו רופא רוחני, והרופא הרוחני, אשר כל העם ישמעו לו, מי הוא? הרב הנמצא בכל מקום, הוא יורה דרך לעם במצות ה׳ ותורתו, הוא יישר ההדורים, ויפשט העקמומיות שבלב בין איש לרעהו עפ״י ד״ת, הוא ישים את השלום על מכונו תמיד.

והנה „בעקרון" התחילו! ונבחר מבחירי בני הישיבה „תורת חיים" האברך הראוי לאותה אצטלא, בר אוריין ובר אבהן, ה״ה כבוד הרה״ג וכו׳ מוהר״ר מרדכי ליב רובין נ״י, בן הרה״ג וכו׳ מו״ה יעקב גרשון נ״י רב דוואשילישאק, וישולח מטעם הרבנים הגאונים שליט״א שבירושלים לכהן פאר בכתר רבנות אשר הולמהו, במושבה הזאת.

ביום השלישי בשבוע העבר ט״ב ימים לחדש שנתנה בו תורה לישראל, זכתה עדת עקרון לקבל פני רבה, אשר בא עם ב״ב להתיישב בתוכה, ובכבוד גדול קבלוהו בבית הנתיבות ברמלה, כי יצאו לקראתו כל זקני העדה, וראשיה, גם המלמדים עם תלמידיהם, (אשר מפי עוללים ויונקים זכתה עקרון לכל הכבוד הזה). נסעו לקראתו בעגלה, ובכבוד גדול הביאוהו במושבה, וביום השבת הזה באו כל בני המושבה אל ביתו לכבדו, ולברכו כי יאריך ימים על כסא רבנותו.

וכל בני־המושבה מודים מאד לכבוד רבני ירושלים בכלל, ולאגדת „שומרי תורה" ולהרה״ג ר״י ווינאגראד ריש מתיבתא „תורת חיים" בפרט על אשר דאגו לרוחניותם ביסוד הת״ת, ומינוי הרב, כי בצוק העתים האלה, אשר מצב א״י בכלל, ומצב המושבה הזאת בפרט, רע הוא מאד, לא יכלו הם בעצמם בודאי להושיע את עצמם, ולהוציא את כל הכסף הנצרך אף לאחד משני הדברים האלה הנחוצים, ולולא קמו רבני ירושלים וחכמיה, והושיטו את עזרתם מקדש מי יודע מה היה אחרית הת״ת, אשר ברוב עמל, ובכמה מלחמות עלה לבני המושבה לדאוג בעצמם לחינוך בניהם, מבלי השפעת בעלי הטובות הידועים מבחוץ אשר אדיר כל תקותם היה להשליט את רוח החפש על החינוך.

וביחוד נותנים בני המושבה תודה כפולה על עצם הבחירה, שבחרו להושיב במושבה איש כזה אשר יפיק רצון מאת כל אחד ואחד ואשר באמת ראוי הוא להיות איש העומד בראש העם, ומקוים כי כשם שעלה בידי הרה״ג רמל״ר הנ״ל הפעם להשיב את שלום המושבה על כנו, ובארח מאד נעלה יכל לסול דרך לקרב את הלבבות כן יצליח תמיד להחזיק את השלו׳ במושבה, והיה לעינים

were underused, because "The young people were distant from him from the day he came, while the older people wanted him to dance to their tune."[15]

In 1908 Rubin returned to Jerusalem, where he became the rabbi of the Yemin Moshe neighborhood. In 1924 he headed the rabbinical court of the Edah ha-Chareidis[16] in Jerusalem – a testament to his piety and scholarship.

Opposite page: **The new rabbi is coming!** "… He was received with great honor at the Ramle train station, for all the elders of the community, the *melamdim* and their pupils (on whose account Ekron merited this entire honor) traveled by wagon to meet him. And they brought him to the moshavah with great honor. This Sabbath, everyone from the moshavah went to his house to pay homage to him and bless him that he retain his rabbinical position for a long time." –*Chavaẓelet*, 4 Tammuz 5664 / June 17 (1904).

Yaakov Yosef Halevi Dzimitrovsky (1908-1910)

Dzimitrovsky was born in Lida, Lithuania, in 1880 and was influenced by the town's rabbi, Mizrachi[17] leader Yiẓchak Reines. After several years in the yeshivah of the famous Rabbi Yisrael Meir Kagan (better known as the Chafetz Chaim)[18] in Radun,[19] Dzimitrovsky made *aliyah* in 1900 and studied at Yeshivat Torat Chaim in Jerusalem. He married a granddaughter of Rabbi Yaakov Chaim Shapira (head of the *beit din* of the Perushim in Jerusalem) and promptly moved to Petach Tikva, where he taught rabbinical students.

Dzimitrovsky's renowned brother-in-law Rabbi Ẓvi Pesach Frank[20] was very impressed with his learning and

---

[15] Naor, *Sefer le-Mazkeret, p. 160.*

[16] The Edah ha-Chareidis (lit. "Ultra-Orthodox Community"), also known as the Badatz, is a prominent organization based in Jerusalem, providing kashrut supervision, *mikvaot,* an *eruv* (an enclosure permitting carrying on the Sabbath) and a rabbinical court. The Edah was established in 1919 by Rabbi Yosef Chaim Sonnenfeld and others who opposed Zionism and the establishment of a secular Jewish state.

[17] The Orthodox supporters of Zionism organized as the Mizrachi movement. Rabbi Reines (1839-1915) founded the Mizrachi movement at a religious Zionist conference in Vilna in 1901, and he served as the organization's first president.

[18] Born in 1838 in Zhetl (today in Belarus), Rabbi Kagan established a yeshivah in Radun in 1869. World-renowned for his piety, humility, and scholarship, he authored *Chafetz Chaim* (by which he is known), on the prohibition of gossip, and *Mishnah Berurah,* a commentary on *Shulchan Aruch.* He died in 1933 and is buried in Radun.

[19] According to other sources, Rabbi Dzimitrovsky studied elsewhere, but his son, Dr. Chaim Zalman Dimitrovsky (he dropped the z), told me that he learned only in the Chafetz Chaim's yeshivah. Conversation with Dimitrovsky, March 23, 2011. Dr. Dimitrovsky, 91, was a professor of Talmud at the Hebrew University in Jerusalem and received the prestigious Israel Prize for Talmudic research in 1994.

[20] Rabbi Frank was the chief rabbi of Jerusalem from 1936 to 1960. He made aliyah from Kovno in 1893. In 1902, he quietly moved to Jaffa to study Torah

character. In a letter dated 23 Iyar 5668 (May 24, 1908), R. Frank suggested that Rabbi Kook urge Ekron's governing board to appoint Dzimitrovsky as rabbi of the colony. R. Frank wrote:

> ... I have discerned his purity of spirit – he is constantly driven to increase the glory and honor of Torah.[21]

Eager to reverse the spiritual deterioration of the moshavot, Rabbi Kook passed Rabbi Frank's recommendation on to the board. Before Dzimitrovsky went to Ekron for his *pruhba* (Yiddish for trial) to "audition," he received some fatherly advice from Rabbi Kook:

> Prepare some nice rabbinic homilies emphasizing the miẓvot connected to the land – particularly *kilayim, terumot,* and *ma'asrot* – because people commonly ask about them.[22]

Dzimitrovsky got the job. Among those who signed his contract were founders Yechezkel Levin, Mordechai Neiman, and Chaim Moshe Press.[23]

Dzimitrovsky quickly proved to be a dynamic speaker, as *Chavaẓelet* reported:

> Harav Ha'Gaon [Yaakov] Yosef Dzimitrovsky, rabbi of the moshavah, spoke on *Shabbat Teshuvah*[24] for two and a half hours, [delivering] a gratifying sermon about the upcoming Holy Days.
>
> The congregants were inspired by his ethical teachings. He also preached tearfully for half an hour after *Kol Nidrei,*[25] inducing the entire assemblage to burst out crying.
>
> The whole moshavah is happy with him, because from the day

---

without distractions. There he became close to Rabbi Kook. A prolific writer, he authored the responsa *Har Ẓvi.*

[21] *Sinai 102* (Sivan-Elul 5705), p. 36.

[22] R. Kook, *Iggrot ha-Re'ayah,* letter 148.

[23] A picture of the contract is found in Arkin, "Beit ha-Knesset," p. 4.

[24] A reference to *Shabbat Shuvah,* the Sabbath preceding Yom Kippur. On this Sabbath, the haftarah opens with "Return (*Shuvah*), O Israel, for you have stumbled in your sin" (Hosea 14:2), and rabbis exhort their communities to repent.

[25] An Aramaic declaration recited in the synagogue before the beginning of the evening service on Yom Kippur.

he arrived he has lectured on rabbinic homilies between *Minchah* and *Maariv*.

While many people used to idle [between the afternoon and evening services], now they run to hear words of Torah and ethical admonishment.[26]

Dzimitrovsky stayed only two years in Ekron. His wife missed her extended family in Jerusalem, and her husband longed for the Holy City's great Torah scholars. But before returning to Jerusalem, Dzimitrovsky detoured to the U.S. and became a rabbi in Lawrence, Massachusetts for about a year, at the behest of some American rabbis he'd befriended. Upon returning to Palestine, he became the rabbi of Jerusalem's Nachalat Shivah neighborhood. He was also involved in a small yeshivah there and never stopped learning. Five years later, in order for his son to associate with children from a more similar background, he and his family moved to the Shaarei Chesed community in Jerusalem.[27]

"Der Ekroner Rav." Yaakov Yosef Halevi Dzimitrovsky

Although Dzimitrovsky left Ekron, Ekron never left him. He was known as the "Der Ekroner Rav" (the rabbi of Ekron) for the rest of his life.[28]

Dzimitrovsky was very close to Rabbi Kook and frequently took his son, little Chaim Zalman, to Rabbi Kook's house in

---

[26] *"Musar Haskel," Chavaẓelet,* 14 Tishrei 5669/October 9 (1908).

[27] Conversation with Dimitrovsky.

[28] Arkin, "Beit ha-Knesset," p. 4.

ספר

דרישת ציון

לחברת ישוב ארץ ישראל

מאר הגאון המפורסם מופת הדור מו"ה **צבי הירש קאלישער**
וצ"ל אב"ד **טאהרן** בעהמ"ח ספר "מאזנים למשפט" על חו"מ וספר
אמונה ישרה על המושכלות ועוד ליסד דעת ודרך ישרה לעלות אל
המסלה העולה בית אל בספרו "דרישת ציון וראשון לציון" לעשות
מסלול לזה בפועל כפינו בחברת ישוב הארץ.

ונלוה עמו **ספר ראשון לציון**

אשר הוסיף המחבר הן בראיות נכוחות אל דרכו בקדש והן
בפלפולים שונים אשר היה לו בזה עם חכמי הדור, עם ההוספה
ראשון לציון ע"י הרב הדרשן מו"ה **נתן פרידלאנד** ז"ל.

וראה זה חדש **קונטרס הר צבי** מ"ם של הלכה, יפרד והיה
לשלשה ענינים נכבדים המה למבינים:

א) אם אפשר להקריב קרבנות בזה"ז. ב) אם אפשר לבנין מקום
המזבח. ג) שו"ת בענין נידולי הר הבית אם המה מותרים.
בדברים המתקבלים וישרים למוצאי דעת.

מאת הרב הגאון וכו' מוה"ר **צבי פסח פרנק** רומ"ץ פעה"ק ת"ו.

ועוד קונטרס "**סמיכת זקנים**" על דבר שאלת הסמיכה בזה"ז
והצעות נכבדות מאת המו"ל, עיין בהקדמה.

המו"ל **יעקב יוסף** במוה"ר **יצחק הלוי דזימיטראווסקי**
מלפנים רב בעקרון באה"ק ובעיר לארענס מאסס באה"ב.

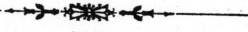

נדפס

פעה"ק **ירושלם** תובב"א

שנת תרע"ט לפ"ק

בדפוס הר"ר **שמואל הלוי צוקערמאן** הי"ו

Jerusalem,[29] where the great rabbi used to ask him about what he was learning.[30]

Opposite Page: **Cover of *Derishat Ẓion*** (4th ed.). Dzimitrovsky borrowed money to publish Kalischer's book.

Passionate about the miẓvah of settling the Land of Israel, Dzimitrovsky obtained a sizable loan to reprint a fourth edition of Rabbi Ẓvi Hirsch Kalischer's classic work *Derishat Ẓion*. Rabbi Frank's approbation appears at the beginning of the book. Dzimitrovsky authored a compendium on his own about the renewal of *semichah*[31] in modern times.

Chaim Zalman told this author that his father never gossiped or spoke ill of anyone; he was a "natural Ẓaddik." People lined up at his door to consult him in all areas of Jewish law. He served as a halakhic authority until the day he died, on 29 Tishrei 5626 (October 25, 1965), at age eighty-five.

The rabbi was also highly involved in the commandments between man and his fellow man. Chaim Zalman related to me that his father mediated disputes between neighbors, and through his contacts in America, he collected funds for the poor who wanted to get married and set up a home.[32]

---

[29] Rabbi Kook moved to Jerusalem after World War I.

[30] Conversation with Dimitrovsky.

[31] *Semichah*, today synonymous with rabbinic ordination, classically refers to the unbroken transmission of rabbinic authority from generation to generation, beginning with Moses. This tradition ended with the dissolution of the Sanhedrin in 358 CE.

[32] Having grown up in Shaarei Chesed (where he currently serves as the rabbi), R. Yehoshua Meir Rosental shared with me his boyhood memories of Rabbi Dzimitrovsky: "I remember he was a righteous man, a Torah scholar, and a distinguished persona. I know Rabbi Shmuel Auerbach [son of the great scholar Rabbi Shlomo Zalman Auerbach, *zt"l*, who also lived in the neighborhood] remembers him." Conversation with Rabbi Rosental, March 30, 2011.

Appendix VII
In the Footsteps of Mazkeret Batya

In recent years, the observance of Shemittah has become increasingly popular. Supported by Keren Ha-Shvi'it (an organization that provides financial assistance for farmers who leave their fields fallow during Shemittah), and donations from Jews worldwide, more and more farmers are committing to following the laws of Shemittah despite the inevitable hardships. Though observance has yet to become common practice, figures for the most recent Shemittah (5768/2007-2008) are impressive:

Northern region[516]	509 farms[517]	58,165 dunams
Central region	1,016 farms	96,585 dunams
Southern region	1,113 farms	138,932 dunams

Below and opposite page: **All over this land.** Communities where Shemittah was observed in 5768/2007-2008 without reliance on the *Heter Mechirah*

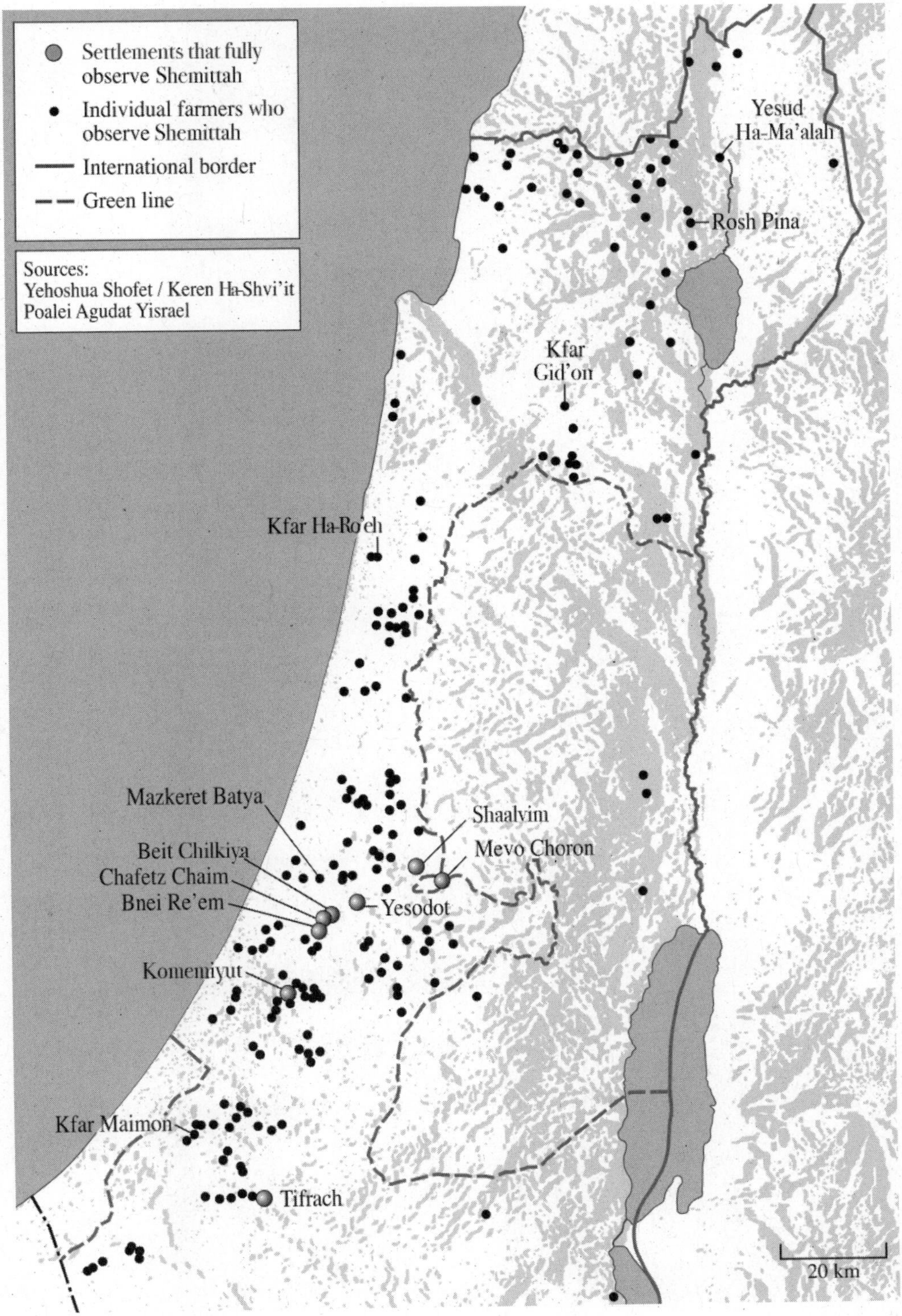

Settlements that fully observe Shemittah
Individual farmers who observe Shemittah
International border
Green line
Sources:
Yehoshua Shofet / Keren Ha-Shvi'it
Poalei Agudat Yisrael
Yesud Ha-Ma'alah
Rosh Pina
Kfar Gid'on
Kfar Ha-Ro'eh
Mazkeret Batya
Shaalvim
Beit Chilkiya
Mevo Choron
Chafetz Chaim
Bnei Re'em
Yesodot
Komemiyut
Kfar Maimon
Tifrach
20 km

From all religious streams. A sampling of the farmers of southern Israel who left their fields fallow during the Shemittah of 5768/ 2007-2008 and were honored by Keren Ha-Shvi'it in the city of Netivot on September 16, 2008/ 16 Elul 5768. Farmers from the north were honored at a ceremony in Afula.

Appendix VIII

Early Hebrew Newspapers, Periodicals and Journals at a Glance

Much of what we know about the First Aliyah period comes from the newspapers of that era. The Jewish press played a role in shaping the opinions of tens of thousands of people regarding *aliyah* to Palestine. The fervently Orthodox in particular were watching how the Shemittah issue played itself out. The sense of anti-religious coercion that came about through what they perceived as the result of an unholy alliance between the secular and the religious (Orthodox rabbis and secular maskilim of Chovevei Ẓion on one hand – Rothschild's secular administrators and the religious colonists on the other) convinced many of them that it was better to stay put in Europe than risk losing their religious autonomy in the Holy Land. The newspapers took sides in the saga of Mazkeret Batya as well – depending on their philosophy and orientation – while the moshavah struggled to make its case. Edmond de Rothschild was also sensitive to how he and his administrators were portrayed during that controversy. The press may have had some influence on Chovevei Ẓion and on the rabbis and policy makers who were sympathetic to their cause by the way they portrayed the economic situation of the settlements.

The Hebrew newspapers also played an important role in that they served as mouthpieces for the various segments of Jewry – the Old Yishuv, the New Yishuv, Perushim, Chassidim, Sephardim, *maskilim*, etc. The following is a brief description of the papers and journals that appear in this book.

SOURCE: *Lexicon of the Hebrew Newspapers of the Eighteenth and Nineteenth Centuries* (Jerusalem: Mossad Bialik, 1992).

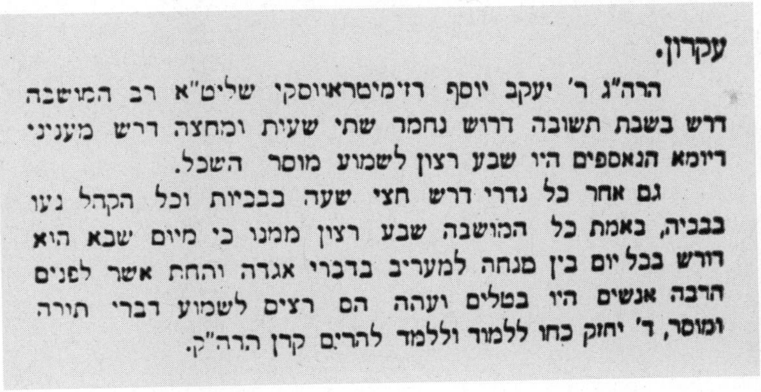

עקרון.

הרה"ג ר' יעקב יוסף רזימיטראווסקי שליט"א רב המושבה דרש בשבת תשובה דרוש נחמד שתי שעות ומחצה דרש מעניני דיומא הנאספים היו שבע רצון לשמוע מוסר השכל.

גם אחר כל נדרי דרש חצי שעה בבביות וכל הקהל געו בבביה, באמת כל המושבה שבע רצון ממנו כי מיום שבא הוא דורש בכל יום בין מנחה למעריב בדברי אגדה והחת אשר לפנים הרבה אנשים היו בטלים ועהה הם רצים לשמוע דברי תורה ומוסר, ד' יחזק כחו ללמוד וללמד להרים קרן הרה"ק.

Great *drashah*! The early Hebrew newspapers reported on everything – from wars, locust plagues, and economics to how well Rabbi Yaakov Yosef Dzimitrovsky's Yom Kippur sermon was received in Ekron.

He said it as he saw it. Yechiel Brill, founder and editor of *Ha-Levanon*. After a visit to Russia where he witnessed the horrible aftermath of the pogroms, Brill began to think along the lines of Rabbi Shmuel Mohilever and Rabbi Mordechai Gimpel Yaffe.

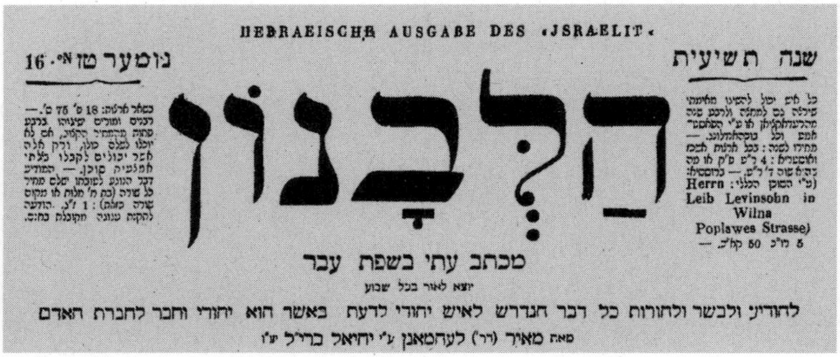

HEBRAEISCHE AUSGABE DES «JSRAELIT»

שנה תשיעית

נומער טז №. 16

הלבנון

מכתב עתי בשפת עבר

יוצא לאור בכל שבוע

Herrn Leib Levinsohn in Wilna Poplawes Strasse)

Did not shy away from controversy. *Ha-Levanon* featured some of the best Orthodox thinkers of the day: Yaakov Lifschitz, Yechiel Michel Pines, Rabbi Shmuel Salant, Dr. Meir Lehmann, Hillel Lifschitz, Yosef Rivlin, and Rabbi Shmuel Mohilever. *Above:* In the December 11, 1872 (11 Kislev 5633) issue, Rabbi Mohilever offers his vision of how to confront the *Haskalah*.

Ha-Levanon (The "Lebanon")[518]

NEWSPAPER

Years of publication:	1863-1886
Places of publication:	Jerusalem, Paris, London, and Mainz (as a Hebrew supplement to Dr. Meir Lehmann's *Der Israelit*)
Editor-in Chief:	Yechiel Brill
Contributing Editors:	Yoel Moshe Salomon, Michel Cohen
Frequency:	Weekly, biweekly, monthly (varied throughout the years)
Main Rival:	*Chavaẓelet*
Mouthpiece of:	Perushim (Lithuanian Jews of the Old Yishuv)

Ha-Levanon was the first Hebrew newspaper to appear on a regular basis in Palestine. At its inception, the paper opposed agricultural colonization of Palestine, because there wasn't a sufficient economic base to support mass *aliyah*. Furthermore, *Ha-Levanon* reflected the view of its reader base, the Perushim, that the Jews in the Land of Israel should dedicate themselves solely to Torah study.

After the Russian pogroms of 1881 Brill had a change of heart, and the paper made a 180° turn and supported Chovevei Ẓion. Furthermore, Brill was against Russian Jews' emigrating to America.

Ha-Levanon brought readers news from the Yishuv in Palestine and adjacent countries, published the positions of moderate and fervently Orthodox rabbis on the burning issues of the day; attacked *maskilim* who called for reforms in Judaism. As time went on, the paper resembled more and more a Torah journal.

שנה שלישית

אלף ושמנה מאות ושמנה עשרה לחרבן ארץ

גליון ה

הַצְּבִי

HAZEWI

Herrn Lipski,
Buchhandlung
Ewraiskaia Ulitza
Haus Gelerter,
Odessa

נערך על ידי בן יהודה בעה"ק ירושלם ת"ו.

Eliezer Ben-Yehuda.
Founder and editor

Ha-Ẓvi (The Deer)[519]

NEWSPAPER

Also published as *Ha-Or* and *Hashkafah*

Years of publication:	1884-1915
Place of publication:	Jerusalem
Editor:	Eliezer Ben-Yehuda
Frequency:	Weekly, daily
Mouthpiece of:	New Yishuv, *maskilim*
Circulation:	300

Ha-Ẓvi was vehement in its opposition to the Old Yishuv and the Chalukah while an avid supporter of the New Yishuv and its philosophy. The paper, supportive of Baron Rothschild and his administrators, eventually received a monthly stipend from the Baron. Its war against the Old Yishuv's leadership peaked with the Shemittah controversy of 1889. It published *Dvar ha-Shemittah* (15 Tevet 5648 [December 30, 1887]), a spirited halakhic defense of the *Heter Mechirah*, by R. Yaakov Mordechai Hirschensohn. (Yiẓchak Hirschensohn, his son, was the license holder of the newspaper.) *Ha-Ẓvi*, in cahoots with *Ha-Meliẓ*, published the news about Rabbi Yiẓchak Elchanan's *Heter Mechirah* only a few days after the article appeared in *Ha-Meliẓ*.

Ha-Ẓvi was the Haskalah's banner paper in the Holy Land. It charged the Old Yishuv with idleness, mismanagement, ignorance, and apathy regarding public sanitation. It also attacked the Sephardim for allowing their people to use missionary hospitals and institutions.

It was in *Ha-Ẓvi* that thousands of Hebrew words were coined by Eliezer Ben-Yehuda.

הוספה להצבי גליון טו

בשורה טובה.

הננו לבשרהו כי פסק הדין על אדות שנת השמטה באה"ק יצא להיתרא מלפני הגאונים הגדולים ר' יצחק אלחנן מקאוונא, ור' שמואל מאהליווער מביאלסטאק, ור' יהושע מקוטנא, ור' זנויל מווארשוי שליט"א. שלשת הרבנים האחרונים היו במותב תלתא לקול קריאת הגרש"מ. והגאון רי"א שלח את פסק דינו גם הוא להגרש"מ בסוף שבוע זה. את הפסק דין הזה ידיעו תיכף להקולוניסטים באה"ק וישלחו להודיעו גם בפאריז.

Shemittah polemics.
Publicizing of Rabbi Yiẓchak Elchanan Spektor's *Heter Mechirah* (without the rabbi's permission)

Yisrael Dov Frumkin, editor. Outspoken and fearless. His increasing alignment with the views of the Old Yishuv earned him the title of "hypocrite" from his detractors.

שנת השש עשרה

№ 28

מחירו לשנה בארץ טירקיי 4 מאגיידי כסף. בעסטרייך 8 פלארין. בצרפת 20 פראנק. בבריטניא ואמעריקא לירא סטערלינג. ברוסיא 6 רו״כ. אדרעססע לסוכן הכללי :
S. Weintraub, Dzika № 42 Local 19 in Warschau.

חבצלת

החפץ להודיע דבר מה לטובתו עליו לשלם בעד כל שורה גרוש וחצי מחיר עלה אחד פויאסטער וחצי. המאסף החותם יקבל עשרה למאה. מכתבים בלתי חפשים ישובו לבעליהם.

מְבַשֶׂרֶת HABAZELETH ציון

מ״ע יו״ל בכל שבוע יבשר וישמיע כל דבר הדרוש לחפץ לבב איש יהודי ·
מאת
ישראל דוב פרומקין

Chavazelet[520] (The Lily)

Newspaper

Years of publication:	1863-1911
Place of publication:	Jerusalem
Editors:	Yisrael Beck (1863-1868), Yisrael Dov Frumkin (1868-1911)
Main rivals:	*Ha-Levanon, Ha-Ẓvi*
Mouthpiece of:	Old Yishuv: Chassidim, Sephardim
Frequency:	Monthly, biweekly, weekly

וביום י״ג לחו׳ תמוז דהאי שתא קראנו עצרה בביהכנ״ס הנדולה המיוחסת לרבן יוחנן בן זכאי זיע״א, אשר לכוללת הספרדים, ושם נתאספו כל הת״ח העי״א גדולים וקטנים, וקרינו תהלים בהכנעה ובלב נשבר, וכשהגענו למזמור ק״ט קראו אותו תלמידי דבי רב (הכל שאין בו חטא) פעמים, ופתחנו דלתות ארון הקודש והדלקנו נרות והחרמנו את אליעזר בן יהודה עורך הצבי, בחרם שהחרים יהושע את יריחו ובשמתא דשמתיה ברק למרוז, בכח שבינת עוזינו ובכח תורתינו הקדושה, ותקעו בשופרות, וענינו כל הקהל קדוש פה אחד הרי הוא מובדל ומופרש מעדת ישראל עד אשר ישוב מדרכו וניחם על הרעה, וכל הקורא במ״ע

Three strikes and you're out. Pronouncement of the Sephardic rabbinate in Jerusalem, published in the 16 Tammuz, 5647/ July 8, 1887 edition of *Chavazelet*, excommunicating Eliezer Ben-Yehuda for his defamatory articles in *Ha-Ẓvi* against the Sephardim

Early on, Yisrael Dov Frumkin was an enthusiastic supporter of Jewish colonization of Palestine and tried to portray the security situation in the country as steadily improving. He also supported educational reforms (similar to those of the *maskilim*) and decried the Chalukah system. He was viciously attacked in *Ha-Levanon* for his reformist positions, which he lobbed back at them in the same venomous tone.

In September 1882, Frumkin started to change course. After seeing how the extremely impoverished Russian immigrants to Palestine were vulnerable to missionaries, he opposed uncontrolled mass *aliyah*. With the establishment of the moshavot, he began to soften his opposition to the Chalukah – he didn't see much difference between the handouts that the moshavot were getting from the Baron and the Chalukah handouts the Old Yishuv was receiving.

If in *Ha-Ẓvi's* opinion the Baron's administration was unassailable, *Chavazelet* depicted it as the most incompetent organization on Earth.

During the Shemittah controversy of 1889, *Chavazelet* sided squarely with the Jerusalem rabbinate and strongly supported Mazkeret Batya. The issue brought the newspaper even closer to the positions of the Old Yishuv.

30 Jahrgang

HAMAGID

שנת השלשים

Erscheint einmal wöchentlich.
Der Abonnementspreis beträgt 12 Mark jährlich im Inlande.
Der Insertionspreis beträgt pro Corpusspaltzeile 20 Pf. bei grösseren Insertions-Aufträgen wird ein entsprechender Rabatt gewährt.
Alle Annoncenexpeditionen nehmen Inserate für „HAMAGID" an. Adresse: Redaction des „HAMAGID," Lyck. Preussen.

המגיד

(נוסד ע״י אליעזר ליפמאן זילבערמאן.)

יצא לאור ע״י

דוד גארדאן זצ״ל.

ויוצא עתה אור מאת בנו דוב גארדאן.

Eliezer Lipmann Silbermann, founder & editor. He started out as a rabbi and *shochet* and became a journalist and publisher.

Ha-Maggid (The Declarer)

NEWSPAPER

Years of publication:	1856-1903
Places of publication:	Lyck (Prussia), Berlin, Cracow, Vienna
Editors:	Eliezer Lipmann Silbermann and David Gordon (1856-1880), David Gordon and Dov Gordon (1880-1886), Dov Gordon (1886-1890), Yaakov Shmuel Fuchs (1890-1903)
Frequency:	Weekly

Ha- Maggid was the first Hebrew weekly. The paper's mission was to keep its readers current with "… what is going on in Europe, Asia, Africa, America, and Australia … the prices of all major merchandise in the major cities – the exchange rate for all kinds of currency… gold … metals … new technologies … etc." *Ha-Maggid* also promised to keep its readers informed of all the latest political developments and to spread the usage of Hebrew as a medium in everyday life (besides its use for religious purposes). That was as far as the paper went regarding the *Haskalah.* It was so mute and non-controversial that even the strictly Orthodox felt comfortable with it in its first years, while the reformist *maskilim* grumbled.

Ha-Maggid was divided into two parts: Part one was devoted to news from around the world – Jewish and general. Part two, printed in Rashi script, was devoted to health, biographies of famous people, linguistics, Biblical research, poetry, and book reviews. It also contained announcements from agunot – women whose husbands were missing.

Ha-Maggid covered all phases of early Ekron's story – the purchase of its land, the departure of the families from Pavlovka, the Baron's visit to the moshavah, and the Shemittah and orchard controversies.

The newspaper's second editor, David Gordon, was an early supporter of Chovevei Ẓion, and under him the paper became the Hebrew voice of the movement.

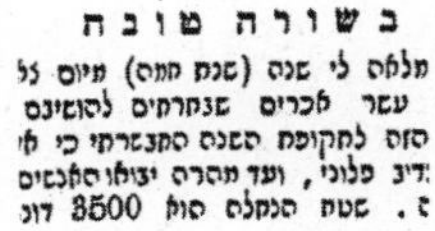
בשורה טובה

Finally! News of the long awaited purchase of land for the settlement that would be named Ekron (November 29, 1883/29 Cheshvan 5644)

Yehuda Leib Gordon, editor. Modernity was his messiah. "Probably the severest critic of his time and a fiery exponent of the *Haskalah*" (*Encyclopedia Judaica*)

Ha-Meliz (The Advocate)

NEWSPAPER

Years of publication:	1860-1904
Places of publication:	Odessa, St. Petersburg
Editors:	Alexander Zederbaum (founder and first editor), Yehuda Leib Gordon
Frequency:	Weekly, daily

Ha-Meliz was the first Hebrew newspaper in czarist Russia. The paper saw its task as to "advocate between the Jewish people and the Russian government" and to bridge the gap between religious faith and rational *Haskalah*. (This was a moderate position that assumed the two were compatible. But starting from 1868, the paper would publish articles that attacked religion.)

Ha-Meliz's calls for religious reform as well as severe criticism of the rabbis came from Yehuda Leib Gordon and Moshe Leib Lilienblum. Gordon wrote biting satirical pieces against the rabbis. But the paper also published essays by "defenders of the faith" such as Yechiel Michel Pines and Rabbi Mordechai Gimpel Yaffe.

The paper was the first to publicize (without authorization) the *Heter Mechirah* of Rabbi Yizchak Elchanan Spektor.

Although the owner of *Ha-Meliz* was pro-Chovevei Zion, and his paper was a mouthpiece of that movement, Gordon did not advocate *aliyah*.

Go to America! Ad in *Ha-Meliz* about ocean liner travel to America. Gordon did not believe that Turkish Palestine was capable of absorbing so many Russian Jewish refugees from the pogroms. He advocated emigration to western countries and the United States.

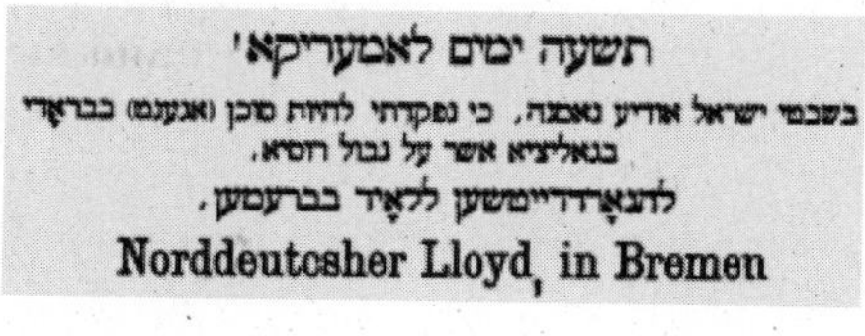
תשעה ימים לאמעריקא!
בשבטי ישראל אודיע נאמנה, כי נפקדתי להיות סוכן (אגענט) בבראָדי
בגאליציא אשר על גבול רוסיא.
לדנאָרדדייטשען ללאָיד בברעמען.
Norddeutcsher Lloyd, in Bremen

הצפירה
HAZEFIRAH.
מכתב עתי מדיני מדעי וספרותי
יוצא לאור מדי יום ביומו

Science lover. Chaim Zelig Slonimski, founder and first editor. He wrote books on mathematics and astronomy (and on Haley's comet) and invented a type of calculator that was patented.

Ha-Ẓefirah (The Dawn)

NEWSPAPER

Years of publication:	1862, 1874-1906, 1910-1921, 1926-1928, 1931
Places of publication:	Warsaw, Berlin
Editors:	Chaim Zelig Slonimski, Nachum Sokolow
Frequency:	Weekly, daily

Ha-Ẓefirah was the first Hebrew newspaper in Poland. Its founder, Chaim Zelig Slonimski , was a self-taught scientist and inventor. Although the paper's stated purpose was to cover Jewish news and history (as well as the latest government edicts), its main thrust was to disseminate knowledge of the practical sciences among Jews.

Slonimski was very careful to avoid controversy so as not to repel the fervently Orthodox. (One of *Ha-Ẓefirah*'s readers was none other than Rabbi Avraham Yeshayahu Karelitz, the legendary halakhic authority better known as the Chazon Ish. Rabbi Karelitz even cites the paper in his magnum opus, *Chazon Ish* [*Orach Chaim/Moed* 141:9].) Slonimski stated that *Ha-Ẓefirah* was no substitute for Talmudic wisdom but rather a reflection of it. He himself wrote Talmudic commentaries that were based on mathematics and astronomy (which appeared in the Zhitomir edition of the Talmud).

When Nachum Sokolow joined *Ha-Ẓefirah* in 1867, he introduced a wide variety of topics, invigorated its writing style, and made it very attractive, so the readership was very broad. The paper carried more and more Jewish news from Europe and Palestine.

Ha-Ẓefirah reported about Mazkeret Batya and the Shemittah controversy, and was quite sympathetic to the struggling farmers who wanted to observe the Sabbatical year against the wishes of the Baron's administrators. The first two decades of the twentieth century marked the high point of *Ha-Ẓefirah*'s circulation, when it became the leading Hebrew newspaper in the Russian Empire.

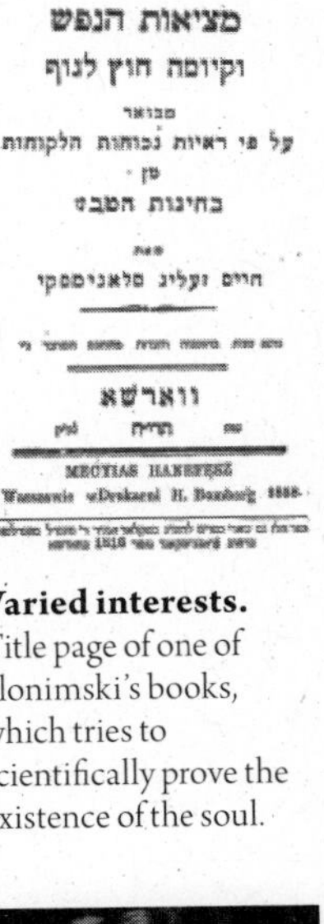
מציאות הנפש
וקיומה חוץ לגוף
מבואר
על פי ראיות נכוחות הלקוחות
מן
בחינות הטבע
מאת
חיים זעליג סלאנימסקי
ווארשא

Varied interests. Title page of one of Slonimski's books, which tries to scientifically prove the existence of the soul.

Nachum Sokolow, editor. He added a lot of journalistic flair and variety to the paper.

Asher Hirsch Ginsberg (Achad Ha-Am), editor. Ginsberg was a Hebrew essayist and one of the foremost pre-state Zionist thinkers. He is known as the founder of cultural Zionism, a secular spiritual alternative to religion.

השלח

מכתב־עתי חדשי

למדע, לספרות ולעניני החיים.

המוציא: קלונימס זאב ויסאצקי.

העורך: אשר גינצברג.

כרך א.

(חוברת א—ו).

חשון-אדר ב׳ תרנ״ו.

Ha-Shiloach[521]

PERIODICAL (MONTHLY)

Years of publication:	1896-1926
Places of publication:	Odessa, Jerusalem
Editors:	Achad Ha-Am, Yosef Klausner

Asher Hirsch Ginsburg, known by his pen name, Achad Ha-Am, was one of the primary (radical) theoreticians who redefined Judaism not as a religion but as a nationality. He was considered the leading intellectual amongst the late-nineteenth-century *maskilim* and their greatest writer. Ginsberg's philosophy was the antithesis of Orthodox Judaism; he was an open atheist who believed that as a consequence of the scientific revolution, religion (and even belief in God) was antiquated. Achad Ha-Am maintained that once the ghetto walls came down and Jews began assimilating, Judaism as a religious way of life would never make a comeback; nor could religion save the Jewish people from total assimilation.

The only remedy, in his opinion, was to create a model Hebrew-speaking culture in Palestine, which would catalyze Jews throughout the Diaspora to preserve their Jewish identity. This became known as "cultural Zionism". (He thought Herzl's idea of creating a Jewish state was a pipe dream. No need for a State of Israel – just a Jewish community in the Land of Israel.) Achad Ha-Am could be called the father of contemporary secular Israeli culture.

Ha-Shiloach was devoted to espousing all trends within Zionism, both the spiritual variety advocated by Achad Ha-Am and the political advocated by Herzl. The journal contained some of the best Hebrew literature of that period. Some very positive articles about Mazkeret Batya/Ekron appeared there.

Klonymous Ze'ev Wissotzky, an Orthodox Chovevei Ẓion supporter, bankrolled *Ha-Shiloach* during its first years.

כנסת ישראל

ספר שנתי לתורה ולתעודה

כולל בתוכו מאמרים כתובים בידי חכמי ישראל וסופריו בכל מקצעות התורה והחכמה:
חקירות דברי הימים ובקרת הכפרות, הליכות עולם, כלכלת העם ונמוסי המדינות,
חכמת הרשים עם ציורים ותמונות אנשי שם, והשקפות החיים והחברה בישראל ובאדם:

ב״ייי חלקים

שנה ראשונה ה׳תרמ״ז

יוצא לאור על ידי

ש״אול פינחס ראבינאוויץ

ווארשא

Knesset Yisrael (Congregation of Israel)

JOURNAL

Years of publication:	1886-1888
Place of publication:	Warsaw
Editor:	Shaul Pinchas Rabinowitz
Frequency:	Annually

Topics ranged from Bible and Talmud to poetry, literary reviews, medical issues, history, and Jewish current events, with a beautiful piece about Mazkeret Batya.

Shaul Pinchas Rabinowitz. Standing, far left, at Chovevei Ẓion convention

5. Friedländer, Kattowitz O/S. 6. Freidenberg, Bialystok. 10. Moses, Kattowitz O S. 13. Rittenberg, Warschau. 15. Freuthal, Kattowitz. 18. Pines, Rosana. 20. Mirkin, Pultawa.

1. Rabinowitz, Warschau. 3. Dr. Chasanowitz, Bialystok. 7. Jasinowsky, Warschau. 9. Schalit, Riga. 12. Dr. Drübinowitz, Rostow a. Don. 16. Luntz, Riga. 19. Wollrauch, London. 22. Meyersohn, Warschau. 23. Davidsohn, Warschau. 25. Löbinger, Kattowitz.

2. Wissozki, Moskau. 4. Klewansky, Kowno. 8. Gordon, Lyk O P. 11. Rab. Mohilewer, Bialystok. 14. Dr. Pinsker, Odessa. 17. Rab. Friedmann, Karlin. 21. Zederbaum, St. Petersburg. 24. Dr. Rabbinowitz, Paris. 26. Deiches, Charkow.

Appendix IX

On 21 November 1882, the "Radom pioneers," as they were known, set out on a harrowing, twenty-day journey to Erez Israel.[1]

The First Leg of the Journey

"Harrowing" is how historian Ran Aaronsohn described the journey of the pioneers who founded Mazkeret Batya. In this section, we will detail the obstacles and dangers faced by Brill and his charges, starting with the very act of leaving czarist Russia.

Obtaining Travel Documents

Starting from 1835, emigration came under provisions of the criminal code, which made leaving from Russia for the purpose of settling abroad a punishable offense.[2] (It was only in 1907 that emigration from Russia was legalized.[3]) Passports were issued only to those planning to be away less than five years and even then the process was expensive (often requiring bribes) and slow.[4] No wonder 75-90% of all departures from that country were illegal.[5]

After the pogroms of 1881-1882, more and more Jews stole across the western frontier into Germany. Between 1881 and 1886, those bound for the United States alone averaged 12,856 annually.[6] Yechiel Brill wanted to redirect that flow to Palestine, but how?

Officially, the farmers couldn't even venture far from Pavlovka:

> Since the reign of Peter the Great, imperial law had forbidden subjects from traveling without an *internal* passport outside their permanent place of residence (a radius of around thirty

---

[1] Ran Aaronsohn, *Rothschild and Early Jewish Colonization* (Jerusalem: Magnes Press, Hebrew University of Jerusalem, 2000), p. 56.

[2] Hans Rogger, "Tsarist Policy on Jewish Emigration," *East European Jewish Affairs* 3:1, p. 27; Eugene M. Avrutin, *Jews and the Imperial State – Identification Politics in Tsarist Russia* (Ithaca: Cornell University Press, 2010), p. 136.

[3] Lloyd P. Gartner, *History of the Jews in Modern Times* (Oxford: Oxford University Press, 2001), p. 259. This was due to the efforts of the Jewish Colonization Organization (ICA).

[4] Gartner, p. 259.

[5] Avrutin, p. 138.

[6] Rogger, p. 28.

ספר
נפש חיה

Partners in "crime." Rabbi Yosef Ber Soloveitchik (left) and Rabbi Chaim Eliezer Wachs of Kalish, author of *Nefesh Chayah* (title page of book at right), broke the law by contributing money to Yechiel Brill's project.

> kilometers) .... [Internal passports were] used as a policing tool ... and to regulate territorial movement.[7]

Czarist Russia was one big prison.

Veiled in Secrecy

In chronicling his travels inside Russia, Brill names no towns or officials, not even major players. He never even specifies Rozhinoy, Pavlovka, or the men selected to go to Palestine! Rabbi Shmuel Mohilever's name appears only as an acronym.

Even assisting emigrants was a criminal act. When Brill records some frantic fundraising, he therefore conceals his donors:

> At the conclusion of the Sabbath, I came to the rabbi of מ' ..., who told me that he'd transfer the money he collected in מ' to the gaon of ב',[8] מוהריב"ם.[9]
>
> ... That evening, I traveled from מ' and arrived at ב' at 11 p.m. After dropping off my luggage at the hotel, I went to the home of the aforementioned rabbi, for I knew that this rabbi never retired before midnight, and that his house would be open to me at this [late] hour. The rabbi was very happy to see me and [pleased with] the work I was doing. We talked a lot about [the project], and he promised to do what he could to help me and ease my worries about the costs of the trip ....[10]

Brill dared not print such sensitive information for fear of the Russian censors and the dreaded secret police, who would use it to sabotage *aliyah*.

In a nutshell, he and the farmers journeyed to Palestine with little money, no documents, no permission, and no fanfare.

---

[7] Avrutin, pp. 91, 92. Emphasis added.

[8] Brisk.

[9] Rabbi Yosef Ber Soloveitchik–מורינו הרב יוסף בער סולוביציק.

[10] *Yesud Ha-Ma'alah*, p. 18. Brill later publicized Rabbi Soloveitchik's support as an unofficial endorsement by a leading rabbinical figure regarding the creation of farming settlements in Palestine.

Leaving Pavlovka

On January 20, 1882, the farmers left Pavlovka and traveled by wagon to Volkovysk,[11] about fifty kilometers (thirty-one miles) northwest. Assuming they traveled six kilometers (3.7 miles) per hour, it would have taken them eight to nine hours to reach their destination. The town had several thousand inhabitants, about half of them Jewish. Brill left his hotel in Volkovysk and met the eleven Pavlovkans at 4 a.m. in the local train station.

The train left at 6 a.m.

Although they might have gone south to Brest, they probably rode west, crossed modern-day Belarus (then known as White Russia), and arrived in Bialystok. (Bialystok was then under Russian control, and Rabbi Mohilever had not yet been appointed rabbi of the town.) From there they traveled southwest to Warsaw, a major train terminal, where they linked up with the Warsaw-Vienna Railway (built in 1857), traversing Poland for 327 kilometers (203 miles).

Drab railroad town. Scene from pre-war Szczakowa. In 1885 the town numbered 162 Jews, or 14.8% of the population. Most of these Jews worked on the railways.

Brill was anxious. A Mainz resident since 1871, he was carrying German identity papers. His travelling with Russian nationals to the Austrian frontier would naturally arouse the suspicion of the police. He had no choice but to leave them and zigzag to Germany before entering Austria.

Brill may also have dreaded getting caught without passports,[12] lacking sufficient bribe money,[13] and the difficulty of obtaining visas into Palestine for Russian Jews, undesirables in the Ottomans' eyes.

---

[11] Brill cryptically refers to the city as V' (ו'). According to Achiezer Arkin, the author refers to Vilna. According to Yerakh Tzur, the reference is to Volkovysk, which was much closer to Pavlovka.

[12] Railroad stops were the only places along the border where inspectors checked travelers' papers consistently. Avrutin, p. 136.

[13] Historian Lloyd P. Gartner of Tel Aviv University points out that "While leaving Russia was illegal, it was overcome by large-scale bribery of border guards on the part of smugglers who guided Jews across for a price." Gartner, p. 259.

Last Stop in Russia

At 3 p.m., the train arrived at its final station in the Russian Empire, "ס"א" (Sosnowiec-Sosnovitz in Yiddish), near the Austro-Hungarian border, about sixty-two kilometers (thirty-eight miles) west, northwest of Cracow.[14]

Brill then counted the money the farmers had collected for the trip. Why hadn't he done so earlier? Was he afraid of pick-pockets? Perhaps when they disembarked in Sosnowiec, he and his charges finally had some privacy. His counting money in front of these men would have made them all look suspicious.

Brill tallied "261 shekels." There was, of course, no such currency at the time. Which currency was it really – rubles? florins? – and why "disguise" it? Apparently, he wanted to cover his tracks.

Brill writes that the farmers continued to Szczakowa (or Shtehkeva in Yiddish) (סצאקאווא),[15] the first town he spells out. For the first time, he separated from them, remaining in Sosnowiec that evening and the next day. When he got word via a mail courier that they'd arrived safely in Szczakowa, on the Austro-Hungarian side of the border,[16] he took the train to Mysłowice (spelled out fully in his book), on the German side.

Gruss von der Drei Kaiser Ecke b. Myslowitz O.S.

Three Emperors' Corner. This 1902 postcard shows the Black Przemsza River (left) and White Przemsza River (right) flowing into the Przemsza River. Before World War I, this spot was a tourist attraction, since it bordered three empires: Germany (left), Austro-Hungary (right), and Russia (between the rivers). Emperors in the photo, from left: Franz Joseph I of Austria, Wilhelm II of Prussia, and Nicholas II of Russia.

Zigzagging

Mysłowice was near the confluence of the Black and White Przemsza rivers, where the German, Russian, and Austrian empires met. Its Jewish population peaked at 900 (out of 14,000) in 1887.

---

[14] Brill, p. 19. By 1880, only 120 Jews lived there (out of a population of 9,318). The first Jew settled in the town in 1859. Source: *www.jewishgen.org/yizkor/pinkas_poland/pol7_00327.html.*

[15] Ibid.

[16] Ibid.

The town also served as a way station for refugees fleeing the Russian pogroms of the 1880s and heading to America[17] – what Brill considered the wrong destination.

Why did Brill zigzag from Russia to Germany when he could have just taken the next train out of Sosnowiec and crossed the border into Austria? As stated earlier, his association with the farmers might have raised the suspicion of the border guards.

Brill's account continues:

> From [Mysłowice] I traveled at nighttime by horse-drawn carriage via a route that takes *three hours* to get to Szczakowa, because the steam locomotive goes from Mysłowice to Szczakowa only once a day – in the morning – and I was sure the farmers would worry if they didn't see me by that evening.[18]

Brill arrived in Szczakowa around 10 p.m.:

> I inquired as to the farmers' whereabouts and was told they had "traveled from here"[19] to a small town about two hours away because of the locals' evil eye toward people who couldn't give a satisfactorily legal answer to the question "Where are you coming from, and where are you going?" I traveled to that town, arriving around midnight. The

Synagogue square. In 1826, a synagogue was built in Mysłowice on the corner of what is today Kołłątaj Street and Mieroszewski Square.

[17] Shmuel Spector, ed., *The Encyclopedia of Jewish Life before and during the Holocaust* (Jerusalem and New York: Yad Vashem, New York University Press, 2001), vol. 2, p. 864.

[18] Brill, p. 19. Emphasis added, because Szczakowa is only 9.7 kilometers (six miles) east of Mysłowice, so the trip shouldn't have taken more than an hour.

[19] נסעו מזה – the same ominous phrase said to the biblical Joseph when he sought his brothers.

Three borders in one. This map, from the 1900 *Andrees Allgemeiner Handatlas*, published in Leipzig, Germany, shows the towns Brill mentions in his travelogue: Sosnowizy (Sosnowiec), Myslowitz (Mysłowice), Szczakowa , and Trzebinia. They were all near each other but in different countries.

> streets were deserted – everyone was asleep. Only one house had lights burning inside. I entered the house and found three men drinking wine, who told me they hadn't seen the people I was looking for. But one man … half asleep … told me that toward evening he'd seen some men with full sacks on their shoulders, walking slowly and searching (because everything was covered with snow) for the road to a certain village. And if they got there, I could find them in the home of the local Jewish dairyman. I went to that village, arriving around two o'clock in the morning. I was happy when I found those I'd selected … a mixture of fear and joy [on their faces].[20]

Although Brill names all the towns they visited once they'd crossed over from Russia into Austro-Hungary, this was an exception. The Jewish milkman apparently provided a safe house for refugees, so Brill wanted to protect this kind fellow's identity. Clearly, even in Austria their troubles were not over.

---

[20] Brill, pp. 19, 20.

> The border province of Galicia in the Hapsburg Empire became a favorite destination … for the people who looked to escape the abject poverty and intermittent violence that plagued the southwestern regions of the empire.… Once emigration increased in volume in 1882, Austrian security police arrested "large numbers" of destitute Russian Jews who fled to border towns such as Szczawnica and Brody without proper documents. Placing [their] gendarmes on high alert, Austrian authorities instructed border patrols to stop people who were traveling illegally and deport them to the Russian Empire.[21]

Brill and company eluded the border patrolmen thanks to a tip from the Jewish dairyman:

> The [milkman] and his wife advised me not to travel together with my men in the steam locomotive that departed from Szczakowa, but to send them ahead of me by horse-drawn carriage to Trzebinia, and from there I could travel with them by train. And I did just as [they] had advised me.[22]

In the Shadow of Hope and Death

Upper Silesia was rich in Jewish history and the stage for momentous things to come.

Trzebinia (טרצעביניא) for instance, sixteen kilometers (ten miles) southeast of Szczakowa, was known in Yiddish as Tchebin and had a distinctly Jewish flavor.[23] The town played an important role in Jewish history prior to World War II. In 1918 the great Rabbi Dov-Berish Weidenfeld settled in Trzebinia, and in 1923 he became the Tchebiner Rav and established the Kokhav mi-Yaakov yeshivah there. Rabbi Ben Ẓion bar Shlomo

---

[21] Avrutin, p. 136.

[22] Brill, p. 20.

[23] In the second half of the nineteenth century, most Jews lived in the center of town, making a living as tradesmen, craftsmen, and storekeepers. Jews also dominated the service industry, until Christians complained to the authorities that it was impossible to hire a wagon-driver on the Sabbath or buy bread on Passover. Eleven Jewish drivers were then fined eighty crowns each. In addition, two drivers were forced to hire non-Jews to operate the wagons on the Sabbath. Any baker who refused to bake bread over Passover was also fined. Source: *www1.yadvashem.org/yv/en/exhibitions/communities/trzebinia/before_holocaust.asp.*

Halberstam, the Bobover Rebbe, resided in Trzebinia from 1932 to 1937 along with many of his followers.

Only eleven kilometers (seven miles) southwest of Sosnowiec, on the German side of the border, was the town of Katowice (Kattowitz). In 1884, delegates from thirty-six Chovevei Ẓion chapters would hold their first international conference there and officially establish the organization.[24] In 1912, the Agudath Israel movement would be founded in Katowice as well.

In stark contrast, another locale in this area would figure in one of the darkest periods in Jewish history. Just nineteen kilometers (twelve miles) south of Trzebinia lay the little town of Oswiecim, better known by its German name – Auschwitz. From spring 1942 until autumn 1944, 1.1 million people from all over Nazi-occupied Europe were murdered in Auschwitz, around 90% of them Jews. En route to Vienna, Brill and the farmers must have passed near this deathtrap on their way to creating a new haven for the Jewish people.

The End of the Line

After arriving in Palestine and suffering under Shmuel Hirsch, the director of the Mikveh Israel agricultural school, the farmers forgot all of Brill's self-sacrifice and accused him of betraying them. Having promised them a homestead in the Promised Land, he searched for months for a suitable site but came up empty-handed. Brill left Palestine heartbroken, never again to see the land he loved so dearly.

The parallel to Moses leading the Jews to the Holy Land, the lapses of ingratitude and suspicion of the Children of Israel towards Moses, and Moses' not fulfilling his mission is striking and inescapable.

---

[24] Chovevei Ẓion was illegal in Russia until 1895, and the Russian authorities forbade the movement's rabbis to attend that first conference.

Appendix X

Resources for Visitors to Mazkeret Batya

The Eran Shamir Village Museum, Mazkeret Batya

The museum is dedicated to the history of Mazkeret Batya. It portrays life in olden times through artifacts, photographs, and documents. The museum tour includes several old buildings, some now under restoration, and the old bucket-chain well. Even as the village is turning into a town, the main street retains much of it's character. The synagogue built by Baron Rothschild in 1927 and the old cemetery can also be visited. Guide assistance in English can be provided by prior arrangement.

Address: 40 Rothschild St. Mazkeret Batya 76804
Phone: 08-934-9525
Fax: 08-935-8345
E-mail: museum@mazkeret-batya.muni.il

Hours: Sun., Tues., Wed., Thurs. – 8:30-1
Mon. – 8:30-1, 4-6
Fri. – 8-12

Admission: Adults, NIS 12
Children, NIS 7
Seniors, NIS 5

Tziyunei Derekh

Tziyunei Derekh is an Orthodox educational project founded by Achiezer Arkin that offers tours of Mazkeret Batya and other locations in Israel. Arkin produced a film that dramatizes the struggle between the farmers of Mazkeret Batya and Baron Rothschild's administrators over the Shemittah issue. The film inspired me to write this book. In June 2009, Tziyunei Derekh opened a museum about Rabbi Shmuel Mohilever, containing photographs, documents, and a film about this great leader. There is a small admission fee, and reservations are required.

Phone: 08-934-0034
Fax: 08-935-2454
E-mail: midrasha.mb@gmail.com
www.midrasha-m-b.org.il

Selected Bibliography and Sources

English

AARONSOHN, Ran. *Rothschild and Early Jewish Colonization.* Jerusalem: Magnes Press, Hebrew University of Jerusalem, 2000.

ANTÉBI, Elizabeth. "Baron Edmond de Rothschild (1845-1934) – from 'HaNadiv' (the benefactor) to 'HaNassi' (the prince)." *Jewish Studies at the Turn of the Twentieth Century*, Vol. II (Leiden: Brill, 1999).

ARIEL, Dov. *Ha-Moshavah Gedera.* Jerusalem: Ben-Zvi Press, 1979.

BEN-ARIEH, Yehoshua. *Jerusalem in the Nineteenth Century – The Old City.* Jerusalem: Ben-Zvi Press, 1984.

BLUMBERG, Arnold. *Zion before Zionism.* Syracuse: Syracuse University Press, 1985.

CHISSIN, Chaim. *A Palestine Diary: Memoirs of a BILU Pioneer, 1882-1887.* New York: Herzl Press, 1976.

DAGAN, Shaul and Ruth. *On the First Road to Zion: Stories of the First Aliyah Colonies.* Haifa: The Arison Foundation, 1998.

DRUCK, David. *Baron Edmond de Rothschild: The Story of a Practical Idealist.* New York: Hebrew Monotype Press, 1928.

ELIACH, Yaffa. *There Once Was a World: A Nine-Hundred-Year Chronicle of the Shtetl of Eishyshok.* Boston: Little, Brown, 1998.

ELIẒUR, Yoel. *Ancient Place Names in the Holy Land.* Jerusalem: Magnes Press, Hebrew University of Jerusalem, 2004.

GRUNFELD, Isidor. *Shemittah and Yovel.* London: Soncino Press, 1972.

LUZ, Ehud. *Parallels Meet.* Philadelphia: Jewish Publication Society, 1988.

MARCHANT, Dovid. *Gateway to Shemittah.* Jerusalem: Feldheim, 2007.

Morris, Benny. *Righteous Victims: A History of the Zionist-Arab Conflict, 1881-2001*. New York: Vintage, 2001.

Morton, Frederic. *The Rothschilds*. New York: Atheneum, 1962.

Naiditch, Isaac. *Edmond de Rothschild*. Washington, D.C.: Zionist Organization of America, 1945.

Rossoff, Dovid. *Where Heaven Touches Earth*. Jerusalem: Guardian Press, 2001.

Schama, Simon. *Two Rothschilds and the Land of Israel*. New York: Alfred A. Knopf, 1978.

Sokolow, Nahum. *Hibbath Zion*. Jerusalem: L. Mayer, 1934.

Stillman, Yedida. *Palestinian Costume and Jewelry*. Albuquerque: University of New Mexico Press, 1979.

Struminger, Laura. *The Life and Legacy of Baroness Betty de Rothschild*. New York: Peter Lang, 2006.

Twain, Mark. *The Innocents Abroad*. New York: Signet Classics, 1966.

Weir, Shelagh. *Palestinian Costume*. London: The Trustees of the British Museum, 1989.

Zohary, Michael. *Plants of the Bible*. Cambridge: Cambridge University Press, 1982.

Hebrew

Aaronsohn, Ran. *Ha'Baron ve'ha-Moshavot*. Jerusalem: Ben-Zvi Press, 1990.

———. *Lechu ve-Nelcha*. Jerusalem: Ben-Zvi Press, 2004.

Aneir, Ze'ev, ed. *Sippurei Moshavot*. Tel Aviv: Ministry of Defense, 1996.

Appel, Yehuda. *Be-Toch Reishit ha-Techiyah*. Tel Aviv: Gutenberg Press, 5696/1936.

Arkin, Achiezer. *Nachshonei ha-Shemittah*. Mazkeret Batya: A. Arkin, 1994.

Brill, Yechiel. *Yesud Ha-Ma'alah*. ed. G. Kressel. Jerusalem: Ben-Zvi Press, 5738.

Chissin, Chaim. *Massa ba-Areẓ ha-Muvtachat*. Tel Aviv: Ha-Kibbutz ha-Meuchad, 1982.

Dinkel, Yaakov Chaim. *Mi-Shvi'it Tarmav ad Shvi'it Tash'sa*. Jerusalem, 2001.

Diskin, Mordechai. *Divrei Mordechai*. Jerusalem: Y. D. Frumkin, 1912.

Droyanov, A., ed. *Ketavim le-Toldot Chibbat Ẓion ve-Yishuv Ereẓ Yisrael*, vol. 2. Odessa: The Committee for the Settlement of Ereẓ Yisrael, 1932.

———. "Aseret Michtavim me'eit A. Bloch le-Gross Mishneihu." *Mi-Yamim Rishonim – Yarchon le-Divrei Yemei ha-Techiyah be-Yisrael*, vol. 1 (June 1934–June 1935).

Elbaum-Dror, Rachel. *Ha-Chinuch ha-Ivri be-Ereẓ Yisrael*. Jerusalem: Ben-Zvi Press, 1986.

Eliav, Mordechai. *Ereẓ Yisrael ve-Yishuvah be-Me'ah ha-Yud-Tet, 1777-1917*. Jerusalem: Keter, 1978.

——— ed. *Sefer ha-Aliyah ha-Rishonah*. Jerusalem: Ben-Zvi Press, 1982.

Friedman, Menachem. "Le-Mashma'uto ha-Chevratit shel Pulmus ha-Shemittah (5649-5650)." *Shalem* 1 (1974).

Ginsberg, Asher Hirsch. *Kol Kitvei Achad Ha-Am*. Tel Aviv: Dvir, 1954.

Izakson, Eliyahu. *Mareh mi-Dor ha-Gesher*. Tel Aviv: Ohr, 1994.

Kahana, Kalman. *Sh'nat ha-Sheva*. Jerusalem: Ha-Machon le-Cheiker ha-Chakla'ut al pi ha-Torah, 1985.

Klausner, Yisrael. *Mi-Katowice ad Basel*. Jerusalem: Ha-Histadrut ha-Ẓionit, 1965.

KOLATT, Yisrael, ed. *Ha-Tekufah ha-Ottomanit.* vol. 1 of *Toldot ha-Yishuv ha-Yehudi be-Ereẓ Yisrael Me'az ha-Aliyah ha-Rishonah.* Jerusalem: Mossad Bialik, 1989.

KOOK, Avraham Yiẓchak Hakohen. *Iggrot ha-Re'ayah.* Jerusalem: Mossad Harav Kook, 5722-5725.

KOSOVSKY-SHACHOR, Yaakov, ed. *Iggrot R. Yiẓchak Elchanan.* Bnei Brak: Y. Kosovsky-Shachor, 2004.

LEVIN, Amihud Y. M. *Eileh Mas'ei.* Mevasseret Ẓion: Kol Mevasser, 5761.

———. "Mikhtav ha-Gaon R' Eliezer Gordon, Av Beit Din ve-Rosh Metivta Telz, al Heter ha-Mechirah bi-Shemittat Tarmat," *Orayta* 9 (2nd Editioṇ) (Netanya: Ha-Mo'aẓah ha-Datit, 5747), pp. 238 – 247.

———. "Mikhtevei ha-Gaon R' Yiẓchak Elchanan, Av Beit Din de-Kovno, be-Inyan Heter ha-Mechirah." *Orayta* 9 (2nd Edition) (Netanya: Ha-Mo'aẓah ha-Datit, 5747), pp. 226 – 237.

LIFSCHITZ, Yaakov Halevi. *Zikhron Yaakov.* Reprint, Bnei Brak, 1968.

LILIENBLUM, Moshe Leib. *Derech La'avor Golim.* Warsaw, 1899.

MORGENSTERN, Arie. *Ha-Shivah li-Yerushalayim, 1800-1860.* Jerusalem: Shalem Press, 2007.

NAOR, Mordechai. *Sefer le-Mazkeret: Mazkeret Batya-Ekron – Me'ah ha-Shanim ha-Rishonot.* Jerusalem: Ben-Zvi Press, 2010.

NEIMAN, David, ed. *Mazkeret Batya (Haytah Ekron).* Tel Aviv: Ha-Merkaz, 1968.

NISSENBAUM, Yiẓchak. *Ha-Dat ve'ha-Techiyah ha-Leumit.* Warsaw: Lewin-Epstein, 5680 (1920).

RABINOWITZ, Shaul Pinchas, ed. "Ekron." *Knesset Yisrael* (5686), pp. 986-987.

REICHMAN, Raphael. "Siftei Yesheinim: Shnei Michtavim Mikhtav Yad ha-Gaon Mordechai Gimpel Yaffe." *Oẓrot Yerushalayim* 140 (5733), ch. 235.

RINOT, Moshe. "Tahalichei Chillun ba-Chinuch ba-Moshavah, 1882-1914." *Ha-Chinuch ke-Mifgash*. ed. Adir Cohen. Haifa: University of Haifa, 5743/1983, pp. 149 – 156.

SALMON, Yosef. "Ha-Immut bein ha-Chareidim la-Maskilim bi-Tenuat Chibbat Ẓion bi-Sh'not ha-Shemonim." *Ha-Ẓionut*. Tel Aviv: Tel Aviv University, 1979.

SCHAMA, Simon. *Beit Rothschild ve-Ereẓ Yisrael*. Jerusalem: Magnes Press, Hebrew University of Jerusalem, 1980.

SCHEID, Eliyahu. *Zikhronot al ha-Moshavot ha-Yehudiyot ve'ha-Masa'ot be-Ereẓ Yisrael u've-Suryah, 1883-1899*. Jerusalem: Ben-Zvi Press, 1983.

SMILANSKY, Moshe. *Perakim be-Toldot ha-Yishuv, 1878-1891*. Tel Aviv: Dvir, 1959.

STAVI (STAVSKY), Moshe. *Ha-Kefar ha-Aravi*. Tel Aviv: Am Oved, 1940.

STERN, Yechiel Michel. *Gedolei ha-Dorot*. Jerusalem: Mechon Minchat Yisrael, 1996.

STERNBERG, Shlomo. *Heter Tarmat*. Jerusalem: Ha-Machon le-Moreshet Yisrael, 1986.

TIDHAR, David, ed. *Encyclopedia le-Chaluẓei ha-Yishuv u-Vonav*. Tel Aviv: David Tidhar, 1947.

TUCAZINSKY, Nisan Aharon, ed. *Torat Rabbi Shmuel Salant*. Jerusalem; Nisan Aharon Tucazinsky, 1998.

TUCAZINSKY, Yechiel Michel. *Sefer ha-Shemittah*. Jerusalem: Mossad Harav Kook, 5766.

TOMER, Ornah. "Beit ha-Kevarot be-Mazkeret Batya." Hebrew University, Jerusalem, 2000. Available through the Eran Shamir Village Museum, Mazkeret Batya.

TROIKES, Y., and Steinman, A. *Sefer Me'ah Shanah.* Tel Aviv: Matar-Troikes Books, 1994.

WISSOTZKY, Klonymous Ze'ev. *Kevuẓat Michtavim she-Nishlachu le-Anshei Shem be-Inyan Yishuv Ereẓ Yisrael.* Jerusalem: Ben-Zvi Press, 5641.

YAVNE'ELLI, Shmuel, ed. *Sefer ha-Ẓionut.* vol. 2, *Tekufat Chibbat Ẓion,* book II. Tel Aviv: Mossad Bialik, 1944.

ZIV, Yehuda. *Rega shel Makom.* Jerusalem: Ẓivonim Press, 2005.

Hebrew Newspapers

CHAVAẒELET. Jerusalem, 1883-1910
HA-LEVANON. Mainz, London, 1881-1886
HA-MAGGID. Cracow, 1884-1889
HA-MELIẒ. St. Petersburg, 1861-1893
HA-ẒEFIRAH. Warsaw, 1889-1893
HA-ẒVI. Jerusalem, 1886-1890

NOTE: Newspaper articles cited in this book can be accessed online at *www.jnul.huji.ac.il/dl/newspapers/index1024.html*

Endnotes

Prologue

[1] I refrain from using the term chaluẓim because in the more narrow sense the word was used to refer to the secular, socialistic pioneers of the Second Aliyah (1904-1914) who often clashed ideologically with the settlers of the First Aliyah. Many of the pioneers of the First Aliyah spoke disparagingly of the chaluẓim. The Jews of Mazkeret Batya should not be termed *Chareidi* as the term is used today, even though they shared many characteristics of contemporary *Chareidim*. Like the *Chareidim* of today, they wore traditional garb, were meticulous in their observance of the commandments and Jewish ritual, and were averse to reforms and modern trends – especially in Jewish education. But they did not necessarily have the identical political mindset and outlook of the *Chareidim* of today, especially concerning Zionism and Jewish nationalism. They were just plain Orthodox Litvaks.
For more on the term *Chareidi*, see note 323.

[2] The others were Rishon Le-Ẓion (1882), Rosh Pina (1882), Zikhron Yaakov (1882), Petach Tikva (1778; re-established 1882), and Yesud Ha-Ma'alah (1883).

[3] Mordechai Eliav, ed., *Sefer ha-Aliyah ha-Rishonah* (Jerusalem: Ben-Zvi Press, 1982), vol. 1, p. xiii.

[4] Ibid., p. xiv.
How many people realize that Zikhron Yaakov, famous for its Carmel Winery, and Rosh Pina (several years after it was abandoned by its founders, who hailed from Safed) were established by a group of Romanian Chassidim from the town of Buhuşi (Moldavia) in 1882? The unique spiritual ethos of these Chassidic pioneers was buried or ignored by secular historians. For example, the settlers' charter of Rosh Pina (clause 58) warns: "... no member of the moshavah is permitted to go out with weapons loaded with lethal bullets ... the purpose of bearing arms is only to make noise [to frighten away the enemy]." Yesud Ha-Ma'alah, adjacent to the Hula swamp in the Galilee, was founded by pious Jews from Mezeridzh, Poland – many of them Torah scholars. The settlement of Hadera (today a city) was founded by deeply pious Jews. One of the initiators of the settlement was Rabbi Moshe Mordechai Epstein, the *rosh yeshivah* of Slabodka and Hebron. (My thanks to Dr. Uri Rottenberg for providing me with this information.)
To appreciate the extent of the Orthodoxy of the first settlers, read Amihud Y.M. Levin's eye-opening introduction to the travelogue *Eileh Mas'ei* (Mevasseret Ẓion: Kol Mevasser, 5761). Read how the first order of business for the pioneers of Rishon

Le-Ẓion, when they arrived at the location of what was to be their new settlement, was to stop and recite the afternoon prayers. This story is told in Ze'ev Aneir, ed., *Sippurei Moshavot* (Tel Aviv: Ministry of Defense, 1996).

Shaul and Ruth Dagan (historians of the First Aliyah) wrote: "... most of the founders of the First Aliyah colonies ... were pious Jews. ... Petach Tikva too, whose founders were from the Old Yishuv in Jerusalem, was an 'Orthodox' colony for all intents and purposes." Dagan, *On the First Road to Zion: Stories of the First Aliyah Colonies* (Haifa: The Arison Foundation, 1998), p. 32.

The religious nature of the First Aliyah was recorded by Moshe Leib Lilienblum in his work *Derekh La'avor Golim* (Warsaw, 1899), p. 84. Lilienblum was one of the secular heads of the Chovevei Ẓion movement.

[5] BILU, an acronym from the words בֵּית יַעֲקֹב לְכוּ וְנֵלְכָה, "House of Jacob, let us go" (Isaiah 2:5), was an organization composed of secular Russian revolutionaries who wished to build a Jewish society in Palestine. BILU was established in 1882 in the aftermath of the pogroms, and its first fourteen members reached Palestine that same year. Religious critics wryly observed that the organization's name omits the initials of the last words of the verse, "in the light of the Lord."

[5A] Eliav, *Aliyah Rishonah*, vol. 1, p. xiv.

[6] Founded by Jews from Safed, it was the only settlement of the First Aliyah that was situated on the Golan Heights, northeast of the sea of Galilee.

[7] Many of the Chovevei Ẓion members were associated with the *Haskalah*. *Haskalah* was the Jewish "enlightenment" movement started in Germany under Moses Mendelssohn. It went through many phases and advocated a number of ideas (some contradictory), such as the study of science, European languages, and other secular knowledge, the taking up of productive trades, the reform of the Jewish educational system (the *cheder*), a renaissance of the Hebrew language and emphasis on the intellectual study of the Bible rather than the Talmud.

[8] To be precise, initially they were not self-sufficient because they relied on the substantial financial support of Baron Rothschild, a Jew who was personally non-observant (though quite sympathetic to religious practice). But their goal, like the rest of the pioneers of the First Aliyah, was to become financially independent.

Chapter 1

[9] Rabbi Mohilever (1824-1898) was a child prodigy who was known as the "*illuy* of Głębokie" (הולבקי, a town near Vilna). He

received rabbinical ordination at the age of eighteen from the Yeshivah of Volozhin. After engaging in business for several years, he served in many prestigious rabbinical posts for about fifty years, the last of which was Bialystok (beginning in1883).

[10] An author and historian, Rabbi Rabinowitz (1845-1910) received ordination from Rabbi Yisrael Salanter but later veered toward the *Haskalah*. Rabinowitz was one of the first activists of the Chovevei Ẓion movement. He translated Heinrich Graetz's monumental *History of the Jews* from German into Hebrew.

[11] See Yiẓchak Nissenbaum, *Ha-Dat ve'ha-Techiyah ha-Leumit* (Warsaw: Lewin-Epstein, 5680/1920), pp. 98-100. For a different analysis of that visit, see Yaakov Halevi Lifschitz, *Zikhron Yaakov* (Bnei Brak, 1968), pp. 93-94. Lifschitz, secretary of Rabbi Yiẓchak Elchanan Spektor, fought the *maskilim* and Chovevei Ẓion. He was the bane of religious Zionists in that he tried to thwart their influence on Rabbi Spektor. The following is a free translation of Lifschitz's version of events:

> During that period when Rabbi Yiẓchak Elchanan Spektor was at the convention [of Jewish leaders] in St. Petersburg, a telegram arrived from Lvov for our Master in Kovno, stating that two great pillars of the Jewish community of England – Mr. Samuel Montague, a member of the British Parliament, along with the Honorable Dr. Asher, the writer and secretary of the Jewish community of London – have arrived (in Lvov), and both have requested that Rabbi Spektor come to Lvov to discuss the [refugee] situation with them.
>
> We sent a copy of the telegram to Rabbi Spektor in St. Petersburg, but there was no way he could leave the convention. When my brother was informed that Rabbi Shmuel Mohilever was staying in Warsaw, I suggested to our Teacher [R. Spektor] to have Rabbi Mohilever travel to Lvov. He agreed and sent a telegram to Rabbi Mohilever. The *gaon* Rabbi Shmuel Mohilever eagerly accepted the invitation. He urged my brother to escort him, but my brother declined for various reasons. But he accepted my brother's suggestion to take with him Shaul Pinchas Rabinowitz ....
>
> ... Rabbi Mohilever realized that the goal of these emissaries [from England] was to inform Rabbi Spektor regarding emigration [from Russia] to England, in order that he should discourage them from coming en mass, so as to prevent incitement of the British people against the Jews there, who were not favorably disposed to absorbing new immigrants ....
> The emissaries inquired about the lives of our Russian Jewish

Mr. Secretary. Yaakov Lifschitz

brethren, but Rabbi Mohilever, who ... served as a rabbi in one of the areas of Poland and was unaware of what the Lithuanian Russian rabbis were trying to accomplish, and as a supporter of Chovevei Ẓion, tried to influence the emissaries toward his line of thinking [i.e., encouraging *aliyah*] ... but they were not interested. So neither side accomplished anything, and all the hullabaloo that came about from the visit of these two dignitaries amounted to nothing. However, if our Teacher had gone to Lvov himself, he would have made valuable suggestions that could have been implemented by them.

[12] Yiẓchak Rafael, ed. *Encyclopedia shel ha-Ẓionut ha-Datit* (Jerusalem: Mossad Harav Kook, 1965), vol. 3, p. 343.

[13] *Ha-Ẓofeh*, February 8, 2006.

[14] Ibid.

[15] One of the greatest rabbinical figures of eastern Europe, Rabbi Soloveitchik (1820-1892) was ordained by the Yeshivah of Volozhin and was a major opponent of the *Haskalah*. From 1854 he co-headed that yeshivah with Rabbi Naftali Ẓvi Yehuda Berlin. In 1878, Rabbi Soloveitchik was appointed rabbi of Brisk. After initially being in favor of Chovevei Ẓion, he soon withdrew his support. He is famous as the author of the work *Beit ha-Levi*.

[16] Rabbi Meisel (1820-1911) was the rabbi of the Polish towns of Lomza (1866-1878), then Lodz (until his death). When Jewish factory owners fired Jews in order to hire cheaper, gentile labor, Rabbi Meisel opened a plant for the unemployed workers. An incredibly industrious communal activist, he established an orphanage, an old age home, a hospital, and elementary schools in Lodz. Wherever he served as a rabbi, Jewish children were never abducted for service in Russian army cantonist regiments.

[17] Rafael, p. 99. According to another source, it was Rabbi Mordechai Gimpel Yaffe, the rabbi of Rozhinoy, who enlisted Rabbis Mohilever and Soloveitchik to announce that the time had come for Jews to colonize the Land of Israel. Yerucham Fishel Pines, *Hesped Mar* (Warsaw: Universal, 5673 [1913]), p. 16.

[18] Y. Troikes and A. Steinman, *Sefer Me'ah Shanah* (Tel Aviv: Matar-Troikes Books, 1994). At this stage, Rabbi Mohilever envisioned businessmen of means to be the agents of *aliyah*, not farmers. The one or two people who would pave the way for the rest would hire local workers, not perform the labor themselves. This is in stark contrast to Yechiel Brill's suggestion, which will be mentioned later.

[19] Nissenbaum, p. 81. Pines, p. 16.

[20] Yechiel Brill, *Yesud Ha-Ma'alah: Parashat Ha'alat Achad Asar ha-Ikkarim me-Russia bi-Sh'nat 1863* (Mainz, Germany, 1863;

reprint, Jerusalem: Ben-Zvi Press, 1978), p. 4.

[21] See Dr. Yerakh Tzur, *Chelko shel Yechiel Brill ba-Hakamat Mazkeret Batya,* on Mazkeret Batya's website: *www.mazkeret.org/BrilsPart.htm.*

[22] About 3% of the Jews in the Russian Empire were farmers (as opposed to 97% of the gentile population). For more information on this fascinating aspect of Russian Jewish life, see Ẓvi Livneh, *Yehudim Chaklaim be-Arvot Russia* (Merchavyah: Sifriat Poalim – Ha-Kibbutz ha-Artzi ha-Shomer ha-Ẓa'ir, 1965).

[23] *Ha-Levanon,* 9 Tammuz 5641 (July 6, 1881).

[24] Brill, p. 7.

[25] Rabbi Kahn was later appointed chief rabbi of France.

[26] Erlanger was a Chovevei Ẓion activist in France, vice president of the Jewish Consistoire there, and a founder of the AIU. He assisted Carl Netter in establishing the first agricultural school in Palestine, Mikveh Israel. Erlanger also managed the Baron's charities and was the liaison between him and Chovevei Ẓion in Russia.

[27] David Druck, *Baron Edmond de Rothschild: The Story of a Practical Idealist* (New York: Hebrew Monotype Press, 1928), p. 23.

[28] Brill, p. 8.

[29] Ibid.

Chapter 2

[30] Achiezer Arkin, *Nachshonei ha-Shemittah* (Mazkeret Batya: A. Arkin, 1994), p. 99.

[31] Rothschild was a member of the Jewish Consistoire of Paris and in 1877 was appointed chairman of the Jewish Charity Committee of Paris, which contributed large sums to the needy Jews of France. In 1881, when pogroms were causing an exodus of Jews from Russia, he and his brother Alphonse were among the founders of the Comité Général de Secours (General Committee for Material Assistance), established to aid Jewish refugees. Ran Aaronsohn, *Rothschild and Early Jewish Colonization* (Jerusalem: Magnes Press, Hebrew University of Jerusalem, 2000), p. 53.

[32] Historian Simon Schama writes that "... there is evidence ... that not once, but on many occasions, [the Baron] openly expressed his opposition to any idea of mass emigration from Russia, or any other part of the Diaspora, to the Land of Israel." Schama, *Beit Rothschild ve' Ereẓ Yisrael* (Jerusalem: Magnes Press Hebrew University of Jerusalem, 1980), p. 59.

[33] Arkin, p. 99.

[34] Ibid., p. 101.

Frederic Morton, in his book *The Rothschilds* (New York: Atheneum, 1962), p.199, puts Rabbi Mohilever's strategy and the Baron's hesitations even more succinctly:

... He had come to Paris hoping to commit to Palestine the innermost fiber of Baron Rothschild's soul.
Edmond answered that he was prepared to contribute the necessary sum – which his visitor had not even mentioned. But Mohilever's Talmudic dialectics steered the interview straight back to the soul again. The Baron, not prepared for a spiritual set-to, kept stressing his willingness to give money; the rabbi would not let go of the innermost fiber. At last the deep black eyes of the old man won out. Edmond promised "... to consult myself and make a trial to see what will result from it."
... For the remaining fifty years of his life, Edmond made a trial of the question, and it made a trial of him.

35 Arkin, p. 101.

35A Mikveh Israel, established in 1870, was the first Jewish agricultural school in Israel. It was founded by Carl [Charles] Netter, also a founding member of the Alliance Israélite Universelle. Netter pioneered progressive educational methods to teach agriculture. The school had a poor reputation amongst some of the Orthodox due to its laxity concerning observance of *halakhah*.
In 1898, Theodor Herzl met Emperor Wilhelm II at the main entrance of Mikveh Israel during Herzl's sole visit to the Land of Israel. Over the years, Mikveh Israel has educated tens of thousands of children. It served as a base for the pre-state defense force, the Haganah.

36 Aaronsohn, *Rothschild*, p. 56.

37 Schama, *Beit Rothschild*, p. 62.

Chapter 3

38 Brill, p. 10.

39 Although Mikveh Israel was established in 1868, it was an agricultural boarding school, not a colony.

40 Brill, p. 11. Brill states there that they arrived in a city he called by the Hebrew letter *vav*. David Neiman, in *Mazkeret Batya (haytah Ekron)* (Tel Aviv: Ha-Merkaz, 1968), p. 41, cites Dr. Yisrael Klausner's opinion that the city was Warsaw. However, G. Kressel, the editor of the Ben-Zvi Press edition of Brill's book understood the *vav* to be an abbreviation of Vilna.

41 Yasinovsky grew up in the Grodno district of Russia, where the farming colony was situated. He was one of the first to join the *Chibbat Ẓion* movement and one of Theodor Herzl's earliest supporters.

42 According to David Tidhar, "shekels" meant rubles. David Tidhar, ed. *Encyclopedia le-Chaluẓei ha-Yishuv u-bonav* (Tel Aviv: David Tidhar, 1947), vol. 1, p. 403. According to Dr. Yisrael Klausner,

Rabbi Mohilever pledged 700 rubles (cited in Neiman, p. 42). As to why Brill did not use the word "rubles," see appendix IX, pp. 371 and 373. He may have been precautious because of the sensitive nature of this illegal undertaking.

[43] Rabbi Yaffe (1820-1891) was Rozhinoy's rabbi for forty years. Instead of a comfortable retirement, he made *aliyah* at the end of 1888 and settled in Yahud, a satellite of Petach Tikva. He was an outspoken opponent of the *Heter Mechirah*. His grandson, Binyamin Yaffe, published a biography of him, *Ha-Rav me-Yahud: Mordechai Gimpel Yaffe* (Jerusalem: Ha-Mador ha-Dati le-Inyenei Ha-Noar ve' he-Chaluẓ shel ha-Histadrut ha-Ẓionit, 1958).

[44] He was known primarily for *Techeilet Mordechai*, his supercommentary on Nachmanides' commentary on the Torah.

[44A] *Pines*, p. 16.

[45] Brother of Chovevei Ẓion activist Yechiel Michel Pines, who will play a major role later in this story.

[46] Ages based on Neiman's *Mazkeret Batya*, p. 37. Though this book puts Yaakov Arkin's age at 34 when he arrived, the Arkin family attests that 34 was the age of his younger brother, Ẓvi. Ornah Tomer, who researched the Ekron/Mazkeret Batya cemetery, confirms that the inscription on Yaakov Arkin's gravestone indicates that no one knew when he was born.

[46A] Aryeh Leib Pines, grandfather of Yechiel Michel Pines (profiled in chapter 25), came to Rozhinoy at the beginning of the nineteenth century and opened a textile factory that employed hundreds of workers. See Meir Sokolowsky, ed., *Rozhinoy: Sefer Zikaron le-Kehillat Rozhinoy ve-ha-Sevivah* (Tel Aviv: Irgun Yotz'ei Rozhinoy be-Yisrael, 5717), p. 58.

The Pines family employed most of Rozhinoy's Jewish laborers (ibid., p. 49), quite possibly including Ẓvi Arkin. Although the factory provided steady employment, the conditions were horrendous. The following description of the weaving industry in Rozhinoy may suggest why Arkin decided to try agriculture and how it prepared him for the rigors of settling the Land of Israel:

> As has been said, there were several weaving enterprises in Ruzhany. The Jewish workers labored in a primitive fashion at simple looms. They worked on a contractual basis and of course were greatly exploited. There were no set work hours. Work began early in the morning and ended late at night. The weavers would even come to the Sabbath Minchah service in their work clothes and their Sabbath overcoat, so they could go to the factory immediately after the Minchah service. They waited impatiently for the first three stars to appear, indicating

> the end of the Sabbath. Then they would quickly recite the Maariv service, remove their Sabbath garb, and immediately go to work until well after midnight, for they had rested on the afternoon of the Sabbath and were able to remain awake until late at night. (ibid., p. 49)
>
> [Some] worked twelve hours a day. … The factory owners considered this to be the norm. (ibid., p. 50)

See also note 495A, below. *Rozhinoy: Sefer Zikaron* can be accessed online at *www.yizkor.nypl.org/index.php?id=2697*.

47 Neiman, p. 158.
48 Dagan, p. 108.
49 Brill, p. 12.
50 *She'eilot u-Teshuvot Rabbi Shmuel Mohilever* (Jerusalem: Mossad Harav Kook, 1980), *Orach Chaim*, 19.
51 Brill, p. 14.
52 See appendix I.

Chapter 4

53 Brill, pp. 13, 14.
54 The blank space refers to Baron Rothschild, who had requested anonymity.
55 The Baron eventually did pick up the tab for their travel expenses.
56 How could Avraham Yaakov Gellman, who was not selected by Brill but joined the others only later, have signed the contract? Furthermore, there are only nine names here instead of ten. These signatures were taken from a condolence letter (pictured at right) written years later by the farmers upon the passing of Shmuel Yosef Fuenn. This exhibit is a mockup for educational purposes only!

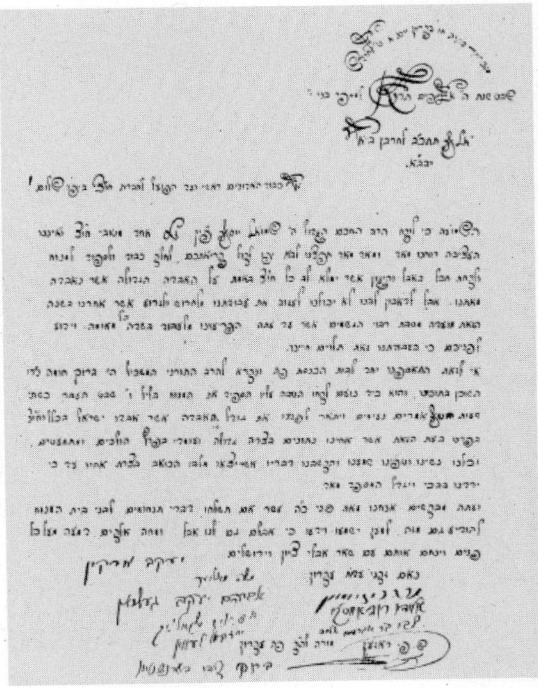

57 Arkin, p. 15.
57A Brill, pp. 18-19; Tidhar, vol. 1, p. 403; According to Dr. Yisrael Klausner it amounted to 598 rubles (Neiman, p. 43).
58 Brill, p. 15.
58A Ibid.
59 From Ezra 7:9 – "For on the first of the first month was the *commencement of the ascent* from

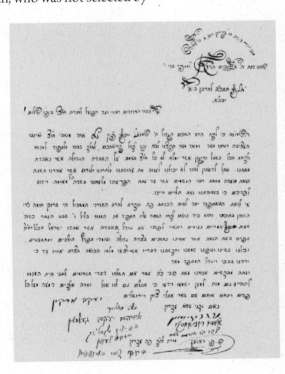

Babylon. ..."

[60] Brill, pp. 16, 17.

[61] Ibid. Rabbi Mohilever was sensitive and could not bear the pangs of a guilty conscience. Brill probably had a thicker skin. They complemented each other well.

[62] *Avot* 2:5.

[63] Mordechai Eliav, *Ereẓ Yisrael ve-Yishuvah be Me'ah ha-Yud Tet 1777-1917* (Jerusalem: Keter, 1978), p. 75.

[64] This was also based on his understanding of Kabbalah. He made two attempts to go to Ereẓ Yisrael: in 1772 and 1782. Both times, he was forced to turn back and saw it as a Heavenly sign.

[65] Dovid Rossoff, *Where Heaven Touches Earth* (Jerusalem: Guardian Press, 2001), p. 169. Eliav, *Ereẓ Yisrael* (p. 85), points out that the Gaon also emphasized the observance of those commandments connected to the Land of Israel.

[66] By the end of the First Aliyah, in 1904, the Jewish population in Palestine had more than doubled to 55,000, with about 2,500 Jews living in twenty-five Jewish agricultural settlements.

[67] Pro-Palestinian historians cite higher figures, while pro-nationalist Jewish authors cite lower ones. For a scholarly example of the latter group, see Moshe Aumann, *Land Ownership in Palestine 1880-1948* (Jerusalem: The Israel Academic Committee on the Middle East, 1976).

[68] Alkalai was the Sephardic rabbi of Zemun, near Belgrade, Serbia. His principal teacher was Rabbi Eliezer Papo, author of *Pele Yoeẓ*. After the Damascus Blood Libel of 1840, he concluded that the only solution to anti-Semitism was the mass return of Jews to Ereẓ Yisrael.

[69] Kalischer, the rabbi of Toruń (a German-speaking city in northern Poland/Prussia), authored *Derishat Ẓion*, which called for taking practical steps to resettle the Land of Israel. He founded a movement that preceded Chovevei Ẓion by two decades. In practical terms regarding actual settlement, the movement accomplished little. But it had a major influence on the thinking of key Jewish leaders in the next generation, such as Rabbi Mohilever, the Malbim, and Rabbi Meir Simchah of Dvinsk.

[70] Not to be confused with the Templar Knights of the Middle Ages, this Protestant splinter group from southern Germany seceded from the Lutheran Church in 1854. Believing that Judgment Day was near, the Templers wanted to be present in Palestine for the "Second Coming." The first large contingent landed in Haifa in 1868. The first two generations of Templers

were pro-Jewish, but the third was influenced by German propaganda and had pro-Nazi leanings. During the Second World War, the British expelled the Templers from Palestine and shipped them off to Australia.

[71] Such as Sarona, a settlement near Haifa.

[72] "Refaim" refers to the giants that lived in the Land of Israel in ancient times (Deuteronomy 2:11). The Valley of Refaim is mentioned in Joshua 15:8. See *Da'at Mikra* (Jerusalem: Mossad Harav Kook, 1970) on that verse.

[73] Jerusalem has greatly expanded, and the neighborhood surrounding Emek Refaim Street today is known as the German Colony.

Chapter 5

[74] The journey at a glance (via land and sea routes):

From	***To***	***Miles***	***Kilometers***
Pavlovka	Volkovysk	31	50
Volkovysk	Trieste, Italy	897	1,444
Trieste	Alexandria, Egypt	1,324	2,132
Alexandria	Jaffa Port, Palestine	290	468
Jaffa Port	Haifa, Palestine	54	88
		TOTAL: 2,596	4,182

[75] 20 Iyar, 5642/May 9, 1882.

[76] Also cited in Eliav, *First Aliyah,* vol. 2, p. 25.

[77] According to Dr. Yerakh Tzur, the editor of Mazkeret Batya's website, Brill was probably referring to the train station of Volkovysk (Vawkavysk in Belarusian), located only 50 kilometers northwest from Pavlovka. Brill only gives us a one letter abbreviation, ו' (the Hebrew letter *vav*). Getzel Kressel, editor of Ben-Zvi Press' edition of *Yesud Ha-Ma'alah,* asserted that it refers to Vilna, the capital of Lithuania. Brill uses the same abbreviation earlier in his work, on pages 11 and 15, where he is referring either to Vilna or Warsaw. The problem with Vilna is that the city is about 204 kilometers (127 miles) away from Pavlovka. It would not make any sense for Brill (who was always strapped for money) to have them pay double by travelling north and then make a u-turn and go south to their first probable transit point, Bialystok, which was only 87 kilometers (54 miles) due west from the Volkovysk train station! Brill also wrote that he met in "*Vav*" the activist Yaakov Ẓvi Zisselman, who led a chapter of Chovevei Ẓion in Pinsk, which was much

closer to Volkovysk than Vilna.
Volkovysk (Vawkavysk in Belarusian) is one of White Russia's oldest towns. According to the 1897 Russian census, the Jewish population of Volkovysk was 5,528, over half of the town's population of 10,323. Brill certainly wouldn't have found it difficult to find appropriate lodging there.

[78] Brill, p. 19, footnote.

[79] So why did Brill, fervently Orthodox himself, give a different reason? We can only assume that Brill knew the real reason and completely agreed with it, but he may have presumed that the minyan argument would not sway the secular Alliance. So he had to come up with a better justification for the additional expense incurred by the eleventh man. Dr. Yerakh Tzur theorizes that Gellman, who was not a farmer, jumped on board at the opportunity to have a farm of his own. He had little to lose and everything to gain if Brill took him along.

[80] Brill, p. 20.

Chapter 6

[81] Brill, p. 20, note.

[82] Ibid., p. 21.

[83] Baumgarten (1828-1908) was an economist, writer, publisher, and communal leader. In his youth, he learned in yeshivot and studied economics at the University of Vienna. Brill refers to him with the honorary title of Ritter von Baumgarten in his book.

[84] Baron Albert Rothschild (1844-1911) was a member of the Rothschild banking family of Austria.

[85] Brill, p. 22.

[86] Established in 1833.

[87] Based on the website: *www.cyberussr.com/hcunn/gold-std. html#france*.

[88] Corfu is a Greek island in the Ionian Sea lying off the coast of Albania. Until the end of the nineteenth century, most etrogim in Europe were cultivated in Corfu. They looked nicer than the etrogim from Palestine, grown mostly by Arab farmers. Rabbi Avraham Yiẓchak Hakohen Kook encouraged Palestinian Jews to grow their own etrogim. When the religious Zionist rabbis banned the purchase of the fruit from Corfu, exports of etrogim from Palestine skyrocketed, reaching 60,000 by World War I. See *Encyclopedia ha-Ivrit*, vol. 7, p. 491.

[89] Brill, pp. 24, 25.

[90] The telegraph linked Europe to Palestine starting in 1864. See Arnold Blumberg, *Zion before Zionism* (Syracuse: Syracuse University Press, 1985), p. 46.

[91] Brill, p. 25.

[92] On the 15th of Kislev (November 26) Rabbi Mohilever sent Brill a letter informing him of this development. The forwarded letter reached Brill in Palestine three weeks later.

[93] Brill, p. 27.

[94] Was he referring to the Biblical story of Jonah? The prophet fled the Land of Israel by boat and told the ship's captain that the raging storm was on account of his sin.

[95] Brill, pp. 27, 28.

[96] Ibid., p. 28.

[97] Obviously, this was a lie, since Russia was not part of the Ottoman Empire. Brill was thinking of bribing the clerk for the necessary documentation.

[98] Based on Ecclesiastes 10:10 – "A feast is made for laughter, and wine makes life glad; and *money answers all things*." An age-old practice in the Middle East, bribery is known in Arabic as *baksheesh*.

[99] Brill, pp. 28, 29.

Chapter 7

[100] Brill, p. 29.

[101] Russian Jews.

[102] Brill, p. 30.

[103] Two weeks later, Brill received a letter from Rabbi Mohilever that had missed him in Trieste, and he got his answer: "I have been informed that a letter has been sent to the director of Mikveh Israel instructing him to warmly receive the guests."

[104] Moyal was one of the pioneers of the Yishuv and of Jewish commerce in Jaffa.

[105] Brill, p. 30, 31.

[106] Ibid., p. 31.

[107] Ibid., p. 32. Why Hirsch received permission for only ten men remains a mystery.

[108] Brill writes: ארבעים, ולא חסר אחת –"forty and *not* minus one" whereas the Mishnah counts "forty minus one" labors prohibited on Sabbath (*Shabbat* 7:2) and lashes to be administered as corporal punishment (*Makkot* 3:10). Brill may wryly be comparing his financial woes to the rigors of both.

[109] The telegram Brill sent didn't arrive in Jaffa for another two days.

Chapter 8

[110] Brill, p. 34.

[110A] The name Mikveh Israel, taken from Jeremiah 14:8, means "the hope of Israel." Hence this chapter's ironic title, "No Hope in Mikveh Israel."

[111] According to historian Ran Aaronsohn, the Baron's chief aides in Paris wanted Hirsch to settle the Pavlovka farmers in Rishon Le-Ẓion, because Rothschild had recently acquired property there. This may explain Hirsch's constant reference to that settlement.

[112] Hirsch's apparent uneasiness extended to both religious and secular Russian Jews. When members of the BILU colonization movement spent time in Mikveh Israel, they too encountered difficulties with him.

[113] Hirsch may not have been bluffing. Rabbis Eliyahu Guttmacher and Ẓvi Hirsch Kalischer corresponded with the Alliance Israélite Universelle, urging that Shemittah be observed in Mikveh Israel in 5635 (1874-1875). Rabbi Kalischer published a letter dated 19 Elul 5634 (September 1, 1874) stating that the Alliance had informed him that it had instructed its administrators at the school to observe Shemittah as he had requested. If that is true, Mikveh Israel was the first modern Jewish settlement to observe Shemittah. Unfortunately, there is no evidence to back this up. See Amihud Y.M. Levin, "She-eilat ha-Shemittah be-Mikveh Yisrael bi-Sh'nat 5635," *Orayta* 9 (5747), pp. 214-225. Ironically, Hirsch later tried to coerce the Pavlovkans to work during the Shemittah of 5649.

[114] In fact, thirty-five years later (1917), Great Britain wrested Palestine from the Turks.

[115] Brill, p. 36.

[116] Ibid.

[117] It was three kilometers (1.86 miles) away, and Brill is quick to point out that he did not violate the prohibition of *techum Shabbat,* walking a long distance in an uninhabited area on the Sabbath. It was customary in those days, he writes, to walk from the city of Jaffa to Mikveh Israel on the Sabbath, for there were "gardens, orchards [citrus groves], and houses all along the way."

[118] Brill, p. 38.

[119] The comment is an attack on Hirsch, who claimed he was too busy to find land for them.

[120] Brill, p. 40.

[121] Ibid., p. 41.

[122] Ibid.

[123] Neiman, p. 159.

[124] Michael Zohary, *Plants of the Bible* (Cambridge: Cambridge University Press, 1982), p. 161.

[125] Brill, pp. 51, 52. To be fair, I must remind the reader that all these stories are taken from Brill's book, *Yesud Ha-Ma'alah*. Brill may have sometimes exaggerated, I believe his account is essentially

credible. Yet the truth is hard to believe. According to Brill, the chief official of the Alliance in Palestine, who was charged with paving the way to help persecuted European Jews settle in the Land of Israel, did not even believe in his mission.

126 He records the letters in *Yesud Ha-Ma'alah* in an entry dated 23 Adar I (April 1).

127 Brill, pp. 71-72.

128 Ibid., pp. 72-73.

129 A man of literary and Biblical knowledge, Brill may have intentionally harked back to the language spoken by the Patriarch Jacob to his adversary Laban, and also alluded to the forty-day mission of the spies sent by Moses to scout the Land of Israel.

130 Brill., p. 75.

Chapter 9

131 Eliav, *Erez Yisrael*, p. 242.

132 Blumberg, p. 3.

133 Yehoshua Ben-Arieh, *Jerusalem in the Nineteenth Century – The Old City* (Jerusalem: Ben-Zvi Press, 1984), p. 314.

133A Brill, p. 91.

134 The custom of praying at gravesites is an old one. According to tradition, Caleb, one of the twelve spies Moses sent to scout the Land of Israel, made his way to the Cave of the Patriarchs in Hebron and prostrated himself there. For further reading, see Yechezkel Shraga Lichtenstein, *Mi-Tumah li-Kedushah: Tefillah ve-Chefzei Mizvah be-Vatei Kevarot va-Aliyah le-Kivrei Zaddikim* (Tel Aviv: Ha-Kibbutz ha-Meuchad, 2007).

135 Brill used the idea of building hotels near holy graves to vent his enduring wrath at Hirsch, commenting sarcastically in the record of his travels: "When I saw this good thing, I said to myself how wonderful it would be if the Alliance Israélite Universelle took it upon itself to build a hostel next to the grave of Netter [i.e., Carl Netter, founder of the Mikveh Israel school], so that when a Jew came to stay overnight in Mikveh Israel, the director would not have to take it upon his honorable self to personally... throw him into the street!"

136 Blumberg, p. 98.

137 From the multimedia presentation at the Rosh Pina Pioneer Restoration Site.

138 Brill received a telegram there from Hirsch and could discern that the message had been sent on the Sabbath (violating Jewish law). The irascible Brill could not restrain his pen: "I learned from this that *Rabbeinu* (our teacher) Hirsch, the *mara d'atra* (halakhic authority) of the Land of Israel, sanctioned the writing of a

telegram on the Sabbath, because in his view the mizvah of settling the land ... is equal in weight to all the other mizvot."

[139] Today Shefar'am is a Druze town about eight kilometers (five miles) east of Haifa Bay. After the Sanhedrin moved from Judea to Usha – in the Galilee – due to Roman persecution in the second century, Shefar'am was its second seat.

Chapter 10

[139A] A paraphrase of Song of Songs 2:15 – "Seize for us the foxes, the little foxes that spoil the vineyards, for our vineyards have tiny grapes."

[140] Brill, p. 104.

[141] Ibid., p. 105.

[142] That's how editor G. Kressel understood the acronym רמ"ך used by Brill. Katz was a member of the first group that settled in Petach Tikva and was an activist in the Yishuv. Alternatively, it refers to(Reb) Michel Cohen, who worked with Brill in setting up the newspaper *Ha-Levanon.*

[143] Brill, p. 108.

[144] Ibid., p. 109. Brill's disembarking from the boat on a Jewish festival did not violate *halakhah.* See *Shulchan Aruch, Orach Chaim* 404:1.

[145] Aaronsohn, *Rothschild,* p. 157.

[146] This section is based on an article (cited earlier) by Dr. Yerakh Tzur on the website of Mazkeret Batya: *www.mazkeret.org/BrilsPart.htm.*

[147] According to Moshe Weiss, the idea to meet Baron Edmond de Rothschild came from Wilhelm Karl von Rothschild, his uncle, when Rabbi Mohilever visited him in Frankfurt in 1882. See Weiss, *For the Love of Zion* (Miami Beach: Moshe Weiss, 1998), p. 39.

[148] P. *xxii.* Originally from Galicia, Kressel (1911-1986) came to Israel in 1930 with the Fifth Aliyah. He documented the early Hebrew press and wrote about the history of the New Yishuv. He was one of the main developers of "bio bibliography" (a bibliography that contains biographical details) in modern Israel.

[149] A region of western Ukraine bordering Poland.

Chapter 11

[150] They were called Radomers because Rabbi Shmuel Mohilever was the rabbi of Radom when he met with Rothschild in 1882.

[151] Shmuel Yavne'elli, ed., *Sefer ha-Zionut* , vol. 2, *Tekufat Chibbat Zion,* book II (Tel Aviv: Mossad Bialik, 1944), p. 237.

[152] Ten years later, in a written testimony submitted to a rabbinical court in Jerusalem involving a suit of Rothschild's administrators vs. the farmers, Ephraim Skolnick, one of the original eleven, wrote, "Because of various impediments, the land deals in which Hirsch was involved never materialized, and much time had

lapsed. We were afraid the process would drag on forever, and we were exasperated. We told Mr. Hirsch that the only option now was to return to Russia. Mr. Hirsch then informed the Baron …" Yavne'elli, book II, p. 237.

[153] Ibid., p. 238. Emphasis added.

[154] Ibid.

[155] Chaim Chissin, *Mi-Reshumot Achad ha-Biluim* (Jerusalem: Ben-Zvi Press, 1990), p. 137.

[155A] Lieut. C. R. Condor, R.E., and Lieut. H.H. Kitchener, R.E., *The Survey of Western Palestine – Memoirs of the Topography, Orography, Hydrography, and Archeology*, vol. 1, part 2, p. 408, sheets VII-XVI – Samaria (London: The Committee of the Palestine Exploration Fund, 1882). (To download p. 408, visit *www.aleph.nli.org.il/nnl/dig/books/bk001197398.html*. A DjVu viewer program comes with the download. On the DjVu menu bar, click NAVIGATE, then GO TO PAGE, and then type "231."

[155B] *Survey*, pp. 252-253. (With the DjVu viewer: NAVIGATE → GO TO PAGE, then type "147.")

[156] Yisrael Kolatt, ed., *Ha-Tekufah ha-Ottomanit*, vol. 1 of *Toldot ha-Yishuv ha-Yehudi be-Ereẓ Yisrael me'az ha-Aliyah ha-Rishonah* (Jerusalem: Mossad Bialik, 1989), part 1, p. 144.

[157] Simon Schama, *Two Rothschilds and the Land of Israel* (New York: Alfred A. Knopf, 1978), p. 77. Quoted from Elie Scheid, *Memoirs* (French), p. 32.

[158] Kolatt, p. 217.

[159] Ran Aaronsohn, *Ha-Baron ve'ha-Moshavot* (Jerusalem: Ben-Zvi Press, 1990), p. 20, note 42.

[160] Moyal hailed from the Maghreb region of North Africa. As a subject of the Ottoman Empire, he had the connections and know-how to deal successfully with the Arabs and their Turkish overlords.

[160A] A subtle psychological factor may also be at play here. The Baron loved to acquire, donating his acquisitions only after holding onto them for a long time. Such was the case with his art collection, which he eventually contributed to the Louvre. Elizabeth Antébi wrote:

> Once asked by Chaim Weizmann why he supported so much archeological research, in particular, to find the ancient tombs of the kings of Judah, the Baron answered that he was excited not by the research in itself, but by "*la possession.*"
>
> Meir Dizengoff, founder and mayor of Tel Aviv, also remembered the day when, riding in 1893 … on the top of Mount Carmel, the Baron looked at the land all around him and ordered: "Buy it for me!"

Elizabeth Antébi, "Baron Edmond de Rothschild (1845-1934): From 'HaNadiv' (The Benefactor) to 'HaNassi' (The Prince)," in Judit Targarona Borrás and Angel Sáenz-Badillos, eds., *Jewish Studies at the Turn of the Twentieth Century*, vol. 2, *Judaism from the Renaissance to Modern Times* (Leiden: Brill, 1999), p. 254.

[161] *Ha-Maggid*, 29 Cheshvan, 5644/November 29, 1883, puts the date at October 21, 1883. But Hirsch's telegram to Paris informing them of the purchase wasn't sent until October 27. Elie Scheid, later one of the Baron's chief administrators in Palestine, wrote in his memoirs that the land wasn't purchased until November 1883. In any case, when the news arrived in Paris, it took everyone by surprise. Historian Ran Aaronsohn surmises that this sudden impact shows us how quickly and unexpectedly the purchase took place. There is a Jewish adage, "*Yeshu'at Hashem ke-heref a'yin*, God's salvation comes as [quickly as] the blink of an eye."

[162] Unbeknownst to Erlanger, Avraham Shlomo Zalman Zuroff came up with the idea almost fifty years earlier. Zuroff is credited with being the first Ashkenazic Jerusalemite to engage in agriculture in modern times. After acquiring a vineyard and a fig orchard near Jerusalem, he was ready for a more ambitious farming project. He wanted to buy some fields outside Aqir and call the settlement Ekron. He sent a memo to Sir Moses Montefiore in 1839, requesting financial assistance for this project, but it never materialized.

[163] Yehuda Ziv, *Rega shel Makom* (Jerusalem: Ẓivonim Press, 2005), p. 211.

[164] Yoel Eliẓur, *Ancient Place Names in the Holy Land* (Jerusalem: Magnes Press, Hebrew University of Jerusalem, 2004), p. 119.

[164A] *Ha-Maggid*, 29 Cheshvan, 5644/November 29, 1883.

Chapter 12

[165] Moshe Stavi (Stavsky), *Ha-Kefar ha-Aravi* (Tel Aviv: Am Oved, 1940), "Entering the Village."

[166] Neiman, p. 34.

[167] Yedida Stillman, *Palestinian Costume and Jewelry* (Albuquerque: University of New Mexico Press, 1979), p. 12.

[168] Shelagh Weir, *Palestinian Costume* (Austin: University of Texas Press in cooperation with British Museum Publications, 1989), p. 48.

[169] Stillman, p. 16.

[170] Arkin, p. 18.

[171] Aaronsohn, *Rothschild*, p. 57.

[172] *Ha-Meliẓ*, 17 Adar 5644/March 14, 1884.

[173] Yavne'elli, book II, p. 242.

[174] In *Ha-Meliz*, 17 Adar 5644/ March 14, 1884, Pines wrote that the wheat they sowed was equivalent to 1,100 pudi. A pud is a Russian weight equivalent to sixteen kilograms (thirty-five pounds).
[175] Based on an estimate of 120-150 dunams per pair of oxen. Aaronsohn, *ha-Baron*, p. 20, note 47.
[176] *Ha-Meliz*, 17 Adar 5644/March 14, 1884.
[177] Ibid.
[178] Arkin, p. 18.

Chapter 13

[179] 14 Elul 5644/September 4, 1884.
[180] Ran Aaronsohn, *Lechu ve-Nelcha* (Jerusalem: Ben-Zvi Press, 2004), p. 121.
[181] Pinchas Ben-Zvi Griyevsky, *Michtavim al Moshavot Erez Yisrael* (Jerusalem: Griyevsky, 5687/1927), vol. 1, p. 7. Another version is that two of the farmers took the building inspector (not the pasha) aside for a drink and discreetly slipped some money into his pocket. The Turk then played Mr. Gullible and expressed "admiration" for their ingenuity. Ultimately, it was the intercession of the Baron and his men with the Turkish authorities that enabled the structures to go up.
[182] Neiman, p. 103.
[183] From a phone conversation with Mazkeret Batya resident and author Achiezer Arkin.
[184] She is the grandmother of Achiezer Arkin, who wrote a book about the Shemittah controversy of 1889.
[185] Aaronsohn, *Rothschild*, p. 179.
[186] Ibid.

Chapter 14

[187] Ornah Tomer, "Beit ha-Kevarot be-Mazkeret Batya." Unpublished research seminar paper, Hebrew University of Jerusalem, 2000, p. 26.
[188] Dagan, p. 105, from an interview with Chaim Maller.
[189] Ibid., p. 108.
[190] Tomer, p. 34. Gellman's ordeal reminds me of the Torah's praise for the Jewish people, who faithfully followed God into "a desolate, *howling* wasteland" (Deuteronomy 32:10). Rashi comments on that verse: "... a place of howling and screaming desert creatures. There too, [the people] were driven by faith, and they didn't say to Moses, 'How can we venture forth into the desert ... ?'"
[191] Tomer, p. 21.
[192] Dov Ariel, *Ha-Moshavah Gedera* (Jerusalem: Ben-Zvi Press, 1979), pp. 47-49.
[193] Simchah Ben Zion, "*Yesod Gedera*," in Le-Noar: Sifriat Erez Yisrael, 2nd edition. (Tel Aviv: Amanut, 5689 - 5701), sec. 19, p. 99.

Chapter 15

194 Dagan, p. 106.

195 Ibid., p. 111.

196 *www.nashbell.com/ver001/welcome/he-zipora.php*. Ẓipporah Maller was one of the few old-timers of Mazkeret Batya who wrote memoirs.

197 Dagan, p. 112.

198 Conversation with Yisrael Arkin, February 25, 2009. This contradicts Tomer, p. 21, who writes that Moshe Maller's daughter's name was Esther and that she married Shlomo Skolnick. Arkin is a Mazkeret Batya old-timer and older brother of Achiezer Arkin, who knows the histories of the village's founding families.

199 Greek for a device used for drawing water from a well: A wheel is turned by an animal walking in a circle, moving a chain of buckets that descend into the well and come up filled with water. The water is then emptied into a trough or canal. *Milon Even-Shoshan* (Tel Aviv: Am Oved/Yediot Acharonot, 2003) s.v. אנטיליה. See also Tosefta, Mikvaot 4:20.

200 Neiman, p. 47.

201 Ibid.

202 Ibid.

203 In those days, they believed in the "bad air" theory – that malaria was carried by microorganisms in the air. While they did see a link between malaria and the swamps, they didn't connect the disease with the mosquitoes that bred there.

204 Avraham Mordechai Levin, father of founder Yechezkel Levin. Arkin, p. 92.

205 Eucalyptus trees were introduced into Palestine by the early settlers for the purpose of draining the swamps. A tree native to Australia and home to the koala bear, the eucalyptus was brought to England in the 1780s. After French colonists in Algeria succeeded in transplanting it there, saplings were brought to Palestine in 1884 and successfully transplanted by Çarl Netter at the Mikveh Israel school. Nili Lifschitz and Gid'on Berger, "Ki ha-Adam Etz ha-Sadeh," *Ariel*, 124-125 (1998), p. 90.

206 On the planting of the eucalyptus trees, see *Chavaẓelet*, 18 Tammuz 5645/July 1 (1885). See also *Chavaẓelet*, 13 Tevet 5646/December 21 (1885), which reports on page one: "Various diseases have infected [Ekron's] residents, and a few people have died."

207 A medical or surgical practitioner without full professional qualifications or status in some east European countries, especially Russia. The word was derived from the German *Feldscher*, which means field shearer and was the term for medieval barber-

surgeons in the army. The barber-surgeon was one of the most common medical practitioners of medieval Europe, generally charged with looking after soldiers during or after a battle. In that era, surgery (and bloodletting) was generally conducted not by physicians, but by surgeon-barbers. The red-and-white-striped poles outside barbershops represented the bloodstained and clean bandages that used to hang in front of surgeon-barbers' shops!

[208] The name Mazia (מזי"א) is an acronym for מזרע ישראל איסורלין, "a descendant of Yisrael Isserlin." Rabbi Isserlin (1390-1460) was a Talmudist and halakhist best known for his work *Terumat ha-Deshen,* which served as one source for *Ha-Mapah,* the glosses of Rabbi Moshe Isserles on the *Shulchan Aruch. Terumat ha-Deshen* is an important source of the practices of Ashkenazic Jews.

[209] Special thanks to Smadar Barak for reviewing the information on Dr. Mazia.

[210] Quinine (extracted from the bark of the South American cinchona tree), the first effective treatment for malaria, debuted in the seventeenth century. It remained the anti-malarial drug of choice until the 1940s, when it was replaced by more advanced medications.

[211] Flies, of course, were a common problem throughout the country. When Mark Twain visited Palestine, as described in his book *The Innocents Abroad* (ch. 45), he observed a girl from a distance. He thought she was wearing shaded glasses, only to discover to his horror that her "glasses" were swarms of flies!

[212] Neiman, p. 103.

[213] Arkin, p. 19.

[214] Neiman, p. 103.

[214A] Neiman, p. 78.

[214B] *Chavazelet,* 26 Iyar 5647/May 20 (1887).

[215] *The duchifat,* normally translated as hoopoe, is listed among the non-kosher birds in Leviticus 11:19. (See Aryeh Kaplan, *The Living Torah* [New York: Maznaim, 1981], p. 319, for other translations of this word.) Nevertheless, on May 29, 2008, it was voted Israel's national bird by tens of thousands of Israeli schoolchildren, soldiers, and diplomats from Israeli embassies and consulates worldwide.

Chapter 16

[216] Mordechai Naor, *Sefer le-Mazkeret: Mazkeret Batya-Ekron – Me'ah ha-Shanim ha-Rishonot* (Jerusalem: Ben-Zvi Press, 2010), p. 112. Naor quotes Professor Shmuel Avitzur, historian, prolific writer, and recipient of the Israel Prize for his lifetime of cultural research:

The farmers of the first moshavot got relief and salvation

> from within. One of the settlers of Ekron, Aharon Zelig Levitta, a master carpenter and very skilled craftsman, developed and created on his own a grain harvester that solved most of [the farmers'] problems. So it was from Ekron – which is Mazkeret Batya – that the grain harvester came to Palestine!

Shmuel Avitzur, "Levitta me-Ekron Boneh Maktzerah me-Etz u-Varzel," *Etmol*, 14 (1977), pp. 9-11.

[216A] Chaim Chissin, *Massa ba-Arez̦ ha-Muvtachat* (Tel Aviv: Ha-Kibbutz ha-Meuchad, 1982), pp. 206-210.

[217] Ibid., p. 210.

[218] Rabbi Moshe Sofer (known by his work *Chatam Sofer*) was born in Frankfurt-am-Main, Germany, in September 1762 (7 Tishrei 5523) and died in Pressburg (now Bratislava) on October 3, 1839 (25 Tishrei 5600).

[219] Ruth 3:2 – "Behold, he [Boaz] is winnowing on the threshing floor of the barley tonight."

[220] *Chiddushei Chatam Sofer*, vol. 1 (Jerusalem: Yerid Ha-Sefarim, 2003), p. 449.

[221] It is clear that this picture was staged. Cows were usually milked in each family's barn. In addition, the subjects are standing too close together, perfectly posed for the photographer. In those days, taking a picture was an event – almost a festive occasion. Most photographers were professionals, as very few people owned cameras. The milk container displayed prominently in the foreground, reinforces the theory that this picture is meant to highlight the advances made by the dairy industry on the moshavah. It looks like this picture was designated for some kind of exhibition or presentation.

[222] 18 Tammuz 5645/July 1 (1885).

[223] Before the families were reunited, the founders employed Arabs from Aqir; and at a much later stage, when their farms expanded, they again resorted to non-Jewish labor.

[223A] See appendix VIII.

[224] Chissin, *Massa*, p. 209.

[225] "Ekron," *Knesset Yisrael* (5646), pp. 986-987. Arkin, pp. 105-106.

[226] He eventually reestablished the company in Israel, where its profile today is comparable to that of Tetley Tea or Nestea in the United States.

[227] Klonymous Ze'ev Wissotzky, *Kevuz̦at Mikhtavim she-Nishlachu le-Anshei Shem be-Inyan Yishuv Erez̦ Yisrael* (Jerusalem: Ben-Zvi Press, 5641), p. 162. Quoted in Arkin, p. 20.

[228] Aneir, pp. 127-130.

Chapter 17

[229] For example, see Brill, p. 35, where he writes that Pavlovkans would not fit in religiously with the people of Rishon Le-Ẓion.

[230] *Ha-Meliẓ* 17 Shvat 5650/February 17, 1890.

[231] Neiman, p. 72.

[232] Also known in Yiddish as *Vachtnacht*. The night before a baby is circumcised, it is customary to gather at his home and recite psalms and prayers. Shmuel Pinchas Gelbard, *Rite & Reason: 1,050 Jewish Customs and Their Sources* (Petach Tikva: Mifal Rashi, 1998), p. 578.

[233] It is customary for firstborn males to fast on the eve of Passover in commemoration of the last of the ten plagues, in which the first-born Egyptians were killed. One may circumvent the fast by attending a *siyum*, even if he has not actually studied the tractate that has just been completed.

[234] Neiman, p. 70.

[235] D. D. "Me-Ereẓ Yisrael: Ha-Yishuv bi-Yehuda bi-Shnot 5658-5659," *Ha-Shiloach* 1899, no. 6, p. 83.
For more on *Ha-Shiloach*, see appendix VI.

[236] *Chavaẓelet*, 28 Elul 5665/September 28 (1905).

[237] "Ekron," *Knesset Yisrael* (5646), p. 986.

[238] Rabbis not pictured: Rabbi Simchah Halevi Bunim Ossowetzky (served in Mazkeret Batya 1884-1888); Rabbi Baruch Chomah (1895-1890); Rabbi Meir Aharon Halevi (1895-1903).

[239] *Shulchan Aruch, Orach Chaim* 128:44.

[240] An astute reader might be wondering how living in the Land of Israel could be less anxiety-producing. In Ekron, for example, the farmers' situation was even more precarious than back in White Russia, because they had to contend with new diseases and face possible physical threats to their lives from their Arab neighbors. Rabbi Yochanan Zweig, dean of the Talmudic University of Florida/Yeshivah ve-Kollel Beis Moshe Chaim in Miami, in a lecture given in 2005 in the Shaarei Chesed neighborhood of Jerusalem, provided an illuminating insight: For many people, happiness is dependent on the tides of fortune and misfortune that are an integral part of the human condition. But people who are fortunate enough to connect to God and sense His closeness are able to feel an inner joy that is not affected by life's vicissitudes. The joy of feeling God's nearness creates an emotional and spiritual stability that does not go away, even when a person hits upon hard times. Perhaps for that reason *Birkat Kohanim* is recited daily only in the Holy Land – for proximity to God's presence facilitates happiness and serenity.

[241] 10 Nisan 5646/April 15, 1886.

[242] Ehud Luz, *Parallels Meet* (Philadelphia: Jewish Publication Society, 1988), p. 67.

Chapter 18

[243] David Green (1886-1973) was born in Plonsk, Poland, where his father was a leader of the Chovevei Ẓion movement. A radical, David joined the Marxist Poalei Ẓion movement while studying at the University of Warsaw. He made *aliyah* in 1906 (and changed his name to Ben-Gurion). He was a founder of the Histadrut, the leader of Mapai, the head of the Jewish Agency, and Israel's first prime minister and defense minister. His strong leadership played a crucial role in the founding of the State of Israel.

[244] Chaim Chissin, *A Palestine Diary, Memoirs of a BILU Pioneer, 1882-1887* (New York: Herzl Press, 1976), pp. 270-271.

[245] Below is a listing of the Baron's trips to Palestine. Due to illness, he did not reach his destination on his fifth trip, but remained in Cairo, where he received Jewish delegations. The second column lists his ports of disembarkation.

April 22, 1887	Jaffa
April 29, 1893	Haifa
January 30, 1899	Tantura
February 15, 1914	Jaffa
March 18, 1924	Cairo
May 10, 1925	Tantura

[246] Aaronsohn, *Rothschild,* pp. 87, 88.

[247] Arkin, pp. 21, 22.

[248] *Ha-Maggid,* 17 Sivan 5647/ June 9, 1887.

[249] 1 Tammuz 5647/ June 23, 1887.

[250] The residents of Ekron felt deeply honored, yet they were reluctant to relinquish the name they had given their settlement. For quite a while, the name Ekron stuck.

[250A] Morton, p. 200.

Chapter 19

[251] Chaim Weizmann, *Trial and Error* (London: H. Hamilton, 1949), p. 67.

[252] Yisrael Klausner, *Mi-Katowice ad Basel* (Ha-Histadrut ha-Ẓionit: Jerusalem, 1965), vol. 2, p. 322. However, Bloch did encourage the building of a nationalist Jewish school in Rishon Le-Ẓion.

[253] By the time Bloch tendered his resignation seven years later, in 1894, he could add a number of accomplishments to his résumé. Under his stewardship, Rishon Le-Ẓion prospered. There was a lot of activity: new housing for the farmers, the building of a synagogue and a winery, the planting of eucalyptus trees, and the introduction of strains of grapevines from India. Eliav, *Aliyah*

Rishonah, vol. 2, p. 409.
[254] Klausner, vol. 2, pp. 322-323.
[255] Chissin, *Massa,* p. 210.
[256] Ibid.
[257] Ibid.
[258] Bessarabia is an area of eastern Europe bounded by the Dniester River on the east and the Prut River on the west. It borders Romania. Once part of the Soviet Union, it is now part of the independent Republic of Moldova.
[259] Aaronsohn, *Rothschild,* p. 104.
[260] Chissin, *Massa,* p. 204.
[261] Ibid., p. 212.
[262] Dagan, pp. 105-106.

Chapter 20

[263] Nisan Aharon Tucazinsky, ed., *Torat Rabbeinu Shmuel Salant* (Jerusalem: N. A. Tucazinsky, 1998), vol. 1, pp. 275-276.
[264] Morton, p. 201.
There were other factors at play, probably more fundamental than Morton's assertion:
Economic waste and ruin:

> If all were to cease for a period of a year, the tremendous sacrifices and the vast sums of money that had been invested in colonization would be wasted ... it would be necessary to start everything anew from the bottom up ... [Druck, p.116]

Proof that Rothschild was wrong about colonizing Palestine:

> And would this not be grist for the mills of those who opposed and ridiculed the colonization work? Would it not justify the argument that the Jews could not rebuild Palestine? Would it not serve as proof to Baron de Hirsch and Veneziani and other philanthropists and leaders that the whole Palestine enterprise was doomed to failure? [Druck, p. 117]

Against the Baron's philosophy of Judaism:

> The Shemittah controversy was not a simple antithesis of secular against religious needs. Edmond was convinced, and so assured by Ẓaddok Kahn, that fidelity to the Torah never demanded that rudiments of life be put in jeopardy. [*Two Rothschilds and the Land of Israel,* p. 100]

Future commitments of economic support:

> Of course the Palestinian militants argued that, since the Baron had the means to support them, it could in no way be asserted that they were in such extremity as to forgo the sabbatical year. That in turn begged the thorny issue of the terms on which such assistance would continue to be provided as a matter of

course. [Schama, *Two Rothschilds*, p. 100]

What kind of Yishuv was now being created?:

Dr. Mordechai Naor pointed out to me that Rothschild was a visionary who envisioned a self-sustaining Jewish community in Palestine (as opposed to the financially dependent Old Yishuv). Rothschild wondered: how could an entire society be self-sustaining if it had to seek financial assistance every seven years? Therefore it is most likely that the search for a *heter* was initiated by Rothschild himself. He did not want to replicate the Old Yishuv that was economically dependent on the Jewish charitable contributions known as the Chalukah. Dr. Naor told me that this was also Rabbi Ẓaddok Kahn's view. Rabbi Kahn had great influence on the Baron and if he had wanted to, could probably have swayed the Baron to have supported the farmers for a year. (Conversation with Dr. Mordechai Naor, January, 2011.)

Personal pride:

The Baron thought it was the height of chutzpah for people who were completely dependent on his largesse and generosity to demand that he support them for not working for a year, even if on religious principles, if there was a halakhic solution that could circumvent that kind of scenario. He also did not want to be taken for some kind of benevolent sucker.

265 *Chavaẓelet*, 1 Iyar 5648/ April 11 (1888).

266 At this point, Rabbi Diskin had not taken a firm stand on the issue. See Mordechai Diskin, *Divrei Mordechai* (Jerusalem: Y. D. Frumkin, 1912). The author was an ultra-Orthodox farmer from Petach Tikva and a relative of Rabbi Diskin.

267 Rabbi Mohilever originally favored the stringency forbidding the *heter*. See Yehuda Appel, *Be-Toch Reishit ha-Techiyah* (Tel Aviv: Gutenberg Press, 5696/1936), p. 285. The more radical *maskilim* in Chovevei Ẓion put pressure on the more moderate *maskil* Shmuel Yosef Fuenn, head of the Chovevei Ẓion chapter in Vilna (who was respected by the organization's rabbinical leaders), who in turn put pressure on Rabbi Mohilever to encourage Rabbi Spektor to come forth with his own *heter*. (See Appel, ch. 21.) The domino effect of the *maskilim* on the organization's rabbis made the mainstream fervently Orthodox wary of joining Chovevei Ẓion.

268 Fruits that have the sanctity of Shemittah, known as Kedushat Shvi'it, cannot be merchandised or taken outside the Land of Israel. For more on Rabbi Trunk's position regarding Shemittah, see: *She'eilot u-Teshuvot Yeshuot Malko*, Yoreh De'ah, siman 55.

269 Yaakov Kosovsky-Shachor, ed., *Iggrot R. Yiẓchak Elchanan* (Bnei

Brak: Y. Kosovsky-Shachor, 2004), vol. 1, letter 115, p. 303. In the case of farmers too poor to hire gentile workers, Rabbi Spektor allowed the *heter* of the three rabbis. The impression of the general public (reinforced by the newspapers) was that Rabbi Spektor had ruled that once the land was under non-Jewish ownership, all forms of work were permitted – even by Jews. The greatest abusers of the *heter* would be Baron Rothschild's administrators.

270 The ruling was the basis of the *Heter Mechirah* implemented by Rabbi Avraham Yiẓchak Hakohen Kook and utilized by the Chief Rabbinate of Israel to this day.

271 The ruling's language and improper dissemination eventually also left it open to widespread abuse. For example, see the letter to the editor defending the farmers who followed the stricter ruling of the Jerusalem Rabbinate in *Ha-Meliẓ*, 22 Tevet 5649/December 26 (1888). Also see the letter of Rabbi Spektor complaining that people were abusing his *heter*: Kosovsky-Shachor, vol. 1, letter 119, p. 308.

272 Such as Shaul Dagan, historian for the Museum of the First Aliyah, in a conversation on October 1, 2007.

273 With a biting tongue, *Chavaẓelet,* 1 Iyar 5648/ April 11 (1888), blasted the Baron's administrators, mockingly associating them with a phrase from Psalms 91:1, "*He who dwells in the hidden place of the Most High*" (referring to God), Whom no one sees but Who is directing everyone below.

> The man *who dwells hidden* in Mikveh Israel [a reference to Shmuel Hirsch] has decided to obtain a *heter* regarding a matter too trivial for a person of his stature to get overly involved in [trying to understand] its details. Truth be told, it is a disgrace for an individual whose Frenchness is greater than his Jewishness, as he has personally testified about himself, to heed the words of a lawgiver [i.e., Moses] who didn't have a trace of Frenchness in him. [The opposition to the *heter* stems from the fact that] by keeping the settlers constantly occupied with their labors, there will be no chance of their catching on to the mischievousness of the administrators, similar to the concept [of Pharaoh in saying about the Israelite slaves,] "Let us greatly increase their workload." … It is not out of love of their people or love for the Yishuv that they sought a *heter,* but out of self-serving love that knows no bounds, and an attitude of subservience to the one *who dwells hidden* in Mikveh Israel, bringing them to a state of total irresponsibility (*hefkerut*) and doing all kinds of sordid things in order to deceive the Baron and convince him that if the settlers observed Shemittah this year the entire Yishuv could not continue to exist, and all his resettlement efforts would be in vain.

[274] Rothschild eventually backed off when Rabbi Spektor's *heter* was widely denounced by many leading rabbis. The Baron gave the farmers the choice of whether or not to work, but those who would not rely on the *heter* would not receive financial assistance that year.

[275] The Shemittah year is calculated according to the Jewish calendar, which begins in the Hebrew month of Tishrei, often corresponding with September.

[276] The issue threatened to tear asunder the fragile coalition between those Orthodox Jews supportive of Chovevei Ẓion and the secular *maskilim* within the movement. Luz, p. 284.

[277] Ibid., p. 74.

[278] Rabbi Guttmacher was born in Borek, in western Poland, in 1796. At the age of nineteen, he entered the yeshivah of Rabbi Akiva Eiger of Posen, where he became a disciple of that famous scholar and studied Kabbalah in addition to traditional Talmudic learning. In 1841, he became the rabbi of Grätz, in the Poznan province of western Poland, where he remained until his death in 1874. During his lifetime, he was known as the *Ẓaddik* of Grätz, and thousands of Jews flocked to him for blessings and advice. Rabbi Guttmacher was also known for his support of Rabbi Ẓvi Hirsch Kalischer and for his extensive collection of funds for institutions in Palestine. Source: YIVO Institute for Jewish Research.

[279] Responsa, *Yoreh De'ah* 114, cited in Kahana, *Sh'nat ha-Sheva* (Jerusalem: Ha-Machon le-Cheiker ha-Chakla'ut al pi ha-Torah, 1985), pp. 124-125. For a more detailed examination of Shemittah observance in Mikveh Israel, see Amihud Y. M. Levin, "She-eilat ha-Shemittah be-Mikveh Yisrael bi-Sh'nat 5635", *Orayta* 9 (1987), pp. 214-225.

[280] It could be credibly argued that it was the ultra-Orthodox Jews of the Old Yishuv who sparked the agricultural revolution of modern Israel. Petach Tikva was established four years before the founding of the Chovevei Ẓion societies in Russia and nineteen years before Herzl convened the First Zionist Congress in Basel, Switzerland. Ironically, when David Green (who later changed his named to David Ben-Gurion), an avowedly secular pioneer, arrived in Palestine in 1920, he found temporary employment as a laborer in Petach Tikva, working for the bearded, pious Jews who lived there – a job that probably saved him from starvation.

[281] Kahana, p. 125.

[282] During the malaria epidemic, the settlers of Petach Tikva did not give up entirely but went on to found the town of Yahud near the Arab village of al-Yahudiyya, about twenty kilometers (12.4

miles) to the south. With the financial help of Baron Edmond de Rothschild, they were able to drain the swamps sufficiently to move back to Petach Tikva in 1883.

[283] Diskin, pp. 16-17.

[284] For more information on the debates regarding the Shemittah of 5642, see *Sefer ha-Yovel li-M'lot Chamishim Shanah li-Yissud Petach Tikva: 5638-5688* (Tel Aviv: Va'adat Sefer ha-Yovel she'al yad Ha-Mo'aẓah ha-Mekomit, 5689), p. 426.

[285] Rabbi Salant sent a letter to *Ha-Levanon* in which he opposed any *heter* for working during Shemittah. *Ha-Levanon, erev Rosh Chodesh Sivan,* 5642/May 18, 1982; cited in Yaakov Chaim Dinkel, *Mi-Shvi'it Tarmav ad Shvi'it Tashsah* (Jerusalem 2001), p. 10.

[286] Letter by A. B. Wolf to Shmuel Yosef Fuenn (chairman of the Chovevei Ẓion branch in Vilna), 14 Shvat 5648 (January 27, 1888) A. Droyanov, ed., *Ketavim le-Toldot Chibbat Ẓion ve-Yishuv Ereẓ Yisrael,* vol. 2 (Odessa: The Committee for the Settlement of Ereẓ Yisrael, 1919-1932), part 2, letter 749, p. 477. It is interesting that Rabbi Moshe Ẓvi Neriah, a supporter of the *Heter Mechirah,* writes that "... the Shemittah questions in Petach Tikva were resolved on their own ... because all the farmers were forced to abandon the land ... and that there were no Jews left to work the land." See Neriah, *Dvar ha-Shemittah* (Jerusalem: ha-Hanhalaha-Arẓit shel Irgun Bnei Akiva be-Ereẓ Yisrael, 5698). This does take into account the testimony of Mordechai Diskin and Rabbi Salant.

[287] For example Moshe Leib Lilienblum wrote to Rabbi Shmuel Fuenn, a year before the Shemittah commenced:

> 26 Tishrei 5648 (October 14, 1887)
>
> Sir! The Sabbatical year, the year of Shemittah, is approaching.... The last Shemittah year, in 5642, scattered the settlers of Petach Tikva in all four directions, and if the rabbis don't make an attempt to find a *heter* for the colonists, then [Shemittah] will be a mortal blow for which there is no cure for the colonists....
> The *gaon* [Rabbi Yiẓchak] Reines of Lida promised me while he was here a few weeks ago that he would try to induce the great rabbis to permit [working] during Shemittah in the upcoming year. But I don't know how urgent this matter is to him. I, for my part, cannot be the one to lobby the rabbis on such a matter, because the involvement of a man like me [who is not religious] will

> create the opposite of the desired effect. The *gaon* Rabbi Shmuel Mohilever told me in Bialystok that he does not want to permit work during the Shemittah year. But I imagine that it is not a prerequisite to [get the *heter*] only from [rabbis] who are trustees [of Chovevei Ẓion]....
>
> Sincerely,
> Moshe Leib Lilienblum

Droyanov, letter 671, p. 328. Later, Lilienblum admitted that malaria, not Shemittah, had ruined Petach Tikva. Appel, p. 304.

288 Menachem Friedman, "Le-Mashma'uto ha-Chevratit shel Pulmus ha-Shemittah (5649-5650)," *Shalem* 1 (1974), p. 456.

289 "A Letter from Jerusalem" to Y. L. Gordon, the editor of *Ha-Meliẓ*. Quoted by Appel, pp. 292-293. Although the author of the letter omitted his name, Menachem Friedman writes that it was probably written by Eliezer Ben-Yehuda. See Friedman, p. 455, note 2.

290 Friedman, p. 456, note 3.

Chapter 21

291 Letter dated October 28, 1888. Droyanov, part 2, letter 853, p. 613.

292 "This religious commandment had many logical reasons in ancient times, based on the societal structure of that period and its laws relating to the land. In modern times, it has no basis and is impossible to fulfill in practice. Of all the ways religion manifests itself by meddling in practical matters, there is none more burdensome for the settler than that of Shemittah. Imagine! A whole year without plowing, seeding, or pruning the vines! To the farmer barely making enough for his sustenance, it is difficult to accumulate enough reserves over a six-year period to enable him not to work during the Sabbatical year, living off what is available." Letter dated October 28, 1888. Droyanov, part 2, letter 853, p. 613.

293 Copies of the actual *heterim* (both Rabbi Spektor's and that of the three rabbis, mentioned in the previous chapter) were not readily available. The farmers had to rely on newspapers, hearsay, and the Baron's administrators, whom they did not trust.

294 Naftali Hertz Halevi was born in Bialystok, Poland. He made *aliyah* in 1884 and was appointed by the leadership of the Old Yishuv as the rabbi of Jaffa. That position made him responsible for the nearby Jewish agricultural settlements as well. Engraved on his tombstone are these words: "He sacrificed himself to ensure that the settlements were established in accordance with the spirit of the Torah." He opposed the *heter*.

295 Ummlebis was an abandoned Arab village purchased by the

settlers of Petach Tikva.

[296] At this point, the only *heter* known to the colonists was that of Rabbi Yaakov Mordechai Hirschensohn, who published it in *Ha-Ẓvi*. It would be another few weeks before Rabbi Spektor's *heter* was publicized.

[297] *Ha-Ẓvi*, 29 Tevet 5648 (January 13, 1888), pp. 2-3.

[298] Klausner, vol. 2, p. 333.

[299] Ibid.

[300] Avraham Menachem Mendel Ussishkin (1863-1941) was a leader of Chovevei Ẓion and the Zionist movement as a whole. In 1923, he was elected president of the Jewish National Fund, which he headed until his death. Jerusalem's Ussishkin Street is named after him.

[301] Klausner, vol. 2, p. 333. Ussishkin's letter to the editor appeared in *Ha-Meliẓ* on 3 Cheshvan 5649/ October 8, 1888.

[302] According to Mordechai Diskin, the majority of the farmers preferred not to rely on Rabbi Spektor's *heter*.

[303] Klausner, vol. 2, p. 334.

[304] Chissin, *Massa*, p. 219.

[305] Rabbi Yaffe, their beloved rabbi from Rozhinoy, arrived on the shores of Palestine two days before Rosh Hashanah. See appendix II.

[306] Klausner, vol. 2, p. 333.

[307] Conversation with Achiezer Arkin.

Chapter 22

[308] On the eve of Sukkot, Bloch left Rishon Le-Ẓion and spent the holiday in Beirut. On Shemini Aẓeret (Thursday, September 27, 1888), he took the train to Jaffa. *Chavaẓelet*, 21 Cheshvan 5649/ October 26 (1888), p. 45.

[309] Chissin, *Massa*, p. 219.

[310] According to Chissin's version of the event, they were all assembled at a town meeting.

[311] Yehoshua Ossowetzky's younger brother worked under Bloch as assistant director of Mazkeret Batya from the end of 1888 until the end of 1889. Aaronsohn, *Rothschild*, p. 128.

[312] *Chavaẓelet*, 21 Cheshvan 5649/October 26 (1888).

[313] Ibid.

[314] Ibid.

[315] Chissin, *Massa*, p. 220.

[316] Ibid.

[317] Emile (Ẓvi) Franck was a high-level administrator, a colony inspector. This was a "national position" in which he was in charge of the regional directors. He shared this high office with Shmuel Hirsch starting in 1887.

[318] Aaronsohn, *Rothschild*, p. 158.
[319] *Chavaẓelet*, 21 Kislev 5649/November 25 (1888).
[320] There was no such position at the time. Either Chissin is misquoting Bloch, or Bloch was mistaken. He meant the greatest rabbis of Russia.
[321] Chissin, *Massa*, p. 220.
[322] Ibid.
[323] It echoed a proclamation made in Jerusalem over 2,500 years ago, in the days of the prophet Isaiah:

> Hearken to the word of the Lord, you who quake [ha-charedim] at His word: Your brethren who hate you, who cast you out, said, "For the sake of my name, the Lord shall be glorified. We will see that you too will rejoice! And they shall be ashamed." (Isaiah 66:5)

In modern times, the term *Chareidim* denotes the fervently Orthodox. And just like today, the ancient verse depicts a struggle between two groups of Jews. (Note: The term *Chareidim* did not come into general use until the 1930s. In the late nineteenth and early twentieth centuries, they were called *adukim*.)

In Isaiah, the ancient opponents of the "*Chareidim*" taunt them, saying: "*We will see that you too rejoice!*" That is, these opponents believe that *they* are the ones who will bring many benefits to *all* segments of society – including the *Chareidim*. The "*Chareidim*" will outwardly rejoice over the benefits they receive. But inwardly, "*they shall be ashamed.*" That is, the "*Chareidim*" will have to admit ashamedly that they were wrong.

But then the Almighty Himself intervenes and responds on the side of the "*Chareidim*:" "*There is a great noise that will come forth from the city [Jerusalem], a call from the palace [the Temple], the voice of the Lord, [signaling that He] will punish His enemies*" (Ibid. 66:6). Who are the "enemies"? In the Biblical text, they are the idol worshippers and their supporters, Jews who mimic and fawn after their gentile neighbors. In the context of the late nineteenth century, the authors of the "*Call from the Palace*" used the term to allude to those who adulate non-Jewish culture and wish to have it adopted by the Jewish masses.

[324] Proverbs 28:21.
[325] *Chavaẓelet*, 21 Cheshvan 5649/October 26 (1888).
[326] Arkin, p. 53.
[327] Ibid., p. 114. He passed away on 27 Tevet 5649 (December 31, 1888).
[328] A play on the name Ekron, whose Hebrew root (עקר) means "uproot".
[329] Droyanov, letter 854, 2 Kislev 5649 (November 6, 1888), p. 615. For additional derogatory remarks about the Jerusalem rabbis, see

Ha-Maggid, 13 Adar I, 5649/February 14, 1889.

[330] Chissin, *Massa*, p. 222.

[331] There was no doctor stationed in Mazkeret Batya, although a doctor would make the rounds of the settlements. Chissin meant that Bloch was forbidding the doctor to ever come back.

[332] Chissin, *Massa*, p. 222.

[333] *Chavaẓelet*, 14 Kislev 5649/November 18 (1888). Cf. Psalms 55:23.

[334] As noted earlier, the pioneers of Pavlovka signed an agreement to go to Palestine on the week of the Torah portion of *Lech Lecha*, in which it is read, "Go ... to the land that I will show you" (Genesis 12:1). They settled in Ekron during the week of the Torah portion of *Va-Yeshev*, in which it is read, "And Jacob settled in the land of ... Canaan" (ibid. 37:1). The day Bloch put up the threatening notice in Rishon Le-Ẓion was November 6, 1888. The Torah reading for that week was *Va-Yeẓei* – "And Jacob left Beer Sheba ..." ibid. 28:10).

[335] Arkin, p. 40.

[336] Rabbi Spektor wrote to Baron Rothschild on 18 Shvat 5648 (January 31, 1888):

> The main motive behind the Baron's drive to establish settlements in the Holy Land is in order to promote the sacredness of the land ....
>
> In my view, it is not worthwhile for the Baron to accept the *heter*. The Baron would be better off through the complete fulfillment of the commandment [of Shemittah], thereby publicly sanctifying the Name of Heaven and the holy Torah.

"Mikhtevei ha-Gaon R' Yiẓchak Elchanan, Av Beit Din de-Kovno, be-Inyan Heter ha-Mechirah," *Orayta 9* (2nd Edition) (Netanya: Ha-Mo'aẓah ha-Datit, 5747), pp. 228-229.

[337] Rabbi Spektor later realized something was going awry in the Holy Land regarding his *heter*. Concerned about its misinterpretation or even outright abuse, he penned a letter dated 25 Nisan 5649 (April 26, 1889) – eight months into the Shemittah year – to Rabbi Yehuda Lubetzky, who headed a congregation of Jews who hailed from Russia and Poland and were currently residing in Paris:

> ... the days of harvesting wheat and grapes are drawing near in the Holy Land, and I have already pointed out in numerous letters that labors forbidden by the Torah may not be performed by Jews during the Sabbatical year but may be performed only by non-Jews. The harvesting of grains and grapes are forbidden by the Torah law.... Therefore, in my name, please inform those responsible

for this matter, so they will be duly informed and not err in this matter, Heaven forbid.
Please make sure to meet with our dear and esteemed activist and friend Michael Erlanger and speak to him about this … so the colony administrators will be informed … *so they won't coerce the colonists to do the harvesting themselves but will have it done by non-Jews* … .
I am sure they will carry out my urgent request … .

Yiẓchak Elchanan
Kovno

Kosovsky-Shachor, vol. 1, letter 119, p. 308. Emphasis added.

338 *Chavaẓelet,* 14 Kislev 5649/November 18 (1888), cited in Arkin, p. 40.

339 Eliyahu Scheid, *Zikhronot al ha-Moshavot ha-Yehudiyot ve'ha-Masa'ot be-Ereẓ-Yisrael u've-Suryah, 1883-1899* (Jerusalem: Ben-Zvi Press, 1983), p. 218.

340 Ibid.

341 *Ha-Ẓefirah,* 11 Adar I, 5649/February 12, 1889.

341A See appendix III – Reliving History: A Letter from Rabbi Mordechai Gimpel Yaffe to His Son-in-Law and Daughter.

Chapter 23

342 *Chavaẓelet,* 26 Tevet, 5649/December 30 (1888).

343 *Chavaẓelet,* 9 Shvat 5649/January 11 (1889).

344 Tidhar, vol. 1, p. 404; Arkin, p. 57.

345 *Ha-Maggid,* 19 Kislev 5650/December 12, 1889.

346 Ecclesiastes 2:14 – "The wise man has eyes in his head …"

347 *Sofer* (Hebrew) = scribe. *Stam* (סת"ם) is an acronym for *sifrei Torah, tefillin, mezuzot.* A *sofer stam,* then, is a scribe authorized to write Torah scrolls, phylacteries and *mezuzot.*

348 *Ha-Maggid,* 24 Nissan, 5649/April 25, 1889.

349 A biblical reference to the meal offering brought by the poor who could not afford animal sacrifices.

350 *Chavaẓelet,* 22 Sivan 5649/June 21 (1889).

351 פקידים ואמרכלים ארץ הקודש באמשטרדם (פקוא"ם) was an organization founded in Amsterdam in 1809 to collect and disburse monies collected from European Jewry on behalf of Jews in Palestine. Its founder was Ẓvi Hirsch Lehren.

352 *Chavaẓelet,* 26 Av 5649/August 23 (1889).

353 Arkin, p. 53.

354 *Chavaẓelet,* 12 Sivan 5649/June 11 (1889). Why the softer touch when it came to Petach Tikva? Arkin attributes it to a fundamental difference in the way the two communities

originated: Rothschild's involvement with Petach Tikva began ten years after its founding, and he did not purchase the land. In contrast, the Baron carried the financial burdens of Mazkeret Batya from its very inception. In the eyes of the Baron's administrators, the moshavah and all therein was his private property. In addition, the residents of Mazkeret Batya acted more aggressively with the Baron's administrators. For example, the farmers refused to hand over their oxen to these officials, as we pointed out earlier, while in Petach Tikva they did return these animals. It should be noted that apparently almost half the farmers of Petach Tikva relied on the *heter*.

355 *Chavaẓelet*, 22 Sivan 5649/June 21 (1889).

356 Chissin, *Massa*, p. 222.

357 What about Erlanger's claim that no one was coerced? It is also peculiar that even though – on the surface – the aim of the sanctions was to force the farmers to work the fields, these orders were issued after the winter and spring wheat planting seasons had already passed!

358 A reference to the Talmud (*Shabbat* 88a), which states that at the time of the giving of the Torah at Mount Sinai, God turned the mountain upside down, suspended it over the heads of the Jews, and said, "If you accept the Torah, fine. But if not, here will be your burial place!"

359 *Ha-Ẓefirah*, 21 Shvat 5649/January 23, 1889.

360 Chissin, *Massa*, p. 222.

361 *Ha-Ẓvi*, 13 Tammuz 5649 (July 12, 1889).

362 Ibid.

363 *Chavaẓelet*, 12 Menachem Av 5649/August 9 (1889).

364 *Der Israelit* was the most influential Orthodox newspaper in Germany at that time.

365 *Chavaẓelet*, 12 Menachem Av 5649/August 9 (1889).

366 *Chavaẓelet*, 26 Menachem Av 5649/August 23 (1889). That a good many people suffered and became quite ill is evident from all accounts, but we may never know if people in Mazkeret Batya actually *died* of hunger. The newspapers generally did not publish the names of such victims, nor do inscriptions on tombstones indicate the cause of death. *Sefer ha-Niftarim* (The Book of the Deceased), written by Avraham Yiẓchak Lefkowitz, is a copy of a handwritten list that was compiled thirty years earlier in Mazkeret Batya's first years. Lefkowitz's list of children who passed away begins with the year 5651(1890-1891). Yet children began arriving at Mazkeret Batya with their parents as early as 5645 (1884); it is hard to believe that no children or infants died during those first, difficult years. Perhaps

Lefkowitz left out some of the names, or the original manuscript from which he copied was missing pages or had illegible information. Another point: The newspapers reported that many sick people were brought to Jerusalem. Whoever died in Jerusalem was buried there (at the Mount of Olives cemetery). It is possible that those Ekronians buried in Jerusalem were not recorded in Mazkeret Batya's burial records. (This information courtesy of Achiezer Arkin.)

367 Rokeach (1854-1915) was a very colorful personality from the Old Yishuv and a resident of Safed. He fought the Chalukah dole system and co-founded the Gei Oni settlement (renamed Rosh Pina). He was a frequent contributor to Yisrael Dov Frumkin's newspaper, *Chavaẓelet*. (Frumkin was his uncle.)

368 I.e., the Ottomans, who monitored the Jewish press.

369 *Chavaẓelet*, 27 Tammuz 5649/July 26 (1889).

370 *Ha-Ẓvi*, 13 Tammuz 5649 (July 12, 1889). The trials and tribulations, the taunts and withering criticism the Mazkeret Batya farmers had to endure did not end when the Shemittah year was over. Their faith was tested again and again. As far as the poor rainfall was concerned, the farmers could have drawn inspiration from their forefather Abraham. He obeyed God's calling to leave his homeland and journey to the land of Canaan, where he was promised blessing, only to encounter a famine there. The Torah states, "And there was a famine in the land, and Abraham descended to Egypt" (Genesis 12:10). Rashi, the classical biblical commentator, writes, "[The famine occurred] in that land [Canaan] alone, to test Abraham if he would question the words of the Holy One Blessed be He, Who had told him to go to the land of Canaan, and now He seemed to be suggesting that he leave it."

The Mazkeret Batya pioneers must have also been familiar with the rabbinic teaching that "It is better to be called a fool one's entire life than to do evil for even one hour before the Lord" (*Kilayim* 5:6). The degradation that the righteous lovingly endure on account of their convictions is considered a great merit for them. (Rabbi Yisrael Meir Hakohen, *Nidchei Yisrael*, ch. 12). A number of explanations have been offered as to why the Torah's promise of blessing for observing Shemittah did not materialize. Among them: It applies only when a majority of farmers fully observe Shemittah when a majority of the Jewish people is living in the Land of Israel; when Shemittah is a biblical requirement and not rabbinic.

Rabbi Avraham Yeshayahu Karelitz also confronted this thorny question. First of all, he writes, the biblical commandment of Shemittah and the promise of blessing are two distinct, independent matters. The latter may be affected by other factors, such as sins committed by the Shemittah observers themselves or by others. Second, the blessing is not a prerequisite for fulfilling the commandment; Shemittah must be observed regardless, even if it entails hardship. Third, the blessing is no excuse for relying on miracles: Shemittah observers must exhaust all natural means of supporting themselves. (However, when no such means are available – such as in wartime – and Shemittah observance would endanger lives [*pikuach nefesh*], one is exempt from this commandment.) See *Chazon Ish al Shevi'it,* 18:4.

371 Diskin, p. 26.

372 *Chavaẓelet,* 21 Adar I, 5649/February 22 (1889).

Chapter 24

373 Arkin, p. 53. Wachs was the rabbi of Kalish until 1884. He was the son-in-law of Rabbi Trunk.

374 *Chavaẓelet,* 29 Adar 5650/March 21 (1890).

375 Regarding the letters of the Jerusalem rabbis to Rabbi Hildesheimer concerning Shemittah and the contribution he made on behalf of the settlers of Mazkeret Batya, see *Moriah* 18, nos. 7-8 (Tammuz 5752), pp. 211-212.

375A The yeshivah was founded in 1875 in the Lithuanian town of Telšiai ("Telshe" in Russian or "Telz" in Yiddish).

376 Amihud Y. M. Levin, "Michtav ha-Gaon R' Eliezer Gordon … al Heter ha-Mechirah bi-Shemittat Tarmat," *Orayta* 9 (5747), p. 244; Arkin, p. 129.

377 Luz, p. 45. Cf. Arkin, p. 128. Rabbi Gordon wrote in July 1889:

> … Before sharing my humble opinion, I would like to relate my personal odyssey regarding the idea of settling Ereẓ Yisrael. For seven years now, I have strongly favored settling the Land of Israel with all my heart, as two previous letters [of mine] written to two of the greatest rabbis of our generation attest. However, to our sorrow and the sorrow of those who fear God, the *maskilim* – the freethinkers of the new generation – have removed the sacred element from this concept, cloaking it in such a manner that the God-fearing cannot be at peace with it. … For this reason, I too withdrew my support for this idea, fulfilling the statement of Rabbi Shimon ha-Amsuni in tractate *Bava Kama* (42b) – just as I am rewarded for my participation, I'm rewarded for withdrawing my participation.

378 Stylistic adaptation of Ecclesiastes 3:7 – "There is a time to remain silent and a time to speak up."

379 Based on Numbers 15:24 which refers to the Sanhedrin, the highest Jewish court in ancient Israel.

[379A] Arkin, p. 119, *www.jnul.huji.ac.il/heb/shmita_01_05.html*

[380] Droyanov, letter 709, 19 Kislev 5648 (December 5, 1889), p. 391.

[381] Rosh Hashanah and Yom Kippur.

[382] ארשת שפתינו, "the utterances of our lips," refers to a High Holy Day prayer. The expression itself comes from Psalms 21:3.

[383] Droyanov, letter 941, 12 Elul 5649 (September 8, 1889), p. 758. Emphasis added.

[384] About half the farmers of Petach Tikva followed the opinion of Rabbi Yaffe, while the remainder relied on the *heter*.

[385] As mentioned earlier, the majority of Russian rabbis opposed the *heter* of Rabbi Spektor. How could Scheid claim something so patently false? Either he was ignorant of the facts, or he assumed that the intended readers of his memoirs would never know.

[386] It wasn't only the Jerusalem rabbis. Even Rabbi Spektor, upon whose *heter* the Baron relied, had suggested that Rothschild support the farmers financially so they wouldn't have to work during Shemittah. In his letter to Erlanger and Kahn on January 31, 1888, Rabbi Spektor wrote, "Therefore it is my view that it is not worth it for the Baron to use the *heter*. The Baron is better off fulfilling the commandment fully, thereby sanctifying the Name of Heaven and the holy Torah in public." (See endnote 336.)

[387] Moshe Leib Lilienblum concurs in his book, *Derech La'avor Golim*. However, as noted above, this statement is inaccurate, for at least half the farmers of Petach Tikva, as well as numerous farmers from other settlements, abstained from working that Shemittah year.

[388] This differs from the testimony of Dr. Chaim Chissin, who wrote that there was a poor harvest that season due to insufficient rain. Chissin, *Massa*, p. 222.

[389] Scheid, Zikhronot, pp. 217-219. Emphasis added. See end of endnote 390.

[390] The Baron made it clear that he had no intention of coercing the Ekronians into working the fields during Shemittah against their religious beliefs. Yet Bloch kept telling them – in the Baron's name – that they had to go back to work. It is doubtful that Bloch would have acted without his superior's knowledge. If the Baron wasn't behind it, under whose authority was Bloch giving his "back to work" orders? Was it coming out of Paris secretly, from Michael Erlanger perhaps? Yet only three weeks after the Baron's letter to Rabbi Kahn, Erlanger informed Leon Pinsker that there would be no coercion of the Shemittah observers. (p. 270; endnote 291.) If not from Paris, was the pressure coming from Elie Scheid in Beirut, or from Shmuel Hirsch in Mikveh Israel? And what could their motives have been? Was Eliezer Rokeach (one of the

contributors to *Chavaẓelet*) on the mark when he said that the administrators, afraid that the colonists would get wind of their indiscretions, wanted to keep them preoccupied?
Another plausible explanation was that the administrators, concerned about the Baron's goal that the settlements become self-sufficient as quickly as possible, may have been worried that the financial losses and setbacks caused by Shemittah observance. Finally, the administrators wanted the colonists to be subservient to the Baron at all costs. (p. 261)

[391] Druck, pp. 123-126 (emphasis is added). This letter can also be found in the original German in Droyanov, p. 778.

[392] Droyanov, p. 779, July 18, 1889, footnote.

[393] He made *aliyah* in 1920. From 1923-1943 he was the principal of the Hebrew Gymnasia high school in Rechavia, Jerusalem.)

[394] Droyanov, p. 779, footnote.

[395] This letter was later publicized by Dr. Yosef Mohilever in the Hebrew newspaper *Ha-Areẓ*.
According to writer Isaac Naiditch (who interviewed Rothschild over a period of fifteen years), the Baron's interest in Jewish colonization began before Rabbi Mohilever's visit. And Rothschild's primary motivation was to stem assimilation:

> "You understand," he said, "everybody makes the mistake of assuming that I joined the Palestine effort because I happened to see a couple of Jews from Russia. The truth is that I arrived at the idea much earlier, when I observed the rapid strides of assimilation among the Jews of France, especially the mixed marriages. I saw great families, once the strongholds of Judaism, become estranged from us. Their children and their children's children leave the fold and Judaism, for which we fought for thousands of years in our history, is disintegrating. I came to the conclusion that we must find a country where Judaism could develop further in the spirit of our great prophets. And I realized that the only place was Palestine, where every plot of ground, every strip of soil, is saturated with the memories of the great eternal works of our prophets."

Isaac Naiditch, *Edmond de Rothschild* (Washington, D.C.: Zionist Organization of America, 1945), pp. 22, 23.

Chapter 25

[396] Tidhar, vol. 4, p. 406.

[397] Chissin, *Massa*, p. 223.

[398] Ibid.

[399] Droyanov, letter 911, 17 Tammuz 5649 (July 16, 1889), p. 714.

[400] Cited in Arkin, pp. 74-75.

[401] Based on the Jewish Publication Society translation of *lechem ha-kelokeil* – לחם הקלוקל (Numbers 21:5), i.e., insubstantial food.
[402] Droyanov, letter 964, 24 Elul, 5649 (September 20, 1889) p. 791.
[403] *Ha-Maggid,* 4 Av 5649/August 1, 1889, p. 238. Cited in Arkin, p.77.
[404] *Ha-Meliẓ,* 11 Sivan 5649/June 10, 1889. Arkin, p. 77.
[405] Diskin, addendum, p. 64.
[406] Droyanov, letter 945, 14 Elul 5649 (September 10, 1889), p. 761.
[407] Ibid. Echoing the words of Pharaoh (Exodus 5:4).
[408] Quoted in Arkin, p. 78.
[409] *Ha-Meliẓ,* 17 Shvat 5650/February 7, 1890.

Chapter 26

[410] *Ha-Ẓvi,* 27 Tammuz 5649 (July 26, 1889) cited in Arkin, p. 80.
[411] *Ha-Maggid,* 19 Kislev 5650/December 12, 1889, pp. 381-382.
[412] Ibid.
[413] Ibid.
[414] A biblical reference: "Do not harden your heart as [in] Meribah, as [on] the day of Massah in the desert" (Psalms 95:8). Meribah was one of the places in the desert where the ancient Israelites exhibited stubbornness. See Exodus 17.
[415] A paraphrase of the verse "He saw a resting place, that it was good, and the land, that it was pleasant, and he bent his shoulder to bear [burdens], and he became an indentured laborer" (Genesis 49:15) – a reference to Issachar. Perhaps Rabbi Salant was hinting by the last words of the verse that it was better for them to be under the thumb of the Baron than to be destitute in Jerusalem.
[416] *Ha-Maggid,* 19 Kislev 5650/December 12, 1889; cited in Arkin, pp. 82-83. This refutes the accusations made by Eliezer Ben-Yehuda and others from Chovevei Ẓion that Rabbi Salant hated the pioneers of the New Yishuv because they were a threat to the Chalukah system.
[417] According to *Chavaẓelet,* 29 Adar 5650/March 21 (1890), the committee distributed 60,962 rubles to the "Ekronim." See Arkin, p. 116.
[418] Rabbi Shaul Chaim Halevi Horowitz (1828-1916) was the rabbi of Dubrovna (White Russia) before he made *aliyah* to Jerusalem in 1883, where he studied under Rabbi Yehoshua Leib Diskin. Rabbi Horowitz was appointed rabbi of the Me'ah She'arim community and founded a Talmud Torah there. He fought any reforms in Jewish education. See Yechiel Michel Stern, *Gedolei ha-Dorot* (Jerusalem: Mechon Minchat Yisrael, 1996) vol. III, p. 944.
[419] Rabbi Shlomo Zalman Baharan (1835-1910) was the driving spirit behind the construction of the Me'ah She'arim neighborhood of Jerusalem. He was also involved in establishing the Beit Yisrael and Beit Yaakov neighborhoods and the Shaare

Zedek hospital.

[420] Rabbi Yosef Chaim Sonnenfeld (1849-1932), a member of the Va'ad ha-Shemittah, was about 40 years old at the time and a rising star within the leadership of the Old Yishuv. Originally from Slovakia, Rabbi Sonnenfeld came to Palestine in 1873 at the age of 24. He became an admirer and disciple of Rabbi Yehoshua Leib Diskin. A great scholar and a man of great piety and humility, Rabbi Sonnenfeld was a fighter who would eventually head the separatist Edah ha-Chareidis and the Old Yishuv community which refused to recognize the Chief Rabbinate, established by the Zionist movement. He also refused to join any umbrella organization with the Zionists. Rabbi Sonnenfeld's opponent was the famous first chief rabbi of modern Palestine, Rabbi Avraham Yiẓchak Hakohen Kook.

[421] *Ha-Maggid*, 19 Kislev 5650/December 12, 1889.

[422] Ibid.

[423] Central Zionist Archives, file A9/72. See also *Chavaẓelet*, 18 Tevet 5650 / January 10 (1890), cited in Arkin, p. 84.

[424] *Ha-Maggid*, 9 Shvat, 5650/January 30, 1890.

[425] Gershon Grah, *Ha-Nadiv Ha-Lo Ya'dua* (Tel Aviv: Modan, 5646), p. 56.

[426] Arkin, p. 140.

Chapter 27

[427] Chissin, *Massa*, pp. 224-226.

[428] Ibid., pp. 226-228.

[428A] Klausner, vol. 3, p. 267.

[429] Chissin, *Massa*, pp. 227-228.

[430] Ibid., cited in Achiezer Arkin, "The Fight Regarding the Orchards in 1893" (unpublished paper).

[431] *Ha-Meliẓ*, 28 Shvat 5653/February 14, 1893.

Chapter 28

[432] Achiezer Arkin graciously provided me with a photocopy of the Central Zionist Archives (CZA) file containing the court transcripts, but the file number he recorded is inaccurate, and the CZA has not found the correct one.

[433] Ibid. In this chapter, all quotations of the trial transcripts are from this source unless noted otherwise.

[434] *Ha-Meliẓ*, 28 Shvat 5653/February 14, 1893.

[435] The implication is that the farmers had hired Arab workers to do certain labors that Bloch wanted them to do themselves. This seems at odds with the directive of the Jerusalem rabbis, who forbade any work during Shemittah, even by non-Jews, except for activities that preserved the trees.

[436] *Ha-Meliẓ*, 28 Shvat 5653/February 14, 1893.

[437] Central Zionist Archives, file no. J15/7128.

[437A] See also Yechiel Michel Pines, "Teshuvah li-She'eilah," republished in Eliav, *Aliyah Rishonah,* vol. 2, p. 265. Klausner, vol. 2, p. 268, adds that the rabbis also required that the administration offer the expellees compensation.

[438] I do not know why the Ottomans objected to the planting.

[439] See page 366.

[440] Asher Hirsch Ginsberg, ed., *Kol Kitvei Achad Ha-Am* (Tel Aviv: Dvir, 1954), p. 216, note 1.

[441] Eliav, *Aliyah Rishonah,* vol. 2, p. 267.

[442] Arkin, *Orchards,* p. 5, note 10.

[443] Klausner, vol. 2, p. 268. All sources in this chapter have been taken from Arkin, *Orchards*.

[444] Eliav, *Aliyah Rishonah,* vol. 2, p. 266.

[445] A. Droyanov, ed., "Aseret Michtavim me'eit A. Bloch le-Gross Mishneihu," *Mi-Yamim Rishonim,* vol. 1 (June 1934 – June 1935) p. 11. Emphasis added.

[445A] Mordechai Naor, *Sefer le-Mazkeret: Mazkeret Batya-Ekron – Me'ah ha-Shanim ha-Rishonot* (Jerusalem : Ben-Zvi Press, 2010), p. 85.

[446] According to Klausner, the colonists, disgusted with Bloch, wanted to vent all their frustrations on his lieutenant Avraham Brill (the local administrator), so they threw a dead dog into Brill's house. This action resulted in some collateral damage as well. Klausner, pp. 268-269. Mordechai Naor does not mention this incident in his book *Sefer le-Mazkeret,* and he told me he never heard of it.

[447] Chissin, *Massa,* pp. 230-231.

[447A] All brackets contain details from Naor's book that either are missing from Chissin's account or contradict it. I've inserted them because Dr. Naor used more than one source to flesh out this story.

[448] Chissin, *Massa,* pp. 230-231.

[448A] Naor, p. 86.

Chapter 29

[449] Ginsberg, pp. 215-216.

[450] Based on I Kings 5:5 – "And Judah and Israel dwelt securely, every man under his vine and under his fig tree, from Dan to Beer Sheba, all the days of Solomon."

[451] Levin, *Eileh Mas'ei,* p. 16, note 8.

[452] Moshe Rinot, "Tahalichei Chillun ba-Chinuch ba-Moshavah, 1882-1914", in *Ha-Chinuch ke-Mifgash,* edited by Adir Cohen (Haifa: University of Haifa, 5743/1983), pp. 149-156.

[453] Ibid., pp. 153-154.

[454] Neiman, p. 65.

[455] Ibid., p. 57. Neiman hated the *cheder*. He lasted only one day there.

[456] The author's grandfather, a staunch Belzer Chassid, could

not prevent his sons from affiliating with the secular Zionist and Communist organizations. But that didn't stop him from intervening when a red line was crossed. He once created quite a scene when he suddenly appeared on a soccer field in his Sabbath attire, which included a *kapote* and *shtreimel,* and yanked one of his sons from the soccer match by his ear.

[457] I heard this from Daphna Shimshoni, the director of the Eran Shamir Village Museum, Mazkeret Batya. It is much like what the secular Zionists did to the immigrants from North Africa in the 1950s.

[458] Rabbi Halevi (1847-1914) was the author of the historical work *Dorot ha-Rishonim* and a founder and leader of Agudath Israel.

[459] R. Avraham Yiẓchak Hakohen Kook, *Iggrot ha-Re'ayah* (Jerusalem: Mossad Harav Kook, 1962) vol. 1, II Adar, 5668, quoted in Rinot, p. 154.

[460] Levin, *Eileh Mas'ei,* p. 63, note 16; Rinot, p. 153.

[461] *Chavaẓelet,* 10 Cheshvan 5669/November 4 (1908).

[462] *Chavaẓelet,* 4 Tevet 5669/December 28 (1908).

[463] Rinot, p. 153.

[464] Certain currents within secular Zionism continued the assault on religion that had been initiated by the radical *maskilim.* Yaakov Weinrot, one of Israel's leading attorneys, who served as one of the Orthodox representatives on the Tal Commission, minced no words in articulating this view of Zionism. "Zionism was never content with gaining national independence," he writes in his addendum to the commission's report. "The mainstream expressed a desire to create a new culture, a new identity, of which a central tenet was the need to wipe out Orthodoxy as a precondition to opening new vistas." *Report of the Commission for Making a Suitable Arrangement Regarding the Enlistment of Yeshivah Students* (Hebrew), April 2000, appendix 3, p. 118.

[465] It would take seventy years for the pendulum to swing in the opposite direction, following the social and religious upheavals wrought by the Six-Day and Yom Kippur wars. The popular Israeli singer/songwriter Arik Einstein composed the song "Hu Chazar bi-Teshuvah" ("He Returned to the Faith"), lamenting the "loss" of his colleague Uri Zohar to Orthodox Judaism. As part of the "*teshuvah* phenomenon," many members of the Israeli secular elite became Orthodox. Ironically, even Einstein's wife, Alona, and their two daughters became religious.

[466] Chaim Nachman Bialik, "Le'vadi," in *Kol Shirei Bialik* (Tel Aviv: Dvir, 1953), vol. 2, p. 141. Bialik, too, eventually succumbed to the "Enlightenment."

Chapter 30

[467] Elizabeth Antébi, author of *Edmond de Rothschild: The Man Who Redeemed the Holy Land* (French), quoting the historian David Landes, professor emeritus of economics at Harvard University. See Antébi's website, *www.antebiel.com/EN/books/rothchild.html.*

[468] Schama, *Two Rothschilds,* p. 318.

Rothschild's gall. Former French president Charles de Gaulle questioned Edmond de Rothschild's Frenchness because of his desire to be buried in the Holy Land, not in France.

[468A] **Burial in a Foreign Land: Pharaoh and de Gaulle**

The late Rabbi Yosef Dov Soloveitchik, dean of the Rabbi Isaac Elchanan Theological Seminary (RIETS), likened Edmond de Rothschild's desire to be buried in the Holy Land to that of the Patriarch Jacob.

Rabbi Soloveitchik infers that Pharaoh was upset and embarrassed by Jacob's request. As Pharaoh tells Joseph, "Go up and bury your father *as he adjured you*" (Genesis 50:6). That is, if there hadn't been an oath, Pharaoh wouldn't have let him go. Likewise, in 1954, when the bodies of Edmond de Rothschild and his wife were transferred from France to Israel, former French president Charles de Gaulle reportedly told Rothschild's cousin James-Henri de Rothschild, "I'll tell you frankly, I don't understand you Jews. I always thought the Rothschilds were devoted and loyal to France and were real Frenchmen, differing only in religion. But tell me, who is a good Frenchman? One who is brought up in French schools,[1] fights for France,[2] contributes to French culture,[3] and is buried in French soil. I cannot imagine a good Frenchman whose body is transferred elsewhere. I could have forbidden [the transfer]. All I had to do was to call the magistrate of Paris and tell him not to grant the permission. But I didn't want to start a fight with the Jewish community."[4]

1. Rothschild attended Condorcet High School, where the French bourgeois sent their children.

2. Rothschild was a soldier in the reserves ("Garde Mobile") in the first Franco-Prussian War.

3. Rothschild served as a member of the French Academy of Fine Arts and bequeathed to the Louvre more than 40,000 engravings and more than 100 drawings by Rembrandt.

4. See David Holzer, T*he Rav Thinking Aloud: On the Parsha – Sefer Bereishis* (Miami Beach: D. Holzer, 2010), pp. 450-452.

[469] In 1899, Baron Rothschild transferred title of his colonies in Palestine to the Jewish Colonization Association (יק"א). In 1924, it was reorganized as the Palestine Jewish Colonization Association

(PICA) and placed under the direction of the Baron's son, James Armand de Rothschild. The property where Ramat Ha-Nadiv was to be built was already part of the lands acquired by PICA.

470 Why did it take twenty years from the Baron's death until his reinterment in the Holy Land? The work was interrupted by the Arab Riots of 1936-1939, World War II (1939-1945), and Israel's War of Independence (1948-1949).

471 Schama, *Two Rothschilds* p. 321.

472 The Rothschild family estate continued to contribute to the building of Israel, including eighteen million Israeli lira for the construction of the Knesset, completed in 1966.

473 Schama, *Two Rothschilds,* p. 323.

474 Pines, *Hesped Mar* p. 21. Yisrael Shurin, *Morei ha-Umah* (New York/Efrat: Torah Umesorah, 1979), vol. 4.

475 *Ha-Ẓofeh,* 25 Kislev 5751/December 12, 1990.

475A Yechiel Michel Tucazinsky, *Sefer ha-Shemittah* (Jerusalem: Mossad Harav Kook, 5766), p. 60.

476 Rabbi Salant opposed the *heter* on halakhic grounds. Note these excerpts from his response to Rabbi Yiẓchak Elchanan Spektor's letter proposing his *Heter Mechirah:*

> 20 Tevet 5648
> Jerusalem
>
> To the Luminary of the Diaspora,
> Rabbi Yiẓchak Elchanan:
>
> I have received your letter dated 22 Kislev regarding what guidelines the colonists should follow in their vineyards in the upcoming [Shemittah] year....
> Your letter mentioned only vineyards but nothing about fields of grain, which is what most of the colonists have (except in Rishon Le-Ẓion, a colony that has planted only grapevines, because the soil there is not suitable for growing wheat).
> You wrote about selling [the land] to a non-Jew for two years. Apparently you opine that selling land for a fixed period does not violate the prohibition of giving non-Jews possession of land [in the Land of Israel] [*lo te'chanem* – see Deuteronomy 7:2]. Undoubtedly, you explain your position in your booklet. But in my humble opinion, at first glance, it does not make sense. If selling land for a fixed, i.e., limited time constitutes a real sale, then we must be concerned about the well-known prohibition of selling lands [to gentiles] in the Land of Israel. And if it is not considered an absolute sale, we must call it "leasing" – and with leasing, the land itself is not considered

> acquired [by the gentile], and the field is still considered belonging to the Jew.
> … I am also unclear about your opinion [regarding who may work the fields after they are sold]. Did you mean that the gentiles who purchased the fields for a two-year period would be the ones to work them during Shemittah, or did you mean the sale would be similar to that of *chametz*?
> Now it is known here that any land sale not conducted properly, through the government legal system, is meaningless. And selling land to non-Jews through the proper legal channels is impossible at this time. The Baron himself would not want it to be done in this manner. And how can the colonists [themselves] sell land that is not registered in their names? For it is understood that most of the colonies were titled in the government records under Mr. Erlanger of Paris.…
>
> Shmuel Salant

Source: *Torat Rabbeinu Shmuel Salant*, pp. 274-276.

In other matters, Rabbi Salant tended to state his opinion but not contend publicly with those who disagreed. So why did he come out *publicly* against the *heter*?

Some clues regarding Rabbi Salant's decision to go public can be found in Friedman's article in *Shalem* which makes some very salient points regarding the Shemittah controversy of 1889:

For the *heter*. Rabbi Alexander Moshe Lapidot

When Rabbi Alexander Moshe Lapidot (for biographical information, see Stern, vol. 3, p. 883) proposed (prior to the Shemittah of 5642/1881-1882) that the rabbis should explore means of exempting the farmers of the moshavot from "the mizvot tied to the land," Rabbi Salant argued that "because of the non-observance [of these commandments] we were exiled from our land" (Friedman, p. 461, note 23).

"Paradoxically, the assessment of the rabbis of the Old Yishuv and that of the nationalist *maskilim* was the same – the issue was not the survival of the moshavot in the Shemittah of 5649, but what would be the character of the country during the upcoming Shemittot: that is, whether the commandment of Shemittah would be observed in the Land of Israel with all the ideological and economic implications – or not" (ibid., p. 466).

Rabbi Salant claimed that if Shemittah was circumvented, "the entire *Shulchan Aruch* will be trampled upon by the colonists." See Droyanov, *Ketavim*, vol. 2, pp. 477-478.

Dr. Chaim Chissin, the BILU pioneer, wrote that the Jerusalem

Rabbinate would have been content to remain silent regarding Rabbi Spektor's *Heter Mechirah* and not intervene, were it not for the raucous activity of Eliezer Ben-Yehuda on behalf of the *heter*. Ben-Yehuda forced these rabbis into taking an uncompromising position. See Chissin, *Memoirs*, p. 466.

477 Y. L. Fishman, "Toldot ha-Rav," *Kovetz Torani-Mada'i* (5697-5698/1937), p. 12, accessed at *www.hebrewbooks.org/22885*.

478 Ibid.

478A Stern, vol. 2, p. 792.

478B Rabbi Ẓvi Yehuda Kook, son of the late chief rabbi Avraham Yiẓchak Hakohen Kook, claimed he was told by Rabbi Yaakov Moshe Charlop that one of the attendees at Rabbi Yaffe's funeral was none other than Rabbi Yehoshua Leib Diskin (then seventy-five years old), who stood for three hours listening to the eulogies. This anecdote appeared in *Ha-Ẓofeh*, 24 Cheshvan 5722/November 3, 1961.

Rabbi Ẓvi Yehuda wrote an article for *Ha-Ẓofeh* about the life of Rabbi Yaffe on the occasion of the seventieth anniversary of his death. Rabbi Ẓvi Yehuda's interest in Rabbi Yaffe stems from family ties. Rabbi Yaffe was the brother of Frieda Batya, who was the mother of Rabbi A. Y. Kook's father, Shlomo Zalman. Thus Rabbi Yaffe was the great-uncle of Rabbi Kook. The article was republished in the book *Li-Netivot Yisrael* (Beit El: Me-Avnei ha-Makom Publications, 5767), vol. 2, p. 33.

If you are planning to visit Petach Tikva, I recommend making a stop at the grave of Rabbi Yaffe in the Segulah cemetery, section 1, row 18, no. 33.

479 Dagan, p. 102.

480 Conversation with Achiezer Arkin, February 21, 2010.

480A "M'at Historia," *Bustenai*, March 14, 1934 (no. 47), p. 17.

481 Tomer, p. 21.

481A "M'at Historia," *Bustenai*, March 14, 1934 (no. 47), p. 17.

482 Tidhar, vol. 1, p. 406.

482A D. D. "Me-Ereẓ Yisrael: Ha-Yishuv bi-Yehuda (Ekron)," *Ha-Shiloach*, Cheshvan-Adar II 5657, vol. 1, p. 355. Also quoted in Naor, p. 122.

Chapter 31

483 Born on July 18, 1929, Eliezer Moshe Arkin was the oldest son of Miriam and Zalman Mendel Arkin. He was fourth-generation Mazkeret Batya and had the blood of a true farmer. In 1942, Eliezer went to study at Mikveh Israel – where his great-grandfather Ẓvi Arkin, one of the founders of Ekron/Mazkeret Batya, had completed his agricultural training in 1883.

Even before graduating, Eliezer joined the Palmach (a Jewish underground army) in 1946 at the age of 17. A few months later, he parted with his friends from the Hachsharat Yiftach training program in Kibbutz Gevat to take part in a squad command course. He completed the course and was cited as an exemplary soldier and battlefield warrior.

In the summer of 1947, the *Exodus* made its way toward Palestine with 4,515 Holocaust survivors seeking escape from the horrors of Europe. Against international law, British forces stopped the ship before it entered Palestine's territorial waters and gained control using tear gas, clubs, and live ammunition. The Jews defended themselves and fought back: three Jews were killed, and another thirty were wounded. The would-be Jewish immigrants were transferred to three ships and forced to return to Europe.

Infuriated by the *Exodus* tragedy, the Palmach decided to retaliate by blowing up the British radar station on Mount Carmel that identified incoming immigrant ships. Eliezer Arkin was one of twelve fighters selected to take part in this operation on the morning of July 21, 1947. The volunteers managed to penetrate the British camp and partially destroy the main facility, but they soon met with heavy fire. Eliezer was severely wounded. Forced to retreat, his friends wanted to evacuate him from the battlefield, but Eliezer insisted that they leave him there. He knew that carrying him would slow them down and result in more casualties. He asked that they take his gun, lest it fall into the hands of the British soldiers.

Eliezer languished alone through the night. The British troops, afraid of mines, waited until morning to enter the area. At daybreak, they ascended Mount Carmel and found Eliezer in critical condition. He was taken to the hospital in Haifa, but instead of providing proper medical attention for massive injuries and blood loss, the British interrogated him about Palmach plans and operations. Despite his pain and suffering, he divulged no information. During the brutal military interrogation, Eliezer died. He was 18 years old. The next day in Mazkeret Batya, thousands of mourners attended his funeral.

484 *Chavaẓelet*, 21 Tevet 5670/January 2 (1910), pp. 1-2.

In a conversation on September 2, 2010, Rabbi Simchah Hakohen Kook (Chief Rabbi of Rehovot and nephew of Rabbi Avraham Yiẓchak Hakohen Kook), told me his uncle had been very supportive of the three Mazkeret Batya farmers who did not want to rely on his *heter* in the Shemittah of 5670 (1909/1910). He also didn't consider his *heter* the best option for the farmers, viewing it only as a last resort. When I asked why so many people think his uncle preferred that all the farmers rely on the *heter* and not be stringent about Shemittah, he replied, "There will always be people who will distort what my uncle said."

He also told me that his uncle wrote to the administrators of the moshavot (then under the Jewish Colonization Association – יק"א) that under extenuating circumstances the farmers could be lenient with regard to some rabbinic restrictions. But if the administrators were going to *coerce* the farmers into relying on his *heter*, then Rabbi Kook would allow no leniencies whatsoever.

See Kook, vol. 1, letters 237, 254, 255).

485 Moshe Michael Ẓuran, "Ha-Sadeh Mushbetet – Ha-Lev Oved," *Hamodia*, 27 Kislev, 5768, Shabbat Supplement, p. 22.

485A Ibid., p. 26.

Appendix II

486 Yaffa Eliach, *There Once Was a World* (Boston: Little, Brown, 1998), p. 257.

487 Adina Ofek writes:

> Since the formal age for enlistment in the Russian army was 18, boys younger than 18 (many even younger than 12) still "eligible" for the draft, were placed in special training and education establishments called Cantonist Battalions. Once they reached the standard draft age of 18, they were formally enlisted in the regular military, and only then would they begin their required twenty-five years of service. According to various records, approximately 50,000 [Jewish] children – many of them as young as eight, nine, and ten years old – were conscripted between the years 1827 and 1854. Nicholas I, zealous in achieving his goals, set out to baptize the Cantonists and make them into "good Russians" before they reached the formal age of enlistment.

Ofek, "Cantonists: Jewish Children as Soldiers in Tsar Nicholas's Army," *Modern Judaism* 13 (1993), p. 277.

488 This was a reversal of the general rule whereby Jews were driven from farms so as not to compete with the gentile farmers.

489 He abdicated the throne, allowing the ascension of his younger brother.

490 This colony was the birthplace of Yiẓchak Lazernitzki, who later changed his family name to Shamir. He became chairman of the Knesset in 1977 and Israel's foreign minister in 1980 before succeeding Menachem Begin as prime minister in 1983.

491 See appendix VIII: Early Hebrew Newspapers, Periodicals and Journals at a Glance.

492 *Ha-Meliẓ*, 16 Tevet 5622/December 19, 1861, p. 158.
The title bespeaks the fact that Jewish farmers were a cultural oddity. See note 22.

Yosef Staravolsky was a member of Chovevei Ẓion from the city of Slonim, near Pavlovka. Although he writes in the first person, he was not one of the farmers. Brill, p. 238, note on p. 18.

493 From Isaiah 44:5 – "This one shall say, 'I am the Lord's,' and this one shall call himself by the name Jacob, and this one shall write [with] his hand, 'To the Lord,' and be called the name Israel."

494 Sapieha was a Polish-Lithuanian noble family. Between the sixteenth and nineteenth centuries Rozhinoy was the main seat of the senior line of this family. They built a magnificent palace there, and owned large estates adjacent to the town.

494A A euphemism. The family was coerced.

495 The November Uprising (1830-1831) – also known as the Cadet Revolution – was an armed rebellion against the Russian Empire in Poland, Lithuania, Belarus, and the Ukraine. Some 70,000 Polish troops were defeated by 180,000 Russian soldiers in a series of battles that included the capture of Warsaw. The estate designated by the czar for the purpose of Jewish agricultural development was previously owned by the Sapieha family who were on the losing side of the revolution.

495A In an article by Yosef Staravolsky entitled "The Founding of Pavlova and Konstantinova," in Sokolowsky, *Rózhinoy: Sefer Zikaron*, p. 51, we read:

> At first, we had bad years, for our land did not yield its produce, and the expenses were great. If not for the Pines woolen-garment factory in Rozhinoy, we would have starved.

According to this account, the Pavlovkans did have an alternate source of income.

However, *Sefer Zikaron* cites the source of the Staravolsky article as "*Ha-Meliẓ*, 1887 (no. 242)" – twenty-six years after his dispatches about Pavlovka first appeared in that newspaper. Furthermore, the article does not appear in the issue cited. So the question of alternate income remains open.

496 A paraphrase of Psalms 55:23.

497 Lamentations 3:41.

498 Deuteronomy 26:15.

499 Deuteronomy 26:7; Haggadah.

500 Psalms 90:17.

501 I Samuel, 16:7 – "And the Lord said to Samuel, 'Look not upon his appearance, or the height of his stature, for I have rejected him, for it is not as man sees, for a man sees through the eyes, while the Lord sees into the heart.'"

502 Genesis 49:15.

503 Deuteronomy 12:20.

504 See Isaiah 58:11.

[505] Based on Jeremiah 29:7 – "And seek the peace of the city where I have exiled you, and pray for it to the Lord, for in its peace you shall have peace."

[506] *Ha-Meliẓ*, 1 Shvat 5622/January 2, 1862, p. 188.

Appendix III

[507] The letter appeared in print in: Reichman, Raphael. "Siftei Yesheinim: Shnei Michtavim Mikhtav Yad ha-Gaon ha-Gadol Mordechai Gimpel." *Otzrot Yerushalayim* 130 (5733), ch. 168.

Appendix V

[508] United States Holocaust Memorial Museum website, *www.ushmm.org.*

[509] Ibid. Another version has it that they were forced to march to Volkovysk. The elites were murdered in the Volkovysk ghetto while the rest were shipped by train to Treblinka. Naor, p. 330.

[510] Today the location of the Israeli city of Ashdod.

[511] A very big assumption made by Tsur Shezaf; may be unfounded but certainly adds spice to his story.

[512] A kibbutz in the western Galilee.

[513] A poet, writer, and stage director who lived in Tel Aviv, 1943-1999. Unlike Arkin, he would not have been aware of the events unfolding in Aqir, as he was only four years old at the time. Like all young commentators, he had to rely on what he was told about historic events to which he was not witness.

[514] Tsur Shezaf, "Adnan al Ghoul," *www.shezaf.net.*

[515] I interviewed him on January 2, 2008.

Appendix VII

[516] A large percentage of the dunams in the north (as opposed to the central and southern regions) are orchards. Keren Ha-Shvi'it subsidizes only those orchards whose owners declare the fruits *hefker* – observing Shemittah in its fullest sense. Orchards that operate under the halakhic leniency of *oẓar beit din* (where the fruits are sold under the auspices of a rabbinic court, and consumers are charged only for labor costs) do not qualify for funding.

There is a big difference between farmers who grow plants used for fodder, which are low-cost per dunam and require very little water, and farmers who grow tomatoes and other crops requiring a lot of irrigation. The latter suffer much greater losses for observing Shemittah, so their compensation must be greater. It should be noted that even with help from Keren Ha-Shvi'it, farmers must sacrifice a great deal not to rely on the *Heter Mechirah.*

[517] Keren Ha-Shvi'it records them as farmers. For accuracy's sake, I have substituted the term "farms." For example, Keren Ha-Shvi'it publicizes that during the most recent Shemittah it subsidized fifty-

four farmers working an area of 2,422 dunams in the moshavah of Beit Chilkiah. (A dunam is approximately one-quarter of an acre.) As of this writing, however, only two farmers are active there: Moshe Kahana and Meir Weil. Yet fifty-four families own land in Beit Chilkiah, almost all of it rented out to these two farmers or to outside professionals. Keren Ha-Shvi'it compensated the families for rental income lost during that Shemittah, but greater compensation went to the farmers, who lost more.

Likewise, for the moshav of Mevo Choron, Keren Ha-Shvi'it lists only one farmer and 3,250 dunams. That means there is one communal farm – Mevo Choron itself, which is a collective – though many farmers live there.

My thanks to Rabbi Ben Zion Kugler, general manager of Keren Ha-Shvi'it, Jerusalem, whom I interviewed September 5, 2010.

Appendix VIII

518 "Lebanon" refers not to the country, but to Deuteronomy 3:25 – "Please let me cross over and see the good land that is on the other side of the Jordan, this good mountain and the Lebanon." Rashi comments: "'And the Lebanon' – this refers to the Holy Temple [in Jerusalem]."

519 The name *Ha-Ẓvi*, "the deer," alludes to the newspaper's license holder, Yitzchak Hirschensohn, because *hirsch* is Yiddish for "deer." Sources: Menucha Gilboa, *Lexicon of the Hebrew Newspapers of the Eighteenth and Nineteenth Centuries* (Jerusalem: Mossad Bialik, 1992), p. 308; *www.jerusalem-stories.com/books/6.htm - chapter* 9.

520 The newspaper was named after a flower appearing in such biblical verses as "I am a *chavaẓelet* of Sharon, a rose of the valleys" (Song of Songs 2:1). Some place the *chavaẓelet* in the Narcissus (daffodil) family, and others define it as a lily. In rabbinic literature, the *chava zelet* symbolizes the Jewish people.

521 The name *Shiloach* (Siloam) is synonymous with biblical Jerusalem's Gihon Spring, cited in I Kings 1:33, 38. More accurately, it is the name of a man-made channel that connected the Gihon to fields:

> In order to irrigate his gardens, and other fields in the Kidron Valley, [King] Solomon built a peacetime channel that was cut into the rock and followed the contour of the eastern slope of the City of David from the Gihon Spring to this area, where the water was collected in a reservoir.... It sent– as the word "Shiloach" denotes – its water from the Gihon to the fields.

Ahron Horovitz, *Jerusalem – Footsteps through Time* (Jerusalem: Feldheim, 2000), pp. 37-38.

Waiting for the Emperor

> [The settlers] couldn't rely ... on the directives of the Sephardic rabbis. Because ... Ashkenazim don't ask Sephardim questions on *halakhah* (because, to our sorrow, our Torah has turned into two – one for each of these two groups – and that which is permissible for one is completely forbidden for the other). FROM PAGE 210.

On October 29, 1898, Emperor Wilhelm II of Germany and his wife visited Jerusalem. In their honor, the Jewish community erected a large and richly adorned arch on Jaffa Road (near today's Clal Building), which proclaimed, "Welcome in the name of the Lord," in Hebrew and German. When the emperor reached the arch, the chief rabbis were waiting for him, holding Torah scrolls. In this rare photograph, to the left of the middle column decorated with branches is Rabbi Shmuel Salant, the Ashkenazic chief rabbi. To the right is Rabbi Yaakov Shaul Elyashar (1817-1906), the Sephardic chief rabbi, after whom Jerusalem's Givat Shaul neighborhood is named. During the Shemittah controversy of 1888, Rabbi Elyashar supported the *Heter Mechirah* (*She'eilot u-Teshuvot Simchah la-Ish, Yoreh Deah,* 26), while Rabbi Salant vigorously opposed it. An exasperated Baron Rothschild, determined not to let the colonists he financially supported "take a Sabbatical," sold his colonial land to a non-Jew through Rabbi Elyashar's *beit din.*

Poles apart. *From top to bottom:* Rabbi Shmuel Salant, the Ashkenazic chief rabbi; Rabbi Yaakov Shaul Elyashar, the Sephardic chief rabbi; the chief rabbis with other dignitaries awaiting the arrival of Emperor Wilhelm II of Germany

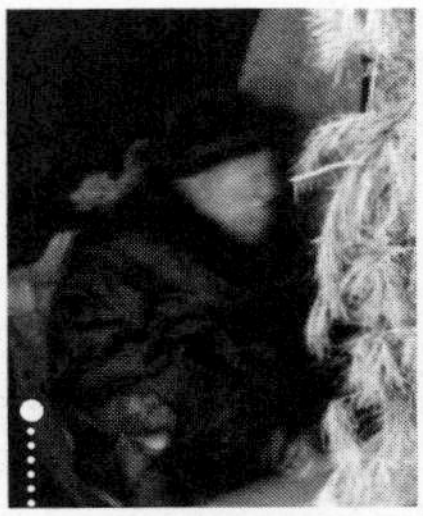

Glossary

ALIYAH	lit. "ascent"; moving to the Land of Israel
AV BEIT DIN	chief judge of a rabbinical court
BARUCH HASHEM	"thank God"
BEIT DIN	rabbinical court
BEIT MIDRASH	hall or room designated for Torah study
BIMAH	synagogue platform on which the Torah is read
CHALUẒIM	early (mostly secular and socialist) Jewish pioneers from 1904 onwards
CHAMETZ	leaven, forbidden on Passover and therefore customarily sold beforehand
CHAREIDI	ultra-Orthodox; see note 323
CHEDER (pl. CHADARIM)	lit. "room"; traditional Jewish school
CHINUCH IVRI	nationalistic Jewish education in which the language of instruction is Hebrew
DAVENING	prayers
DERECH EREẒ	lit. "the way of the land"; pursuits necessary to maintain society, such as earning a living, ethics, and good manners
DRASHAH	sermon
EREẒ YISRAEL	Land of Israel
ETROG (pl. ETROGIM)	citron, used for ritual purposes during Sukkot
EZRAT NASHIM	women's section of the synagogue
FELLAHIN	(Arabic) Arab peasant farmers
GABBAI (pl. GABBAIM)	person who helps organize the synagogue service; duties include choosing who leads the prayers, opens the ark, or is called to the Torah
GALICIA	province of the Austro-Hungarian Empire, extending from southern Poland to the western Ukraine and containing many Chassidic communities

GAON (pl. GEONIM)	genius
GERUSH	Ottoman coin also known as a piastre; one hundred gerush equaled one Ottoman lira or pound
HAFTARAH	portion from the Prophets, chanted – often by bar mizvah boys – in the synagogue on Sabbath mornings
HALAKHAH (adj. HALAKHIC)	Jewish law
HARROW	an agricultural implement with spike-like teeth or upright disks, drawn chiefly over plowed land to level it, break up clods, uproot weeds, etc.
HASKALAH	the Enlightenment
HAVDALAH	ceremony marking the end of the Sabbath or festivals, including blessings over wine, spices, and candlelight
HEFKER	ownerless
HETER	HALAKHIC ruling rendering an act or object permissible
ILLUY	prodigy
KADDISH	mourners' prayer
KAPOTE	long, black coat originating in eastern Europe and now worn chiefly by very Orthodox or Chassidic Jews
KEHILLAH	Jewish community
KIDDUSH	(1) prayer recited over wine, grape juice, or liquor to sanctify the Sabbath and holidays; (2) refreshments served after Sabbath morning prayers, beginning with the recitation of Kiddush

KOLLEL	(1) charitable organization supporting Diaspora communities transplanted to Palestine; (2) program of full-time, paid Torah study
LANDSMEN	fellow townspeople
LITVAK (adj. LITVISH)	non-Chassidic Jews with roots in the former Grand Duchy of Lithuania, which included present-day Belarus, Lithuania, northern Ukraine, and northeastern Poland
MA'ASROT	agricultural tithes distributed to the Levites or the poor
MAARIV	evening prayer
MASKILIM (sing. MASKIL)	supporters of the HASKALAH, including *radicals*: • proponents of assimilation and Russification • secular Jewish nationalists, who wanted to reform Judaism *moderates*: • Jews of varying levels of observance who wanted Jewish education to emphasize Bible, Hebrew, and secular studies
MECHANCHIM	educators
MELAMED	a religious studies teacher for boys in a Jewish school, especially a CHEDER
MENTSCHEN	upstanding persons
MIKVEH	ritual bath
MINCHAH	afternoon prayer
MITNAGDIM	opponents of Chassidism
MIẒVAH (pl. MIẒVOT)	religious commandment
MOSHAV	semi-collective farming community where members work for themselves but share equipment and market their produce together

MOSHAVAH	non-collective (farming) community, sometimes containing cooperatives; in Mazkeret Batya, for example, several families founded a dairy
MUSAR SHMUESS	moral instruction
NACHAS	satisfaction
NETILAT YADAYIM	ritual washing of the hands with a cup before the eating of bread
OẒAR BEIT DIN	a rabbinical court that makes produce grown during the Shemittah year available to the public, charging only for labor, not for the fruit itself
PAYOT	sidelocks
PERUSHIM	Lithuanian Jews of the Old Yishuv
PILPUL	intricate halakhic discourse
POSEK (pl. POSKIM)	authority on Jewish law
RABBOSAI	"Gentlemen!"
REBBE	Chassidic leader
REBBETZIN	rabbi's wife
REBBI	teacher
ROSH CHODESH	first day(s) of the Hebrew month
ROSH YESHIVAH	yeshivah dean
SCHNORRER	beggar
SELICHOT	penitential prayers said on fast days and during the High Holy Day season
SHADCHAN	matchmaker
SHAS	Talmud
SHECHINAH	Divine Presence
SHELICHIM	envoys, emissaries
SHELOSHIM	lit. "thirty"; thirty-day mourning period
SHEMITTAH	Sabbatical year

SHEMURAH MATZAH	strictly kosher matzah
SHIUR (pl. SHIURIM)	Torah class
SHIVAH	lit. "seven"; seven-day mourning period
SHOCHET	ritual slaughterer of kosher animals
SHTETL	village
SHTREIMEL	fur hat originating in eastern Europe and now worn chiefly by Chassidic Jews
SHUK	marketplace
SHUL	synagogue
SHULCHAN ARUCH	Code of Jewish Law
SIMCHAH	joyous occasion
TALLIT (pl. TALLITOT)	prayer shawl with ẒIẒIT fringes on all four corners
TALLIT KATAN	tunic-like mini-TALLIT with ẒIẒIT fringes on all four corners
TALMUD TORAH	Jewish school
TANACH	acronym for Torah, Nevi'im (Prophets), Ketuvim (Writings); the Bible
TERUMOT	produce donated to a *kohen,* as mandated by the Torah
TIKKUN CHAẒOT	midnight prayer mourning the destruction of the Temple and Jerusalem
TUR YOREH DE'AH	volume of the *Tur,* a code of Jewish law that was composed by Rabbi Yaakov ben Asher (1270-1340) and served as the basis of the SHULCHAN ARUCH
VA'AD	committee, council
YIDDISHKEIT	Judaism
YIZKOR	memorial prayer

YOM KIPPUR KATAN	mini-Yom Kippur on the day before ROSH CHODESH, marked by fasting and prayer for forgiveness, so one can begin the new month free of sin
ẒADDIK	righteous person
ZAYDE	grandfather
ẒIẒIT	fringes worn on four-cornered garments, reminding the wearer to observe all the commandments
ZT"L	an acronym for *zecher tzaddik liv'rachah*, "may the memory of the righteous one be for a blessing"

Illustration Credits

[Page | **Caption** | *Source*]

1 **Founders Street, Mazkeret Batya**
Tzvi Willner

2 **Faces of Mazkeret Batya**
Eran Shamir Village Museum, Mazkeret Batya

3 **Chaim and Guta Glick with son Noach**
Eran Shamir Village Museum, Mazkeret Batya

3 **Yisrael Arkin and daughters**
Eran Shamir Village Museum, Mazkeret Batya

5 **Comrades in arms**
Eran Shamir Village Museum, Mazkeret Batya

6 **America replacing Israel as the Promised Land**
By courtesy of the Oster Visual Documentation Center, Beit Hatfutsot, Tel Aviv

6 **Yosef Weidenfeld**
Amihud Yitzchak Meir Levin, Eileh Masei

7 **Misleading**
Mordechai Eliav, ed., Ha-Aliyah ha-Rishonah, *Ben-Zvi Press*

9 **On the run**
Beth Hatefutsoth, Photo Archive, Tel Aviv, Zusia Efron Collection

11 **Visionary**
Picture collection, Department of Archives, the Jewish National and University Library, Jerusalem

11 **Signatories**
Yechiel Michel Stern, Gedolei Hadorot

13 **Yechiel Brill**
Picture collection, Department of Archives, the Jewish National and University Library, Jerusalem

13 **Bread of affliction**
Central Zionist Archives

14 **The Baron's Inner Circle**
Museum of Rishon Le-Ẓion, Historical Archives

16 **Imposing**
Bibliothèque nationale de France

17 **The main man**
Reproduced with the permission of The Rothschild Archive

19 **Where history was made**
Dr. Mordechai Naor

23 **Poster kids**
Picture collection, Department of Archives, the Jewish National and University Library, Jerusalem

24 **What they left behind**
Eran Shamir Village Museum, Mazkeret Batya

25 **Rozhinoy's rabbi**
Achiezer Arkin

25 **Yaakov Arkin, Moshe Maller, Ẓvi Arkin**
Eran Shamir Village Museum, Mazkeret Batya

25 **Yaakov Laskovsky**
Shmuel Press, great-grandson of Yaakov Laskovsky

26 **Chaim Moshe Press/Yechezkel Levin**
Eran Shamir Village Museum, Mazkeret Batya

26 **Ephraim Skolnick**
Achiezer Arkin

26 **Dov Rudovsky**
*Studio Fisch; www.tidhar.tourolib.org/*tidhar/view/1/406

27 **Camouflaged currency**
Shutterstock Images

29 **What's wrong with this picture?**
Eran Shamir Village Museum, Mazkeret Batya

31 **Brill's nemesis**
David Druck, Baron Edmond de Rothschild- The Story of a Practical Idealist

33 **Poor and proud**
Matson Photograph Collection, Library of Congress

34 **Four hundred years**
Matson Photograph Collection, Library of Congress

36 **In their Sunday best**
Matson Photograph Collection, Library of Congress

37 **Uncle Abdul doesn't want you**
Ben-Zvi Press

39 **Minyan man**
Central Zionist Archives

40 **Center of culture**
Wikipedia

41 **One kreuzer, 1881, Austria**
Münzen Hofmann Coins, Innsbruck, Austria

41 **Emanuel Baumgarten**
Yaakov Lifschitz, Zikhron Yaakov

41 **Baron Albert Salomon Rothschild**
Österreichische Nationalbibliothek Photo Archives, Vienna

42 **Magyar money**
Münzen Hofmann Coins, Innsbruck, Austria

46 **Bon voyage**
Central Zionist Archives

48 **Steamship**
Eitan Osaphim- Stamps, Coins & Judaica

49 **Etrog City**
Münzen Hofmann Coins, Innsbruck, Austria

50 **Dawn of a new era**
Central Zionist Archives

51 **Dear friend**
Oded Yarkoni Archives of the History of Petach Tikva

51 **Mayhem!**
Matson Photograph Collection, Library of Congress

52 **Jaffa boatman**
Central Zionist Archives

52 **Welcome mat**
Matson Photograph Collection, Library of Congress

53 **Gateway to Palestine**
Picture collection, Department of Archives, the Jewish National and University Library, Jerusalem

56 **The Bobbsey twins**
Matson Photograph Collection, Library of Congress

61 **Jaffa sunshine**
Ely Schiller, Ariel Publishing

62 **Extensive**
Matson Photograph Collection, Library of Congress

63 **Fieldwork**
Ely Schiller, Ariel Publishing

67 **Imposter**
Grasses of Iowa Website, Iowa State University

71 **Superhighway**
Ely Schiller, Ariel Publishing

71 **Entrance to Bab El Wad**
Ely Schiller, Ariel Publishing

71 **Carriage on the Jaffa - Jerusalem Road**
Picture collection, Department of Archives, the Jewish National and University Library, Jerusalem

72 **Western Wall**
Matson Photograph Collection, Library of Congress

72 **Lemonade Vendor**
Ely Schiller, Ariel Publishing

72 **Closed for the Sabbath**
Matson Photograph Collection, Library of Congress

72 **Jerusalem Jew**
Matson Photograph Collection, Library of Congress

73 **The shuk**
Ely Schiller, Ariel Publishing

73 **Street Scene – Jewish Quarter**
Ely Schiller, Ariel Publishing

73 **Jewish Quarter with Churvah Synagogue**
Ely Schiller, Ariel Publishing

74 **The only game in town**
Central Zionist Archives

74 **Trekking**
Central Zionist Archives

75 **Caesarea**
Matson Photograph Collection, Library of Congress

76 **A must-see destination**
Ely Schiller, Ariel Publishing

77 **David Kosviner**
Amihud Yitzchak Meir Levin, Eileh Masei

79 **From ship to shore**
Central Zionist Archives

81 **The tired typesetter**
Israel Postal Authority

116 **Centenarian**
Eran Shamir Village Museum, Mazkeret Batya

117 **Grist for the mill**
Ely Schiller, Ariel Publishing

117 **Burning bush**
Sam Finkel

119 **Idealist**
Eliyahu Izakson, Mareh mi-Dor ha-Gesher

120 **A one man show**
Achiezer Arkin

121 **In your eye**
Central Zionist Archives

124 **Ra-ta-tat**
Eyal Tal Bartov

124 **Graceful**
Eyal Tal Bartov

124 **Wise guy**
Eyal Tal Bartov

125 **Under the pear tree**
Sam Finkel

125 **Climbing the walls**
Eyal Tal Bartov

125 **Mousetrap**
Eyal Tal Bartov

125 **Deadly**
Eyal Tal Bartov

125 **Sting operation**
Jan Ove Rein, The Scorpion Files

126 **Faster than a speeding sickle**
Ben-Zvi Press

127 **My son the doctor**
Central Zionist Archives

127 **When it rains, it pours**
Achiezer Arkin

129 **Threshing in Ekron**
From the film: Jewish Life in the Land of Israel – 1913, *Jerusalem Cinamateque, Israel Film Archive*

130 **A quiet afternoon**
Photo Archives, Keren Kayemet le-Yisrael/KKL

131 **Page from Chidushei Chatam Sofer**
Jerusalem: Yerid Ha'sefarim Publishers, 2003

132 **Bringing in the sheaves**
From the film: Jewish Life in the Land of Israel – 1913, *Jerusalem Cinamateque, Israel Film Archive*

132 **Milking this picture for all it's worth**
Israel Government Press Office

133 **A land flowing with milk and honey**
From the film: Jewish Life in the Land of Israel – 1913, *Jerusalem Cinamateque, Israel Film Archive*

134 **Village of Ekron in the Land of Yehuda**
Achiezer Arkin

135 **A farmer from the neighboring settlement of Gedera**
Ely Schiller, Ariel Publishing

136 **Mr. Tea**
Central Zionist Archives

137 **Starting all over**
Eran Shamir Village Museum, Mazkeret Batya

138 **Letting the light seep in**
Central Zionist Archives

139 **A farmer's study companion**
Tzvi Willner; Eran Shamir Village Museum, Mazkeret Batya

140 **L'chaim**
Central Zionist Archives

141 **Cover page of Tractate Berachot**
Ron Sofer, Eran Shamir Village Museum, Mazkeret Batya

141 **Original set of Talmud**
Ron Sofer

142 **Pied Piper**
Eran Shamir Village Museum, Mazkeret Batya

142 **The chairmen**
Eran Shamir Village Museum, Mazkeret Batya

143 **Departures**
Eran Shamir Village Museum, Mazkeret Batya

143 **Technicalities of kindness**
Eran Shamir Village Museum, Mazkeret Batya

143 **Seal of approval**
Ben-Zvi Press

202 **The real McCoy**
Photo courtesy of Rabbi Yaakov Chaim Dinkel

204 **Notable contributor**
Yechiel Michel Stern, Gedolei Hadorot

206 **Lover of Ereẓ Yisrael**
Yechiel Michel Stern, Gedolei Hadorot

206 **Not a Time to Be Silent**
Picture collection, Department of Archives, the Jewish National and University Library, Jerusalem

208 **Rabbinical head**
Achiezer Arkin

208 **Secular head**
Central Zionist Archives

212 **Mr. Medallions**
Central Zionist Archives

214 **Royal rage**
Reproduced with the permission of The Rothschild Archive

217 **In his younger years**
Mossad Harav Kook

220 **Moderate *maskil***
Central Zionist Archives

220 **Radical *maskil***
Central Zionist Archives

221 **A complex man**
Central Zionist Archives

226 **Symbol of the Old Yishuv**
Israel Postal Authority

227 **Learning the art of earning**
Central Zionist Archives

228 **Me'ah She'arim's spiritual leader**
Yechiel Michel Stern, Gedolei Hadorot

229 **Like two heads of state**
Central Zionist Archives

230 **Historic irony**
Sam Finkel

231 **Peacemaker and philanthropist**
Central Zionist Archives

232 **Rothschild's rabbi, Ẓaddok Kahn**
Wikipedia

242 **The farmers' rabbi**
Achiezer Arkin

243 **I want justice!**
Central Zionist Archives

246 **Eloquent**
Eran Shamir Village Museum, Mazkeret Batya

247 **"So many became…"**
Eran Shamir Village Museum, Mazkeret Batya

248 **Michael Erlanger**
Museum of Rishon Le-Ẓion, Historical Archives

250 **The verdict is in**
Central Zionist Archives, file J15/7128

251 **The bottom line**
Central Zionist Archives, file J15/7128

254 **Like a tornado hit it**
Achiezer Arkin

255 **Smiling for the camera**
Central Zionist Archives

256 **We're sorry**
Central Zionist Archives, file no. J15/5011

258 **Sons of the founders**
Achiezer Arkin

259 **The missing head**
Museum of Rishon Le-Ẓion, Historical Archives

260 **Critic**
Central Zionist Archives

263 **A new generation emerges**
Eran Shamir Village Museum, Mazkeret Batya

264 **Generation gap**
Eran Shamir Village Museum, Mazkeret Batya

264 **The Torah as a way of life**
Central Zionist Archives

266 **Tanach as an academic subject**
Central Zionist Archives

267 **Making the grade**
Eran Shamir Village Museum, Mazkeret Batya

268 **The competition**
Eran Shamir Village Museum, Mazkeret Batya

269 **Under the table**
The Israel Museum, Ansky Collection, 1912-1914

Index

Note: Numbers in *italic* refer to **illustrations** and **illustration captions**.

Footnotes are indicated with a page number followed by "*n.*" and the footnote number (ex: 370 *n.* 11).

Endnotes are indicated with only "*n.*" or "*nn.*" and the endnote number (ex: *nn.* 222, 435).